A Man's Journey with God

Seminar Edition

Wellington Boone

A Man's Journey with God

Seminar Edition

A man's personal accountability journal . . .

between you and God

Man Hunt Seminar Edition

APPTE Publishing

Atlanta, Georgia

A Man's Journey with God Seminar Edition

A man's personal accountability journal . . . between you and God

www.WellingtonBoone.com

APPTE Publishing

5875 Peachtree Industrial Blvd Ste 300

Norcross, GA 30092

The following abbreviations are used to identify versions of the Bible used in this book:

KJV *King James Version,* also known as the *Authorized Version.*

NASB Scripture quotations taken from the New American Standard Bible®,
Copyright © 1960, 1962, 1963, 1968, 1971, 1972, 1973,
1975, 1977, 1995 by The Lockman Foundation
Used by permission. (www.Lockman.org)

NLT Scripture quotations are taken from the Holy Bible, New Living Translation, copyright ©1996, 2004, 2007, 2013, 2015 by Tyndale House Foundation. Used by permission of Tyndale House Publishes, Inc., Carol Stream, Illinois 60188. All rights reserved.

NKJV Scripture taken from the New King James Version®. Copyright © 1982
by Thomas Nelson. Used by permission. All rights reserved.

The Message Scripture quotations from THE MESSAGE. Copyright © by Eugene H. Peterson 1993, 1994, 1995, 1996, 2000, 2001, 2002. Used by permission of NavPress. All rights reserved. Represented by Tyndale House Publishers, Inc.

Nouns and pronouns referring to Deity are capitalized throughout the text of this book unless they are included within a direct quotation, in which case the original capitalization is retained.

Includes Footnotes, Bibliographic References, Historical Timeline,
Illustrations, Portraits, Annotated Index.
ISBN-13: 978-0-9974710-0-7

Printed in the United States of America
April 2016

Portions of this book are adapted from *A Man's Journey with God* (APPTE Publishing, 2016), *Your Journey with God* (AAPTE Publishing, 2015) and *My Journey with God Signature Edition* by Wellington Boone (ProVision Publishing, 2002). Original portraits by Avery Sean Bush from the 2002 edition are included in this book.

A Man's Journey with God

I will complete the pages of
my consecration journal
in the back of this book
each day for 30 Straight
Days of Consecration

If I miss a day, I will start over again at the beginning
until I can complete 30 straight days.
Then I will have established the
character-building habits of a
consecrated devotional life.

Fellowship of Finishers

Certificate

I, ______________________

(My Name)

completed the 30-Day Journey

in *A Man's Journey with God*

From ______________________ ***(starting date)***

To ______________________ ***(ending date)***

In the Year of Our Lord

____

The Significance of 30 Days of Consecration

If you repeat anything for 30 days, you can develop new habits.

The number 30 has special significance:

Jesus was 30 years old when He was released into ministry.
David was 30 when he became king.
Joseph was 30 when he stood before Pharaoh.

Because you completed your journal for 30 straight days
you have developed new habits of consecration that can last a lifetime.

"Therefore, brethren, be even more diligent to
make your call and election sure,
for if you do these things you will never stumble."

2 Peter 1:10 NKJV

,

"A highway shall be there, and a road, and it shall be called the Highway of Holiness. The unclean shall not pass over it."

Isaiah 35:8 NKJV

"And I sought for a man among them, that should make up the hedge, and stand in the gap before me for the land, that I should not destroy it: but I found none."

Ezekiel 22:30 KJV

"I was told by the man that stands at the gate,
at the head of this way, that if I called here,
you would shew me excellent things,
such as would be a help to me
in my journey."

John Bunyan—*Pilgrim's Progress*

Contents

Section 3. Daily Practices of Consecration

Section 4. Lifetime Exercises in Consecration

Section 5. Resources and Index

Your Personal 30-Day Consecration Journal

Timeline for People and Events in *A Man's Journey with God*

A.D. **33** Modern history is dated A.D. "In the Year of Our Lord" from the conception or birth of Jesus Christ. He was crucified, died on the cross, and was resurrected in A.D. 33. He lives forever!

200-900	Apostles' Creed
325	Nicene Creed
c.385 to c.461	Saint Patrick
500	Athanasian Creed
1369-1415	John Hus
1483-1546	Martin Luther (age 62)
1500s	Protestant Reformation and Birth of Reformed Churches
1509-1564	John Calvin (age 54)
1514-1572	John Knox (age 58)*
1560	Presbyterianism Begins
1564 approx.	Puritans Begin
1592	Congregational Church Begins.
1592-1670	John Comenius (age 78)
c.1600-1776	Colonial Charters of the American Colonies
1600 approx.	Slavery in America 17th Century to 1865 (end of Civil War)
1609	Baptists Begin
1628-1688	John Bunyan, author of *Pilgrim's Progress* (age 59)
1640s	Quakers (Society of Friends). Founder, George Fox (1624-1691)
1644-1718	William Penn, Founder of Pennsylvania (age 73)
1640s	Westminster Confession and Catechisms
1691-1747	Theodore Jacob Frelinghuysen (age 56)
1700-1760	Ludwig Von Zinzendorf (age 59)
1701	Yale founded as a school for ministers
1703-1758	Jonathan Edwards (age 54)
1703-1791	John Wesley (age 87)
1707-1788	Charles Wesley (age 80)
1714-1770	George Whitefield (age 55)
1718-1747	David Brainerd (age 29)
1720 and beyond	First Great Awakening in American Colonies
1722	Moravian Church Begins
1723-1780	William Blackstone (age 56)
1725-1807	John Newton (age 82)
1727	Moravian Revival Sends Out Missionaries
1729	Holy Club (John and Charles Wesley, George Whitefield, others)
1731-1800	William Cowper (age 68)
1740s	Methodist Church Begins

1745-1816	**Francis Asbury (age 70)**
1746	Princeton founded for ministers, first called College of New Jersey
1759-1833	William Wilberforce (age 73)
1760-1831	Richard Allen (age 71)
1761-1834	William Carey (age 72)
1763-1817	James McGready (age 54)*
1769	Dartmouth founded as Christian school for Native Americans
1772 1844	Barton W. Stone (age 71)
1775-1783	American Revolution
1775-1863	Lyman Beecher (age 87)
1786-1865	Arthur Tappan (age 79)
1788-1873	Lewis Tappan (age 85)*
1792-1875	Charles Finney (age 82)
1800s	Underground Railroad
1800s	Benevolent Empire begins
Early 1800s	Second Great Awakening
1801	Cane Ridge Revival and beginning of Camp Meetings
1803-1895	Theodore Weld (age 91)
1805-1879	William Lloyd Garrison (age 73)
1805-1898	George Müller (age 92)
1809-?	Jeremiah Lanphier
1809-1865	Abraham Lincoln (age 56)
1811-1884	Wendell Phillips (age 72)
1812-1815	War of 1812
1813-1887	Henry Ward Beecher (age 73)
1817	American Sunday School Union begins
c.1817-1895	Frederick Douglass (age 77)*
1829-1912	William Booth (age 83)
1834-1892	Charles Spurgeon (age 57)
1837-1899	Dwight L. Moody (age 62)
1839	*Amistad* slave mutiny
1844	YMCA Young Men's Christian Association founded in London
1846	American Missionary Association
1852	*Uncle Tom's Cabin* by Harriet Beecher Stowe published
1856	Third Great Awakening begins
1860-1931	C. T. Studd (age 70)
1861-1865	American Civil War

1861-1939	James Naismith (age 78) Invented basketball in 1891 for YMCA.
1862-1932	Julius Rosenwald (age 69)
1862-1935	Billy Sunday (age 72)
1865	Slavery ended by the 13th Amendment to the U. S. Constitution
1865	Salvation Army founded
1866-1961	Charles Harrison (C. H.) Mason (age 95)
1870-1922	William Joseph Seymour (age 52)
1870-1935	John G. Lake (age 65)
1873-1929	Charles F. Parham (age 55)
1874-1917	Oswald Chambers (age 43)
1878-1950	Evan Roberts (age 73)
1890	*In Darkest England and The Way Out* by William Booth
1898	Spanish American War
1906-1915 approx.	Azusa Street Revival
1907	Church Of God In Christ (C. H. Mason)
1912-1984	Francis Schaeffer (age 72)
1914-1918	World War I
1914	Assemblies of God founded
1918 to present	Billy Graham (William Franklin Graham, Jr.)
1930 to present	Pat Robertson (Marion Gordon Robertson)
1935 to present	Jay Grimstead
1939-1945	World War II
1940 to present	Bill McCartney, co-founder of Promise Keepers
1950-1953	Korean War
1952 to present	Franklin Graham (William Franklin Graham III)
1960-1975	Vietnam War
1973	Roe v. Wade Supreme Court decision legalizes abortion
1979	Nobel Peace Prize awarded to Mother Teresa, speaks against abortion
1990	Founding of Promise Keepers men's movement

The age in parentheses is the age at death. If marked "*" age at death is approximate because exact month of birth or death is not available.

Introduction

A Man's Journey to Pleasing God

I remember very clearly the moment that I knew I was saved because I was absolutely terrified! I had been a soldier in Vietnam, and I thought that was bad, but when the glory and presence of the living God filled my room I was so frightened of His power that I couldn't move. I felt if I made one mistake He would kill me. I did not hear Him say anything. I just knew I was in His presence.

From that time on—more than 40 years ago—I knew that I was saved and that I wanted more than anything else to become accountable to God in everything. I remember crying hard and saying, "I just want to please you! I just want to please you!" That is what *A Man's Journey with God* will help you to do—just please God!

In the first part of this book you will learn a system of private accountability like the saints of the past that uses faith, prayer, and spiritual disciplines from the Bible to give your life eternal purpose and meaning.

At the end of the book you will find a 30-day consecration journal where you will develop new habits of spiritual intensity as Holy Spirit teaches you privately about habits of holiness using a practical, Bible-based work-through guide. You will experience the joy of knowing that you have pleased God by walking in Christ-like character.

God's goal is your Christ-likeness *Romans 8:29 KJV*	*"For whom he did foreknow, he also did predestinate to be conformed to the image of his Son, that he might be the firstborn among many brethren."*

When I was in that room alone with God, after I overcame the fear I was filled with a totally different emotion—joy! I was filled with joy that a holy God had accepted me and I could live for Christ instead of living for the devil as I had been doing for far too much of my life.

That is how I started the greatest adventure of my life. I learned how to become privately devout and develop an intimate relationship with God. Then I began to teach others how to change their lives, too. That became my ministry, and I have been ministering to others ever since.

Some questions to consider as you start this journey:

Am I truly saved?

Do I have a consciousness of sin and a quickness to repent?

Do I seek to know God and live a Christ-like lifestyle?

Do I pray and live sacrificially for others, as Jesus did?

Are people's lives changed because I am there?

Do I have a contrite spirit toward God?

Am I totally devoted to a life given over to God?

Life given over to God *Romans 11:36 KJV*	*"For of him, and through him, and to him, are all things: to whom be glory for ever. Amen."*

As you go about your daily affairs, do you make choices based on your need to please God? Do people get a witness that you are the real thing? Is Jesus so alive in you that you are making a significant difference in your home, church, community, and nation? If you cannot answer all of these questions with a positive response, you still have time to learn. Even if no one else will change, you can make changes in yourself, beginning with the way you manage each day, *starting now*. You can learn how to strive for a clear conscience—with no offenses between you and God—and succeed!

Striving for a clean conscience *Acts 24:16 NKJV*	*"I myself always strive to have a conscience without offense toward God and men."*

Everything comes from God. He is our Source. He is the most important Person we could ever please. The greatest goal that we could ever have is pleasing God. That takes holiness, because His nature is holy. All of us are born with a sin nature—an unholy side. However, after you are born *again* and receive Christ you now have Christ in you, the hope of glory.[1] You can develop new habits of holiness and become more like Christ every day, just like great Christian men in history.

Before you begin your 30-day journey, you will read in this men's manual about biblical principles and effective practices that are the foundation of the life-changing exercises in your journal at the end of the book. You will be inspired to become like our perfect role model, Jesus, Who was fully accountable to His Father every day of His life on earth.

---

[1] See Colossians 1:27.

You Are Accountable to God for Your Life

Many of the greatest men of God in the past recorded the events of their daily lives in their journals. They also held themselves accountable in writing each day in two areas:

1. How they spent their time in godly pursuits

2. What they did with their money

These people recognized that daily practices of accountability prepared them for that Great Day when God would ask them to give an accounting of their lives before the Judgment Seat of Christ. They wanted to be ready to hear Him say "Well done" when they died because they had sought that same "well done" approval every day that they were alive.

Features of This Edition

A Man's Journey with God has the same life-changing spiritual practices that made a difference in the lives of people using other editions that I have written in the past. It also contains helpful additions specifically for men and a revised navigation system for the digital edition (sold separately) that make this book even more effective.

You will find the word "consecrated" often in this book because it means dedicating yourself fully to the service and worship of God. Here are the sections that you will read on your way to a life of consecration:

Section 1, Becoming Like Christ, explains the significance of Christ, Who is not only your Savior but also your Role Model. You will be challenged to become like Him in personal consecration, defeat the devil's influence on yourself and others, restore the influence of the church on the culture, and personally bring spiritual revival and godly standards to all areas of society. That is what I call "Total Domination," which means taking responsibility for every area of life."

In Section 2, A Man's Consecrated Prayer Life, you will develop a prayer life characterized by humility, repentance, forgiveness, and obedience. You will create daily prayer lists. You will build strength for an extraordinary prayer life. As a consecrated man, you will learn how to pray all night and also how to make each day count for God.

In Section 3, Daily Practices of Consecration, you will work out with daily consecration practices like a yearly through-the-Bible reading schedule, daily meditations on the Word, managing your money as a good steward, serving others, and keeping a daily accountability journal between you and God.

Section 4, Lifetime Exercises in Consecration, shows you how to continue growing once you have completed your 30-day journal by developing lifetime habits of consecration. These include the Eightfold Anointing, personal partaking of communion, fasting, and study of the Word and other resources privately and under submission to a local pastor.

Your Personal 30-Day Consecration Journal that starts on page 345 is your actual 30-day journal. You will be challenged to complete 30 straight days. If you miss a day, you start over. Each day you will write personal insights in your journal. You will study the daily meditation, read your assignment in the Bible read-through, create prayer lists, serve others and recommit yourself to do the will of God. You will ask before you go to bed at night, *"May I go to sleep now, Father?"* You will receive fresh insights from God, which you should write down in your journal—both this one and another notebook or journal with more pages for your revelations.

Each day, you will become more sensitive to God's purpose for your life. You will learn how to please Him. Pleasing God will become your most important goal every day. You will sacrifice sleep, food, and fellowship with others just for the privilege of being with Him. You will develop a passion for accomplishing God's will in earth as it is in heaven—both the entire earth, which is the world around you, but even more important, in your earth, which is the ground of your heart. That's right, God's focus will be your heart—the area that needs to be changed first! God will help you, through Jesus Christ, with Holy Ghost as your Guide.

In the back of the book, ***Bible Reading Guide,*** provides you with a daily Through-the-Bible reading guide for one year. You can start on any day and begin reading from that point. You will also find an annotated **Index** on page that contains important information on the biblical and historical foundations provided in this book as well as useful study topics and readings by other authors on vital subjects.

Learning from the lives of great Christians. The chapters of this book are filled with examples of godly men who will be a tremendous inspiration to you. Just reading these vignettes will inspire you to persevere, as they did, and keep going for your 30 straight days. Reading the personal examples from men in the Bible and Christian men in history will fuel your excitement for your own pursuit of holiness. You will see what God did in these men's lives when they sought after Him and you will believe that He can use you as He used them—if you will be consecrated

You will want to launch off these brief vignettes and read biographies and books that these people have written. You will find many links to resources in the charts, footnotes, and Index.

Put yourself under personal accountability to God. Your goal is to gain more intimacy with God by willingly becoming personally accountable and transparent, relying on your Guide, Holy Spirit, to bring you into holiness. As the Bible says, *"He who called you is holy, you also be holy in all your conduct, because it is written, 'Be holy, for I am holy.'"*[2]

Finish Your 30 Straight Days Because You Are a Finisher!

In sports, everybody finishes. Did you ever hear of a pro game where the players quit before the final whistle? Of course not. Be a man!

Join the Fellowship of Finishers

Complete your journal in 30 straight days

1. Visualize the goal. Your goal is Christ-likeness—a real man who thinks, acts, and looks like Jesus.

2. Understand what it takes to get there. This book provides you with a proven, process-driven series of 30 consecutive days of building consecration habits.

3. Decide that you will finish. If you miss a day, you start all over again until you complete 30 consecutive days. This is significant training for manly leadership.

4. Ask Jesus to pioneer finishing for you. Don't assume that you can be righteous on your own. You need Jesus now and for your lifetime. Remember that He has called you and will help you to finish well.

> *"And the very God of peace sanctify you wholly; and I pray God your whole spirit and soul and body be preserved blameless unto the coming of our Lord Jesus Christ. Faithful is he that calleth you, who also will do it."*[3]

5. Allow the Holy Spirit to be your Guide into the holy life from now on.

---

[2] 1 Peter 1:15-16 NKJV.

[3] 1 Thessalonians 5:23-24 KJV.

Endure to the end

Keep your eyes focused on the goal, as Jesus did when He "for the joy that was set before Him, endured the cross, despising the shame, and is set down at the right hand of the throne of God."[4]

It takes endurance to go all the way to the cross, but that is where you find true joy. Jesus in you becomes the champion of finishing for you. Remember that He pioneered finishing. With Christ in you, you can finish anything that begins in God's purpose for your life. Athletes play to the finish and they play to win. Christians never have a losing mentality. Jesus didn't, and neither do you.

Jesus came to finish *John 4:34 KJV*	*"My meat is to do the will of him that sent me,* ***and to finish his work.****"*

How This Journal Frees You to Run Your Race and Win

Running without the weight of sin *Hebrews 12:1-2 KJV*	*". . . let us lay aside every weight, and the sin which doth so easily beset us, and let us run with patience the race that is set before us, looking unto Jesus the author and* ***finisher of our faith****."*

You can have the assurance that in that Great Day God will say to you, "Well done, my good and faithful servant."[5] You can have the assurance that God will say to you, "Well done," in the future if you live your life now so that He says, "Well done," to you *every day*.

ManHunt challenges you to judge yourself honestly and admit when you are living righteously and when you are not.

The definition of a real man is not someone with the lowest moral standards but the highest moral standards. You can be that man.

---

[4]Hebrews 12:2 KJV.
[5]Matthew 25:21 NLT.

When you are a man, you want to be honest about the level of your spirituality, especially between yourself and God. You don't want to live with guilt, because you are ordained to be free.

Your journal will locate you. Your journal will show you where you are on the map of your personal walk with God and then give you directions about where to go next so that you can lay the foundation of a future holy life. Once you meet God, you will never want to turn back.

If you judge yourself, you will not be judged.[6] All day long you will keep account of yourself before God. At the end of the day, after you complete your journal, you can judge for yourself where you are, just as God will be able to judge you at the end of your days on earth. Your journal will show you what you have thought, read, and done all day that you now have to offer to God at night. You can grade yourself on a scale of 1 to 10, or A to C. When you ask God, "May I go to sleep now, Father?" if you do not have a sense of His approval, you can make the corrections, and then go to sleep in peace.

*If you miss a day, keep starting over until you have completed 30-straight days***.** In 30 days you can create new habits that will produce godly character, spiritual success with God and man, and, prayerfully, a greater level of personal significance. Remember, if you miss a day, start again.

Start a Spiritual Revolution with Personal Notes in Your Journal

A revolution is begun with the spoken word, but it is carried with the pen. Talk is cheap. When you *write* personal notes in your journal, you will be carrying out the revolution that God is working every day in your heart.

Become a revolutionary writer. Write what God shows you in the Word of God and prayer. Record what God does in your life daily. You can be more open with God in prayer if you open up with Him on paper.

Use this as a starter journal on your Highway of Holiness. This book is not intended to be a lifetime journal. *A Man's Journey with God* is just a starter journal. I have not tried to provide everything for you or to give a full treatment of any subject. This is just a seed to help launch you on the highway of holiness, where your Companion, Holy Spirit, will teach you to be holy.

---

[6] 1 See Corinthians 11:31.

"A highway shall be there, and a road, and it shall be called the Highway of Holiness. The unclean shall not pass over it."
Isaiah 35:8 NKJV

Continue on after the initial 30 days. After you finish your 30-day journal, you will be encouraged to continue your own journey with God.

Don't be afraid of what others would think if they read your journal. Keep it in a secret place, but remember that someday your secret strivings might be the key to unlock someone else's spiritual prison, if your journal were released to the world. Along the way, I will give you some examples of men whose journals became classics of the Christian faith.

St. Patrick (*c*.385-*c*.461)
He won Ireland to the Lord but hesitated to expose himself in writing

"For this reason I had in mind to write, but hesitated until now; I was afraid of exposing myself to the talk of men, because I have not studied like the others, who thoroughly imbibed law and Sacred Scripture, and never had to change from the language of their childhood days, but were able to make it still more perfect. In our case, what I had to say had to be translated into a tongue foreign to me, as can be easily proved from the savour of my writing, which betrays how little instruction and training I have had in the art of words; for, so says Scripture, by the tongue will be discovered the wise man, and understanding, and knowledge, and the teaching of truth."

Saint Patrick, *Confession*

Consider how your revelations could empower the next generation. Earlier generations could credit their spiritual growth to reading not only the Bible but also books and journals by great men of God. *A Man's Journey with God* helps you to create a consecration journal that future generations could read to receive inspiration for a lifetime of service to the Lord. Even if you keep it private forever, consider selecting and expanding some of your notes into published excerpts in book form.

With today's technology, every man can become an author and reach people worldwide with his insights and honest reflections on his life.

Section 1

Becoming Like Christ

It's not what you're going through.
It's how you're going through it.

It's not what you have,
but what you can handle.

The Significance of Numbered Days

"So teach us to number our days, that we may apply our hearts unto wisdom."[7]

7

Completion

Genesis gives 7 days for the creation of the earth. Solomon completed his temple in 7 years.[8] Revelation speaks of the 7-fold Spirit of God, 7 churches, 7 spirits, and 7 lamp stands. You may want to fast first for 7 days. When you succeed, you will have a sense of completion.

8

New Beginnings

After creation and God's day of rest, a new day of life on earth began on the 8th day, or the beginning of a new week. You will be anointing yourself 8 ways to start anew each morning.

21

Days that Daniel fasted

Daniel fasted for 21 days. You may need to consecrate yourself on a 21-day Daniel fast of vegetables and water.

30

Time to Set New Habits that Release You into Ministry

If you repeat something for 30 days, you can develop a habit. If you will use this journal for 30 straight days, you will develop new habits of consecration. Jesus was 30 years old when He was released into ministry. David was 30 when he became king. Joseph was 30 when he stood before Pharaoh and received a new assignment.

40

Time of Testing

Jesus fasted for 40 days before the devil came to test him.[9] Israel spent 40 years in the wilderness.[10] God caused it to rain on the earth 40 days and 40 nights.[11] After you complete 30 days, go on and reach 40 days. Press past your time of testing.

50

Jubilee—the Lord's Release

In Israel on the 50th year, all debts were to be canceled (Leviticus 25). Fifty also represents the release of the Holy Spirit. The outpouring of the Holy Spirit came on Pentecost, 50 days after Passover. After you finish your 30 days to establish a new habit, then maintain your new lifestyle to go on to 40 days, past the time of testing. After that, go to 50 days for the Lord's release.

---

[7]Psalm 90:12 KJV.
[8]See 1 Kings 6:38.
[9]See Matthew 4:2.
[10]See Numbers 14:33.
[11]See Genesis 7:4.

Chapter 1

Jesus Christ,
Every Man's Role Model

"Before I shaped you in the womb, I knew all about you.
Before you saw the light of day, I had holy plans for you."[12]

God wants every man to look like Jesus, but Jesus didn't leave a picture of Himself so we could compare ourselves to how He looks physically. He had no intention of giving you a photograph so that you could put it up in your house and show everyone. *You* are an expression of Jesus—to the degree that you surrender.

The photograph that God wants to show that represents who He is has your face painted on it.

Christ lives in me
Galatians 2:20 KJV

"I am crucified with Christ: nevertheless I live; yet not I, but Christ liveth in me: and the life which I now live in the flesh I live by the faith of the Son of God, who loved me, and gave himself for me."

Everything that Jesus did represented His Father. He said, "If you have seen me you have seen the Father."[13] He did the things that pleased His Father.[14] When He said, "If you have seen me you have seen the Father," He wasn't talking about how the Father looked physically. He wasn't talking about His complexion or His hair color or His skin pigmentation. He was dealing with the *ways* of the Father.

When the guys in the ghetto have a son, they call him "Mini Me." They still have some sense that they have reproduced themselves. When Jesus is your life, everything that you say or do or think is representative of Him in every way. Others could model their lives after

---

[12]Jeremiah 1 *The Message.*
[13]John 14:9.
[14]John 8:29.

you because you are an example of Jesus' life. When you see Him in the future, you will look like Him.

The Character of Jesus Looks the Same in Any Culture

If you are White, Asian, Black, Hispanic, or any other culture, you don't need a picture of Jesus on your wall that looks like someone from your culture. The degree to which you look like Jesus in your character is what counts, and that corresponds to the degree to which you have surrendered in your inner man.

How do you know when you are beginning to develop the character qualities of Jesus? Here are some of the ways you can be a "Mini Me" like our Father and His Son, Jesus Christ:

You no longer look at life from an unspiritual man's perspective, which is "beneath." You look at life from God's biblical worldview perspective, which is "above."

Not of this world *John 8:23 NKJV*	*Jesus said, "You are from beneath; I am from above. You are of this world; I am not of this world."*

Your thinking has been transformed and you live by the Word of God. You love to think righteously according to His commandments and the witness of the Holy Spirit. Unrighteousness thoughts have no appeal.

Living by every word of God *Deuteronomy 8:1-3 KJV*	*"All the commandments which I command thee this day shall ye observe to do, that ye may live, and multiply, and go in and possess the land which the Lord sware unto your fathers. And thou shalt remember all the way which the Lord thy God led thee these forty years in the wilderness, to humble thee, and to prove thee, to know what was in thine heart, whether thou wouldest keep his commandments, or no. And he humbled thee, and suffered thee to hunger, and fed thee with manna, which thou knewest not, neither did thy fathers know; that he might make thee know that man doth not live by bread only, but by every word that proceedeth out of the mouth of the Lord doth man live."*

Prayer is an attraction to you. God's Spirit draws you often into secret prayer.

Praying without fainting *Luke 18:1 KJV*	*"And he spake a parable unto them to this end, that men ought always to pray, and not to faint."*

Your priorities in prayer have begun to change. You want to seek God's face, not His hands. Instead of seeing prayer as spiritual *wel*fare—seeking handouts from God—you see prayer as spiritual *war*fare and an opportunity to get to know God and become more like Jesus.

You love Him and want Him to use you to accomplish *His* purposes instead of wanting Him to accomplish yours.

You become willing to stand for principles, even if you stand alone.

You understand rank and respect authority, like the sons of Issachar.

Keeping rank *1 Chronicles 7:1;* *1 Chronicles 12:38 KJV*	*"Now the sons of Issachar were, Tola, and Puah, Jashub, and Shimron, four. . . . All these men of war, that could keep rank, came with a perfect heart to Hebron, to make David king over all Israel."*

Your attitudes display reverence for God and compassion for your fellow man. You don't judge people by their outward appearance.

You love being with God's family. You can see others' needs and shortcomings, including those of other Christians, but you can handle that, because your heart is aflame with the compassion of Jesus.

You pray and meditate on the Word and you set aside quantities of time every day for personal devotions because it is your life. The Word puts everything in the right perspective. It gives you the confidence to do great things for God, like Moses, who took the presence of God and delivered two million people from bondage.

You know you can do even greater things than Moses,
***because God was <u>with</u> Moses,* but He is <u>in</u> you.**

Understanding life through Jesus in you *1 John 5:20-21 KJV*	*"And we know that the Son of God is come, and hath given us an understanding, that we may know him that is true, and we are in him that is true, even in his Son Jesus Christ. This is the true God, and eternal life."*

Answering the Disciple's Call to Holiness

I met a pastor who said he was hard-pressed to find anyone he knew whom he could call holy—not someone holy by legalism, but by lifestyle, someone whose life could be modeled after, like Jesus.

This journal will give you an opportunity to become that person—a true disciple of Jesus, a "disciplined one" who demonstrates with personal devotion and a holy lifestyle that Jesus did not give His life in vain. Your holiness standard will prove that the Holy Spirit is real.

You may be a gifted communicator, wealthy businessman, best-selling author, or pastor, but if people can't see the holiness of the Lord[15] in your life, you have not achieved the level of success that God wants.

You may be a teacher who is theologically sound and practically relevant, but if you are not getting alone with God in the prayer closet of total surrender, why should God reproduce after your life? You could not walk into a roomful of people you have never met and feel confident in saying, "I represent Jesus."

As the Scripture says, "Now then we are ambassadors for Christ, as though God did beseech you by us."[16] Until you have totally given yourself over to God by faith, you are not able to walk in Christ-likeness. But once you do and the fruit of the Holy Spirit[17] comes forth in your life, you legitimately represent Him in your thoughts, words, and deeds.

[15]See Numbers 6:8.
[16]2 Corinthians 5:20 KJV.
[17]See Galatians 5:22-23.

Answer the call to a contrite spirit. In America's colonial era, before we became a nation, Theodore Frelinghuysen preached the following message to church members whom he believed were too proud to be truly converted. Their humble response to his call to a contrite spirit helped launch America's First Great Awakening.

A sermon about repentance that helped launch the Great Awakening in colonial America

Theodore Jacob Frelinghuysen (1691-1747)

***"In a contrite spirit** are found: a deep sense and clear perception of sin. . . . Heart-felt disquietude and sadness. . . . an open and free confession of sin. By reason of a sense of the greatness of his sins, he knows not whither to look or turn: . . . **Thus he is driven out of himself, to the sovereign grace of God in Christ,** for reconciliation, pardon, sanctification, and salvation."*[18]

If you are dissatisfied with your level of consecration and Christ-likeness, *A Man's Journey with God* will give you an opportunity to turn your life around and have a new beginning.

When you become more consecrated, you will increase your ability to hear God's voice. Jesus could hear God because He *is* God. He is holy, harmless, and undefiled.[19] When you become like Jesus, you become more holy, more harmless, and more undefiled, and you can hear God more clearly. Hearing God more clearly is an inevitable result of the process of consecrating yourself.

You may not be able to change anybody else right away. You may not be able to change your family or your church, but you can change yourself through your commitment to consecration. Then you will be able to hear God when He tells you what everybody else needs.

Jesus was the firstborn of many brethren.[20] We are His kinfolk. We have the same Father.

As we will say often, Jesus is our role model for the consecrated life. He did not demand to have His needs met. He came to meet the needs of others. He came to die—not only *in* the flesh on the cross but also *to* the flesh in the daily decisions He made. He is calling us to be conformed to His image—to become just like Him. That's a place of victory for us and a great satisfaction to the Father.

---

[18] This quote was captured in Issue 23 of *Christian History* magazine, a valuable resource published by *Christianity Today*. Several of the original issues like this one are available online. Issue No. 23, subtitled "Spiritual Awakenings in North America" is well worth reading. It is available online at https://www.christianhistoryinstitute.org/uploaded/50cf796bc8bdb7.30632672.pdf. Accessed February 2016.

[19] See Hebrews 7:26.

[20] See Romans 8:29.

Jesus, firstborn of many more men like Him *Romans 8:29 NKJV*	*"For whom He foreknew, He also predestined to be conformed to the image of His Son, that He might be the firstborn among many brethren."*

Consecrating Yourself Daily to Do the Will of God

When you consecrate yourself, you prepare yourself daily and diligently[21] to be a man of God and do everything God might call on you to do. As you seek God daily and study His Word, ask Him to purify your heart, change your motivations, and help you to become more like Jesus.

As the Holy Spirit sheds light on the unholy areas of your life, ask God to perfect you and get you in shape for the battles to come in the unknown future. When you fall, get back up and give Him praise.

When God saved you, He saw you as His child. He welcomed you into His family. God loves you, and because He loves you, just like any father, He wants you to grow up to be just like Him. He wants you to grow beyond the baby stage and come to full age where you are a man of God who sees beyond his own personal needs and brings a spiritual revolution.

We are called children of God *1 John 3:1 NKJV*	*"Behold what manner of love the Father has bestowed on us, that we should be called children of God!"*

Children love spending time with a father who loves them. When you know God as your Father, you love being with Him. When you spend time with Him in the intimacy of the prayer closet, He shares His heart with you. He gives you a passion to reach others who don't yet know Him as you do. After a while, you begin to look like Him, and people are drawn to you because you look like Jesus to them. They love spending time with you because it is like spending time with God. Then you can teach them how to know Him in the same way you do.

[21] See Proverbs 8:17.

Sacrifice is your reasonable service

Romans 12:1-2 KJV

"I beseech you therefore, brethren, by the mercies of God, that ye present your bodies a living sacrifice, holy, acceptable unto God, which is your reasonable service. And be not conformed to this world: but be ye transformed by the renewing of your mind, that ye may prove what is that good, and acceptable, and perfect, will of God."

Your Heart Will Be Affected by *A Man's Journey with God*

The practical and spiritual exercises in *A Man's Journey with God* will give you an opportunity to develop a new level of heart intimacy with God. In your prayers, ask Him what He wants you to do—what you were born to do. As you listen for His voice and do whatever He tells you, don't be surprised if He begins to give you an awareness of the need for revival and spiritual awakening in your community and nation.

When God sees He can trust you, He may entrust you with significant assignments that might eventually transform history. That's where revivals come from.

Praying Men Bring Revival

Events leading to revival in church or spiritual awakening in society

1. **Someone prays.** Some man gets serious about God and prays.

2. **He sees a desperate need.** He sees the desperation of those around him to know Jesus Christ as Lord and Savior.

3. **He yields to God.** He submits himself to the requirements of God for his own life even as he prays for others to change.

4. **He goes after God with intensity.** He seeks the Lord until God comes upon him, and then He seeks God for those who need to be saved or to yield more fully to His Lordship.

5. **He takes responsibility for bringing the next revival.** He commits himself fully to the responsibility of bringing revival to his city, culture, nation, or generation, and goes after it, regardless of the personal cost.

Start a Revolution by Your Writing

When you spend this much time with God, He will speak to you. Write down in your journal what He says. You have the potential to start a revolution with the revelations that God will give you.

Remember what we said—a revolution is started by the spoken word, but carried by the printed page. Remember, someday someone might put your words in print to inspire others, as happened with many of the other books and journals of famous people that you will be reading here.

When your life is an awesome testimony to the reality of God, people can live off the substance of your dedication.

PERSONAL NOTES

Chapter 2

What Can Happen When Christ Brings Revival

"Wilt thou not revive us again:
that thy people may rejoice in thee?"[22]

One of the greatest revivals in American history began in New York City in 1857 when a layman who believed in prayer distributed a flyer inviting people to pray. Jeremiah Lanphier had been converted to Christ in Broadway Tabernacle (pastored by Charles Finney before he moved to Oberlin College). Lanphier had been given the assignment as "city missionary" for the Dutch Reformed Church in Manhattan, which, like many other churches in America in that day, was losing members. He wrote an invitation to noonday prayer and distributed it in leaflets.

History-Making New York Revival

Revival historian J. Edwin Orr described what happened after that first New York City prayer meeting as it quickly grew into a widespread movement that swept the nation and affected the world.

> ***In response to his advertisement, only six people out of a population of a million showed up.*** *But the following week there were fourteen, and then twenty-three when it was decided to meet every day for prayer. By late winter they were filling the Dutch Reformed Church, then the Methodist Church on John Street, then Trinity Episcopal Church on Broadway at Wall Street.* ***In February and March of 1858, every church and public hall in down town New York was filled.***

[22] Psalm 85:6 KJV.

How Often Shall I Pray?

Handbill distributed by Jeremiah Lanphier before revival hit New York City, 1857[23]

"As often as the language of prayer is in my heart; as often as I see my need of help; as often as I feel the power of temptation; as often as I am made sensible of any spiritual declension or feel the aggression of a worldly spirit.

"In prayer we leave the business of time for that of eternity, and intercourse with men for intercourse with God.

"A day Prayer Meeting is held every Wednesday, from 12 to 1 o'clock, in the Consistory building in the rear of the North Dutch Church, corner of Fulton and William Streets (entrance from Fulton and Ann Streets).

"This meeting is intended to give merchants, mechanics, clerks, strangers, and business men generally an opportunity to stop and call upon God amid the perplexities incident for those who may find it inconvenient to remain more than five or ten minutes, as well as for those who can spare the whole hour."

"Horace Greeley, the famous editor, sent a reporter with horse and buggy racing round the prayer meetings to see how many men were praying. In one hour he could get to only twelve meetings, but he counted 6,100 men attending. *Then a landslide of prayer began, which overflowed to the churches in the evenings. People began to be converted, ten thousand a week in New York City alone. The movement spread throughout New England, the church bells bringing people to prayer at eight in the morning, twelve noon, and six in the evening. The revival raced up the Hudson and down the Mohawk, where the Baptists, for example, had so many people to baptize that they went down to the river, cut a big hole in the ice, and baptized them in the cold water. When Baptists do that they are really on fire!"*[24]

Edwin Orr, revival historian

[23] J. Edwin Orr, *The Light of the Nations Evangelical Renewal and Advance in the Nineteenth Century* (Grand Rapids, MI: Eerdmans, 1963).
[24] J. Ibid.

Revival fires spread by prayer meetings from America to nations

> ***"Trinity Episcopal Church in Chicago had a hundred and twenty-one members in 1857; fourteen hundred in 1860. . . .*** *Then that same revival jumped the Atlantic, appeared in Ulster, Scotland and Wales, then England, parts of Europe, South Africa and South India, anywhere there was an evangelical cause. It sent mission pioneers to many countries. Effects were felt for forty years. Having begun in a movement of prayer, it was sustained by a movement of prayer."*[25]

Impact on Churches from Third Great Awakening

It was spread by people who started lay prayer meetings but were also committed to building up their churches

Lay prayer meetings spread the revival. Revival was spread to other cities by prayer meetings, not preaching. Limits were set on the time that an individual could pray and how long the meeting would last. Entire communities were shut down for prayer, once, twice or even three times a day. Every meeting place in town might be filled.

Prayer led by lay people and heartily supported by pastors. Businessmen and other lay people were the driving force, with ministers like Henry Ward Beecher eager to assist. Charles Finney, the revival preacher, said, "The general impression seemed to be, 'We have had instruction until we are hardened; it is time for us to pray.'"[26]

Denominations worked together. New churches were planted across America. New converts joined churches. One million church members were revived. Church membership increased. Chicago's Trinity Episcopal Church, for example, went from 121 to 1,400 members.

---

[25] *Ibid.*

[26] Charles G. Finney, *The Autobiography of Charles G. Finney*. Chapter XXXIII, "Revivals in Boston in 1856-58." Online source: www.gospeltruth.net.

Impact on Families and Cities from Third Great Awakening

One in 30 Americans were converted to Christ and some cities had no unconverted citizens

One American in 30 converted to Christ in one year. Out of a national population of about 30 million, one million were converted.

Bold and lasting. Converts were bold and conversions were lasting. Some towns had no remaining unconverted citizens. New York City had 10,000 conversions in one week.

Conversations were on spiritual topics. Everyone was talking about what God was doing and what one must do to be saved. Newspapers reported favorably.

Spiritual depth built in families. Families prayed and studied the Bible together, applying spiritual principles to their lives.

First Awakening and a Consecrated Man: David Brainerd

Earlier in America's history, an obscure 18th century missionary to Native Americans named David Brainerd (1718-1747) had an impact on the American colonies in spite of personal doubts and debilities.

David Brainerd's experience at Yale

David Brainerd was born on April 20, 1718, in Haddam, Connecticut, as the son of devout Puritan parents who died before he reached the age of 15. In 1741 he enrolled at Yale, which at that time was a school for training ministers. As a sophomore, he had to leave school because of an illness that was probably tuberculosis, the disease that presumably caused his death at the age of 29. Upon his return to Yale, tensions had developed between leaders of the spiritual awakening that was taking place in the American colonies and those at Yale who considered the revivalists' "enthusiasm" to be too excessive. Yale trustees promised to expose and then expel any student who persisted in making negative comments about the spiritual condition of the trustees or faculty.

David was accused of making negative comments in private against the leaders and expelled. He humbly apologized and asked to return. The great theologian Jonathan Edwards, whose message "Sinners in the Hands of an Angry God" helped launch the First Great Awakening, befriended David and described how well he handled himself during this crisis.

"'I was witness,' says Mr. Edwards, 'to the very christian [sic] spirit which Brainerd showed at that time; being then at New-Haven, and one whom he thought fit to consult on that occasion.
"'There truly appeared in him a great degree of calmness and humility; without the least appearance of rising of spirit for any ill-treatment which he supposed he had suffered, or the least backwardness to abase himself before those, who, as he thought, had wronged him. What he did was without any objection or appearance of reluctance, even in private to his friends, to whom he freely opened himself.
"'Earnest application was made on his behalf, that he might have his degree then given him; and . . . many arguments were used, but without success. He desired his degree, as he thought it would tend to his being more extensively useful; but still, when he was denied it, he manifested no disappointment nor resentment.'"

The Works of Jonathan Edwards, Volume One, Chapter XIII[27]

Brainerd Honored God in His Youth

The author of Ecclesiastes gives a charge to youth to honor God and remember Him in the midst of life's trials and triumphs. Brainerd was an example of these words of wisdom:

"Don't let the excitement of youth cause you to forget your Creator. Honor him in your youth before you grow old and say, 'Life is not pleasant anymore.' Remember him before the light of the sun, moon, and stars is dim to your old eyes, and rain clouds continually darken your sky."[28]

---

[27] Available online at Christian Classics Ethereal Library, www.ccel.org.
[28] Ecclesiastes 12:1-2 NLT.

The Apostle Paul told Timothy to disregard those who criticized him for his youth but to press on and be an example of love, faith, and purity.

> *"Don't let anyone think less of you because you are young. Be an example to all believers in what you say, in the way you live, in your love, your faith, and your purity."*[29]

Responding to injustice with serenity

Jonathan Edwards, who might have been David Brainerd's father-in-law if he lived, recognized admired his rare qualities of humility in the face of personal injustice. He said that David "manifested no disappointment nor resentment."

Answering the sacrificial call to ministry

Because David Brainerd turned to God in the midst of his trials, he was able to hear God's voice when He called him away from the academic life and even away from the security of civilization. He became a missionary to the Native Americans, traveling day and night on horseback, preaching for a long time with no visible results.

During this time, he kept a personal journal that can still be read today. In fact, his commitment to follow God in the midst of discouragement and physical infirmities has inspired centuries of godly men not to give up.

In 1749, after David's untimely death, Jonathan Edwards published an edition of Brainerd's personal journal. His transparency in recording the personal struggles of a Christian eventually affected the spiritual destiny of nations. His perseverance in the face of affliction inspired major Christian leaders like John Wesley and William Carey, who reached nations with the Gospel.

John Wesley, founder of the Methodist Church, supplied copies of Brainerd's journal to his ministers and said, "Let every preacher read carefully over the Life of Brainerd."

William Carey, missionary to India, regarded Edwards' *Life of Brainerd* as a sacred text.

David Livingstone, British missionary to Africa; Andrew Murray, South African pastor; Jim Elliot, who was later martyred by the Auca Indians—all drew inspiration from *Brainerd's Journal*.

---

[29] 1 Timothy 4:12 NLT.

Trials and Challenges of Missionary David Brainerd

1741. Enrolled at Yale (then a school for ministers), rose to top of class, expelled. Criticism of a professor stirred a controversy during First Great Awakening.

1742. Licensed to preach as a Presbyterian. First message to Indians, August 12, near Connecticut-New York border.

1743. Minimal impact on Indians at Kaunameek, near Stockbridge, Massachusetts. Some response. Depressed by worldliness of church. Plagued by illness and hardship.

1744. Minimal impact on Indians at Delaware River in Pennsylvania. Some interest but he failed to achieve widespread response and was ill most of the time.

1745. Minimal impact on Iroquois on Susquehanna River. A few stirrings in the people but he failed to achieve success.

Brainerd refused to give up his vision for evangelism. Finally, in 1745, Brainerd's interpreter, Moses Tautomy, on a brief trip with Brainerd back to Delaware, gave his life to Christ, along with his wife. Then God gave Brainerd his first new convert, a woman, and a spiritual awakening broke out. These conversions and the experience of spiritual fathering brought him such joy that it seemed like heaven.

Vision of heaven because of Brainerd's love for his new converts

David Brainerd (1718-1747)

"After public worship a number of my dear Christian Indians came to my house; with whom I felt a sweet union of soul. My heart was knit to them; and I cannot say I have felt such a sweet and fervent love to the brethren for some time past; and I saw in them appearances of the same love. This gave me something of a view of the heavenly state; and particularly that part of the happiness of heaven, which consists in the communion of saints.[30]

[30] *The Life and Diary of the Rev. David Brainerd, Part III.* A.D. 1742. July-November. 25. 329. Online at Christian Classics Ethereal Library, www.ccel.org.

Spiritual Awakening of Delaware Indians in 1745 at Crossweeksung (near Trenton, New Jersey) *Breakthrough for dedicated missionary, David Brainerd*	*"My soul, my very soul, longed for the ingathering of the poor heathen; and I cried to God for them most willingly and heartily; I could not but cry."*[31] (*Brainerd's Journal*, July 26, 1745, 13 days before spiritual awakening at Crossweeksung) *July 1745.* Breakthrough conversion of interpreter Tautomy and wife. *August 8, 1745.* Conversions of Indians, who began coming from miles around. *August 25, 1745.* Baptized 25 people. *1745-1747.* Set up Christian community, schools for children and adults.

Impact of Brainerd's life on Yale, Princeton, and Dartmouth

In addition to Brainerd's missionary work among the Native Americans his life also affected the founding and renewal of at least three of what we now know as the prestigious Ivy League schools—Yale, Princeton, and Dartmouth.

In colonial times, the first colleges that were founded that we know today as Ivy League schools were Harvard and Yale. They were both founded by Christians for the education of ministers.

Yale, founded in 1701 by Congregationalists. When Brainerd was expelled from Yale in the midst of America's First Great Awakening, Jonathan Dickinson and Aaron Burr, Sr.,[32] tried to get Brainerd reinstated but without success. Nevertheless, his life and witness had an impact and Yale experienced later revivals.

Princeton, founded as College of New Jersey, 1746. Dickinson and Burr were so disturbed by the policies in place at Yale that they founded a new school, College of New Jersey, which became Princeton University.

[31] *Life and Diary of the Rev. David Brainerd.*

[32] Aaron Burr, Sr., was the son-in-law of Jonathan Edwards and a founder and president of Princeton University (then called College of New Jersey and founded for the education of ministers). His son, Aaron Burr, Jr, became vice president of the United States under Thomas Jefferson. (Aaron, Jr., also had an infamous duel with Alexander Hamilton where Hamilton died.)

Founding of Dartmouth, 1769. Eleazar Wheelock (a Congregationalist) read in Brainerd's diary about his work with the native Americans. Then he went to the Iroquois and Algonquin tribes. He then founded a school to educate them and moved it to Hanover, New Hampshire, where he named it "Dartmouth."

COLLEGES FOUNDED IN FIRST GREAT AWAKENING

Princeton (1746). Founded as College of New Jersey in Princeton, New Jersey, by Presbyterians (Ivy League)

University of Pennsylvania (1751). Founded as the Academy in Philadelphia, Pennsylvania, by Quakers (nonsectarian) (Ivy League)

Columbia University (1754). Founded as King's College in New York City, New York, by Anglicans (Ivy League)

Brown University (1764). Founded as Rhode Island College in Providence, Rhode Island, by Baptists who were also slave traders (Ivy League)

Rutgers University (1766). Founded as Queen's College in New Brunswick, New Jersey, by Dutch Reformed (not Ivy League)

Dartmouth (1769). Founded in Hanover, New Hampshire, by Congregationalists (Ivy League)

Other American colleges founded in earlier years were also created as Christian schools for the education of the clergy: Harvard (1636, Puritans), William and Mary (1693, Anglicans), Yale (1701, Congregationalists).

"If the foundations be destroyed, what can the righteous do?"[33]

Will you take the challenge of restoring these schools to their original Christian calling through a spiritual awakening?

[33]Psalm 11:3 KJV.

Brainerd Mission gives Christ to Cherokee before Trail of Tears

In 1747 Brainerd had to give up his beloved mission because of failing health and went to stay at the home of Jonathan Edwards where Edwards' teenage daughter Jerusha nursed him in his final illness at the Edwards home. David had considered marriage to Jerusha, but chose instead his mission to the Indians. David died at the age of 29 and Jerusha died four months after his death. Her father was comforted in knowing that both of these young people had pursued the will of God as they knew it.

In 1817, 70 years after David Brainerd's death, the American Board of Commissioners for Foreign Missions founded the Brainerd Mission. It was an interdenominational outreach organized by Congregationalists. Many Cherokee were converted to Christ and made advances in community development but in 1830 these Christian Native Americans were driven off their land by President Andrew Jackson and forced to march to Oklahoma in the "Trail of Tears" where 4,000 died along the way.

However, the zeal of these missionaries was not in vain as they worked in the name of Jesus and followed the example of Brainerd. Many of the survivors kept the faith. Future Cherokee descendants would include Christian leaders like Oral Roberts, who reached millions for Christ.

Your call to ministry will be unlike anyone else's call

"I never, since I began to preach, could feel any freedom to enter into other men's labours and settle down in the ministry where the gospel was preached before."

David Brainerd's Journal, May 12, 1745, three months before spiritual awakening among Native Americans

Chapter 3

Courage of a Man Who Is Like Christ

My prayer is, Lord, make me so yielded now that
I will not have to cry over my failures when I get to heaven.
Provoke me now to come up another level in holiness and total consecration. Help me to sow seeds of destiny
into others' hearts so that they desire above all else to know You and to become like
Your Son, Jesus Christ, in every thought, word, and deed.

A Man's Journey with God gives you a unique perspective on how you are growing spiritually. Most men don't have any practical way to privately measure their development in God. This book is not a read-through. It is a work-through. It challenges you to develop the habits of consecration that helped Christians of the past to become more like Christ.

In the "Timeline at the beginning of the book, you can see not only what society was doing but also what the church was doing at the same time. Most history books don't cover much about what the Christ-like people were accomplishing but that is the only history that matters to God.

At the same time that the devil is doing his work, the church is doing greater work but most of the time nobody else knows about it. Humility doesn't mean not being known. God gave David a name when he was king. You have a destiny and a purpose that God created you for and you must not die until you fulfill His will. Your life must demonstrate Christ-likeness.

In this ManHunt movement you are called to be good ground to spend the rest of your life for only one purpose—the cause of Christ. If anything causes you to hesitate, put it on the altar. Say to the Lord, I am dying to that.When you stand for God, people may mock you and say you are "so heavenly minded that you are no earthly good." If they do, quote back to them what Jesus said about heavenly standards in the Lord's Prayer:

"Thy kingdom come. They will be done. In earth, as it is in heaven."[34]

[34]See Matthew 6:10, Luke 11:2.

In *A Man's Journey with God* I have given you something that will allow you to record a 24-hour daily self-judgment of how you spent your time. It's a self-accountability journal between you and God. I have given you just one line for each hour but you can get another journal to write more and document your day. This will enable you to record what you planned to do and what you actually did from the time you awakened in the morning until you went to sleep. *You are accounting for entire 24-hour periods every day for 30 days.*

Maybe you got up at 5:00 AM. You prayed for 45 minutes and read the Scriptures. Make a little note of it. Then you ate breakfast and got dressed. That took an hour.

You went to work. Write what you did at work. You talked to people. You write it all down.

Let's say one day you looked at a football game. Maybe you bought a lottery ticket or played a slot machine. Whatever you did, write it down. Write down how long you talked on the phone. How long did you look at television programs? Which ones? How did they affect you?

Seeing yourself in a new way by documenting your day

This will be an opportunity to record your life for one day outside of what you thought about yourself before you did the documentation. If you document your life now, you can observe yourself objectively. You have to say, "This is me right here," because you have written it all down.

What is being recorded in the Book of Life in heaven is probably going to be way more than you wrote down for 24 hours. I am asking you to do it for 30 straight days. This is a journal of your Christian life and your level of Christ-likeness. Did you talk to anyone about Christ this month? You can look back and see what you wrote down. How long did you pray? You don't have to show it to anybody. God already sees it.

You may discover that you have a false picture of your dedication level. You may hang around Christians who are not living anything or you may act like you are a serious Christian but *you* are not living anything. You are living in deception.

Your journal is your release into truth. The truth about yourself will set you free. You won't have to cover up any more. You won't have to wonder if you are a sincere Christian. Your standard is Christ. How much can you develop in the next 30 days so that what someone could read in your journal would represent the life of a true man of God?

Following in Jesus' steps

What is Christ-likeness? The whole New Testament gives you a picture of what the apostles saw in Jesus and what God revealed to them to bring themselves and others closer to being like Christ. So does the witness in your own heart if you are in tune with God. Here is one concise description of the life and gift of Christ from the Apostle Peter that can be a model for you if you will give yourself to Him. Jesus died as a martyr. You can die a *bloodless* martyrdom to your old sins and your old way of life. Follow Him in His suffering and follow Him in His resurrection.

Characteristics Peter saw in Jesus

"For God called you to do good, even if it means suffering, just as Christ suffered for you. He is your example, and you must follow in his steps.

> *He never sinned,*
> *nor ever deceived anyone.*
>
> *He did not retaliate when he was insulted,*
> *nor threaten revenge when he suffered.*
>
> *He left his case in the hands of God,*
> *who always judges fairly.*
>
> *He personally carried our sins*
> *in his body on the cross*
>
> *so that we can be dead to sin*
> *and live for what is right.*
>
> *By his wounds*
> *you are healed.*

"Once you were like sheep
who wandered away.
But now you have turned to your Shepherd,
the Guardian of your souls."[35]

[35] 1 Peter 2:21-25 NLT.

Courage to Be a Man of God in an Age of Sodomy

Billy Graham's wife Ruth Graham once said that if God didn't judge America He would have to repent for Sodom and Gomorrah.

God should be able to count on Christian men to set the standard for society according to the Bible. God should be able to send a sinner to your church because He knows that when that person gets there you will have answers for him and the love that he needs.

Calling out a specific sin—sodomy

Let us be clear about a specific sin—sodomy. God judged Sodom and Gomorrah for the sin of a man lying with a man, which God calls an abomination. God starts declaring His stand in the Old Testament.

> *"If a man practices homosexuality, having sex with another man as with a woman, both men have committed a detestable act [an abomination].*[36] *They must both be put to death, for they are guilty of a capital offense."*[37]

Ever since the beginning of creation, sodomy has been a sin. Even without the Bible, every civilized society recognized that sodomy was unnatural and most passed laws against it. Some made it punishable by death. It was that wicked.

God took a stand in the New Testament, also. Below is one of several passages condemning the practice of sex between men.

> *"And don't forget Sodom and Gomorrah and their neighboring towns, which were filled with immorality and every kind of sexual perversion. Those cities were destroyed by fire and serve as a warning of the eternal fire of God's judgment. . . . Like unthinking animals, they do whatever their instincts tell them, and so they bring about their own destruction" (Jude 7, 10 NLT).*

[36] The King James Version uses the word "abomination."
[37] Leviticus 20:13 NLT.

God's answer for "gays"—You're a Eunuch! We need you!

God judges those who live by their lusts and engage in sex with the same gender. It is not a sin to have a predisposition but it is a sin to interpret it as being "gay" and act it out.

God's answer for these men is obvious, yet most of us have missed it all these years.

Jesus' definition of a eunuch

Jesus said in Matthew 19: "Some are born as eunuchs, some have been made eunuchs by others, and some choose not to marry for the sake of the Kingdom of Heaven. Let anyone accept this who can."[38]

1. Some are born as eunuchs
2. Some are made eunuchs by others (such as when the Babylonians castrated young male prisoners like Daniel)
3. Some choose not to marry for the sake of the Kingdom of Heaven

Gays on earth have missed their calling. If the eunuch community would walk in Daniel's dedication level, it would be a culture of godliness.

- Following everything God would want.
- Giving themselves over totally
- Unioned with the purposes of God
- Communion with the voice of God
- Assignment to progress in God
- Spending their lives faithfully according to His reason for creating them

Examples of biblical eunuchs:

- Daniel and the Hebrew men Shadrach, Meshach and Abednego, who were leaders in the administration of King Nebuchadnezzar. When those Hebrew boys were captured, they were most likely castrated, which was a common practice.
- John the Baptist, Jesus, Paul, Nazarites

[38] Matthew 19:12 NLT.

Extraordinary abilities of Kingdom eunuchs

In the church today, we are probably not recognizing when we have eunuchs among us who are single men free from the lust of the flesh, the lust of the eyes, and the pride of life.[39] We should celebrate them and thank God for them and utilize their abilities. We need to welcome them as family so they will not be attracted by the counterfeit fellowship of the gay community. They love serving. They need Jesus as their First Love.Throughout the Bible, especially in the Old Testament, history records the extraordinary administrative ability of eunuchs like Daniel. Likewise, many of today's "gays" are notable for their administrative skill and entrepreneurial ability. However, they use their skills to advance the kingdom of same-sex marriage instead of the Kingdom of God.

Pat Robertson described *The Secret Kingdom*

One of the Christian leaders whom I greatly admire is Dr. Pat Robertson, founder of the Christian Broadcasting Network and Regent University. I have had an opportunity to watch his life and see his worldwide impact for the Kingdom of God for the past three decades.

Several years ago he wrote a book called *The Secret Kingdom: Your Path to Peace, Love, and Financial Security* (Word Publishing, 1992) where he described with great clarity principles that God put in place that work in all seasons of history. I recommend that you read it.

Dr. Robertson explained that there is a visible world and an invisible world and "From the beginning to the end, the Bible teaches that these two dimensions are real and very powerful."

As you compare the visible and invisible dimensions of the Secret Kingdom in your life with the contrasts that you have just read about, follow this advice from Paul in Ephesians 5:

> *"Carefully determine what pleases the Lord. Take no part in the worthless deeds of evil and darkness; instead, expose them. It is shameful even to talk about the things that ungodly people do in secret. But their evil intentions will be exposed when the light shines on them, for the light makes everything visible. This is why it is said, "'Awake, O sleeper, rise up from the dead, and Christ will give you light.'"*[40]

---

[39] 1 John 2:16 KJV.

[40] Ephesians 5:10-14 NLT.

Chapter 4

God's Call to Christ-likeness

When I ask most people, "What is the calling of God on your life?" they usually tell me about something they do—ministering in the inner cities, pastoring a church, going to another nation as a missionary, reaching students on college campuses. *That is the wrong answer.*

The primary calling of God on the life of every Christian is not something you DO. It is something you ARE.

You are being transformed into the likeness of Jesus Christ.

That call to Christ-likeness takes consecration. It takes courage. It takes integrity, truthfulness, and consistent intimacy with God. The application of that calling may vary, but the primary calling remains the same. The Bible says that this calling to Christ-likeness is a predetermined pattern for everyone who is truly saved. You are predestined to become like Jesus, if you will yield.

Predestined to become like Christ

Romans 8:29-30 KJV

"For whom he did foreknow, he also did predestinate to be conformed to the image of his Son, that he might be the firstborn among many brethren."

God's highest priority for you is not your good deeds. Lots of people on earth do "good deeds" but inside they are messed up. Many are not even saved. They are motivated by pride and their need to feel good about themselves but do not give glory to God.

The fruit God wants to see in your life is Christ-likeness.

He wants you to know Him and become like Him in every way.

When you are like Christ, then you can build on that right relationship with God all of the good deeds and soul-winning that He tells you to do. However, it will be birthed out of your intimacy with Him, not out of pride or need for man's approval.

What are you accomplishing with your time?

Sometimes we get so busy that it seems there are not enough hours in the day. Where do we find more time to pray, let alone do a 30-day journal? Many people will rob their time with God to get more time to do other things. However, whatever you are doing with that time, no matter how well intentioned, cannot substitute for your time with God.

The Bible says that all of your righteousness is as filthy rags (Isaiah 64:6). Works don't amount to anything without a right relationship with God. You can't do something evil—outside of the will of God—and then boast that good has come of it (Romans 3:8). That won't do. First, you become like Jesus. Then you try to do what He would do in every situation.

- Jesus would spend time with the Father every day.
- Jesus would go to the heathen in spite of tremendous obstacles, as David Brainerd went to the Native Americans.
- Jesus would challenge church members to be truly converted, as did Theodore Frelinghuysen.

Don't just GO to church; BE the church

What excuses have you been giving God for your lack of commitment to your quiet time or the weakness of your dedication? Will those excuses stand in that Great Day? Consecration into Christ-likeness is a battle against the powers of darkness that oppose Christ and the Church. If you don't watch out, you can *go* to church and never *be* the Church. That is why you must be constantly on the alert through your personal accountability system.

The Greek word for "church" is *ekklesia*, which means a "calling out," called out to serve. It is a high calling, the highest calling on earth.

When you are called out, you are not like the crowd. You are Zacchaeus in the tree,[41] or James and John by the sea,[42] or Matthew at the tax collector's table,[43] who left everything when Jesus called them.

I need supernatural help!

A Man's Journey with God is calling you to a high standard of holiness but it is not higher than the standard of God. If the standard seems too hard for you to attain, then you are in the right place! You are seeing that you need God's supernatural help! You cannot attain this standard on your own. Paul saw that he had not attained the standard but he didn't give up. He kept pressing toward the mark like a champion.

Pressing toward the mark

Philippians 3:12-13 KJV

"Brethren, I count not myself to have apprehended: but this one thing I do, forgetting those things which are behind, and reaching forth unto those things which are before, I press toward the mark for the prize of the high calling of God in Christ Jesus."

You can become like Jesus, but not until you follow Him just as passionately as the escaping slaves followed the North Star. Even in your darkest hours He will help you to find the way.

This was Paul's testimony:

For Christ, I willingly suffer the loss of all the things

Philippians 3:7-10 KJV

"But what things were gain to me, those I counted loss for Christ. Yea doubtless, and I count all things but loss for the excellency of the knowledge of Christ Jesus my Lord: for whom I have suffered the loss of all things, and do count them but dung, that I may win Christ, And be found in him, not having mine own righteousness, which is of the law, but that which is through the faith of Christ, the righteousness which is of God by faith: That I may know him, and the power of his resurrection, and the fellowship of his sufferings, being made conformable unto his death."

[41] See Luke 19.
[42] See Matthew 4:21.
[43] See Matthew 9:9-13.

You Can Be Holy if You Make Him Lord

Oswald Chambers was converted to Christ as a teen under the great British preacher **Charles Spurgeon**. Millions of copies of Chambers' classic devotional book *My Utmost for His Highest* are now in print. Created from his messages by his wife after his death and first published in 1927, it remains in the top ten religious best-sellers.

Oswald Chambers

(1874-1917)

Excerpt from his daily devotional, *My Utmost for His Highest*

"Beware of placing our Lord as a Teacher first. *If Jesus is a Teacher only, then all he can do is to tantalize me by erecting a standard I cannot attain. What is the use of presenting me with an ideal I cannot possibly come near? I am happier without knowing it. What is the good of telling me to be what I never can be—to be pure in heart, to do more than my duty, to be perfectly devoted to God? I must know Jesus Christ as Saviour before His teaching has any meaning for me other than that of an ideal which leads to despair.* ***But when I am born again of the Spirit of God, I know that Jesus Christ did not come to*** **teach** ***only: He came to*** **make me what He teaches I should be.** *The Redemption means that Jesus Christ can put into any man[44] the disposition that ruled His own life, and all the standards God gives are based on that disposition."*[45]

In that excerpt Chambers challenges us about how we are relating to Jesus. If you keep trying to be more holy and failing, maybe you are relying too much on your own strength without seeking real power from God. You are holding God at a distance. You are using Jesus as a Teacher when you should be yielding to Him as Lord.

---

[45]Oswald Chambers. *My Utmost for His Highest* (Grand Rapids, Michigan: Discovery House, 1935, 1963, 1992). Daily devotionals from this book are available online.

Chapter 5

Fantasy Christianity

Fantasy football and fantasy Christianity kind of go together. Too many men see Christianity as a fantasy. However, the true religion where you should be challenged to lose your life for your beliefs is Christianity, not Islam.

All of the apostles except maybe John the Revelator died as martyrs. They found out that faith in Jesus was real and they were willing to die for it.

No Christian in natural history has lived up to the standards of the Bible, but that doesn't mean you shouldn't try. Unless you set your standard to become like Jesus, some area of the world will stay in regression because you are missing in action.

Disciple nations—that means to change them!

Before Jesus ascended, He gave us an assignment. He said to disciple nations. Did He mean you should go there and change a whole nation? Change them to what? They already have structure. They have systems of authority. They have economic systems. Yet He said, Whatever I taught you, you teach them and it's non optional. In other words, I'm not going to go over there and negotiate with you. I am coming to change you.

What do you think the recruits do when they join ISIS? They change priorities. They change their goals. They are deceived by the cause but they understand commitment. They have a zeal to change nations. Somebody's teaching allowed each nation on earth to become what it is, for evil or good. Somebody's information built the chair that you are sitting on right now. You have to decide what to do with the information and revelation that you read in the Bible and what you hear from your pastor and other men of God. You have to pray and listen for instructions.

When your faith becomes real and not fantasy, it will affect your life and your fulfillment of God's calling.

"Those who listen to instruction will prosper; those who trust the Lord will be joyful."[46]

Jesus said:

"Anyone who listens to my teaching and follows it is wise,

like a person who builds a house on solid rock."[47]

He also said that whoever listens to Him and adheres to His teachings will be raised up as a new man. This new man will not be common. He will not be like you until you have decided that this word is true and you are going to change everything you previously had decided for your life and hear Him instead. All of us have already proven what we can do with our lives on our own. I guarantee if you are serious about God you want to be better than your past. Let me just go on record. I do. I don't want to stay the same.

No ceiling on your potential for growth

With no ceiling on my potential for growth and Almighty God as my Father, why would I want to accomplish only what I have accomplished to date? Why would I want to function as a mere human when I am born of God? Something has to break in you to become something more as a Christian. No man can define that level for you. That's why you need to devote more attention to hearing God. You and I have to satisfy the One who made us. Our Creator is on a ManHunt to find a godly man to stand in the gap. I have decided to become that man. If you think it is a fantasy that Jesus died for your sins to give you a new life, repent of your sins now and ask Him to come into your heart. That is the pathway to life. Stop right now and give Him your life.

Giving Your Gifts to Reach the Generation

What gifts has God given you that, if they were dedicated to Him, could reach the hearts of the sinners of the world?

What excuses have you given for holding back your gifts?

If you don't see that you have gifts, ask God to show you.

---

[46] Proverbs 16:20 NLT.

[47] Matthew 7:24 NLT.

Then I shall see *1 Corinthians 13:12 KJV*	*"For now we see through a glass, darkly; but then face to face: now I know in part; but then shall I know even as also I am known."*

What is the point of a ManHunt? Seeing what is wrong around you and taking the responsibility to cleanse the land.

"Again the word of the Lord came to me: 'Son of man, say to the land, "You are a land that has not been cleansed or rained on in the day of wrath."'"[48]

However, before you can cleanse the land you've got to get clean yourself. God was talking to us through Ezekiel. He was not talking through a perfect man but through a man named Ezekiel who was willing to be cleansed and write down what God told him for future generations. David said in Psalms 110:3 KJV, "Thy people shall be willing in the day of thy power." God is looking for people who will give themselves totally over to God so He can make a difference in their lives and use them to accomplish his goals for the earth. He has goals that He wants to accomplish through you. He is the only One with the authority to set goals. You don't set goals until you ask God if these are His goals, too.

Going on a ManHunt for Other Men

God is on a ManHunt for you, and He wants you to be on a ManHunt for other men to win them to Jesus. Why would you win a person to Jesus? What is supposed to happen to them? Do they just miss hell and go to heaven?

No, those who are saved should run the nations if they are consecrated and committed to govern by the same underlying biblical principles that are the foundation of America.

Where can you apply Christian principles? Everywhere. What's supposed to happen to people once those principles are established? Orderly structure and blessing. They are to be both learned and applied, not just heard. Biblical principles that are fixed, uniform, and universal are not only good for this world but will also apply in the next world. We are all going to die naturally but spiritually there is no death. We

[48] Ezekiel 22:23-24 NLT.

go to the next world. If you are born again, Jesus has prepared a place for you and you will have a function there and so will those who are saved on a ManHunt.

"Therefore be imitators of God, as beloved children" (Ephesians 5:1 NASB).

We are called to imitate God not only in this life but also in the next life. To what degree do you imitate Him now?

God has men here on earth now who have received Him and have become His messengers. So many other men are far from God and would say right away, "I'm not a minister." What are you then? Because the word minister means to serve. You mean you don't hear anything from God?

Do you need to have a designation and a pastor's title in order to hear something from God and become His messenger? Don't you have any relationship with God? Any sense of assignment? Is there nothing you can say that could make a difference?

The issue is not whether or not you are a minister by official title. God's issue is whether you have been available to Him or not by setting aside significant time for prayer. Jesus said, "It is written, My house shall be called the house of prayer."[49] You pray because you believe that you are a house of prayer. Someone is listening and something will happen when you talk to Him. That is not fantasy. That is reality.

My Prayer for You

I'm asking you, Lord, don't let a single one of the men reading this book die until the reason you brought them into the earth is fulfilled. I pray that each one of them would receive that mindset.

—That they would say to you, Not my will, God. Thy will be done.

—That they would break yokes and bondages and limitations.

—That they would be so surrendered to you that they would understand that the only limitations on them are those you give them. Nothing else would be strong enough to stop them from doing Your will because the Lord would be at hand in these men.

—You spoiled principalities and made a show of them openly.

—You gave a demonstration of what we are supposed to do.

Let them receive that now. In Jesus' name. Amen.

[49] Matthew 21:13 KJV.

Chapter 6

The Devil Is Defeated

Can you see eternal truths at work in spite of your circumstances? Seeing the truth takes spiritual eyes. That is why you need the Holy Spirit to lead you past your misconceptions and into unseen truth.

Holy Spirit guides you into all truth
John 16:13-14 KJV

"Howbeit when he, the Spirit of truth, is come, he will guide you into all truth: for he shall not speak of himself; but whatsoever he shall hear, that shall he speak: and he will shew you things to come. He shall glorify me: for he shall receive of mine, and shall shew it unto you."

Jesus is always glorified by the Holy Spirit's witness to your heart. The devil's lies may sound true at first, as they did when the snake talked to Eve in the Garden, but you will not be fooled if you put those lies to the holiness test. If your thoughts are unholy and they do not glorify Jesus, they are not from God. Just ask the Holy Spirit.

Get All the Snake Out of You, Man!

In the ghetto where I come from, when a man didn't stand up for himself we would say he is a sissy or a punk. We would rather die than not be man.

In the Garden of Eden (Genesis 3) Adam failed the test to be a man. He lost his authority. He was a punk. Not only that. He was henpecked.

Adam had a "God-said." God told him personally not to eat off the tree of the knowledge of good and evil.[50] The woman had an "Adam-said." Adam told the woman what God had said. She didn't hear that word herself. When the serpent came to the Garden and started talking to her and she agreed, the man was standing right there beside her but he did not speak up and tell her she was wrong. She was deceived but Adam was not.

---

[50] See Genesis 2:16-17.

"For God made Adam first, and afterward he made Eve. And it was not Adam who was deceived by Satan. The woman was deceived, and sin was the result."[51]

Adam willfully disobeyed God. He had a chance to be a real man and stand up for his woman but instead he was a punk. God had given him authority and dominion over the serpent. Adam was the one who named the snake, but at that crucial moment he did not walk in his authority from God. He allowed the woman to decide something that went against what God had said to him. He was henpecked. As a result, God had to judge him directly. The weight of judgment fell on the man.

When the woman ate, nothing happened in heaven. When she gave it to the man, there were no recriminations. But when the man ate, that was a cataclysmic moment. Their eyes were suddenly opened and they hid.

Adam's violations came under the three main categories of all sin—"the lust of the flesh, and the lust of the eyes, and the pride of life."[52]

When God came He went straight to the man. He told Adam:

"Because you have listened to the voice of your wife, and have eaten from the tree about which I commanded you, saying, 'You shall not eat from it'; Cursed is the ground because of you; In toil you will eat of it All the days of your life.

He said to the man, "You listened to the voice of your wife and did what I commanded you not to do." Adam was supposed to be promoted out of the garden, but because he failed to follow God he was kicked out.

You and I have inherited our sin nature from Adam. The Bible says we are born in sin. However, God wants you to be born *again*. He wants to prepare you to become like the Last Adam, Jesus, so that He can trust you to rule—not only over a garden, or your present jurisdiction, but over worlds.

This life is just a seed life. God is using your circumstances on earth to get all of the snake out of you now so that He can use you in the future to rule in eternity.

You are being positioned to rule and reign with Christ, and He doesn't allow snakes to be kings with Christ. God cast the devil out of heaven, so He certainly doesn't want us to bring the devil back up in there again by acting like snakes.

---

[51] 1 Timothy 2:13-14 NLT.

[52] 1 John 2:16 KJV.

Abundance *John 10:10 KJV*	*"The thief cometh not, but for to steal, and to kill, and to destroy: I am come that they might have life, and that they might have it more abundantly."*

The devil tells lies about God ("You shall not surely die," Genesis 3:4) and is the accuser of the brethren[53] so when Christians are deceived they fight harder against God and other Christians than they fight against the devil! They let the devil use them for his purposes because they are not consecrated.

When the devil fights to keep you separated from God and fighting against Christians, resist him. Don't give in. You have the promise of the Word of God. If you resist the devil, he will flee.[54]

Defeat the devil from the inside out

God wants to do a remodeling project inside your inner man so that you are transformed more and more into His likeness. He wants you to give up your old Adamic, snake-like nature and put on a new nature, the holy nature of Jesus. Jesus defeated Satan and made a show of him openly because he was consecrated. You can do the same.

Jesus showed up the devil *Colossians 2:15 KJV*	*"And having spoiled principalities and powers, he made a shew of them openly, triumphing over them in it."*

God has given you the potential to become Christ-like and gain the same power that Jesus has over the devil.

Jesus gives you power over the devil *Luke 10:18-19 KJV*	*"And he said unto them, I beheld Satan as lightning fall from heaven. Behold, I give unto you power to tread on serpents and scorpions, and over all the power of the enemy: and nothing shall by any means hurt you."*

Because Jesus is holy, you can be holy in your inner man. You can become free of every evil force that keeps you from being like Him. All of your conduct can become the fruit of Christ-likeness as you develop your inner holiness.

---

[53] See Revelation12:10.
[54]See James 4:7.

Fruit of the Holy Spirit *Galatians 5:22-23 NKJV*	*"But the fruit of the Spirit is love, joy, peace, longsuffering, kindness, goodness, faithfulness, gentleness, self-control. Against such there is no law."*

The devil is a liar

When you believe in God and understand His power, everything in life looks good instead of bad. Joy becomes your testimony. The world becomes a theater for displaying God's glory.

"The heavens declare the glory of God; and the firmament sheweth his handiwork."[55]

The devil has none of the positive attributes of God. Don't let the devil steal your health or your relationships or anything else that God has given you. Don't listen to your thoughts when the devil accuses those close to you and tries to turn you against them. Drive him out!

My mother had a great approach to the devil. She called him a "lying rascal"! She was not afraid to tell him off. Jesus said in the Great Commission mandate that part of our inheritance as Christians is the ability to cast out devils. Don't let the devil get away with anything that takes you out of the nature and character of God and what He has determined to establish on the earth.

Jesus did not hesitate to include in the Lord's Prayer, "Deliver us from evil" or you could say, "Deliver us from the evil one." That's part of the power that He gives us in His Kingdom, in earth as it is in heaven. Amen!

Deliver us from evil *Matthew 6:13 KJV*	*"And lead us not into temptation, but deliver us from evil: For thine is the kingdom, and the power, and the glory, for ever. Amen."*

God calls you to be holy, like Christ. If that were not possible, He would not have given you that standard. ***You can be holy.***

[55] Psalm 19:1 KJV.

Chapter 7

Holiness—God's Answer for an Unclean Land

"Thou art the land that is not cleansed"
(Ezekiel 22:24 KJV).

The prophet Ezekiel was not a perfect man, like Jesus, but God used him because he was a man who was willing to be cleansed and then go out on assignment to cleanse the land. God could speak to the nation through Ezekiel's prophetic writings.

God is looking for men today who are willing to give themselves totally over to God so that He can speak through them as He spoke through Ezekiel. When you willingly yield to God, you receive power to be holy. God makes a difference in your life and you become clean and willing to cleanse the land in you and the land you live in. As the Bible says:

"Thy people shall be willing in the day of thy power" (Psalms 110:3 KJV).

God has the power to clean anything. Not one negative thing in the culture is too much for God to handle. Nothing intimidates God. He is almighty!

God is seeking men of significance who know Him, honor Him, and glorify Him and show other people how to be made clean. God will impart His authority and power to you once He sees that He can trust you.

As you present yourself to God daily by completing your 30-day personal accountability journal, He will see whether or not He can trust you and you will see if God can trust you, too.

God is doing something special in your life. As a man of God you should cultivate the idea that something positive is about to happen. Don't be overtaken by negatives. Anticipate something good and anticipate that you will be used to make good things happen.

When you are attuned to God through prayer and consecration, you can use your trials to develop spiritual strength. This life is a tried life. You grow in God through your trials.

As you grow chronologically, you are tried in natural ways. You are tried as a child at about age 5 when you first go to school. Then each grade level is a tried level. You learn. You're tested on what you learn. If you're effective in what you are learning and can remember it for a test, then you are promoted to the next grade. There is a constant progression.

Remember, the goal of ManHunt is for you to progress into that man who will stand in the gap whom God describes in Ezekiel 22:30, to become that man God is seeking but has not been able to find.

"And I sought for a man among them,
that should make up the hedge, and
stand in the gap before me for the land,
that I should not destroy it: but I found none."
(Ezekiel 22:30 KJV)

Holiness—God's Answer to Pornography

You can't watch TV, movies, or sports and not realize that there are some fine women out there on display. If you had a chance and no one was looking, would you have sex with her? She looks like she has nothing on but her underwear. She is shaking her stuff. She is saying to the whole world not only "Look at me" but also "I will give you some of this."

If she said to you, "I'll give you some," would you take it? Or are you a man of God standing strong for the sake of other men tempted to live by their lusts?

If God is not in you and your body is not the temple of the Holy Ghost, you are a piece of bread to her. You have to see that she is just a woman who needs God.

If I could look in her eyes, she would be uncomfortable with me looking in her eyes because I would not be admiring her looks. I would know she's a whore. She's not selling sex in the streets but she's selling it on national television. She does that for money.

You call yourself a Christian man. Christ is in you. (Now I'm really getting in your mess.) If you lust after some fine-looking woman or a *picture* of a woman and entertain ungodly thoughts, would Jesus say to you when you get to heaven, "Well done, you good and faithful servant. I loved it that you enjoyed that woman showing her stuff and throwing sex up in your mouth"?

Man, don't you know He can see you now?

I'm getting older but I'm not blind. Let me tell what I do. When something like that comes up on TV that I was not expecting, I turn away quickly and I think about how sorry I feel for her. I pray, "Father, convict her. If she once made a commitment to the Lord, send her back to church."

You don't know those women. Do you think what you are seeing is reality? If you do, you're a knucklehead. You are living in the realm of nothingness. People are hiding out. They don't want you to see who they really are. You are having sex with demons.

I am responsible for my actions and my reactions. I am not only accountable to God but also to my spiritual sons. If I lusted after one of those women, to that degree I would be the seed to put the spirit of lust in all my sons. Every son reproduces after his own kind.

I am not only pure in relation to God. I am pure in relation to you. As the old hymn says, "I would be true, for there are those who trust me; I would be pure, for there are those who care."[56]

As I am pure, my expectation is that you are pure when I am your dad. Nobody has to watch over you because you are lusting and dribbling all at the mouth at some nasty woman who looks clean but is of the devil. The devil doesn't go around showing you that he is nasty. He looks clean. He masquerades as an angel of light. That means his daughters look like they are really nice people. They look clean to you, but like the man says, "Dirt is what dirt does."

When you are holy, like God, you have power over sin, both in yourself and others. When Christians are holy, like God, together they become a unified, transforming force in society.

The Holy Ghost comes upon you when you are born again, but because of Adam's Fall something in your nature resists yielding to God, even after you are saved. You still want to be in charge. You may admit that you need to change but you do it on your timetable, not God's. You still listen to the devil too much without rebuking him and turning away. God cannot use you until you are yielded to His holiness. He is watching your life to see how much He can trust you to do what He would do. He is deciding where He will place you now and in the next world.

Revivals and spiritual awakenings are birthed when people enter an intense search for personal holiness and God responds to them and gives them the power to save sinners.

Unbelievers respond to a Christian whose heart's desire is to be holy. They become born again and begin to clean up their lives with a resulting transformation of society. They love the will of God more than the sin nature they inherited from Adam, that nature that makes them want to hide from God.[57]

---

[56] Howard A. Walter, "I Would Be True." Public domain. Available online.
[57] See Genesis 3:8..

Holy People of God

Jesus. *"And the angel answered and said unto her, The Holy Ghost shall come upon thee, and the power of the Highest shall overshadow thee: therefore also **that holy thing** which shall be born of thee shall be called the Son of God."*[58]

John The Baptist. *"**For Herod feared John, knowing that he was a just man and an holy, and observed him**; and when he heard him, he did many things, and heard him gladly."*[59]

Prophets. *"As he spake by the mouth of his **holy prophets**, which have been since the world began: That we should be saved from our enemies, and from the hand of all that hate us."*[60]

Barnabas. *"For he was a good man, and **full of the Holy Ghost** and of faith."*[61]

Families with One Believer. *"For the unbelieving husband is sanctified by the wife, and the unbelieving wife is sanctified by the husband: else were your children unclean; **but now are they holy**."*[62]

You. *"I beseech **you** therefore, brethren, by the mercies of God, that ye present your bodies a living sacrifice, **holy**, acceptable unto God, which is your reasonable service."*[63]

Holiness Disciplines Can Empower College Students

One of the most influential Christians in history is John Wesley (1703-1791), founder of the movement that became the Methodist denomination. In 1729, when he was in his mid-twenties, John came to reside at England's famous Oxford University, where his brother Charles was a college student.

The young men were members of a large and godly family of 19 children, although 13 of them died young. Their father, Samuel Wesley

[58] Luke 1:35 KJV.
[59] Mark 6:20 KJV.
[60] Luke 1:70-71 KJV.
[61] Acts 11:24 KJV.
[62] 1 Corinthians 7:14 KJV.
[63] Romans 12:1 KJV.

(1662-1735), was a clergyman and he and his wife Susanna raised them in a strong Christian home. Therefore, it was only natural that Charles would start what we would call today a Bible study among his fellow students.

When John arrived at Oxford, he soon became involved in the group and became the group's leader. They developed standards and were accountable to one another about when they got up in the morning and what they did all day. If a young man was considering marriage, he would talk to the others about the bride he had chosen. They had a standard of visiting prisons and the poor.

John Wesley was a contemporary of George Whitefield, who was also a member of this group, and both had a significant impact on reaching people for Christ on a global scale—especially England and colonial America. You could possibly say that Whitefield was even more famous than Wesley in the early stages because of his preaching skill and also his insight. God was with him.

They had formidable challenges at Oxford. Their fellow students ridiculed them and were actually the ones who gave them the name of "Holy Club" as a form of mockery. Later, when Whitefield was preaching in England and America, I have seen pictures that folks drew of people throwing animal parts at Whitefield his preaching brought such an incredible conviction of sin. That documentation is easily available in *Christian History* magazine (online) published by *Christianity Today*. It chronicles people historically and describes the challenges of evangelists in that day.

However, although Whitefield greatly impacted the culture and his preaching skill was notable, he never created a following. John Wesley had a significant impact not only through the Holy Club they created at Oxford but also through lifelong standards that he incorporated into a new movement eventually called the Methodists.

There were several noted members of the group. In addition to John Wesley and George Whitefield, there was Charles Wesley, John's brother, was a great Psalmist, a writer of songs that are still familiar today, thousands and thousands of them. But Wesley was the administrator. He was the leader and he has been given credit for what the Holy Club became.

On the next page are some of the remarkable global accomplishments that resulted from the holiness disciplines and discipleship model of John and Charles Wesley in the early 18th century.

Impact of the Disciplines of John and Charles Wesley

John Wesley (1703-1791)

- Led student Holy Club at Oxford University whose members included George Whitefield (1714-1770), who led a major spiritual awakening in America, and John and his brother Charles, who led a spiritual awakening in England.
- Rode over 250,000 miles on horseback, equal to ten times around the globe at the equator.
- Preached over 40,000 sermons.
- Wrote 5,000 sermons, tracts, and pamphlets.
- Fought against slavery.
- At his death, left in place a thriving movement that became the Methodist Church, which now numbers millions worldwide.

Charles Wesley (1707-1788)

- Wrote over 6,500 hymns, many of which are still in hymnals today. Titles include "Love Divine, All Loves Excelling," "Christ the Lord Is Risen Today," "Hark! the Herald Angels Sing," "O For a Thousand Tongues to Sing."
- Godly leader in Holy Club and Methodists.

Church Movements with Methodist Roots[64]

- 10.1 million United Methodists world-wide
- African Methodist Episcopal (AME), 2.5 million members in 30 nations
- African Methodist Episcopal Zion (AME Zion), 1.4 million members
- Foundation of other Christian movements, including Salvation Army, Church of the Nazarene, Wesleyan, Holiness—memberships of tens of millions more

[64]Online source United Methodist Church archives at http://archives.umc.org and World Council of Churches.

Amazing Love!

A hymn by Charles Wesley usually called by the first line,
"And can it be that I should gain"

"And can it be that I should gain
An interest in the Savior's blood?
Died He for me, who caused His pain—
For me, who Him to death pursued?
Amazing love! How can it be,
That Thou, my God, shouldst die for me?
Amazing love! How can it be,
That Thou, my God, shouldst die for me? . . .

"Long my imprisoned spirit lay,
Fast bound in sin and nature's night;
Thine eye diffused a quickening ray—
I woke, the dungeon flamed with light;
My chains fell off, my heart was free,
I rose, went forth, and followed Thee.
My chains fell off, my heart was free,
I rose, went forth, and followed Thee."[65]

Wesley's Personal Resolutions

"With regard to my own behavior, I now renewed and wrote down my former resolutions.

"1. To use absolute openness and unreserve with all I should converse with.
"2. To labor after continual seriousness, not willingly indulging myself in any the least levity of behavior, or in laughter; no, not for a moment.
"3. To speak no word which does not tend to the glory of God; in particular, not to talk of worldly things. Others may, nay, must. But what is that to thee? And,

[65]Charles Wesley, "And Can It Be that I Should Gain?" (1738). Available online.

"4. To take no pleasure which does not tend to the glory of God; thanking God every moment for all I do take, and therefore rejecting every sort and degree of it which I feel I cannot so thank Him in and for."[66]

Writing Your Personal Resolutions

John Wesley was able to define his resolutions. Can you define the underlying Christian principles that are the foundation of your faith and lifestyle? Have you defined personal principles of holiness for yourself? Where do you apply your principles? Could someone with your principles run the culture in a way that pleases God? During and after the 30-day consecration journey, take time to look back at what you are seeing, hearing, and writing. Maybe you will be able to encapsulate personal rules that will guide your behavior from now on.

Accountability and Eternity

A lot of people are not impressed with the idea of heaven because the only way heaven is pictured is the opposite of going to hell. And of course the way hell is described nobody wants to go there. How many people are excited to know that if they are not saved they may be going in the lake of fire and burning forever and ever? Fire and brimstone. The Lake of Gehenna. Who wants to go there? So I choose heaven.

But what do you do in heaven? Hardly anybody describes a typical cay in heaven and when they do they basically say you're going to be like the 24 elders throwing your diadems and singing songs like the choir of heaven. Some people think they will be angels and sit on a cloud.

However, the same God who can create an earth full of trees and a solar system full of planets is able to do something far greater than that in eternity. Most Christians have some anticipation of what God will do with Israel, but what applies to the nation of Israel naturally applies to the Israel of God spiritually. If you are a Christian, that affects you. That is why you need to prepare yourself now for your role in eternity. You are the creative work of God's hand. You would not be living unless God had determined that you should be alive.

---

[66] *The Journal of John Wesley*, available online at Christian Classics Ethereal Library, http://www.ccel.org/ccel/wesley/journal.i.html.

You are challenged to compromise every day. You have to decide daily if you want to keep pressing toward a new level in God, or let the devil win and ruin your life. No exceptions.

Scores of people are not as sensitive as you are about God. Jesus never did anything significant with masses. He always did it with the remnant. The question is, who is the remnant? Is it you? The word actually means "that which is left."

Somebody will always be exceptional in a day of mediocrity. If you say you are born of God, there is something great in you waiting to emerge. You can't say you are really a Christian, that God is your Father, and there's not a potential in you that nobody has seen yet. I am talking about what God can do through vessels of clay.

When you look around at the men God uses, He often uses people whom other people miss. He ordained it in creative order to use humanity to show deity. The men He uses are not necessarily the most gifted and qualified naturally but they are the ones who said, "Even so, Lord, use me."

If you can call upon God and He can respond on the basis of what you say to Him, who else does He have who is better for Him to talk to?

But if you think of prayer as religion, then why do it? There's nothing happening.

God said the prayer of faith shall save the sick. Now, if you are praying because you are confident that something will happen when you finish, that is serious and you are part of the remnant.

Holiness Applied to Society: William Booth
Founder of the Salvation Army

William Booth (1829-1912), founder of the Salvation Army, published his book *In Darkest England and the Way Out* in 1890 to describe not only the despicable problems of society in England but also the solutions—if only Christians would obey the Bible.[67]

General Booth dedicated his book to the memory of his wife Catherine, who was a vital partner in his founding of the Salvation Army in 1865 and died shortly before the book was published.

Today the Salvation Army is active in 124 countries. Committed to reaching souls for Jesus Christ, they shelter the homeless, visit prisoners, feed the hungry, deliver those on drugs and alcohol, and rescue

[67]His book recalled the title *In Darkest Africa* by Henry Morton Stanley (1841-1904), the journalist and explorer who had earlier searched for and found missionary David Livingstone.

those in need.[68] That is an example of Christ-likeness, holiness, and bringing heaven to earth that all people can follow. If we, as the Church, can change into the likeness of Jesus like that, everything we do will function more like heaven on earth.

"Time, experience, criticism, and, above all, the guidance of God will enable us, I hope, to advance on the lines here laid down to a true and practical application of the words of the Hebrew Prophet: 'Loose the bands of wickedness; undo the heavy burdens; let the oppressed go free; break every yoke; deal thy bread to the hungry; bring the poor that are cast out to thy house. When thou seest the naked cover him and hide not thyself from thine own flesh. Draw out thy soul to the hungry—Then they that be of thee shall build the old waste places and thou shalt raise up the foundations of many generations.'"[69]

William Booth

(1829-1912)

Jesus prayed for earth to become like heaven, and Jesus is still praying. The Bible says that He ever lives to pray for us.[70] Our homes can become like heaven. Our churches and schools can become like heaven. Neighborhoods and ultimately nations can become like heaven—if we have heaven inside of us, in our hearts!

As it is in heaven

Matthew 6:9-10 KJV

"After this manner therefore pray ye:
Our Father which art in heaven,
Hallowed be thy name. Thy kingdom come.
Thy will be done in earth, as it is in heaven."

When God gives you a passion for souls, the church becomes a sending station instead of a resort location. Pastors no longer boast about how many people come to church on a Sunday morning, but how many are sent out to save people from hell.

[68]See detailed statistics from the Salvation Army International online at http://www.salvationarmy.org/ihq/statistics.
[69]William Booth, *In Darkest England and the Way Out* (Salvation Army, 1890). Available online at Gutenberg.org. See also Isaiah 58.
[70]See Hebrews 7:25.

Chapter 8

Saved from Hell

Charles Thomas "C. T." Studd was a professional athlete (cricket player) in England when God called him and six other men already established in their careers to go into missions work. He was one of the "Cambridge Seven," willing to leave everything and join the China Inland Mission under Hudson Taylor. The men said, "For years in England we have been debtors. . . . and the knowledge of this precious Jesus, who to most of us is everything in the world, is absolutely wanting to thousands and millions of our fellow-men and women today."[71] God gave them a relentless vision for saving souls.

C. T. Studd

(1860-1931)

Missionary to China, India, and Africa

Rescue Within a Yard of Hell

"Some want to live
within the sound
of Church or Chapel bell;
I want to run a rescue shop
within a yard of hell."[72]

"If Jesus Christ be God and died for me, then no sacrifice can be too great for me to make for Him."[73]

[71] Online at http://www.WholesomeWords.org.
[72]The organization he founded in 1913 was called the Heart of Africa Mission, now called Worldwide Evangelisation for Christ (WEC International) and serving 49 countries. His son-in-law, Norman Grubb, took over leadership in 1930 and served until 1965. Quotes and short bio online.
[73]Quote found on a postcard on his desk that became the motto of his organization.

Studd didn't separate the people's personal needs from their need to be rescued from hell—not only hell on earth but also hell in the next world. Hell is a real place that is the eternal destiny of those who do not receive Jesus Christ as their Lord and Savior. Jesus Himself taught about hell, and His teaching on hell is just as true as His teaching about loving your neighbor, whether people want to admit it or not.

Hell was not made for humans

Hell was not made for you or any other person. It was created for the devil and his angels.[74] However, hell will become your eternal destiny if you continually reject Christ.

People choose to go to hell when they exclude themselves from heaven by becoming "dogs, and sorcerers, and whoremongers, and murderers, and idolaters, and whosoever loveth and maketh a lie."[75]

Lying, hypocrisy, adultery, and other sins will send you to hell just as much as murder. Even the stubborn refusal of a rich man to share his wealth with a poor beggar is punishable by eternal death in hell.

Reality of hell according to Jesus *Luke 16:22-24 NLT*	*Jesus said, "Finally, the poor man died and was carried by the angels to be with Abraham. The rich man also died and was buried, and his soul went to the place of the dead. There, in torment, he saw Abraham in the far distance with Lazarus at his side.* *"The rich man shouted, 'Father Abraham, have some pity! Send Lazarus over here to dip the tip of his finger in water and cool my tongue. I am in anguish in these flames.'"*

We know from that story of Jesus that personalities are recognizable in hell. There is fire in hell. There is remorse in hell. If we can't love the devil out of you, we will have to scare the devil out of you to save you.

---

[74]See Jude 1:6.
[75]Revelation 22:15 KJV.

Inadequacy of the law—need for Jesus' blood

Wrath is God's "strange work."[76] God by nature shows you Who He is—unconditional in His love, truly eternal in His character. He has provided a way of escape from hell through the blood of His Son. No matter how righteous you are, your good deeds alone cannot gain you entrance into heaven. Compared to Jesus' righteousness, all of your righteousness is as filthy rags.[77] The Law exposed the exceeding sinfulness of sin[78] and the inadequacy of our attempts at righteousness. That is why we need Jesus and His blood.

When you see that you are unable to succeed in meeting the standards of God, that is the place where the Lord comes with His mercy. That place of failure and repentance is where the Lord finds you and you are broken enough to let Him have His way with you.

God's grace is unconditional and unmerited. We not only don't deserve it, we actually deserve the opposite. He should have killed us all long ago, because He says that the wages of sin is death.[79] None of us could have met the conditions of God, the Judge of all, because He is holy. Everything about God is pure. That shows the greatness of his love, and that is why He deserves our homage.

Other than His unconditional love and grace—His unmerited favor—there is no reason why He should have sent Jesus to save us—the Lamb slain from the foundation of the world—because God is all knowing and is everywhere at once, not subject to time but the Creator of time, transcending every wall or barrier that we could put up. He knew when He created man that man would fail, but He made provision for our failure before He ever created us.

God's challenge—your free will

He's a great God! If I were to say He was challenged in any area of His creation, it would be in creating man with a will, the power to choose. The only place in His creation where He tolerates willfulness is in mankind made in his image. Everything else He judges immediately.

---

[76]See Isaiah 28:21.
[77]See Isaiah 64:6.
[78]See Romans 7:13.
[79]See Romans 6:23.

God judged Lucifer in the heavens. He judged the angels who followed Lucifer. The earth and everything else, including animal life, suffered immediately from Adam's transgression.

Adam was relegated to die immediately after he sinned but it was a spiritual death. His death was separation from God. Without a life source of revelation from God there was no real life in Adam, so the issue of Adam's death was the breaking of fellowship.

Heavenly Minded People Are Effective People

The whole matter of eternal realities is understated. Remember, when you hear people say that if you are heavenly minded you are no earthly good that doesn't correspond with the prayer that Jesus prayed, "Thy will be done in earth as it is in heaven." When you are spiritually minded, that is the only time when you are some good in the earth.

If you look back historically at the models we have of people helping other people, the most outstanding examples of sacrificial love are Christians. In America, Christians built the first universities and hospitals. They had the vision to fight for freedom. They were able to defeat slavery and help one another escape. Until you see heaven's reality and have that restoration of union with God, you will be ineffective in bringing the kingdom of heaven to the earth in the way that Jesus prayed.

As in heaven, so in earth

Luke 11:2 KJV

"And he said unto them, When ye pray, say, Our Father which art in heaven, Hallowed be thy name. Thy kingdom come. Thy will be done, as in heaven, so in earth."

Man cannot attain to God's level. It is too wonderful for us.[80] You may look good in terms of man's ability because you can accomplish a certain amount through intellectualism, discipline, training, and work ethic, but in order to accomplish the great things of God you must have a life-emanating force that comes only from God.

Adam did not need air to live. He lived by the substance of revelation. God breathed on him and man became a living soul.

[80]See Psalm 139:6.

In Genesis 2:7 (KJV) it says, "And the Lord God formed man of the dust of the ground, and breathed into his nostrils the breath of life."

When God spoke Adam into existence, He created him first as a spirit. That is the same miracle that happens to every one of us when we are born again. God spoke Adam into existence by revelation. A new being was created who had a revelation of Who God was. That is what happened to you when you were born again. You became a new being, someone saved from subjection to the world's way of thinking into the liberty of God's way of thinking.

New creature *2 Corinthians 5:17 KJV*	*Therefore if any man be in Christ, he is a new creature: old things are passed away; behold, all things are become new.*

When you are a new creature in Christ, you have received the love of God and live with an appreciation of that love. Maybe your circumstances haven't changed since you were saved, but your heart has changed. Maybe you don't fit this world, but you fit heaven. Maybe people in this earth don't like you, but God loves you. Maybe you don't carry the name of the wealthy people in this earth, but you carry the name of Jesus, the creator of wealth.

Created in the image of the One Who owns it all

God made you in His image and likeness. He owns the universe. He placed you here on the earth to be like Him. You don't know what you are talking about if you say God doesn't want us to be rich.

Before the woman came, Adam owned everything. We are impressed if somebody owns 500 acres, or a house with 5,000 square feet or 10,000 acres. Your great granddaddy Adam owned everything on earth.

If Adam owned everything and God gave it to him, then nothing could make Adam more important than he already was. In other words, money couldn't make him special. Houses couldn't impress him. Position couldn't add to him. There was nothing on the earth that could take Adam out of character until the devil came and deceived the woman to make him think he lacked something. He didn't lack anything. God had already given it all to him.

Adam named the snake. He was under Adam. So what did the snake have to say of any significance to the one who named him? Nothing. Adam should have said, "How can you tell me anything, dummy? I named you. I defined you. You are a snake. You have no importance. You don't talk unless I give you my permission, especially to my woman."

That is important. Most of your troubles come because you listen to people who are under the standard of where you are called.

What can you get that has more value than you have as a child of God? Things are not valuable until you touch them. It is stupid to go after money instead of serving God. It makes no sense to chase money because it cannot give you value. The search for riches without God is a deception. Money is nothing but a medium of exchange.

This life on earth is only a seed life. Money is temporary. You won't need money in eternity. Eternal wealth is in your future. That is why you want to cleanse your conscience and purify your heart now. You don't need to be bound by the mindset of this earthly life when you can be released into your future.

Released into a higher life through humility

Your mind can be released into a higher life. The key is humility.

He will lift you up if you move closer to Him

James 4:8-10 KJV

"Draw nigh to God, and he will draw nigh to you. Cleanse your hands, ye sinners; and purify your hearts, ye double minded. Be afflicted, and mourn, and weep: let your laughter be turned to mourning, and your joy to heaviness. Humble yourselves in the sight of the Lord, and he shall lift you up."

Chapter 9

Miraculously Healed

"And he said unto them, Go ye into all the world, and preach the gospel to every creature. He that believeth and is baptized shall be saved; but he that believeth not shall be damned. And these signs shall follow them that believe; ***In my name shall they cast out devils;*** *they shall speak with new tongues; They shall take up serpents; and if they drink any deadly thing, it shall not hurt them; they shall lay hands on the sick, and they shall recover."*[81]

One of the places where Jesus made an open show of the devil's weaknesses and His superiority was through miracles, signs, wonders, and healings. Because God is the Creator and Sustainer of all life on earth, He is able to do miracles in the earth, which is His creation.[82]

When you get a true revelation of Who God is through His Word, the intimacy of prayer, and your life experiences, you come to realize through faith that nothing is impossible for God.[83]

When you read through the Bible, you come across many passages where God heals the sick, casts out devils, and raises the dead. Jesus is our role model for miracles, including feeding 5,000 people, calming a storm, and cursing a fig tree that withered.

In the history of the Church, many other Christians through the centuries have also seen signs and wonders occur in their ministries, including John Wesley and the circuit riders who hosted camp meetings.

Modern-day preachers have also been given these gifts of healing and miracles, signs, and wonders—not only healing the sick but also raising the dead. God has the power to do anything He wants to do when it comes to His creation, including miracles for today.

---

[81]Mark 16:15-18 KJV.
[82]See Exodus 34:10.
[83]See Matthew 17:20.

As you read about miracles and healings, your faith will come alive that God can do the same mighty works today. You will be willing to face down ridicule and doubt because God is with you.

"I tell you the truth, anyone who believes in me will do the same works I have done, and even greater works, because I am going to be with the Father."[84]

Blessed with Health and Healing: John G. Lake

Before God used John G. Lake (1870-1935) in a miraculous way to bring supernatural healing to people, he was surrounded by sickness. As a child, eight of the 16 children in his family died from sickness. When he was 16, he was saved and joined the Methodist Church. God healed him of sickness at that time but he became sick again. He had heard about the healing ministry of Alexander Dowie, who founded Zion, Illinois, as a Christian community, so he went to him, and God healed him again. After that, several other family members were healed through Dowie's prayers.

A turning point in Lake's life and ministry came as he sought God for his wife, who was ill. His Bible fell open to Acts 10:38.

Healing all who are oppressed of the devil
Acts 10:38 KJV

"How God anointed Jesus of Nazareth with the Holy Ghost and with power: who went about doing good, and healing all that were oppressed of the devil; for God was with him."

His friends had been counseling him to resign himself to her death but when he saw in the Bible that sickness was of the devil, and not of God, he was filled with faith. He contacted everyone he knew and told them he was going to pray for his wife Jennie at 9:30 a.m. the next morning and that God would heal her.

The next morning at 9:30 a.m., he laid hands on his wife and she was instantaneously healed. He went on to many successful years of healing ministry, both in South Africa and the United States. During the first five years he was in Spokane, Washington, he and his team recorded 100,000 healings, and understandably it became known as the healthiest city in America!

[84] John 14:12 NLT.

This generation needs healing of body, soul, and spirit

God is a Healer. The Bible says that clearly and consistently. This generation needs healing—not only physical healing but also healing from emotional and psychological wounds.

I believe God heals diseases and infirmities because the Bible says so. Therefore, I will pray for people to be healed and I will expect God to answer.

Healing is a spectacular demonstration of God's power. Paul said it was an affirmation of His role as an apostle.

"And my speech and my preaching was not with enticing words of man's wisdom, but in demonstration of the Spirit and of power."[85]

It is legitimate for you to ask God to give you an apostolic affirmation through gifts of healing and miracles, signs, and wonders. You can ask Him to prove that your message is from God by affirming it with physical healings. We could not pray one prayer if God did not give it to us. All that we have comes from God. You are not better than someone else because you can pray for the sick and they recover. You are not necessarily missing God if you have not seen anyone healed. The gift of healing comes from God, who distributes it as He will.

However, if you are consistently seeking God in secret and reading and following the Scriptures in a life of consecration, you can expect to see God intervene miraculously in your life and the lives of those for whom you pray.

Not all who heal are of God

Not all those who are used to heal people are godly. If you look back historically in the Church, you will see that sometimes those with a healing ministry had terrible character, but God still used them to heal people. The gift speaks of the Giver, Who is God, not the person administering the gift. Give God the glory.

---

[85] 1 Corinthians 2:4 KJV.

No boasting *1 Corinthians 4:7 NKJV*	*"And what do you have that you did not receive? Now if you did indeed receive it, why do you boast as if you had not received it?"*

Access to the supernatural realm is not limited to God's people. The devil uses it, too. In Pharaoh's court the heathen were able to duplicate many of Moses' miracles. That takes us all the way back to God again. Know God. Seek Him daily. Then you will recognize the real thing.

Healing instantaneously or by medical help is still from God

God can heal someone instantaneously, or He can heal someone gradually, through a process. A healing process may begin with prayer by the elders of the church, as in James 5:14-18, and may also include proper rest, diet, and exercise, and especially fellowship with God and obedience to His Word. It may involve medicine.

"Every good gift and every perfect gift is from above, and cometh down from the Father of lights, with whom is no variableness, neither shadow of turning."[86]

Life and health *Proverbs 4:20-23 KJV*	*My son, attend to my words; incline thine ear unto my sayings. Let them not depart from thine eyes; keep them in the midst of thine heart. For they are life unto those that find them, and health to all their flesh."*

Salvation includes wholeness and healing

The Bible says clearly that salvation through Jesus Christ includes spiritual, physical, mental, and emotional healing. Wholeness of spirit, soul, and body comes through salvation. Christ came to die so that we might be healed.

The Greek word for "to heal" in the following passage is *iasthai*,[87] which means to cure, literally or figuratively. It is translated as "heal" or "make whole." The Lord's healing power was present with Jesus!

---

[86]James 1:17 KJV.
[87]Strong's number 2390.

"And it came to pass on a certain day, as he was teaching, that there were Pharisees and doctors of the law sitting by, which were come out of every town of Galilee, and Judaea, and Jerusalem: and the power of the Lord was present to heal them."[88]

Healing and Wholeness—Blessings from God

Exodus 15:26. If you obey, "I will not make you suffer any of the diseases I sent on the Egyptians; for I am the Lord who heals you" (15:26 NLT).

Deuteronomy 28:1-14; 30:19-20. "I have set before you life and death, blessing and cursing: therefore choose life" (30:19 KJV).

Psalms 91:16; 103:3; 107:20; 118:17. "With long life will I satisfy him" (91:16). "He sent out his word and healed them" (107:20 NLT).

Proverbs 4:20-23. My words "bring life to those who find them, and healing to their whole body" (4:22 NLT).

John 10:10. "I am come that they might have life, and that they might have *it* more abundantly" (10:10 KJV).

Isaiah 53:4-5. ". . . and with his stripes we are healed" (53:5 KJV).

Jeremiah 30:17. "'I will give you back your health and heal your wounds,' says the Lord" (30:17 NLT).

Matthew 10:1. ". . . his twelve disciples, he gave them power against unclean spirits, to cast them out, and to heal all manner of sickness and all manner of disease" (10:1 KJV).

Mark 11:23-24; 16:17-18. "What things soever ye desire, when ye pray, believe that ye receive them, and ye shall have them" (11:24). "And these signs shall follow them that believe" (16:17 KJV).

---

[88] Luke 5:17 KJV.

Romans 4:17-21. "[Abraham] staggered not at the promise of God through unbelief; but was strong in faith, giving glory to God" (4:20 KJV).

Romans 8:11; 8:26-28. "Holy Spirit helps us in our weakness" (8:26 NLT).

2 Corinthians 10:4-5. ". . . and bringing into captivity every thought to the obedience of Christ" (10:5 KJV).

Galatians 3:13-14. "Christ hath redeemed us from the curse of the law, being made a curse for us" (3:13 KJV).

Ephesians 6:10-17. "Wherefore take unto you the whole armour of God, that ye may be able to withstand in the evil day" (6:13 KJV).

Philippians 2:13; 4:6-7; 4:13. "I can do all things through Christ which strengtheneth me" (4:13 KJV).

2 Timothy 1:7. "For God hath not given us the spirit of fear; but of power, and of love, and of a sound mind" (1:7 KJV).

Hebrews 10:23, 35-36; 11:11; 13:8. "Jesus Christ the same yesterday, and to day, and for ever" (13:8 KJV).

James 5:14-18. "And the prayer of faith shall save the sick" (5:15 KJV).

1 John 3:21-24. "And whatsoever we ask, we receive of him, because we keep his commandments, and do those things that are pleasing in his sight" (3:22 KJV).

3 John 2. "Beloved, I wish above all things that thou mayest prosper and be in health, even as thy soul prospereth" (2 KJV).

Revelation 12:11. "And they overcame him by the blood of the Lamb, and by the word of their testimony; and they loved not their lives unto the death" (12:11 KJV).

See also 1 Kings 8:56; Joel 3:10; Matthew 8:2-3; 8:17-19; 21:21; 1 Peter 2:24, and many others.

By His stripes you were healed

1 Peter 2:24 KJV

"Who his own self bare our sins in his own body on the tree, that we,
being dead to sins,
should live unto righteousness:
by whose stripes ye were healed."

Sometimes when the Bible speaks of "healing" or "salvation" the words are a translation of the Greek verb *sozo* and the noun *soteria,* which include not only salvation in the sense of deliverance from sins but also deliverance from danger and suffering. *Sozo*[89] means to be made whole.

For example, Jesus said to the woman with the issue of blood, *"Daughter, be of good comfort; thy faith hath made thee whole."*[90] The word translated "whole" in the KJV is *sozo*. The issue of blood stopped and she was also made whole.

Oral Roberts—When Someone Is Not Healed

The late evangelist Oral Roberts (1918-2009) was one of the most famous Christian leaders of the 20th century. He believed in praying for the sick for divine healing and wholeness—body, soul, and spirit. When he was 17 years old he could have died from tuberculosis but his family refused to give up on him and continued to pray until he was healed. That was a life-changing experience of faith at work, believing for the miraculous. Through his tent meetings, revivals, television ministry, Oral Roberts University, and international missions trips he preached on the theme of "Seed-Faith" and millions were healed.

In his book *Better Health and Miracle Living* he wrote that even though he was always willing to pray for healing, he never forgot that his main goal was to point people to God and salvation in Jesus Christ. This was especially important if someone was dying and might not yet know Jesus as Savior. He always encouraged people to seek medical care in addition to believing God for their healing. He said he felt better if they would do everything they could. He built a hospital in addition to a prayer tower and counseled medical doctors to pray for divine guidance.

---

[89] Strong's Greek 4982.
[90] Matthew 9:22 KJV.

Sometimes you pray but the person dies

Dr. Roberts always cautioned people that he was not a "faith-healer" because only God heals—and sometimes He does not. He saw instances when he prayed for someone terminally ill and they still went home to be with the Lord within a short time. However, many times their passing was dramatically changed. Some experienced the presence of the Lord in wholeness of body, soul, and spirit. They became peaceful and calm. Some were no longer in pain. They were able to settle their affairs and interact with their families in love in the final days.

> *"I am called of God to pray for people, to give them my very best. It's thrilling to see miracles work but no one knows how it hurts when you pray, and seemingly the person is helped, but then he dies.*
> *Still, I have to obey God's calling on my life and pray for those who seek my prayers."*
>
> Oral Roberts, *Better Health and Miracle Living*

Chapter 10

Jesus—Bearing His Cross and the Crucified Life

"Even the mystery which hath been hid from ages and from generations, but now is made manifest to his saints: To whom God would make known what is the riches of the glory of this mystery among the Gentiles; which is Christ in you, the hope of glory."[91]

When you have been born again into the reality of the Kingdom, you have Christ in your heart. You no longer just talk religion. You have the hope of glory. The Lord is real. You have Him in your heart and you will not let Him go. Jesus makes the cross a reality in your heart.

He is the Savior of the world.
Author and Bishop of our souls
The Resurrected Christ
The Exalted One on the right hand of the Father
The soon returned and coming King
Jesus will receive the kingdom up in glory.
Jesus will glorify His people and rule and reign forever.

You embrace Him. You call His name. You cry out for the seal of His eternal reality inside of you.

Jesus, the Precious One
The Lamb slain from the foundation of the world
Jesus, Author and Finisher of our faith
Sustainer of Life Our Propitiation, the Great Sacrifice for our sins

[91] Colossians 1:26-27 KJV.

When you are born again, an eternal transaction takes place. He not only delivers you from hell when you die physically but also from hell on earth because you have been dead spiritually. Jesus destroyed principalities and powers and made a show of them openly by the integrity of His name. Death, hell, and the grave could not keep Him. His name had too much power because He is so full of light.

Every other religion is dead religion and altogether nothing. Jesus is the only one Who is real. He was crucified, died, and was buried in a tomb but darkness could not hold Him. On the third day He was raised from the dead. He is alive today. He is not only a fact of history but also a very present reality.

Spurgeon preached Christ crucified and revived the church

Charles Spurgeon (1834-1892) was a great preacher who never tired of telling people how to find their way to the cross. Each week this pastor found new ways to challenge sinners with the message of Jesus. He preached his first message when he was only 19 years old and became the most popular preacher in London.

People came to Christ through his ministry because they loved his non-compromising, consistent commitment to truth. He never had to advertise because people told other people and they came by word of mouth until attendance reached 10,000 every Sunday.

He always took people on the road to Christ

Spurgeon referred to an old pastor's advice on evangelism that you need to keep "running along the road towards the great metropolis—Christ." He said he would always find a way to preach about a road to Christ in his sermons. He said, "I will make a road, I would go over hedge and ditch but I would get at my Master, for a sermon is neither fit for the land nor yet for the dung hill, unless there is a savour of Christ."[92]

Is anyone drawn to Christ through the Word of God in you? How often do you speak to sinners? Maybe you are not called to pastor a church of thousands, or maybe you are, but do your words count? Are they making a difference in this generation?

[92] Charles H. Spurgeon, Sermon No. 242, "Christ Precious to Believers (March 13, 1859). Online at www.spurgeongems.org.

"When the Lord shall be pleased to restore to his Church once more a fervent love to Christ, and ***when once again we shall have a ministry that is not only flavoured with Christ, but of which Jesus constitutes the sum and substance****, then shall the Churches revive . . . only let God the Holy Spirit give to us once again the bold and clear preaching of Christ crucified in all simplicity and earnestness, and the dwarf shall swell into a forest giant, each expanding bud shall burst into foliage, and the cedar shall tower aloft again, until the birds of the air shall lodge in the branches thereof. I need offer you no apology, then, for preaching on those matters which engrossed all the time of the apostles, and which shall shower unnumbered blessings on generations yet to come."*[93]

Charles Spurgeon

(1834-1892)

"We Preach Christ and Him Crucified" was the motto of Spurgeon's ministry and Metropolitan Tabernacle Church

Spurgeon increased his church by preaching the Gospel

"Somebody asked me how I got my congregation," he once said. "I never got it at all. I did not think it was my duty to do so. I only had to preach the Gospel."[94]

Near the end of his life, his neighbor, Robert Taylor, a Presbyterian minister, asked him to briefly express his Christian faith. "It is all in four words," he said. "Jesus died for me."[95]

Preaching the cross is power

1 Corinthians 1:18 KJV

"For the preaching of the cross is to them that perish foolishness; but unto us which are saved it is the power of God."

[93] Charles Spurgeon, "Death and Life in Christ," Sermon No. 503 (April 5, 1863). Available online.
[94] W. Y. Fullerton, *Charles Haddon Spurgeon: A Biography,* Chapter 7, "The Great Tabernacle." Online source "The Spurgeon Archive," www.spurgeon.org.
[95] Ibid., Chapter 13, "A Chapter of Incidents."

Think of your own life. Is Christ precious to you? Spurgeon said if Christ is not precious to you, "then rest assured you have not a true and saving faith." If you do not call His name, you are not saved. At the end of each day, are you satisfied that you have gone to the cross and taken others on the road to the cross to the extent that God has allowed?
Have you lived every possible moment for Jesus? If you were to die young, as Spurgeon did, which of your works would survive the fire and earn from God a "Well Done"?

Chapter 11

Sacrificing Your Money for the Purposes of God

One man who took God at His word regarding money was Lewis Tappan (1788-1873). Tappan's faith in Christ led him to give away such large sums of money that they actually influenced the course of American history in such moral causes as the abolition of slavery and education of the freed slaves, temperance, and honoring the Sabbath day.

A few years ago a popular movie called *Amistad* directed by Steven Spielberg told the story of slaves from West Africa who were captured and sold illegally. In 1839 they mutinied on a slaving vessel and commandeered the ship. They were captured in America but American abolitionists fought for their freedom and won.

The man chiefly responsible for funding their defense and persuading the former president of the United States, John Quincy Adams, to serve as their lawyer was Tappan. He mobilized benefactors to finance the slaves' defense and after the trial these benefactors formed the American Missionary Association.

Benevolent Empire—unified by Christian charity

In a wave of Christian unity birthed out of the early 19th century Christian revivals, Arthur and Lewis Tappan, evangelist Charles Finney and others among the Presbyterians, Congregationalists, Methodists, Baptists and Episcopalians sought to influence society in what Finney said was "being useful to the highest degree possible."

This unified wave of charity was so huge that it came to be called the "Benevolent Empire." Benevolence was not only done for its own sake but also as a means to reach the lost and win them to Christ. Finney said that anyone who claimed to be a Christian would of necessity be involved in the reform of society. Otherwise, they were backslidden. Charity was the obligation of a Christian whom Jesus had called to both love God and love his neighbor as himself.

Changing society is a great way to spread the Gospel

Almost all Christians involved in those evangelical revivals believed that changing the ethics of society and transforming lifestyles were of nearly equal importance to preaching the Gospel.

One of the societies founded as part of what came to be called the Benevolent Empire was the American Sunday School Union. Its mission included not only teaching Bible verses but also instilling in children Christian ethics and educational skills like reading and arithmetic. In an age before the widespread availability of public schools, this might be the only education the children ever received outside the home.

Christians working together for the reform of society through faith in Jesus Christ created major interdenominational movements like these in 19th century America:

- American Board of Commissioners for Foreign Missions (1810)
- American Education Society (1815) founded as the American Society for Educating Pious Youth for the Gospel Ministry
- American Home Missionary Society (1826)[96]
- American Bible Society (1816)
- American Tract Society (1826)[97]
- American Sunday School Union (1817)
- American Temperance Society (1826)
- American Anti-Slavery Society (1833)[98]
- American and Foreign Anti-Slavery Society (1840)[99]
- American Missionary Association (1839)[100]

The American Missionary Association became a major force in the education of former slaves after the Civil War, including the founding of Black schools such as Fisk University and Atlanta University. Arthur and Lewis Tappan also contributed heavily to Oberlin College, which admitted both Blacks and women, and to the revival crusades and pastorate of evangelist Charles Finney, who became president of Oberlin in 1852.

---

[96] This group resulted from the combined efforts of the Congregational, Presbyterian, Dutch Reformed, and Associate Reformed Churches to financially assist congregations on the American frontier until they could become self-sufficient. It was diverse. Some members owned slaves while others spoke out for abolition. It became predominantly Congregational later in the 19th century.

[97] Included tracts not only on how to be born again but also on social issues like the evils of slavery.

[98] First president was Arthur Tappan. Other leaders included Lewis Tappan, William Lloyd Garrison, Frederick Douglass, Theodore Weld. They advocated the immediate emancipation of slaves because slavery was a crime against humanity.

[99] Formed when the Tappans and others withdrew from the American Anti-Slavery Society because they felt it gave too much emphasis to women's rights. Their focus was the abolition of slavery.

[100] Developed from the defense committee that won freedom for the slaves in the *Amistad* trial. In contrast to other missionary agencies that accepted the existence of slavery, it was active in defeating slavery and raising the status of Blacks in America. Merged with other organizations in 1846.

Lewis Tappan

(1788-1873)

Wealthy Christian businessman who changed American history

Founder of agency that became Dun and Bradstreet

Lewis Tappan's life demonstrated the biblical principles in *A Man's Journey with God.* He believed that God gave him wealth and he should use it in a godly way. This included the principle of biblical integrity, which led him to found a credit rating agency called the Mercantile Agency that became Dun and Bradstreet.

God Gives You Power to Get Wealth and to Give

When you allow the Lord to use your finances, you can focus on Him as not only your source of money but also a provider of creativity to earn an increase that you can apply to good deeds in His name.

"But thou shalt remember the Lord thy God: for it is he that giveth thee power to get wealth, that he may establish his covenant which he sware unto thy fathers, as it is this day."[101]

God does that which is true to His nature, which is to give. He expects you to do the same. When you are a faithful steward of your finances, you do basic bookkeeping and close out your books each night before you go to sleep. How much did you earn? How much did you spend? What did you spend it for? What bills need to be paid immediately? Did the bank record your activity accurately for the previous day? What did you invest? What did you give away?

[101] Deuteronomy 8:18 KJV.

"He who is faithful in what is least is faithful also in much; and he who is unjust in what is least is unjust also in much. Therefore if you have not been faithful in the unrighteous mammon, who will commit to your trust the true riches? And if you have not been faithful in what is another man's, who will give you what is your own?"[102]

[102] Luke 16:10-12 NKJV.

Chapter 12

Unifying the Church by Prayer

Ludwig von Zinzendorf (1700-1760), from the time he was a child, knew that he would dedicate his life to serving the Lord. When he was in his early twenties, he used his inheritance to purchase an estate. There he allowed hundreds of Moravian Christians trying to escape religious oppression to settle and form a community called Herrnhut, which means "The Lord's Shelter." For the rest of his life, his prayers and his lifestyle were dedicated to meeting others' needs.

This group of Moravians he gathered was known as Unitas Fratrum or Unity of Brethren. Eventually the Moravian Church spread to America. In 1736 a group of Moravians sailed to the colony of Georgia, where they had founded a settlement. On board the ship was John Wesley, future founder of the Methodist Church. The Moravians' calm faith in Christ in the midst of a raging storm at sea so impressed the young man that he recognized that he did not know God as they did. Through Bishop August Spangenberg and other Moravians, Wesley was born again and later launched a spiritual revolution that changed the world.

Christian unity births prayer meeting that lasts 100 years

Nearly ten years earlier on one crucial day in 1727, Zinzendorf challenged the Moravians on his estate with their lack of Christian love toward one another in the community. He showed these Christians what they needed to do so that they could come together in unity. It was a milestone in their development into one of the greatest missionary movements in history, and soon they began the longest prayer meeting ever recorded. On August 27, 1727, the Moravians started a round-the-clock prayer meeting that lasted for 100 years. Initially, 24 brothers and sisters each devoted one hour to the Lord to intercede for the church and the Herrnhut community. At least one person was praying 24 hours a day.

A great missionary movement was birthed when men declared they were willing to become slaves if they could win slaves in the West Indies to Christ. As their number increased, so did their intercession, to include the churches, missionaries and countries where they lived, government authorities—everyone whom the Lord brought to their attention.

Zinzendorf's challenge to come into Christian unity

Jesus knew that man was already disposed to love himself so He told us to renounce self-love and instead love others as ourselves. Unity is not built on self-love. It is built on death to the self-life.

"If you want to be my disciple, you must hate everyone else by comparison—your father and mother, wife and children, brothers and sisters—yes, even your own life. Otherwise, you cannot be my disciple."[103]

Ludwig von Zinzendorf

(1700-1760)

Used his earthly wealth to become a unifier of the brethren, making a commitment to live in love and encourage others to do likewise

"On that day, the Count made a covenant with the people, in the presence of God. The brethren individually engaged to belong entirely to the Saviour. They were ashamed of their religious quarrels, and were unanimously disposed to bury them in oblivion. They also sincerely renounced self-love, self-will, disobedience, and freethinking. They were desirous of becoming poor in spirit; none of them sought a preference above the rest; and each one wished to be taught by the Holy Spirit in all things."[104]

[103] Luke 14:26 NLT.

[104] Rev. August Gottlieb Spangenberg, *The Life of Nicholas Lewis Count Zinzendorf* (London: Samuel Holdsworth, 1838), p. xxiv.

Jesus sanctified Himself for us so that we would become one with Him and with one another. The Moravians caught the vision.

Beyond partisanship and personal problems to meeting others' needs

Like the Moravians, the Church today must grow beyond disunity and personal-problem praying to a place of fellowship and consideration for the needs of others. When our problems and disputes no longer have the ability to overtake us and distract us from fulfilling His will, we will become a unified force to bring change—in earth, as it is in heaven.

You please God when you sanctify yourself for the sake of others as Jesus did in his great high priestly prayer. When you pray for unity, that we may all be one, you follow in His steps.

Self-love is the enemy of unity, so let it die

The world celebrates self-love and the Church endorses it by saying that you can't love others unless you first love yourself, but that is not what Jesus said. Jesus said that He sanctified Himself so that we might be sanctified. He gave us His glory so that we might be one and the Church might be made perfect in oneness. Unity in the Church is a miraculous sign and wonder that the world is still waiting to see.

Jesus prayed, "And for their sakes I sanctify myself, that they also might be sanctified through the truth. Neither pray I for these alone, but for them also which shall believe on me through their word; That they all may be one; as thou, Father, art in me, and I in thee, that they also may be one in us: that the world may believe that thou hast sent me. And the glory which thou gavest me I have given them; that they may be one, even as we are one: I in them, and thou in me, that they may be made perfect in one; and that the world may know that thou hast sent me, and hast loved them, as thou hast loved me."[105]

[105] John 17: 17-23 KJV.

Moravian Church—Unitas Fratrum (Unity of Brethren)

Originated in Bohemia and Moravia, the future Czech Republic. Movement was begun to reform the Roman Catholic Church a century before Martin Luther published his 95 theses in 1517.

John Hus (1369-1415), Czech reformer. Professor of philosophy and rector of the University in Prague. Preached at the Bethlehem Chapel in Prague. Was falsely accused of heresy, burned at stake on July 6, 1415.

Followers of John Hus formed the movement Unitas Fratrum (Unity of Brethren).

1517, Unitas Fratrum Movement had 200,000 members and more than 400 parishes. Hymnal, catechism, printing presses for the Bible in their own language.

1547, Bitter persecution. Relentlessly reduced numbers and influence.

John Amos Comenius (1592-1670). Moravian leader still known today for his progressive views of education. He was offered the first presidency of Harvard but declined.

1722, Revival of the Moravian Church through Zinzendorf. Young Count Nicholas Louis von Zinzendorf, pietist nobleman in Saxony, built community of Herrnhut on his estate that became a haven for Moravian refugees.

1727, Spiritual renewal for Moravian Church in Herrnhut. Repentance and unity of Christians, onset of 24-hour prayer movement lasting 100 years.

1732, First Moravian missionaries sent to slaves in the Caribbean. They were willing to become slaves, if necessary, to reach them. Missions to North America, Africa, India, Europe.

John Wesley
(1703-1791)

1735. Mission to the colonies of Georgia and South Carolina. In 1736 Moravian leader August Gottlieb Spangenberg developed a relationship with John Wesley, also on a mission to Georgia, that had a profound spiritual impact on Wesley and his development of the Methodist Church.

1741, Established Bethlehem, Pennsylvania, On Christmas Eve, 1741, Zinzendorf visited this American settlement of Moravians and named it "Bethlehem." It succeeded because of their faith, unity, discipline, willingness to work, and communal system.

Moravians also settled in New Jersey, Maryland, and North Carolina, where they founded Wachovia Bank (later bought by Wells Fargo).

When you live on the side of selflessness and forgiveness, give your love freely, and pray for others, you are like God, because God so loved the world that He gave His Son Jesus.[106] Before His Son demonstrated His love by dying for us, He commanded us to love one another in the same way.

"This is my commandment: Love each other in the same way I have loved you. There is no greater love than to lay down one's life for one's friends."[107]

[106]See John 3:16.
[107] John 15:12-13 NLT.

My prayer for you

Lord, don't let a single one of the men reading this book die until the reason You brought them into the earth is fulfilled. I pray that each of them will receive the mindset to say to You, "Not my will, God. Thy will be done." Break the yokes of their bondages and limitations. Help them to be so surrendered to You that they understand that their only limitations are ones that You give them. Nothing is strong enough to stop them from doing Your will because the Lord will be at hand in them.

The devil is not a worthy foe for them. You defeated the devil and gave that to us as an example of your power. It's said in your Word you spoiled principalities and made a show of them openly. You weren't just giving us a testimony of what You could do, Lord. You were giving a demonstration of what we are supposed to do.

I pray in the name of the Lord that You not only loose them from limitations but by the Spirit of God there is an unlimited sense that what You put in their hearts can be easily accomplished because You are the One Who is doing it and You don't have a worthy foe. You are greatly to be praised! You're not challenged by anything! Whatever You decide is going to happen.

Thank you, Lord. In Jesus' name, Amen.

Chapter 13

Revitalizing the Church by Racial Reconciliation

"After this I beheld, and, lo, a great multitude, which no man could number, of all nations, and kindreds, and people, and tongues, stood before the throne, and before the Lamb."[108]

In1893, a young Black man from Tennessee by the name of Charles Harrison Mason (1866-1961) was deeply depressed after being divorced by his wife of only two years. His wife had outward beauty but apparently did not have the inner substance to handle the call of God on her husband's life.

Charles Harrison Mason
(1866-1961)

"Endure Hardness"

First message theme of C. H. Mason, Founder of Church of God in Christ

"Thou therefore endure hardness as a good soldier of Jesus Christ"
(2 Timothy 2:1-3 KJV).

That same year, Meyer and Brothers of Chicago published *An Autobiography: The Story of the Lord's Dealing with Mrs. Amanda Smith, The Coloured Evangelist.* After Mason read about this former slave's experiences with God, he claimed entire sanctification[109] for his own life

[108] Revelation 7:9 KJV.
[109] "Entire sanctification" means a post-conversion experience whose end-result is complete holiness.

and began to teach it as a second work of grace available to all believers. It was a turning point in his life of faith.

As a child, Mason had prayed earnestly with his mother and the neighbors, all former slaves who had known great hardship. His first sermon came from 2 Timothy 2:1-3, "Thou therefore endure hardness as a good soldier of Jesus Christ." Holiness and hardness, both well known by the slaves, became marks of his future ministry. However, this intensity separated him from mainstream Baptists and Methodists, who until then had been the major influence on Black American Christians. In 1897, he and his fellow ministers formed a new denomination by a name revealed to him one day in Little Rock, Arkansas—Church Of God In Christ. (Today it is often abbreviated as COGIC.)

Mason Goes to Azusa Street

In 1906, C. H. Mason was seeking the Lord for greater consecration and more spiritual depth in his life when he heard about the Rev. William J. Seymour at Azusa Street in Los Angeles and went there to find out about the baptism of the Holy Spirit with the evidence of speaking in tongues.

William Seymour

(1870-1922)

Pastor of Apostolic Faith Mission at Azusa Street in Los Angeles

William Seymour, a Black preacher blind in one eye, had learned about this baptism from Charles Parham in Houston, Texas, even though in Parham's segregated Bible classes Seymour had to sit in the hallway, separated from White students!

In Los Angeles, Seymour held revival meetings in a simple building on Azusa Street. Mason said that when he arrived, "The first day in the meeting I sat to myself, away from those that went with me. I began to thank God in my heart for all things, for when I heard some speak in tongues, I knew it was right, though I did not understand it. Nevertheless, it was sweet to me."

Remarkably, in those days of racial segregation, the Azusa Street meetings were attended by people of all races, worshiping in harmony, and the future worldwide impact of the revival would reflect that diversity.

"Nearly twenty-five percent of the world's Christians count themselves among the Charismatic and Pentecostal family of Christian Movements, yet few know how Pentecostalism began. The Azusa Street Mission and Revival tells the story of the small racially-inclusive group that gathered in Los Angeles in 1906 and changed the world of Christianity. With little more than a printing press, a trolley stop and a powerful message, the revival that began at Apostolic Faith Mission on Azusa Street rapidly crossed more than race lines—into Mexico, Western Europe, Scandinavia and West Africa—and began to change the landscape of Christianity."[110]

While attending the Azusa Street meetings, Mason was filled with the Holy Spirit and began to speak in tongues. Seymour considered tongues to be a sign of unity, like the day of Pentecost, crossing racial lines. He said, "Don't go out of here talking about tongues: talk about Jesus." Frank Bartleman, a minister and historian of the movement, said,

"The color line has been washed away in the Blood."

Mason as a spiritual father—half of his ministers were White

Since few of the White men at Azusa Street who were receiving the gift of tongues were accepted by their own denominations, Mason became a spiritual father to those who wanted to be ordained, including White ministers, in his Church Of God In Christ.

COGIC historian Ithiel Clemmons wrote, "He appears to have been the only early convert who came from a legally incorporated church body and who could thus ordain persons whose status as clergymen was recognized by civil authorities. . . . As a result, scores of White ministers sought ordination at the hand of Mason. Large numbers obtained credentials carrying the name CGIC. In the years 1909-14, there were as many White Churches of God in Christ as there were Black, all carrying Mason's credentials and incorporation."[111]

---

[110]Cecil M. Robeck, *The Azusa Street Mission and Revival: the Birth of the Global Pentecostal Movement* (Nashville: Thomas Nelson, 2006).
[111]Ithiel Clemmons, "C. H. Mason." *Dictionary of Pentecostal and Charismatic Movements.* Stanley M. Burgess, Gary B. McGee, editors (Grand Rapids, MI: Zondervan, Regency Reference Library, 1988).

"Mason dreamed of an integrated church and believed that all races were entitled to equal rights and authority. From COGIC's inception, Mason ordained and allowed whites to join his denomination. From 1907 to 1914, Mason ordained hundreds of white ministers. In 1914, a group of whites left COGIC and established the Assemblies of God. Throughout his tenure, Mason continued to integrate COGIC. A white COGIC pastor named Leonard P. Adams pastored Grace and Truth in Memphis, and COGIC's first general secretary was a white man named William B. Holt. Mason also conducted integrated funerals, baptisms, and worship services. At the height of Jim Crow, Mason allowed blacks and whites to sit next to each other in church. In the 1930s, Edward Hull 'Boss' Crump told Mason he could not continue to allow blacks and whites to sit together. However, Boss Crump did not stop Mason from holding integrated meetings. Mason used COGIC as a platform to fight against segregation and encouraged blacks and whites to embrace racial unity."[112]

Spiritual father to Whites who left him to return to segregation

Within a few years after Mason's trip to the interracial environment at Azusa Street, old racial differences resurfaced and disrupted the harmony that the Holy Ghost had brought to the Pentecostals.

Some of Mason's White pastors secretly planned to separate themselves into a new denomination that became the Assemblies of God. COGIC historian Ithiel Clemmons wrote, "By 1913 it had become increasingly clear that as Pentecostals moved toward denominationalism, they would follow the segregating practices of American culture. The color line that had been washed away in the blood of Jesus at the Azusa Street revival reappeared."[113]

However, Mason was a man of such godly character that when he found out about the plans of his White spiritual sons he traveled to their organizational meetings to bless them, and from then on continued to

[112]Elton H. Weaver III, "Charles Harrison Mason (1866-1961)." *Tennessee Encyclopedia of History and Culture*. Tennessee Encyclopedia online.
[113]Ithiel Clemmons, op. cit.

speak in their conferences, encouraging them in a deeper walk with God. Decades later, some of the White Pentecostals looked back and repented for the segregating practices of their denominations. The Assemblies of God issued this statement repenting for a century of racism.

White Pentecostals in Assemblies of God repented after a century of racism

"It is right that we repent of racism and ask our black brothers and sisters for forgiveness for failing to keep and treasure the shining ideal of Jesus and the 20th-century Azusa Revival." —Assemblies of God, Resolution 25, Revised "Use of Black Ministries"

The ministers ordained by Mason eventually went on to found many other denominations, and the Church Of God In Christ, along with other Pentecostal and holiness denominations, became a dominant force in the spread of Christianity among Blacks. Millions of people of all races were eventually affected by this one man's dedication and his commitment to seek deeper levels in God for his life.

Mason prays to resolve jealousy between bishops

A story is told about two of Mason's bishops in the Church Of God In Christ who came to him with a dispute over their territories. Instead of counseling them through it, he said, "Let's get down on our knees and pray." After four hours, they stopped praying and started arguing, so he said, "Let's go before the Lord in prayer." Back to prayer another four hours. When they stopped praying, they said, "But Bishop, what about my territory?" So he said, "Let's go before the Lord again in prayer." After 12 hours of prayer, one bishop said, "Bishop Mason, he can have my territory." And the other said, "No, Bishop, he can have *my* territory." And Bishop Mason got up off his knees. He hadn't counseled them into agreement. He had prayed them into agreement and humility.

Pride is an enemy to unity. It is one of the chief weapons of the devil, the accuser of the brethren.[114] If you don't want to do the devil's

[114]See Revelation 12:10.

work, don't prolong disputes with other Christians. It is better to die to yourself than disrupt the unity that Jesus prayed and died for.

Unity[115]	UNITY (Hebrew *yahad*, adverb "unitedly"). Used to signify a oneness of sentiment, affection, or behavior, such as should exist among the people of God (Psalm 133:1). The "unity of the faith" (Ephesians 4:13; Greek *henotes*, "oneness") is the unanimity of belief in the same great truths of God, and the possession of the grace of faith in a similar form and degree.

William Seymour

*"'**We belong to the whole body of Christ'** is a phrase that might well be applied to the band of worshipers who gathered together in the Azusa Street Mission in April of 1906. . . . Seymour cannot be claimed only by the blacks, or the Pentecostals; he belongs to the whole body of Christ—of all nations, races, and peoples. And the baptism in the Holy Spirit, with the accompanying gifts and graces does not belong only to the Pentecostals, but to the whole body of Christ—indeed unto 'as many as the Lord our God shall call' (Acts 2:39)."*

Frank Bartleman,[116] *Minister and unofficial historian of Azusa Street*

"By the year 2000, the spiritual heirs of Seymour, the Pentecostals and charismatics, numbered over 500 million adherents, making it the second largest family of Christians in the world. Today, practically all Pentecostal and charismatic movements can trace their roots directly or indirectly to the humble mission on Azusa Street and its pastor."[117]

Vinson Synan, "Pentecostalism: William Seymour"

[115] *New Unger's Bible Dictionary,* Moody Press of Chicago, Illinois. Copyright (C) 1988.
[116] Frank Bartleman, *Azusa Street* (first published in 1925).
[117] Vinson Synan, "Pentecostalism: William Seymour." *Christian History*, Winter 2000. Available online in *Christian History* archives at *Christianity Today*. Used by permission.

Chapter 14

Warning Nations of Judgment

"The battle shall appear strong, which you are to suffer, but the Lord himself shall be your comfort.

Flee from idolatry, and stand with Christ Jesus in this day of his battle, which shall be short and the victory everlasting!

For the Lord himself shall come in our defence with his mighty power; he shall give us the victory when the battle is most strong; and he shall turn our tears into everlasting joy.

He shall consume our enemies with the breath of his mouth, and shall let us see the destruction of them that now are most proud, and that most pretend to molest us. From God alone we abide redemption (Zech. 2; Ps. 46, 57, 61; Rev. 7, 22; Ps. 55)."

John Knox[118]

John Knox (c.1514-1572), a founder of the Presbyterian Church and one of the foremost leaders in the Protestant Reform Movement, was born in Scotland and became a clergyman persecuted for his faith.

In a day when the civil government controlled the church, Knox proclaimed that God was the Head of the church and "Presbyterian" or representative church government was the biblical model. Church leaders were not appointed by kings or other political rulers. The people elected elders or "presbyters" to oversee the churches.

While in the service of King Edward VI of England, Knox revised the text of the *Book of Common Prayer* but he was forced to leave the country when the Catholic Mary Tudor ascended the throne.

[118]John Knox, "A Godly Letter of Warning or Admonition to the Faithful in London, Newcastle, and Berwick (1553). Extracted from: *Selected Writings of John Knox: Public Epistles, Treatises, and Expositions to the Year 1559* .Online source Hanover College at http://history.hanover.edu/link-lists/knox.html. Accessed April 2013.

During his time in exile, he studied under John Calvin in Geneva, Switzerland. He pastored an English church in Geneva and also communicated with the churches in Scotland by letters. Some of his letters were published to challenge leaders to standards of righteousness.

In 1559 he returned to Scotland to lead the Protestant rebellion against the French-Catholic regent of Scotland, Mary of Guise. She died suddenly the next year and her daughter, Mary Queen of Scots, took the throne.

Mary Queen of Scots reportedly said, "I fear the prayers of John Knox more than all the assembled armies of Europe." Mary later fled to England where Elizabeth I placed her under house arrest and eventually executed her. Knox boldly challenged the heads of England and Scotland to repent for this execution and the murder of Christian martyrs.

Knox and Calvin had a profound influence on the development of America's representative form of government, the freedom of the Church, and biblical worldview foundations for American society.

John Knox's prayer of repentance for national sins

"God the Father of our Lord Jesus Christ, by the power of his Holy Spirit, so illuminate and so move your hearts, that clearly you may see, and perfectly understand, how horrible has been your fall from his verity; how fearful and terrible it is to fall into his hands without hope of mercy; and what is that his unspeakable mercy which yet again he offers unto you; and that it may please his eternal goodness to endue you with such wisdom, prudence, and fortitude, that seeing his good pleasure in his word revealed, without all fear you may follow the same, to the advancement of his glory, to the consolation of his afflicted church, and to your everlasting comfort, through our only Mediator, Redeemer, Peacemaker, and Lawgiver, Christ Jesus our Lord, whose Holy Spirit rule your hearts in his true fear. So be it."[119]

If a nation repents

. . .

Jeremiah 18:7-8 NKJV

"The instant I speak concerning a nation and concerning a kingdom, to pluck up, to pull down, and to destroy it, if that nation against whom I have spoken turns from its evil, I will relent of the disaster that I thought to bring upon it."

[119] John Knox, "A Brief Exhortation to England" (1559). Online at Still Waters Revival Books, http://www.swrb.com/newslett/actualNLs/briefexh.htm. Accessed February 2016.

William Wilberforce

The film *Amazing Grace* is a story of the 19th century career of British statesman William Wilberforce (1759-1833). It was released in February 2007 to celebrate the 200th anniversary of the parliamentary vote that banned the slave trade in the British Empire as a result of his leadership. He was influenced by Christian leaders like John Newton, a pastor and former slave trader who wrote the lyrics to the beloved song *Amazing Grace,* which is featured in the film title and throughout the film.

Wilberforce was elected as a Member of Parliament at age 21 and represented various constituencies for the next 45 years. Like other Christians you are reading about in *A Man's Journey with God,* he kept a spiritual journal. In 1787 he recorded what he saw as his destiny:

"God Almighty has set before me two great objects,
the suppression of the Slave Trade and
the reformation of manners" [a term for social justice].

William Wilberforce, 1787

William Wilberforce

(1759-1833)

Wilberforce challenged politicians to consider their decisions in light of God's eternal judgment upon them.

"A man who acts from the principles I profess, reflects that he is to give an account of his political conduct at the judgment seat of Christ."[120]

He called society back to its biblical foundations to honor God and avert God's judgment. Strong foes fought against Wilberforce for his stand on ending the slave trade but he was eventually successful because he sought the Lord's will and refused to yield.

[120] Christopher D. Hancock, "Profiles in Faith: William Wilberforce (1759-1833) The Shrimp Who Stopped Slavery." *Christian History* (Winter 1997). Online at http://www.christianitytoday.com.

Judgment Seat of Christ *2 Corinthians 5:10-11 NKJV*	*"For we must all appear before the judgment seat of Christ, that each one may receive the things done in the body, according to what he has done, whether good or bad. Knowing, therefore, the terror of the Lord, we persuade men."*

In 1788, John Wesley, an outspoken opponent of slavery, wrote to William Wilberforce, charging him to press on against the evil of slavery in England and America that was such a vile affront to God.

Wesley, from his deathbed, charges Wilberforce to end slavery on earth	*"O be not weary of well-doing. Go on in the name of God, and in the power of His might, till even American slavery, the vilest that ever saw the sun, shall vanish away before it."*[121]

Preaching Judgment and Joy to New Nation: Francis Asbury

Francis Asbury (1745-1816) was the first significant leader of the Methodist Episcopal Church in America, following Thomas Coke who returned to England after a short term.

Like Wesley, Asbury was a brilliant organizer and he developed a ground-breaking system of circuit riders to serve as pastors to the colonial nation. He personally rode an estimated quarter of a million miles and preached 16,000 sermons.

Can he preach? Does he have a horse?

Circuit riding on horseback was so essential that these questions were asked of every candidate for the Methodist ministry:

(1) Is this man truly converted?
(2) Does he know and keep our rules?
(3) Can he preach acceptably?
(4) Has he a horse?[122]

[121]Robert Isaac Wilberforce and Samuel Wilberforce, *The Life of William Wilberforce, Volume 1* (J. Murray, 1838), p. 297.
[122]Timothy K. Beougher, "Asbury." *Christian History*, Issue 45, p. 3. Available online from *Christianity Today*.

As a result of Asbury's riding and that of his faithful ministers, plus their camp meetings, the number of Methodists in America grew during his lifetime from 1,200 people to 214,000 members and 700 ordained preachers.[123]

Circuit riders preached holiness, God's judgment, and joy

Biographer Ezra Tipple described how their preaching of God's judgment along with the joy of the Lord brought people to Christ:

> *"The early Methodist itinerants had little to do with the questions of the day—The newness of the nation, the widely scattered peoples, the long journeys, the absence of church organizations, led the preachers to confine themselves to comparatively few subjects, but these were vital. They took their stand on fundamental and essential truths.*
>
> *"They had no time to discuss questions of doctrine or to debate mooted questions of theology. They entered a village, sounded the alarm, held up the cross, and were gone.*
>
> *"**What every preacher tried to do in every sermon was to answer the one great question, What must I do to be saved?** Thus he preached God in his infinite holiness and justice and love, and a doctrine of sin most effective in producing the profoundest sense of guilt and peril.*
>
> *"The final judgment in the array of its solemnities and issues was heralded in all its awesome imminence and reality. So also was Christ, the Saviour, joyously preached—preached in the fullness of his grace and the pathos of his love. The salvation offered in his name was free and full, and realizable in a present assurance and joyous experience."*[124]

[123]Source of statistics—Asbury University website, www.asbury.edu.

[124]Ezra Squier Tipple, *Francis Asbury: The Prophet of the Long Road* (New York, Cincinnati: The Methodist Book Concern, 1916). Public domain. Available online at www.Archive.org.

Highlights in the Life of Francis Asbury (1745-1816)

Born in England to godly parents. Began working at age 11 as a saddler to support himself. Converted to Christ in barn at age 15 and was overtaken with joy. Began holding meetings and teaching others the Scriptures.

Licensed at age 17, entered full-time ministry at 21. Committed himself to America and left behind parents in England at age 26 to launch the work.

Known for his life of prayer. Arose at 4:00 or 5:00 a.m. daily for two hours of prayer and study before the day's journey by horse. Read and studied again at night in the home where he was given lodging.

Disciplined, committed to self-improvement and sacrifice for others. Read daily the Old Testament in Hebrew, a language that he taught to himself. He never married.

"In the night I had a sore throat, but through the help of God I go on, and can not think of sparing myself:

"'No cross, no suff'ring I decline
Only let all my heart be thine.'

"I want to breathe after the Lord in every breath."[125]

Bishop Francis Asbury

Read books constantly. Read at least 100 pages/day, his personal rule. As a circuit rider, he carried books in his saddle bags or a box.

Stayed in America during Revolution. Asbury disobeyed Wesley and stayed in America—sometimes in hiding—during the American Revolution to continue to build the church. When it was over, he was able to resume his work because he had not publicly sided with the British.

Opposition to slavery. Slavery split the Methodist Church just like other denominations. Like John Wesley, Asbury was adamantly opposed to slavery and spoke out against it.

Personal zeal for the Gospel and warning of God's judgment. Asbury rode 5,000 miles a year on horseback. When he was too sick to ride, which happened frequently, one biographer said he had to be tied in the saddle to remain upright. Eventually had to resort to a wagon but he never stopped. Preached 16,000 sermons. Like Jonathan Edwards in New England, when he warned people of God's judgment people became agitated, it was so real.

---

[125]"Francis Asbury," *Harper's New Monthly Magazine* (New York: Harper and Bros, Volume 33, Issue: 194, July 1866), 213. Cornell University Library.

Ordained new preachers, including Blacks. Asbury ordained 700 preachers, including Blacks like Richard Allen; blessed Allen's founding of the African Methodist Episcopal Church. He organized America into circuits, each with dedicated preachers on horseback who covered several churches. Because of the grueling pace, more than half of the circuit riders died before the age of 33, but the toughest, Peter Cartwright of Illinois, continued to ride and minister for 71 years.

Phenomenal increase in Methodists. At his death, the Methodist Episcopal Church was the largest denomination in the United States, about one in 40 of the entire American population.

Commitment to literacy. Although Asbury had never completed his own education in England, he founded five schools and many other schools would follow that were named after him. His Sunday Schools not only taught children the Bible but also reading, writing, and arithmetic.

Mindset of Global Christianity

John Wesley and William Asbury remind us that God thinks on a global level. He not just looking at America. God created the earth, winds, waters, and people of the earth. As a matter of fact, everything you can see that has life all came from God. In an era of limited options for transportation those men crossed oceans on unstable ships and rode horseback until they died just to warn people of God's Judgment and His answer in the blood of Jesus.

Even then, no man, even the most spiritual, can come close to the love that God has for His people. In His redemptive story God has already shown His love. God so loved world that he gave His only Son. He didn't allow His Son to be excused from the cross. He didn't prevent His suffering. He allowed Him to die before He could be raised and win our salvation. Jesus paid a price and we pay a price.

God could have told Jesus, "I will keep you from pain. I am just going to impute to the people righteousness on the basis of intent." No, Jesus had to go through suffering and die. God showed His love for the just and the unjust because His Son died for the whole world.

God's justice is another issue. We must get God's perspective on justice, a biblical world view where we look at life from the perspective of the Bible and God in every situation.

When people suffer and die, we have compassion for them in the challenges that they are going through. We are afraid to say what God is doing. We are afraid to look at the circumstances that allowed tragedies to happen. We are not bold enough to say that God is almighty and He could have stopped that but He did not. Most people are more into circular reasoning according to their own laws of nature that these things just happen and there is no reason to it.

Collateral damage in God's judgments

Either God has lost control and He does not care about people or the earth He created or He is still in control and He is trying to get something across and there is collateral damage.

In every judgment of God in the Bible, not only the wicked were judged but also the righteous suffered collateral damage. When there is a war some innocent people get killed. Terrorists are cowards who hide out among the innocent and our weapons are often not precise enough to kill only the unrighteous people and leave the righteous alive.

There are some things that God reserves for the day when we all have to face Him. Whether you think about it or not, this life on earth is not the only life you will live. This life is only preparation for the next life. How you live today will be recorded for tomorrow. When you correct your present, your future will be much greater.

Hardly anyone preaches messages about hell. No circumstance that goes on in the world today comes close to how great hell is. I heard a preacher say that you are going through on earth and hell couldn't be any worse. Man, what are you saying? Do you understand what hell is? Eternal separation from God. No chance for repentance. Fire and pains that do not abate. Physical pain, emotional pain at a level you can't even explain.

Nothing on earth comes close to eternal separation from God and the eternal fires of hell. God's judgment is real, but so is His justice. Jesus came to satisfy His justice. He died so that we would not be condemned to hell but would be saved from God's judgment to live with Him forever.

"For God loved the world so much that he gave his one and only Son, so that everyone who believes in him will not perish but have eternal life. God sent his Son into the world not to judge the world, but to save the world through him.

"There is no judgment against anyone who believes in him. But anyone who does not believe in him has already been judged for not believing in God's one and only Son."[126]

[126] John 3:16-18 NLT.

Section 2

The Consecrated Prayer Life

PERSONAL NOTES

Chapter 15

Approaching God with Humility

When you have questions about your life in Christ, you need to go to the source. You need to seek God. The proper way to approach God is with humility.

You may have heard the old saying "Prepare to meet your Maker." When you meet with God in prayer, you are meeting your Maker. He made you. He made everyone you know. He made the earth and all of creation. He has allowed you to have an audience with Him, but that does not give you any rights other than what He gives you.

Your starting place is acknowledging that God is greater than you

God is greater than your understanding, and therefore you are willing to place your entire trust in Him. You are willing to submit yourself to Him and acknowledge and obey Him. "Trust in the Lord with all thine heart; and lean not unto thine own understanding. In all thy ways acknowledge him, and he shall direct thy paths."[127]

In this chapter, you will find five basic steps that will help you to approach God in prayer in such a way that He will accept you and interact with you in the way that you need.

1. Humble yourself and submit to God.
2. Ask God to judge your heart.
3. Repent of any known sin and receive the cleansing of the blood of Jesus.
4. Forgive others and seek their forgiveness.
5. Obey God.

[127]Proverbs 3:5-6 KJV.

1. Humble Yourself and Submit to God

When you yield to God, you are saying that you are willing to purify your heart. Purity is the fruit of personal humility in repentance, forgiveness, and obedience to God. When you enter the presence of the Lord with humility, trusting in the blood of Jesus, you can come without condemnation—without a feeling of guilt.

No condemnation to those in Christ Jesus *Romans 8:1-2 KJV*	*"There is therefore now no condemnation to them which are in Christ Jesus, who walk not after the flesh, but after the Spirit. For the law of the Spirit of life in Christ Jesus hath made me free from the law of sin and death."*

You enter the throne room with boldness and confidence—not from a position of arrogance but from a position of humility. You are fearless not because you are "macho" but because you are humbly trusting in Someone greater than yourself. Your manner of speaking is appropriate for a child acknowledging the dignity of his Father. Your heart and your words have the purity of meekness. You expose yourself to Him totally.

Purified language of prayer *Zephaniah 3:9, 12 NKJV*	*"For then I will restore to the peoples a pure language, that they all may call on the name of the Lord, to serve Him with one accord. . . . I will leave in your midst a meek and humble people, and they shall trust in the name of the Lord."*

Cane Ridge Revival, camp meeting on the frontier

Bishop Francis Asbury, on one of his many journeys, traveled to Tennessee in 1794 and lamented that greed had replaced faith on the frontier: He said, "When I reflect that not one in a hundred came here to get religion, but rather to get plenty of good land, I think it will be well if some or many do not eventually lose their souls."

There was a spiritual vacuum on America's frontier but Christians refused to yield. In the face of widespread crime and debauchery along with a decline in church attendance they came together regardless of their denominations and prayed for revival.

One of the first to see a manifestation was the Rev. James McGready, a Presbyterian frontier pastor of three small churches. He was known for his fire and brimstone messages but he was also a humble man of God.

In June 1800 his church at Red River in Logan County, near the border of Kentucky and Tennessee, sponsored a meeting called a "communion," because taking communion was a highlight of the event. Ministers from several denominations preached and about 500 were in attendance. Nothing too unusual happened until the fourth and final day when the Holy Spirit fell on the people and they began screaming and falling down unconscious, slain in the spirit.

The June communion at Red River had such a dramatic effect that another meeting was scheduled for July in Gasper River, Kentucky. Once again there were supernatural manifestations as a wave of repentance swept through the crowd. Children began to preach and multitudes who had come from miles around were saved.

25,000 come to Cane Ridge and find Christian unity

Barton W. Stone, the Presbyterian pastor of churches in Cane Ridge and Concord, went to Logan County to see McGready and then scheduled a camp meeting for Cane Ridge, Kentucky, in the summer of 1801. This time 25,000 people poured in from many states and denominations. Roads were clogged with people. Once again, the outstanding features were Christian unity, evangelism, and miracles.

"This was not a sectarian meeting, although it was held at a Presbyterian meeting house. Baptists, Methodists, and Presbyterians were simultaneously engaged. Perfect friendship, unanimity, and brotherly kindness prevailed. They had come together, to the help of the Lord against the mighty, and 'Zion was terrible as an army with banners.'

"The meeting lasted six days--the last sermon that was delivered on the occasion, was by a Methodist preacher, by the name of Samuel Hitt. It is known only to God, how many were converted at this meeting. There were no means, by which, even to ascertain how many professed religion. The object of the meeting was not to build up any sect or party; but to bring sinners to the Savior.

When the meeting was over, the people returned to their homes and friends.--There were many there from Ohio, and some from Tennessee, and the excitement spread with the people, and the young converts joined the churches of their choice; and the good work of reformation went on with irresistible force, and appeared like carrying every thing before it.

"Many were fully persuaded that the glorious millennial day had commenced, and that the world would soon become the Kingdom of our Lord Jesus Christ."[128]

Work of unity through humility remains to be done

A recurring theme of the camp meetings was the terrors of hell and the glories of heaven. Consider carefully these personal questions:

Do you believe that earth can become like heaven, with all nations assembled in one accord?[129]
Do you believe that the prayer of Jesus for unity in John 17 can be answered?
Will you persevere to that end, even if it means death to your own preferences and the sacrifice of your pride?
Can God begin anew with you?

God is ready—are you? *Isaiah 65* The Message	*"I've made myself available to those who haven't bothered to ask. "I'm here, ready to be found* *By those who haven't bothered to look.* *"I keep saying 'I'm here, I'm right here.'"*

[128]Levi Purviance, *The Biography of Elder David Purviance* (Dayton: B.F. & G.W. Ells, 1848), 301. Online at http://docsouth.unc.edu/nc/purviance/purviance.html.
[129]See Revelation 7:9.

2. Ask God To Judge Your Heart

If you say that you are willing to repent and yield, God is not impressed with superficial words. He looks at your heart.[130]

God looks on the heart *1 Samuel 16:7 KJV*	*"But the Lord said unto Samuel, Look not on his countenance, or on the height of his stature; because I have refused him: for the Lord seeth not as man seeth; for man looketh on the outward appearance, but the Lord looketh on the heart."*

Before you try to impress God with your prayers, ask Him to judge your heart. Allow Him to deal with your intents and motivations. When you first go before the Lord in prayer, ask God for His assessment of you. Are you in right relationship? Are there any issues between you and God? If He speaks a divine peace into your heart, you know that you are in harmony and can proceed to pray for yourself and others. If not, you can find out what you need to do to get yourself straight.

Acceptable in His sight *Psalm 19:14 KJV*	*"Let the words of my mouth, and the meditation of my heart, be acceptable in thy sight, O Lord, my strength, and my redeemer."*

3. Repent Of Any Known Sin And Receive The Cleansing Of The Blood of Jesus

In the 18th century a talented poet named William Cowper lived in the home of the great preacher John Newton, author of "Amazing Grace." Cowper had recurring times of depression and in a time of momentary insanity tried several times to take his own life.

Restored to his right mind and full of guilt, he repented, was washed from his sins, and wrote this song:

[130]See 1 Samuel 16:7, Acts 1:24, Revelation 2:23.

There Is a Fountain Filled with Blood

"There is a fountain filled with blood drawn from Emmanuel's veins;
And sinners plunged beneath that flood lose all their guilty stains.
Lose all their guilty stains, lose all their guilty stains;
And sinners plunged beneath that flood lose all their guilty stains.

"The dying thief rejoiced to see that fountain in his day;
And there have I, though vile as he, washed all my sins away.
Washed all my sins away, washed all my sins away;
And there have I, though vile as he, washed all my sins away."

William Cowper
[pronounced "cooper"]
(1731-1800)

When the camp meetings began 100 years after his death, the people rediscovered Cowper's song and wrote a new tune to it, rejoicing in the blood that cleanses from sin. Those washed in the blood have access to God. The man blind from birth whom Jesus healed said, "God does not hear sinners; but if anyone is a worshiper of God and does His will, He hears him."[131] If you have sin in your life, you need to repent. Don't hide out. Don't try to make excuses. Simply say, "I'm sorry. Please forgive me."

God hears the righteous *Proverbs 15:29 KJV*	*"The Lord is far from the wicked: but he heareth the prayer of the righteous."*

Unrepentant Christians who are not walking at the level where God has called them need to be restored first before God will listen to them. If you repent, then God hears, forgives, and cleanses you by the blood of Jesus.

God forgives and cleanses *1 John 1:9 KJV*	*"If we confess our sins, he is faithful and just to forgive us our sins, and to cleanse us from all unrighteousness."*

You need the covering of Jesus' blood now—not just to gain access to the Father when you die and go to heaven, but to walk every day now in the light of His righteousness.

[131]John 9:31 NKJV.

The blood cleansing is as important for walking in Christ-likeness in this life as it is for reaching the next. If you do not let Him cleanse your conscience from dead works, you will not be able to serve the living God.[132] We need to restore an appreciation for His blood.

The blood of Jesus has the ability to:

- Obliterate your sins
- Allow you access to the Father
- Give you a consciousness of holiness
- Give you relief from past guilt

His blood still speaks.[133] If He were still alive as a man on the earth and you could inject one drop of His blood into your veins, a rush of purity would flood through you. You would instantly be able to live forever.

Power in the blood of Jesus

In 1899, Lewis Jones, who had been a Moody Bible Institute classmate of evangelist Billy Sunday, wrote a song called "There Is Power in the Blood" at a camp meeting in Mountain Park, Maryland.

Wonder Working Power in The Blood

Words and music by Lewis E. Jones

(1865-1936)

"Would you be free from the burden of sin?
There's power in the blood, power in the blood;
Would you o'er evil a victory win?
There's wonderful power in the blood.

"There is power, power, wonder working power
In the blood of the Lamb;
There is power, power, wonder working power
In the precious blood of the Lamb."[134]

---

[132]See Hebrews 9:14.
[133]See Hebrews 12:24.
[134] Online hymn source.

When you sin and you don't know God, feelings of condemnation can be so great that you wish you were dead. However, a Christian who sins and repents in a godly way has a different kind of sorrow. You are sad that you have disappointed God, Who loves you, but you know that you can return to Him and repent. This produces life through His blood.

Godly sorrow produces repentance *2 Corinthians 7:9-10 NKJV*	*"Now I rejoice. . . that your sorrow led to repentance. For you were made sorry in a godly manner, that you might suffer loss from us in nothing. For godly sorrow produces repentance leading to salvation, not to be regretted; but the sorrow of the world produces death."*

4. Forgive Others and Seek Their Forgiveness

Forgiveness is a characteristic of God, but sometimes *unforgiveness* describes Christians' attitudes more than forgiveness. Most of the sinners I know are Christians. If I had held onto everything that others have ever done wrong to me I would be an emotional wreck and unable to communicate with God, but God gave me a good forgetter!

Forgive and be forgiven *Matthew 6:14-15 KJV*	*Jesus said, "For if ye forgive men their trespasses, your heavenly Father will also forgive you: But if ye forgive not men their trespasses, neither will your Father forgive your trespasses."*

***When you can't seem to break through in prayer,
examine your heart. Do you have sin in your heart?
Are you harboring unforgiveness?
If you seem to be coming against strongholds
when you are praying, is the problem in you?***

If you are saved but you are still holding unforgiveness against someone, if you are mad at a cousin or upset with your wife, you have strongholds in your life. You are in sin, and God cannot hear your prayer.

Marital harmony affects prayer effectiveness

If a man is out of harmony with his wife, he needs to humble himself and honor her by asking for her forgiveness, so that God can restore him to fellowship with Himself.

Husbands to honor wives *1 Peter 3:7* *NKJV*	*"Husbands, likewise, dwell with them with understanding, giving honor to the wife, as to the weaker vessel, and as being heirs together of the grace of life, that your prayers may not be hindered."*

Forgiving enemies: Frederick Douglass

Black Americans have received unfair treatment throughout our history, but we have also had a supernatural ability to forgive, especially because of our Christian experience. I would say that among most Blacks I know, those who are bitter and unforgiving are the exceptions, not the rule. God has given us great spiritual victories as we have forgiven our enemies.

A dramatic example of forgiveness occurred following the Civil War through an eloquent former slave, Frederick Douglass. Sometime after he achieved his freedom, he wrote a remarkable letter to his former slave master, Thomas Auld of Maryland.

> *"I shall make use of you as a means of exposing the character of the American church and clergy—and as a means of bringing this guilty nation with yourself to repentance. In doing this I entertain no malice towards you personally. There is no roof under which you would be more safe than mine, and there is nothing in my house which you might need for your comfort, which I would not readily grant. Indeed, I should esteem it a privilege to set you an example as to how mankind ought to treat each other. "I am your fellow-man, but not your slave."*[135]

Frederick Douglass, Letter of forgiveness to his former slave master:

Douglass had escaped from his master in 1838 with the help of his fiancée Anna Murray (whom he later married). He settled with his wife to raise a family in the North with the support of Northern abolitionists

[135]*The Liberator* (Boston), September 22, 1848. Published in the *International Library of Negro Life and History, "I Too Am America," pp.* 85-90.

like William Lloyd Garrison (1805-1879) who first heard Douglass speak at Nantucket Island, Massachusetts.

In the Preface to Douglass's autobiography *Narrative of the Life of Frederick Douglass,* Garrison wrote that he challenged the other white men with him at that Nantucket meeting, "I appealed to them, whether they would ever allow him to be carried back into slavery,—law or no law, constitution or no constitution. The response was unanimous and in thunder-tones—"NO!" "Will you succor and protect him as a brother-man—a resident of the old Bay State?" "YES!" shouted the whole mass, with an energy so startling, that the ruthless tyrants south of Mason and Dixon's line might almost have heard the mighty burst of feeling, and recognized it as the pledge of an invincible determination, on the part of those who gave it, never to betray him that wanders, but to hide the outcast, and firmly to abide the consequences."[136]

A brilliant, self-educated man, Douglass became a powerful public speaker on behalf of the abolition of slavery. Years later, he paid his master for his freedom with $700 he had obtained from friends. Honored with public service appointments rarely given to Blacks of his era, Douglass became the Marshal of the District of Columbia in the administration of President Rutherford B. Hayes. Under President James Garfield's administration, he received the federal appointment of Recorder of the Deeds of the District of Columbia. He received his third appointment as Minister-Resident and Consul-General to the Republic of Haiti under President William Henry Harrison.

He wrote three autobiographies. In 1848 in Rochester, New York, he became the founder and editor of the anti-slavery newspaper, *The North Star*. (The name of the paper refers to the crude navigation system mentioned earlier that was used by the slaves to escape to the North by following the North Star.[137])

Douglass was a Christian who wrote in biblical terms.

He said, "The slave is a man, 'the image of God,' but 'a little lower than the angels;' possessing a soul, eternal and indestructible; capable of endless happiness, or immeasurable woe; a creature of hopes and fears, of affections and passions, of joys and sorrows, and he is endowed with those mysterious powers by which man soars above the things of time and sense, and grasps, with undying tenacity, the elevating and sublimely glorious idea of a God."[138]

---

[136] William Lloyd Garrison, "Prelude," *Narrative of the Life of Frederick Douglass*. Online at http://www.gutenberg.org/files/23/23-h/23-h.htm#link2H_PREF. Accessed February 2016.

[137] See also page 46.

[138] Frederick Douglass, "The Nature of Slavery. Extract from a Lecture on Slavery," at Rochester, December 1, 1850. Online at Wikiquote.

5. Obey God

"Yes, Adam's one sin brings condemnation for everyone, but Christ's one act of righteousness brings a right relationship with God and new life for everyone. "Because one person disobeyed God, many became sinners. But because one other person obeyed God, many will be made righteous."[139]

Adam chose volitionally to disobey God. Because Adam disobeyed, all who are born under Adam are born with a spirit of disobedience and a tendency to sin. The Bible says:

> *"Once you were dead because of your disobedience and your many sins. You used to live in sin, just like the rest of the world, obeying the devil—the commander of the powers in the unseen world. He is the spirit at work in the hearts of those who refuse to obey God. All of us used to live that way, following the passionate desires and inclinations of our sinful nature. By our very nature we were subject to God's anger, just like everyone else. But God is so rich in mercy, and he loved us so much, that even though we were dead because of our sins, he gave us life when he raised Christ from the dead. (It is only by God's grace that you have been saved!) For he raised us from the dead along with Christ and seated us with him in the heavenly realms because we are united with Christ Jesus. So God can point to us in all future ages as examples of the incredible wealth of his grace and kindness toward us, as shown in all he has done for us who are united with Christ Jesus.*[140]

The passage from Ephesians 2:3 above says, "By our very nature we were subject to God's anger, just like everyone else." When you disobey God, the sin you commit is a manifestation of something going wrong in the invisible realm. Something inside of you is in rebellion against God. You are in sin and spiritually dead. Jesus came as a perfect sacrifice for your sins. When you are united with Him, you come to life. You are spiritually alive! He has just raised you from the dead. The reward of your obedience is eternal life.

[139] Romans 5:18-19 NLT.

[140] Ephesians 2:1-7 NLT.

God is angry at our disobedience but pleased with our obedience. Hearing from God is a fruit of obedience. It is an issue of heart purity.

"Who may climb the mountain of the Lord?
Who may stand in his holy place?
Only those whose hands and hearts are pure,
who do not worship idols
and never tell lies.
They will receive the Lord's blessing
and have a right relationship with God their savior." [141]

God wants to wash you with His Word until you have been cleansed from all the filth of the world. Just as a newborn baby fresh from his mother's womb must be washed, a newborn Christian must be washed with the water of the Word.

You might be wondering, Why am I going through these trials? God is using your circumstances to expose the real you. He wants you to see yourself as He sees you—the good, the bad, and the ugly. He wants you to see your potential but also to see how your dead thinking is keeping you from realizing your potential.

Revival came to Wales when a man obeyed God

One of the most powerful revivals of the early twentieth century occurred in Wales, led by a ministerial student named Evan Roberts who had prayed fervently for his own brokenness with the words, *"Plygni, O Arglwydd!"*—"Bend us, O Lord!"—in the Calvinistic Methodist Church that he was attending. Within six months, 100,000 souls had been saved from that plea and his consistent call to those whom he reached with his message that it was time for all people everywhere to obey God.

[141]Psalm 24:3-5 NLT.

Evan Roberts Said to Obey the Holy Spirit

Young Evan Roberts gave to the Welch Revival what became known as the Four Points:[142]

1. Put away any unconfessed sin.
2. Put away any doubtful habit.
3. Obey the Holy Spirit promptly.
4. Confess Christ publicly.

Evan Roberts

(1878–1950)

When the people obeyed God, a wave of revival swept not only the church but also the community through the Welsh Revival of 1904-1905.[143] ***Roberts was also in communication with the leaders of the Azusa Street revival in Los Angeles, as the Holy Spirit swept across continents.***

After Roberts had been used by God to launch the revival, a woman reportedly told him that he should step out of the public's eye. He did what she said and left the public spotlight. The momentum of the revival ceased without his presence but the fruit of that awakening continued for years to come.

[142]Alvin L. Reid, "A Human Spark to the Work of God." Online source.
[143]See J. Edwin Orr, *Prayer and Revival*. Online source.

Wales Transformed By Revival (1904-1905)

Crime stopped. No robberies, burglaries, rapes, murders, embezzlements. No cases to try.

Policemen idle. Formed quartets and sang at prayer meetings.

Alcoholism down. Taverns went bankrupt.

No cursing. Slowdowns in the mines—horses didn't understand commands without curse words.

Moral standards. Illegitimate birth rate dropped 44 percent.

Church growth. People started returning to the churches.

How about you? Are you the next Evan Roberts for your country or community? Could you cry out to God, "Bend me!" until a nation fell at Jesus' feet?

Chapter 16

Prayer Priority List

"Don't be afraid, Daniel. Since the first day you began to pray for understanding and to humble yourself before your God, your request has been heard in heaven. I have come in answer to your prayer."[144]

I see at least five priorities for personal prayer. The way that it is listed here is the way that God wants you to pray—from the inside out. Daniel understood that before he prayed for his nation first he had to pray for understanding and humble himself so that he would be in right relationship with God. In the next five sections you will read about these topics of prayer that are also included in the daily consecration journal:

Priority 1—Right Relationship with God
Priority 2—Family Needs and Destiny
Priority 3—Fivefold Ministry
Priority 4—Leaders—Local, State, Nation, World
Priority 5—Other Needs

Joy in His presence
Psalm 16:11 NKJV

"You will show me the path of life;
in Your presence is fullness of joy;
at Your right hand are pleasures forevermore."

Daniel was a man of passionate and prolonged prayer. Likewise, in David Brainerd's journal of his work among the Native Americans that was mentioned earlier, he records time and again the passion that he had for prayer. Sometimes he had to tear himself away from prayer to keep his commitments because of his desire to stay in God's presence.

---

[144]Daniel 10:12 NLT.

Desire to spend every moment for God **David Brainerd** (1718-1747)	*"I felt an intense desire to spend every moment for God. God is unspeakably gracious to me continually. In times past, he has given me inexpressible sweetness in the performance of duty. Frequently my soul has enjoyed much of God; but has been ready to say, 'Lord, it is good to be here.'"*[145]

When God comes upon you in prayer, you forget about your problems and focus on His presence. In His presence, all problems are no problem. He can handle anything. He isn't backing down off of anything.

After Paul had the Damascus Road experience with Jesus,[146] he was blind for three days and he didn't eat or drink. That's because God was going to give him a new way of seeing things as He saw them, and a new diet to eat—the substance of God.

Feeding on Jesus *John 6:57-58 NLT*	*"I live because of the living Father who sent me; in the same way, anyone who feeds on me will live because of me. I am the true bread that came down from heaven. Anyone who eats this bread will not die as your ancestors did (even though they ate the manna) but will live forever."*

Typically during our time in prayer we talk to God about all the *temporary* things that we are dealing with. However, the atmosphere of the prayer closet is totally changed when we become quiet and allow Him to reveal to us *eternal* things related to His future kingdom.

Time to be still *Psalms 46:10-11 NKJV*	*"Be still, and know that I am God; I will be exalted among the nations,* *I will be exalted in the earth!* *The Lord of hosts is with us;* *the God of Jacob is our refuge."*

Knowing information about God's acts is not the same as receiving revelation about His ways.

---

[145] *The Life and Diary of the Rev. David Brainerd*, Part III. A.D. 1742. July-November. 25. 329 (public domain). Online http://www.ccel.org/ccel/edwards/works2.ix.html.
[146] See Acts 9.

Learning ways of God *Psalms 103:7 NKJV*	*"He made known His ways to Moses, his acts to the children of Israel."*

Revelation comes by spending personal time with God in secret and studying His Word in the environment *where* He is and the context of *Who* He is. You can read the Bible all the way through with a hardened heart and still only know God outwardly. Heart knowledge comes from secret, submitted prayer.

Light shining in our hearts *2 Corinthians 4:6 NLT*	*"For God, who said, 'Let there be light in the darkness,' has made this light shine in our hearts so we could know the glory of God that is seen in the face of Jesus Christ."*

Coming into the light through prayer

Tell all darkness to flee from your heart as you prepare yourself to be the Bride of Christ. Prayer is the light that keeps darkness out of your heart.

If you have been in the dark in a spiritual sleep,
wake up and turn on the light.
If you are having too little effect on
those around you, you are having
too little intimacy with God in prayer.

When you are in the light of God's secret place, you do not hide from God. You don't put on. You are transparent. You are wide open. You fit heaven. The light of the Lord comes into your heart and it never goes out. Light fits heaven, and it fits your heart. There are no shadows in heaven. There are no shadows in your heart—only pure light.

Time alone with God

God's highest priority for prayer is that you would spend time with Him alone developing your personal relationship with Him. Out of your relationship come personal insight, healing, needs met, and growth into Christ-likeness. Also out of your relationship come answers to prayer on behalf of others. When you know God privately, you know how to please Him openly and how to pray according to His will.

Jesus calls you to the closet of secret prayer

Matthew 6:5-6 NLT

"When you pray, don't be like the hypocrites who love to pray publicly on street corners and in the synagogues where everyone can see them. I tell you the truth, that is all the reward they will ever get. But when you pray, go away by yourself, shut the door behind you, and pray to your Father in private. Then your Father, who sees everything, will reward you."

Do you remember how much you loved to pray when you were first born again? Prayer is simply greeting and talking with God. As in any form of communication, there is the one who gives and the one who receives, the one who speaks and the one who listens. Revelation comes when you listen in your personal time with God in secret, reading His Word to understand Who He is, and who He wants you to be. Your heart becomes tender in secret.

Jesus prayed in secret before day

Jesus is God, yet He understood the importance of secret prayer. The Bible says that He rose a great while before day to pray.[147] The Scripture says, "I love them that love me; and those that seek me early shall find me."[148] "Early" also means "earnestly." Getting up early, before day, demonstrates to God and your family that you are in earnest in seeking God. When you pray in secret a great while before day, you receive substance of the spirit world from God. You take on His nature. When you

[147]See Mark 1:35.
[148]Proverbs 8:17.

pray in secret for others, what you speak comes to pass, because the creative work that supplies their needs has already begun in the closets of your secret prayer.[149]

Saved People Pray in Secret: Jonathan Edwards

Jonathan Edwards, the 18th century theologian whose preaching helped launch the First Great Awakening, said that those who make excuses for neglecting secret prayer are hypocrites, and not truly saved. They are not drawn by faith to commune with God.

Jonathan Edwards
(1703-1758)

Hypocrites *"in a great measure leave off the practice of secret prayer. They come to this pass by degrees. At first they begin to be careless about it, under some particular temptations. Because they have been out in young company, or have been taken up very much with worldly business, they omit it once: After that they more easily omit it again. Thus it presently becomes a frequent thing with them to omit it and after a while, it comes to that pass, that they seldom attend it. Perhaps they attend it on Sabbath days, and sometimes on other days.*

But they have ceased to make it a constant practice daily to retire to worship God alone, and to seek his face in secret places."[150]

[149] See Matthew 6:5.
[150] Jonathan Edwards, "Hypocrites Deficient in the Duty of Prayer." Online source.

Life of Jonathan Edwards (1703-1758)

- Entered Yale before 13th birthday (age 12), graduating four years later at head of class.
- In 1729, succeeded his grandfather, Solomon Stoddard, as pastor of the prestigious Congregational church in Northampton, Massachusetts.
- In 1734, six people were suddenly converted in his church, then 30 or more every week, and America's First Great Awakening was launched.
- In 1741, preached the famous sermon "Sinners in the Hands of an Angry God" at Enfield, Connecticut. Parishioners screamed and held onto the pillars of the church, fearing they would fall into hell.
- Wrote many scholarly works and is considered America's greatest theologian. He explained history as God's work, based on His scriptural promises, interspersed by periods of the outpouring of His Spirit.
- Edited journal of David Brainerd, a missionary to Native Americans who died in his home at the age of 29. This journal is credited with inspiring some of the greatest missionaries in history.
- In 1750, he was removed as pastor of the Northampton church because of his commitment to high standards for church members and his requirement of proof that members were truly saved.
- From 1751-1757, he served in Stockbridge, Massachusetts, including ministry to the Native Americans.
- In 1757, he became president of Princeton, but died a few months later from smallpox.

Edwards' descendants for generations were evidence of a godly seed of pastors, judges, college presidents, and elected officials, including a Vice President of the United States, with accomplishments so great that the family record was included in *Ripley's Believe It or Not*.

Priority 1—Right Relationship with God

*"Therefore I exhort **first of all** that supplications, prayers, intercessions, and giving of thanks be made **for all men**, for kings and all who are in authority."*[151]

First prayer priority—not *civil* government but *self*-government

You may have heard that the first priority in prayer is to pray for governmental authorities, based on Paul's words to Timothy: However, that is not the point that Paul is making.

It is important to pray for leaders but your first priority is to get yourself right with God.

With God, the first level of government is self-government. How you take authority over the competing forces inside of you determines who you are before God and what kind of a Christian you are becoming—from the inside out.

When on the inside you are out of control, always lusting after needs and fighting for what is best for yourself, you can't fight for God and His will. You can't be an instrument of others' change on His behalf.

You must fight the battle for your soul and relationship with the Father before fighting for your family and the world. Self-government says that you can ignore the demands of your flesh.

The environment of prayer and holiness is self-regulating. It is the basis of your righteousness and integrity. It causes you to do the right thing at the right time, even when no one else is looking.

When you are self-governed, you do not need an accountability group to keep you in line because your honor is based on an internal accountability system that has developed between you and God alone.

---

[151] 1 Timothy 2:1-2 NKJV.

Exposing your inner conflicts
James 4:1-3 NKJV

"Where do wars and fights come from among you? Do they not come from your desires for pleasure that war in your members? You lust and do not have. You murder and covet and cannot obtain. You fight and war. Yet you do not have because you do not ask. You ask and do not receive, because you ask amiss, that you may spend it on your pleasures."

Change of Heart: Charles Finney

The future American revivalist Charles Finney (1792-1875) as a young man had an intellectual approach to Christianity. His debates over theology made his Presbyterian pastor doubt if he would ever be saved, but God was working in his heart. Finney was studying the law by reading William Blackstone's *Commentaries on the English Law*, which was the custom for lawyers in that day. He found so many references to the Bible in Blackstone that he bought a Bible—his first. Suddenly, as Derek Prince would say, while he was reading the Bible, the Bible started reading him. He saw that he was not in right relationship with God. His heart was evil, and filled with pride.

Under deep conviction, he escaped from the law office to the woods, where God spoke to him about his heart, and he "fastened upon [these convictions] with the grasp of a drowning man." He was thoroughly converted in that secret place with God, and from then on he never lost the conviction that his heart must be always pure before God. Eventually, Finney went on to bring about the conversion of half a million people and change the course of world history through his influence on society.

Finney knew that you can study the Bible with your mind, but until you see its application to your heart you will not be driven to change into Christ-likeness. You will be unwilling to die to yourself and sacrifice everything to serve Christ. You will not comprehend with your mind in the time and space realm of earth that you are an eternal being whose life in the here and now is only a preparation for the life to come. You will be unwilling to yield fully to the need for complete holiness, or what Amanda Smith and C. H. Mason called "entire sanctification."

"Are you willing to make the sacrifices?"
Charles Finney

"Do you wish for a revival? Will you have one? If God should ask you this moment, by an audible voice from heaven, 'Do you want a revival?' would you dare to say, 'Yes?' 'Are you willing to make the sacrifices?' Would you answer, 'Yes?' 'When shall it begin?' ***Would you answer, 'Let it begin tonight, let it begin here, let it begin in my heart NOW'?*** *Would you dare to say so to God, if you should hear his voice to-night?"*[152]

Authority of an Intercessor: Father Nash

The first time Charles Finney met the man whom God would eventually call to cover him in intercessory prayer, the Rev. Daniel Nash was active in the church where Finney was being licensed. Finney saw him praying publicly but noted later in his autobiography that Nash was "in a very cold and backslidden state."[153]

The next time Finney met this man, who had become known as "Father Nash," Finney observed that he was a changed man. Shortly after that meeting where Finney met him, he had suffered a major crisis with his eyes and had to remain in a dark room indefinitely. Finney wrote:

> *"He could neither read nor write, and, as I learned, gave himself up almost entirely to prayer. He had a terrible overhauling in his whole Christian experience; and as soon as he was able to see, with a double black veil before his face, he sallied forth to labor for souls."*

When Finney met him again at Evans Mills, New York, where Finney had been praying for revival, Father Nash was full of the power of prayer. One sinful man listed only as "D" was particularly profane, resistant to the Gospel, and disruptive at revival meetings. However, after Father Nash prayed fervently about this man, Finney reported, Nash left town but soon "D" came trembling into one of the meetings, a broken man.

---

[152]Charles G. Finney, *Lectures on Revivals of Religion*. Lecture 2, "When a Revival Is to Be Expected." Online source.
[153] Chapter 4, "His Doctrinal Education and Other Experiences at Adams." C. G. Finney, *An Autobiography*. John Clark, ed. 1908 Edition of the 1876 work. Online at http://truthinheart.com/EarlyOberlinCD/CD/Finney/Biography/autob04.htm. Accessed February 2016.

Finney wrote:

> *"He then proceeded to make one of the most heart-broken confessions that I almost ever heard. His confession seemed to cover the whole ground of his treatment of God, and of his treatment of Christians, and of the revival, and of everything good.*
> *"This thoroughly broke up the fallow ground in many hearts."*

Calling men to be intercessors

Father Nash is an example of a man who found his calling as an intercessor and specifically applied this gift to the work of an evangelist who was changing a nation, Charles Finney.

In most churches today, the lead intercessors are women. The Bible speaks repeatedly about *men* praying through every period of biblical history. Where are the *men* today who will pray at the altars for the unsaved and obstinate unbelievers like "D"? Where are the *men* who will pray for the cities and nations? How many men are praying daily for revival and awakening, beginning in their own cities? It is my prayer that out of this book *A Man's Journey with God* many men will recognize their call to prayer.

Impact of Revivals of Charles Finney

- **Converts**. 500,000 people converted to Christ.
- **Philadelphia** (1829-1830). Christian Unity. Thousands saved.
- **Lumberjacks** took revival to camps with no clergy. 5,000 saved.
- **Rochester, New York** (1830-1831). Leading lawyers, physicians, and businessmen saved. Converts entered ministry. Revival moved to 1,500 other towns and villages.

- **Theodore Weld**, converted to Christ through Finney, became radical American abolitionist after seeing that all slavery was sin. Weld wrote *The Bible Against Slavery* and *Slavery As It Is*.
- **Benevolent Empire**, inspired by Finney's ongoing emphasis on social change as a requirement for converted Christians, brought together many denominations and focused on the church as leader in areas of education, personal virtue, prohibition of alcohol, defeat of slavery, and respect for God and the Sabbath. By 1834, its annual budget was **today's equivalent of $130 million**, which rivaled the budget of the federal government.
- **Arthur and Lewis Tappan**, wealthy businessmen in Benevolent Empire, were greatly influenced by Finney's teachings and supported him financially, in spite of some disagreement on focus.
- **Second president of Oberlin College** (1851-65), which broke ground by admitting Blacks and women, and was a seedbed for abolition activists who attacked slavery in every way possible.
- **YMCA** was founded in England in 1844 by George Williams, who had been influenced by the writings of Charles Finney.
- **James Naismith** (1861-1939), a Presbyterian minister and physical education teacher at the YMCA International Training School in Springfield, Massachusetts, invented the sport of basketball in 1891 to occupy the boys during the cold winters and also teach them Christian character.

Caring about Sin, Converted to Change Society

Finney preached that true conversion to Christ affects all areas of your personal life and ministry and revivals are God's primary means of reforming both the Church and the world.

Only those truly converted can bring social reform. Once someone is saved, God will lead him to reform the institutions of law, civil government, and all of culture according to the Bible.

If you do not see that, he said, you are not truly converted.

Charles Finney

(1792-1875)

When the unconverted subdue their consciences for a long time, he said, ". . . the presence of sin and its daily practice is no source of grief or trouble to them."

"Many do not care to be saved from their sins. *This is not the kind of salvation which they would have. If they could be saved* in *their sins, they would like that full well. But they have no desire to be saved* from *their sins. The punishment they would gladly avoid if they conveniently could; but the presence of sin and its daily practice is no source of grief or trouble to them. . . . Some have a sort of desire, but yet are not willing to be saved from sin. They have seen so much of the hatefulness of sin as to wish to be saved from it; just as many drunkards wish to be saved from their cups, but you cannot for their life get them to sign a temperance pledge. This is often the case with sinners. They mistake their desires for a willingness; but they are not really willing.* ***They often pretend they are willing, but if you push them you will find they are not. They will draw back and will not go straight forward in the gospel path of faith in Christ Jesus and of self-renunciation."***[154]

Opposition of Lyman Beecher to Finney

In 1827, when Lyman Beecher (1775-1863) was minister of Hanover Street Congregational Church in Boston, he openly opposed Finney's "new measures" and Finney's plan to hold revival meetings in Boston. Beecher reportedly said, "Finney, I know your plan and you know I do; you mean to come to Connecticut and carry a streak of fire to

[154]Charles G. Finney, "Jesus, a Savior From Sinning (April 25, 1849). Text of the sermon: "Thou shalt call His name Jesus, for He shall save His people from their sins" (Matthew 1:21). Online source.

Boston: but if you attempt it, as the Lord liveth I'll meet you at the state line, and call out all the artillery men, and fight every inch of the way, and then I'll fight you there."[155] However, when Beecher heard reports of the results of Finney's revivals he headed a delegation to bring him in.

Areas of Controversy in Ministry of Charles Finney

- **"Anxious bench"** provided at front of church. If God was dealing with a person, he could sit there, waiting and praying.
- **Meetings** were long and frequent, sometimes daily.
- **New converts** were allowed to join churches immediately.
- **Women prayed publicly**.
- **Language of prayer** was personal, less formal.
- **Anyone** could make a decision to be saved.
- **Free will**: Those who believed in a certain interpretation of predestination disputed his teaching that an individual could make a decision to accept or reject the Gospel, stating it was God's decision. Others who had felt doomed by predestination received hope they could be saved.
- **Reality of hell:** Unitarians and Universalists opposed his teaching that unsaved people went to hell, calling it scare tactics.
- **Christian perfection:** Some disputed his biblical teaching that Christians have a limitless capacity for repentance and change; therefore, God can perfect them.

Priority 2—Family Needs and Destiny

Charles Dickens once wrote that "Charity begins at home and spreads abroad." Those closest to you in your home are the ones who see if your Christian life is legitimate as they watch you and hear your

[155] *The National Cyclopaedia of American Biography*, p. 463.

prayers on their behalf. Your family becomes your first opportunity to demonstrate your devotion to God and create a loving environment, "in earth as it is in heaven." Your family looks like what the world would become if you were in charge. They are the first fruit of your dedication.

According to creative order, first you pray for yourself, then your family, before you pray for those outside the home. You are responsible under God for maintaining a holy lifestyle and praying for your family.

Defeating the will of the devil in the family

Every family has four wills:

- Your will and each individual's will
- The family's will
- God's will
- The devil's will

In the first family, when Adam refused to intervene as the devil tempted Eve, the devil was allowed to exert his will. The devil's will showed up again in Cain through generational transfer.

If the devil's will can be transferred generationally, so can the will of God. It is up to you to determine which will should win.

All authority is delegated authority. God gives authority to the heads of families. He expects the head of a family to exercise self-government first, and then to fulfill godly government in the home.

If you don't give the devil any authority in your house he can't take authority. You are in charge. When you take authority in your house, you claim your rightful jurisdiction on behalf of God.

If you can take authority in your house, you can take authority in the earth, because you have been given a greater authority than what God has delegated to the devil—the authority of Jesus.

God created you in His image and likeness. He saved you. He created your family to look like Him as a spiritual entity on the earth, according to creative order, but the visible transformation of your family will not happen by accident. It will take concerted prayer and consecration and a commitment to do the will of God, not anyone else.

Men Who Pray for Their Families

If you are the man of the house, you are under the authority of God. It is your duty to submit to Him before you try to enforce your authority on anyone else. If you are not submitted to God, you cannot expect anyone else in your family to submit to you voluntarily.

Because of generational digression, men have been falling away from God and neglecting spiritual responsibilities in the home; therefore, their families are under a curse.[156]

Children of this generation have experienced unnecessary pain because of the prayerlessness of their fathers but God can "turn the heart of the fathers to the children, and hearts of children to their fathers."[157] A godly man builds his household through his prayers and consecration. Every man is supposed to get a God-said for his family. He intercedes for their needs and seeks God's will for their lives, beginning before they are born. His words impart a blessing that can last for generations.

Value of a Praying Wife: Charles Finney

Nineteenth-century evangelist Charles Finney knew in advance that he needed the kind of wife who was a pious, praying woman. He knew his own weaknesses and the great call upon His life, and he knew he could not get there on his own strength.

He did find a godly woman to undergird him in prayer. Lydia Andrews knew him before he was saved and prayed for his conversion. He was converted in 1821, and they were married in 1824. Whenever he held revivals, she would organize women's prayer meetings, which he considered essential to the work.

[156] See Malachi 4:6.
[157] Malachi 4:6 KJV.

Charles Finney

(1792-1875)

Finney sought a woman who would become a praying wife

"I can well remember that, in my own case, full one year before I was married, ***I had an irresistible conviction on my mind that I should lose my soul if I were to marry any other than a pious wife.*** *I knew I could not pray for myself. An ungodly wife would not pray for me, but would only strengthen me in my sins. I therefore came fully to the conclusion that I should never marry any other than a pious woman. I had never heard my father or my mother pray, and had no reason to suppose they ever prayed for me. Hence, perhaps I felt the more need of a praying wife. But I have often heard other men say the same in regard to marrying pious wives."*[158]

When Lydia died in 1847 he was devastated but his soul-searching brought him to another level of dedication. He married his second wife Elizabeth a year later and she became even more active, including public speaking and leading prayer meetings. At her death, Finney married again, to a third godly woman, who eventually outlived him. In an age when women almost never had a public role, he put his wives forward into public prayer and public speaking, and encouraged other women to be Christian leaders as well. He knew the value of a praying woman.

Committed to Praying Over Children: George Müller

When you pray for the children in your family, you have the opportunity to speak into them their future destiny. The old mothers used to pray over me when I was a child in church, and their prayers for my *consecration* worked a power of *concentration* in me so that I was able to excel in school. They did not "despise my youth"[159] but rather exhorted me to get all of God that I could, because, as they said, "Son, these are dark and evil days." When I was a young man my mother's prayers carried me

[158] Charles G. Finney, "On Persevering Prayer for Others." January 17, 1855. Online at http://www.gospeltruth.net.
[159] See 1 Timothy 4:1.

for years when I was backslidden and didn't even know if there was a God. She kept praying for the rest of her life.

George Müller (1805-1898), a German by birth whose famous faith carried several orphanages in 19th century Bristol, England, has been an inspiration for generations of people, but until he reached the age of 20 and was saved, he was a scoundrel who cheated his pastor/father and everyone else he met.

After he was born again and was married, he and his wife decided that they would never ask for money for their ministry and would never give definite answers when asked if they had a need. They would simply renew their prayers. He relinquished his small preacher's salary and placed an offering box in the chapel, and committed himself never to go in debt and never to ask anyone but God for money.

God gave Müller the equivalent of $7.5 million for his orphans, by prayer

Müller said, "Oh, how good, kind, gracious and condescending is the One with Whom we have to do! I am only a poor, frail, sinful man, but He has heard my prayers ten thousands of times."[160]

He never had a large bank balance. He trusted God. Once when he had £3000 (British pounds) someone asked if that made it easier for him to trust God, but he said, "No, I find myself apt to trust the £3000!"

Your name must stay in the earth

Children are a father's blessing. It's a sad day when men view pregnancy and fatherhood as a curse and pressure women to abort their own children in the womb. The Bible says that the fruit of the womb is God's reward.[161]

Müller's experience, beyond meeting the physical needs of the children, was his understanding of children's sensitivity to spiritual nurturing. He said that most people expect too little of children spiritually and therefore undervalue any efforts that could be made on their behalf. He urged Christians to have the patience to pray for children and teach them about Jesus, because he knew that they were good ground.

When you are rich toward God, He rewards you with natural and spiritual children. You love them and nurture them in the ways of righteousness. You pray for them all their lives.

---

[160] *The Kneeling Christian* (author unknown). From Chapter 8, "Does God Always Answer Prayer?" Online at Christian Classics Ethereal Library, www.ccel.org.

[161] See Psalm 127:3.

Children represent your legacy. They carry your name. Your name represents integrity. Your name has to stay in the earth through them.

George Müller

(1805-1898)

Spiritual nurturing of children

"As far as my experience goes, it appears to me that believers generally have expected far too little of present fruit upon their labours among children."[162]

After five years of preaching, publishing, education of children, and ministering to the poor, Müller announced in a meeting that he was starting an orphanage for the miserable street children who had won his heart. However, he did not take up an offering. After he made his announcement, one person handed him ten shillings and a Christian woman volunteered for the work. After five more days of prayer he had enough money to get started. That was the beginning of years of miraculous provision for children's orphanages all over the world. By the time he died in 1898, God had given him the equivalent of seven and a half million dollars for orphans. Tens of thousands lined the streets for his funeral.

Müller's Miracles

- Spent 68 years in ministry.
- Never specifically asked for money.
- Answered 3,000 letters each year, without a secretary.
- Traveled extensively to talk about his work.
- Raised $7.5 million for orphanages and other work in his lifetime, more than any other individual before him in history.

[162]Arthur T. Pierson, *George Müller of Bristol and His Witness to a Prayer-Hearing God* (Old Tappan, New Jersey: Fleming H. Revell Company, 1899). Available online at Christian Classics Ethereal Library, www.ccel.org, and other resource sites.

- Cared for 10,023 orphans. More than 3,000 orphans won to Christ.
- Read the Bible more than 200 times, half of them on his knees
- Traveled 200,000 miles in 42 countries, preached to 3 million people.

A Father's Confrontation of His Prodigal Son

Some years ago, the late wife of evangelist Billy Graham, Ruth Graham, wrote a book about her journey through the youthful spiritual turmoil of her son Franklin. She called it *Prodigals and Those Who Love Them*. You would never know it today, but at one point in his life, Franklin Graham—who now heads both the Billy Graham Evangelistic Association and Samaritan's Purse—was once a prodigal.

Franklin was an absolute rebel who acted more like one of his father's opponents than his son. As a young man in his twenties, Franklin smoked and drank, rode a motorcycle, and shot machine guns for fun, while still trying to keep a foothold in the door of the Church.

As Franklin tells it, on his 22nd birthday in 1974 his father once again confronted him with the same truth with which the elder Graham has confronted millions of people during his decades in ministry: the love of God and the claims of Jesus Christ on his life.

Billy Graham told his son, "You can't continue to play the middle ground. Either you're going to choose to follow and obey Him or reject Him." Without committing himself, Franklin went off on a trip to the Holy Land, but in a hotel room near Jerusalem, God got hold of him and wouldn't let him go. As Jesus said in the Parable of the Prodigal Son in Luke 15, he "came to himself."[163]

Franklin said later, "I put my cigarette out and got down on my knees beside my bed. I was His. . . . The rebel had found the cause."

He said that the verse from the Bible that meant the most to him at that time was Romans 8:1:

"There is therefore now no condemnation to them which are in Christ Jesus."[164]

I know Franklin didn't have perfect parents, even though they're famous Christian leaders, but he did have parents who loved him, believed in him, prayed for him, and didn't condemn him. They tried to show him the way out. Maybe that gave him the hope and perseverance to find out how much God loved him and believed in him, too.

---

[163] Luke 15:17 KJV.
[164] Romans 8:1 KJV.

Parents, like God, don't give up on prodigals

Parents who refuse to give up on their wayward children are just like God. They don't stop valuing them when they became an embarrassment and a source of frustration because that is not like the Father. Our Father is like the Prodigal's father. We can come to Him with a wasted life, having ruined ourselves financially and every other way, and He's just glad to see that we've come home. Jesus said:

> *"And he arose, and came to his father. But when he was yet a great way off, his father saw him, and had compassion, and ran, and fell on his neck, and kissed him. And the son said unto him, Father, I have sinned against heaven, and in thy sight, and am no more worthy to be called thy son. But the father said to his servants, Bring forth the best robe, and put it on him; and put a ring on his hand, and shoes on his feet: And bring hither the fatted calf, and kill it; and let us eat, and be merry:*
> *For this my son was dead,*
> *and is alive again; he was lost, and is found.*
> *And they began to be merry."*[165]

God longs to see unconditional love like that in parents everywhere because it is absolutely awesome when parents act like God!

Godly parents love the real person inside

At the end of Jesus' parable, the elder brother had his say. He was mad! He didn't see why his brother should be given a party after the terrible things he had done. His standard of value was based on accomplishment and he challenged his father's judgment by calling his attention to his own superior value, in his eyes, because he had followed the letter of the law. He didn't see that his father had given his blessing.

What heaven has commanded, earth must obey.
Find out what heaven has commanded for your family relationships and pray that back to God. Discover the great causes that God has destined for you to win, and dedicate your life to them. Give the devil good reasons to fight against you and ultimately you will win.

[165] Luke 15:20-24 KJV.

Praying for Your Family as Jesus Prays for You

Develop a family prayer list and pray for members of your family every day. Pray for your children and their spouses and children, if they are grown; pray for your parents, your siblings, your in-laws, and others. Never stop praying! Jesus never stops praying for us. "He is also able to save to the uttermost those who come to God through Him, since He always lives to make intercession for them."[166]

Do you have the ambition that any of your children might become President of the United States or is your highest ambition that they obtain a C-average on their grade report? Do you have a vision for your spouse to do great things for God or is it more important that your spouse focus on you and your needs? What vision does Jesus have for you? For your family?

Pray for them with patience as you believe that Jesus prays for them, and with the intensity that you hope He is praying for you. Your vision and prayers on behalf of your spouse and children will help them break through into the destiny that God has for them.

Patience to bring fruit to perfection *Luke 8:14-15 KJV*	*"And that which fell among thorns are they, which, when they have heard, go forth, and are choked with cares and riches and pleasures of this life, and bring no fruit to perfection. But that on the good ground are they, which in an honest and good heart, having heard the word, keep it, and bring forth fruit with patience."*

Be longsuffering with your family's faults as God is toward us,[167] believing God to change them. When you pray, have mercy, remembering your own weaknesses and need for God's mercy.

Mercy triumphs over judgment *James 2:12-13 NKJV*	*"So speak and so do as those who will be judged by the law of liberty. For judgment is without mercy to the one who has shown no mercy. Mercy triumphs over judgment."*

[166] See Hebrews 7:25 NKJV.
[167] See 2 Peter 3:9.

From His throne of mercy Jesus is "touched with a feeling of their infirmities."[168] Be like Him. Don't dwell on their faults. How would you feel if God constantly reminded you of your shortcomings as clearly as you remind others of theirs? He doesn't nag you. He prays for you.

Jesus lives to pray *Hebrews 7: 24-25 NLT*	*"But because Jesus lives forever, his priesthood lasts forever. Therefore he is able, once and forever, to save those who come to God through him. He lives forever to intercede with God on their behalf."*

Jesus' prayers and steadfast love on your behalf have so much power that they can carry you into your destiny. You need to have that kind of prayer and steadfast love for your family.

Do you ever wonder what Jesus is saying as He prays for you every day? Stop a moment each day and ask Him to show you so that you can fulfill His prayers. Then try to pray for your family with the same zeal that you want Jesus to have when He prays for you.

In both the Old Testament and the New, the men of God who had an impact on their generation were the priests, the prophets, and the kings. A lot of men think they should be king of their house—king of the castle!—but in order to be the man of God your family needs, you need to take on the spiritual offices of priest and prophet.

Any man can throw his weight around, but you want to become like Jesus in your home and love your wife as Christ loves the Church.

If you want heaven in your home, stop trying to be king and start being priest and prophet. Every man should be both priest and prophet.

As priest, go to God daily on behalf of your family. Your home will be called a house of prayer when you as a man of God can be called a house of prayer.

As prophet, go to your family daily on behalf of God. You can give your family a "God said" when God has said something to you in prayer because you were in a position to hear Him.

God is looking for people who will carry their families and this generation in prayer. Don't let Him be able to say that in our generation He could find no one to stand in the gap. Stay faithful in prayer.

"And I sought for a man among them, that should make up the hedge, and stand in the gap before me for the land, that I should not destroy it: but I found none."[169]

---

[168] Hebrews 4:15 KJV.

[169] Ezekiel 22:30.

Would Jesus find you in faith, praying for your family?

Luke 18:7-8 NKJV

"And shall God not avenge His own elect who cry out day and night to Him, though He bears long with them? I tell you that He will avenge them speedily. Nevertheless, when the Son of Man comes, will He really find faith on the earth?"

Believe in your family. Become like God who says "I believe in you" while you're still a rebel or unproven and then sows into you what's necessary to bring your change.

The prodigal's father gave him the family money and then he gave him a ring and a party because he sensed that those gifts were what the young man needed to bring his change.

Never stop sowing love into your family

When the prodigal's father sowed those gifts into his wayward son, he was in reality sowing love. The money was gone that he had given his son, but he still gave more. Jesus used him as an example of God the Father's love because he was still ready to give.

That father is also an example of how we give everything to God. When you take everything you have that God gave you and give it over to God, that's the starting place. You start out by giving your whole life to God. Then your life becomes a lifestyle of giving.

God's love and acceptance make it possible for you to accomplish the things that please Him. Condemnation and judgment could never accomplish what is accomplished by giving. We love because God first loved us. When we love, we are like God.

We give because God first gave to us. When we give we are like God, especially when the one who receives is not worthy of the gift.

Priority 3—Fivefold Ministry

"And he gave some, apostles; and some, prophets; and some, evangelists; and some, pastors and teachers; For the perfecting of the saints, for the work of the ministry, for the edifying of the body of Christ" (Ephesians 4:11-12 KJV).

The "fivefold ministry" are leaders who provide salt and light in the Church and the world. If they hide their sin and allow sin in others, so will the world, but they are to be salt and light to the world.

Fivefold ministers carrying light into the world

Every genuine revival in the Church has also had a positive influence on the world. Whenever the Church has been in a backslidden or formalistic condition without a true relationship with Jesus, sin has flourished in the world.

However, when Christians are in right relationship with Jesus, the church shines and the world receives the light of life "because as he is, so are we in this world."[170]

You are the light, so let your light shine

Matthew 5: 14-16 KJV

"Ye are the light of the world. A city that is set on an hill cannot be hid. Neither do men light a candle, and put it under a bushel, but on a candlestick; and it giveth light unto all that are in the house. Let your light so shine before men, that they may see your good works, and glorify your Father which is in heaven."

Society flourishes when true Christians control the culture

The direction of our culture is not determined by outside forces stronger than the Church. We are God's elect. We should be in charge.

Like Adam in the Garden before the Fall, Christians have been ordained to have dominion but we have abdicated our responsibility. We should pray for the Church to have more influence in society by praying for those who lead us in the Church.

[170] 1 John 4:17 KJV.

Fivefold Ministry Offices in the Bible

Apostle

Apostles are pioneers or missionaries with the authority of Christ who are set apart and sent out with a life-giving message backed by miraculous powers. Everywhere they go they preach the Gospel with sound doctrine and plant churches.

Jesus selected 12 apostles from the disciples after a long night in prayer (Luke 6:12-15).

Paul listed apostles first in the foundation of the Church (1 Corinthians 12:28 KJV).

Since Judas was one of the original 12, one of the first actions of the early church was to replace him with another apostle (Acts 1:26).

Prophet

Prophets are both foretellers and forth-tellers. They predict the future and also speak forthrightly to the people with messages from God that bring to light actions in their own day.

Paul listed prophets second in the foundation of the Church (see 1 Corinthians 12:28 KJV).

Jesus warned apostles and prophets of persecution and death for their faith (Luke 11:49).

Paul said that the Holy Spirit would reveal to Christ's "holy apostles and prophets" truths that had never been known in previous generations" (Ephesians 3:5).

Evangelist

A preacher of the Gospel, a messenger sent out to announce the good news about Jesus Christ—His life, teachings, death, resurrection, and ascension to heaven. Jesus, the 12 apostles, Paul (1 Corinthians 9), Philip (Acts 21:8), Timothy (2 Timothy 4:5) were evangelists.

Jesus said, "I must preach the Good News of the Kingdom of God in other towns, too, because that is why I was sent" (Luke 4:43 NLT).

Peter told Cornelius, "God chose me from among you some time ago to preach to the Gentiles so that they could hear the Good News and believe" (Acts 15:7 NLT).

Gospel of the kingdom (Matthew 24:14 KJV). Gospel "of the grace of God" (Acts 20:24 KJV). The "gospel of Christ" (Romans 1:16 KJV). The "gospel of peace" (Romans 10:15). The "glorious" and the "everlasting" gospel (1 Timothy 1:11; Revelation 14:6).

Pastor

A "shepherd" who feeds, protects, and brings order and well-being to a "flock"

"Jesus, the Good Shepherd (John 10) had compassion on the masses who were "confused and helpless, like sheep without a shepherd" (Matthew 9:36 NLT). At the eternal judgment Jesus will separate His true sheep from the goats (see Matthew 25:32).

Shepherd after God's own heart, guiding others (Jeremiah 3:15 NLT). Appointed by the Holy Spirit, he guards his heart as he shepherds the Church, purchased with Christ's blood (Acts 20:28). Like Timothy, he "genuinely cares about your welfare" (Philippians 2:20 NLT).

Teacher

Instructor, master. Jesus was a Teacher sent by God (John 3:2). "Rabbi" means "Teacher" (John 1:38). Teachers receive and teach truths "to other trustworthy people who will be able to pass them on to others" (2 Timothy 2:2 NLT). "All scripture is given by inspiration of God, and is profitable for doctrine, for reproof, for correction, for instruction in righteousness" (2 Timothy 3:16 KJV).

"Obey your spiritual leaders, and do what they say. Their work is to watch over your souls, and they are accountable to God. Give them reason to do this with joy and not with sorrow. That would certainly not be for your benefit" (Hebrews 13:17 NLT).

The Church is more than a place that provides Sunday services and opens its doors for special occasions like deaths, weddings, and national disasters. When people come to church they should see that they have been missing something because the Church has strong leaders and biblical principles with practical relevance for every area of their lives.

Christians Who Take Responsibility for Their Communities

After the Civil War, the first building to be raised in the freed slaves' new communities was the church. The pastor was the town leader. He was not limited to giving a message on Sunday morning. He was into everything—from confronting men with their responsibilities to their families to building schools and starting banks and insurance companies. Businessmen came out of the church. The community flourished because Christian pastors and leaders were in control.

Some of the well-intentioned government programs for the freed slaves ended in disaster because the motivations were often based more on politics than principle.

When the Freedman's Bank failed and many of the nation's Black citizens lost what little savings they had, pastors and Christian businessmen rose up and created banks for their own people.

When tax money for schools went mostly to the Whites, the Black churches raised their own money for schools.

Thomas Sowell gave some remarkable statistics about the role of the American church in his book *Ethnic America*. He said that the Black population went from being almost totally illiterate after the Civil War to being 75 percent literate only 50 years later.

How did it happen? Because Christians and other private citizens believed they, not the civil government, had a responsibility for the state of the culture.

The Black churches raised almost seven times as much money as the federal government's Freedman's Bureau spent on schools for Blacks.

Christians Influencing Culture After the Civil War

Black Church *(Most had been enslaved and had no personal assets.)*

- Built churches in every community.
- Raised $24 million to build schools *(roughly equivalent to $240 million today).*
- Discipled their people into citizens with Christ-like character

American Missionary Association *(Mostly White Christians from the North)*

- Worked in the public forum for the abolition of slavery.
- Sent secret guides to lead slaves to freedom.
- Planted hundreds of anti-slavery churches
- Founded 500 predominantly Black schools for children and adults.
- Founded 10 predominantly Black colleges

  Atlanta University
  Berea College
  Dillard University
  Fisk University
  Hampton Institute (now Hampton University)
  Howard University
  Huston-Tillotson College
  Le Moyne College
  Talladega College
  Tougaloo College

- Created help programs for Native Americans, Asians, and migrant laborers.

It was the goal of the American Missionary Association to bring "full and equal privileges of citizenship to the black population of the United States during the latter half of the 19th century, leading into the 20th century. The Association did so under the doctrine that to deny these rights would serve to subvert the teachings of Jesus, thus those who attempted to deny these rights performed sins against God and man." [171]

With a strong anti-slavery focus, they developed schools for Black teachers so that the race could become self-sufficient and take over the responsibility of educating their own people.

[171] "The American Missionary Association." Online at http://northbysouth.kenyon.edu/1998/edu/charleston/ama.htm. Accessed February 2016.

God Is Watching the Church

Can God count on your prayers for your church and the fivefold ministry? Will your prayers make the difference in their effectiveness in reaching and changing the world?

When much is given, much is required
Luke 12:48 NKJV

"For everyone to whom much is given, from him much will be required; and to whom much has been committed, of him they will ask the more."

World Peace Is Dependent on Prayer

World peace depends on what happens in the prayer closets of Christians, including prayers on behalf of the fivefold ministry. God builds the whole earth from the foundation of His Church. The eyes of the Lord are on *His Church.* He is coming for *His Church.*

Pray for leaders *in the Church* and pray to become a leader yourself. When the Church is strong, its people have been transformed into the image and likeness of Christ. Everything else in the world can be changed and restored to suit God.[172]

We need to come to this place in the Lord where we are not just praying for God to do something. We are actually making something happen. This comes from a devotion or realization that you are one with Christ. This comes from consecration.

There is a correlation between consecration and what you can do in God. Once you consecrate yourself to God, you forget about what you can't do. There is a correlation between believing and doing great things and not doing things because of your self-consciousness.

[172]"And they that shall be of thee shall build the old waste places: thou shalt raise up the foundations of many generations; and thou shalt be called, The repairer of the breach, The restorer of paths to dwell in" (Isaiah 58:12 KJV).

When you think too much about yourself, you don't do great things. You think about failing the Lord or what you don't know or the fact that you didn't pray long enough today.

Once you consecrate yourself over to the Lord and say, "Lord, my life is your life," then you do that which becomes natural in Christ to do.

You are the fruit of the apostles, prophets, pastors, teachers, and evangelists who perfected you for the work of God. My calling is apostolic. Jesus told the apostles to go and make disciples of nations so I disciple nations by discipling leaders. I expect fivefold leaders to go to the nations with the Gospel. They fulfill the Bible at all costs.

Once again, the theme of this book comes from Ezekiel 22:30

"And I sought for a man among them, that should make up the hedge, and stand in the gap before me for the land, that I should not destroy it: but I found none."

One of the ways that you stand in the gap, of course is prayer.

When you make your prayer list, write down the names of Christian leaders whom you admire, as well as those whom you have criticized, and pray for all of them, trusting God to perfect them and use them greatly to change the world.

Priority 4—Praying for Leaders— Local State, Nation, World

Cities, states, nations, and the world need prayer for God's help. Christians don't just *reform* society. They *transform* it by bringing people to Jesus. But before we can transform society, we must be transformed ourselves through a continuing encounter with the love and Lordship of Jesus Christ.

After you pray for yourself, your family, and the fivefold ministry, you pray for leaders in the marketplace. You start by praying for those leaders closest to you at the local level—such as those in authority over you in the community—then you pray for leaders of the state, the nation, and the nations of the world. That is the proper order—praying from the inside out.

There are five sovereign spheres of government:

- Individual (self-government)
- Family
- Church
- Civil government
- Free associations

Each sphere has a degree of sovereignty from every other sphere, but all need the prayers of the saints.

Pray for city leaders *Jeremiah 29:7 KJV*	*"And seek the peace of the city whither I have caused you to be carried away captives, and pray unto the Lord for it: for in the peace thereof shall ye have peace."*

Take responsibility to pray for your leaders

Cities, states, and nations need God, and God needs someone like you to pray and be His prophet in the public arena on His behalf.

Corporations need His standards of integrity, fairness, and compassion. Schools and universities need His wisdom to be His instruments in the lives of the youth.

You can win your city, your nation, and the nations of the world if you see them with the eyes of revelation through your prayer life and personal involvement. Just as God told Abram that he could have all the lands he could see, you can have all the lands that you see. Once you see, you can go where you see, with God. You can declare that your nation and all of the nations you see will someday be ruled by men of God.

Claiming ground as far as your eyes can see *Genesis 13:14-15 NKJV*	*"And the Lord said to Abram, after Lot had separated from him: "Lift your eyes now and look from the place where you are—northward, southward, eastward, and westward; for all the land which you see I give to you and your descendants forever."*

Times of great national crisis should remind our leaders of our nation's dependency on God. President Lincoln and Congress understood that and issued this call to fasting and prayer in 1863 during the Civil War.

President Abraham Lincoln declares day of humiliation, fasting and prayer[173]

Calling on God in midst of Civil War

Lincoln called the people to "recognize the hand of God in this terrible visitation" and to "sorrowful remembrance of our own faults and crimes as a nation and as individuals, to humble our selves before him and to pray for His mercy, to pray that we may be spared further punishment, though most justly deserved."

Pastor of World Leaders— Billy Graham

One of the greatest examples in our time of a Christian who has maintained favor with world leaders is Billy Graham. He has kept faithfully to his calling as an evangelist to the masses and at the same time has been welcomed to the inner circle of American presidents, the queen of England, and even leaders of former Communist countries.

Dr. Graham has maintained the highest moral character. He is consistently one of the most admired men in the world, yet he has not become proud, or unreachable, and he has not fallen into sin. He has maintained standards of Christ-likeness.

Become a New Elijah to a Nation

Elijah was an Old Testament prophet who had access to leaders in high places of power. Perhaps God will show you in prayer that you are to be a new Elijah. The prophet Elijah was in conflict with Ahab, king of Israel, because Ahab had married Jezebel, daughter of the pagan king of Tyre. He had also joined in the practices of other religions, and established a center of Baal worship in Samaria. Elijah pronounced God's judgment on Israel in the form of a drought, then escaped and lived in Zarephath, where God kept him alive through miraculous means at the home of a widow.

[173]The war began in 1861. Lincoln called this day of prayer and fasting for April 30, 1863.

Lord turned hearts back to Him *1 Kings 18:37-39 KJV*	*"Hear me, O Lord, hear me, that this people may know that thou art the Lord God, and that thou hast turned their heart back again. Then the fire of the Lord fell, and consumed the burnt sacrifice, and the wood, and the stones, and the dust, and licked up the water that was in the trench. And when all the people saw it, they fell on their faces: and they said, The Lord, he is the God; the Lord, he is the God."*

Elijah—just a man, but his prayers brought a national revolution

At the end of three years, Elijah appeared and challenged Ahab and his prophets of Baal to a contest on Mount Carmel, to prove who was really God. Ahab and the prophets failed to awaken their god, but Elijah succeeded in a miraculous way.[174] That gave him the platform to proclaim who was the God of Israel, and the people fell down in worship of the true and living God.

Elijah was a man like us. He had passion when he prayed for Israel. In his private time, he carried a whole nation's destiny into the face of God in order to change the consequences of their sin.

In the Bible, we are not only told that we can pray like Elijah but also that we can get the results that Elijah was able to get.

Elijah prayed and rain stopped for three years *James 5:17-18 KJV*	*"Elias was a man subject to like passions as we are, and he prayed earnestly that it might not rain: and it rained not on the earth by the space of three years and six months. And he prayed again, and the heaven gave rain, and the earth brought forth her fruit."*

Would there be a revolution in earth if everyone prayed the way that you pray? Could God use your prayer life as a model for the generation?

Do you have a sense of certainty that others' needs will be met, based on your level of passion as you pray for them?

[174]See 1 Kings 18.

You might have churches exploding everywhere, all over the world. You may be receiving plaudits in anniversary services and people are coming from miles around to hear you preach. Your church may have sufficient finances for several building projects. However, you still need to judge yourself against the great leaders of the Bible and the Church.

Suppose I had the goal of being naturally rich and I met that goal. However, if I were not like God, I would still not be a success. If I kept the credit for myself I would be dishonoring God Who made me and gave me all that I have.

You must live with the witness of Christ's return. If on the inside you don't have the witness of a dedicated life, you will never be satisfied. Jesus could come at any time so live right now, as far as you know how, with Holy Spirit telling you that you don't have to change a thing to be ready to face Him on that day. When God shows you a place where you need to repent, obey Him instantly so that you are always ready for His return.

Israel—Entrepreneurs Building on God's Covenant

When you pray for nations, pray for the Jews and Israel because God's chosen people are unique among the people of the earth.

One of my favorite books is *Start-Up Nation: The Story of Israel's Economic Miracle* by Dan Senor and Saul Singer. The authors document how modern-day Israel has become a nation of entrepreneurs and creative geniuses, especially in this digital age. Israel's success demonstrates in a practical way the entrepreneurial capabilities of a called-out people whom God has given power to create wealth.

God gives you power to create wealth

Deuteronomy 8:18 KJV

"But thou shalt remember the LORD thy God: for it is he that giveth thee power to get wealth, that he may establish his covenant which he sware unto thy fathers, as it is this day.

When God made a covenant with Abraham, it was an everlasting covenant with Israel. The world may reject Israel's claim to its land but God stands by His Word forever. He still chooses them as His people.

Everlasting covenant with Israel *Psalm 105:8-10 KJV*	*"He hath remembered his covenant for ever, the word which he commanded to a thousand generations. Which covenant he made with Abraham, and his oath unto Isaac; And confirmed the same unto Jacob for a law, and to Israel for an everlasting covenant."*

Israel represents God's elect. When you bless Israel, you will be blessed, but when you curse Israel, you incur God's wrath.

God will bless those who bless Israel, ***and curse those who curse Israel*** *Genesis 12:2-3 KJV*	*"I will bless thee, and make thy name great; and thou shalt be a blessing: And I will bless them that bless thee, and curse him that curseth thee: and in thee shall all families of the earth be blessed."*

Christians pray earnestly for God's blessing on Israel:

- Pray for the peace of Jerusalem.

Pray for the peace of Jerusalem *Psalm 122:6-9 KJV*	*"Pray for the peace of Jerusalem: they shall prosper that love thee. Peace be within thy walls, and prosperity within thy palaces. For my brethren and companions' sakes, I will now say,* *Peace be within thee."*

- Pray that America will remain a friend of Israel, even if all the rest of the world treats Israel as an enemy.
- Pray that Israel will acknowledge Jesus as their Messiah.

Jesus was crucified on Passover

Moses instructed the Israelites on the night they escaped from Egypt to kill a lamb or goat and smear the blood on top and sides of their doorframes. This was the first Passover.

> *"When you enter the land the Lord has promised to give you, you will continue to observe this ceremony. Then your children will ask, 'What does this ceremony mean?' And you will reply, 'It is the Passover sacrifice to the Lord, for he passed over the houses of the Israelites in Egypt.*
> *And though he struck the Egyptians,*
> *he spared our families.'"*[175]

Jesus came first to the Jews.

John the Baptist prophesied that Jesus was the Lamb of God slain for the sins of the world.[176]

Jesus was crucified during the Jewish Passover.

Holy Ghost came with fire on the Jewish Pentecost

After Jesus' death, burial, and resurrection He told His disciples to stay in Jerusalem until they received power to be His witnesses, which also means the power to be His martyrs.[177]

Holy Ghost came at the Jewish Pentecost when His disciples—Jews—received the Baptism in the Holy Ghost and fire. The first people to hear the Gospel preached after the Holy Ghost came were Jews from many nations who were in Jerusalem to celebrate Pentecost. They spoke many languages but miraculously they understood the words of the apostles because they spoke the words given to them by the Holy Ghost.

---

[175] Exodus 12:25-27 NLT.
[176] See John 1:29.
[177] See Acts 1:8.

Suffering of Jews in Modern History

In 1998 I was privileged to participate in a Jubilee celebration honoring the 50th anniversary of the State of Israel that was established at great sacrifice in 1948. On their website they declare that it was a "rebirth; the framework for a democratic Jewish state founded on liberty, justice, and peace, as envisaged by the biblical prophets."[178] Today the population is approximately 8.3 million people of whom about 6.1 million are Jewish.

State of Israel offered a new beginning after the Holocaust

The State of Israel was created soon after the Holocaust in Nazi Germany and German-occupied territories in which six million Jews were murdered. The Holocaust was a horrific act of genocide led by Adolph Hitler and the Nazi Party to destroy the Jewish race. Hitler was a eugenicist. He believed that his race was the only noble one and that Jews belonged to a lower race that must be eliminated.

Before those mass murders took place, officials in each city persecuted and killed Jews and destroyed their businesses. They forced them to live in overcrowded ghettos as in earlier centuries. The ghettos were surrounded by walls with locked gates. Anyone leaving would be shot. In the Warsaw Ghetto, for example, 400,000 Jews lived in only 1.3 square miles. With little food and sanitation many died of starvation and disease. Beginning in 1942 the Jews were deported to extermination camps where the massive killings took place that have come to be called the Holocaust.

Refusing to yield to a ghetto mentality

Jewish ghettos in Europe during World War II had visible walls and locks but a ghetto can also have invisible walls imposed from without, such as walls of prejudice. They may also have invisible walls imposed from within, such as the so-called "crab" syndrome where anyone trying to rise above their circumstances is pulled back by jealousy among those who have not yet made it. Nations have tried to destroy the Jews and are still trying to overrun Israel. It is surrounded by enemies but Jews have refused to embrace the ghetto mentality. The issue is authority. Who has the right over your life and your future?

---

178 Online at http://mfa.gov.il/MFA/AboutIsrael/State/Pages/The%20State.aspx.

Israel chose to take authority by building a nation. In the ghettoes when the Jews had no water or food they literally survived by God Himself. They refused to abandon their core principle that they are the people of Abraham, Isaac, and Jacob and God's chosen people.

Someday Jews will recognize Jesus as Messiah and be saved

The Bible says that there will come a future time when Israel will be saved. As we pray for Israel and learn from their example of entrepreneurship built on God's covenant we eagerly anticipate that day.

Israel will mourn for the One they have pierced

Zechariah 12:10 KJV

"And I will pour upon the house of David, and upon the inhabitants of Jerusalem, the spirit of grace and of supplications: and they shall look upon me whom they have pierced, and they shall mourn for him, as one mourneth for his only son, and shall be in bitterness for him, as one that is in bitterness for his firstborn."

Paul is our example of compassionate prayer for Israel

As an Israelite himself, the Apostle Paul advised us to never lose hope that his own people, God's chosen people, would eventually turn from their unbelief in Jesus and be grafted in again to His tree.

"Dear brothers and sisters, the longing of my heart and my prayer to God is for the people of Israel to be saved. I know what enthusiasm they have for God, but it is misdirected zeal. For they don't understand God's way of making people right with himself. Refusing to accept God's way, they cling to their own way of getting right with God by trying to keep the law. For Christ has already accomplished the purpose for which the law was given. As a result, all who believe in him are made right with God."[179]

"And if the people of Israel turn from their unbelief, they will be grafted in again, for God has the power to graft them back into the tree."[180]

[179] Romans 10:1-4 NLT.
[180] Romans 11:23 NLT.

Priority 5—Praying for Other Needs

As you continue your prayer list each day, you will remember many other needs for your family, friends, fellow Christians, and others in the world. Perhaps you will be called to put those prayers into action like Ludwig von Zinzendorf, who in his early twenties dedicated his wealth to providing a place for Christian refugees to live in safety. He gave them not only safety but a heart for love, unity of the saints, continual prayer, and sacrificial missionary journeys to reach the lost.

Looking out for the needs of others

Philippians 2:1-4 KJV

"Therefore if there is any consolation in Christ, if any comfort of love, if any fellowship of the Spirit, if any affection and mercy, fulfill my joy by being like-minded, having the same love, being of one accord, of one mind. Let nothing be done through selfish ambition or conceit, but in lowliness of mind let each esteem others better than himself. Let each of you look out not only for his own interests, but also for the interests of others."

Coming Together to Reach Nations: William Carey

William Carey (1761-1834) is called the "father of modern missions." Even though he was preceded by other missionaries like the Moravians, he has been given that unofficial title because of his tireless efforts and widespread influence on restoring the church's vision for missions. From his time on, missionary activity increased dramatically, eventually crossing all denominations to reach nations.

Carey also had a burden for Christians to unite. He believed that unified praying on behalf of others would resolve many of the differences among Christians and bring about a new level of evangelism.

William Carey

(1761-1834)

Missionary to India

Calling Christians to unite through unified prayer

"Many can do nothing but pray, and prayer is perhaps the only thing in which Christians of all denominations can cordially, and unreservedly unite; but in this we may all be one, and in this the strictest unanimity ought to prevail. Were the whole body thus animated by one soul, with what pleasure would Christians attend on all the duties of religion, and with what delight would their ministers attend on all the business of their calling."[181]

In 1792 he preached a message entitled "Expect Great Things from God, Attempt Great Things for God" that resulted in the creation of the Baptist Missionary Society. Carey's mission field was India, but he not only had a burden for those in India who did not know Jesus as Savior. He also had a heart for sinners everywhere.

Effectiveness of William Carey's Ministry

- Scriptures translated into 40 languages
- College founded at Serampore, India
- India opened to missions
- Edict passed prohibiting *sati* (burning widows on the funeral pyres of their dead husbands)
- Indians converted to Christ
- Final request: "When I am gone, say nothing about Dr. Carey—speak about Dr. Carey's God."

William Carey's life is a testimony of what one man can do.

[181]William Carey, *An Enquiry Into The Obligations Of Christians To Use Means For The Conversion Of The Heathens.* This excerpt available online at http://www.grace.org.uk.

Stay in God's Will When Praying for Other Needs

Israel in the wilderness needed water. When Moses prayed for their need God told him specifically how to meet that need.

"Moses and Aaron turned away from the people and went to the entrance of the Tabernacle, where they fell face down on the ground. Then the glorious presence of the Lord appeared to them, and the Lord said to Moses, 'You and Aaron must take the staff and assemble the entire community. As the people watch, speak to the rock over there, and it will pour out its water. You will provide enough water from the rock to satisfy the whole community and their livestock.'"[182]

However, when Moses went back and saw the people's strife and unbelief he let their lack of character offset his obedience to God. He stood angrily before them and struck the rock twice with his staff instead of speaking to it to bring forth water as God had told him in prayer.[183]

Watch out for distractions when God tells you how to help others

Watch out. You need to maintain such a sense of awareness of God's power that you can keep that awareness no matter what else is happening. You can impart His power to others in perfect obedience to His instructions because that sanctifies the Lord before the world.

Later, when God told Moses to impart his spirit into the life of Joshua, the man whom He had chosen to lead the people of Israel in place of Moses, the Lord said:

"Take Joshua son of Nun, who has the Spirit in him, and lay your hands on him."[184]

---

[182]Numbers 20:6-9 NLT.
[183]See Numbers 20:11.
[184]Numbers 27:18 NLT.

Moses was not representing himself when he laid his hands on Joshua. He was representing God. When you touch someone's life you touch them for God. You restore a sense of God's reality to their being.

Moses imparted a right spirit to Joshua. He passed on his supernatural ability to lead the people. He passed on the ability from God to be able to handle the hard cases and the ability to delegate authority.

Stay on fire and willing to sacrifice for others' needs

When churches stay in existence for a number of years, they may develop more religion than passion for worldwide revival. There is a danger that they will have church services but no longer be a service church. The members will have no desire to sacrifice for those in need nor to pray until something happens. They will forget about becoming like Jesus and changing the rest of the world to become like Him.

Jesus, because of His passion, went to Gethsemane and then Golgotha. When you have His passion, you can pray for a city, a community, or a generation to know Him and God can give you the ability to persevere to the fulfillment of what you see.

Having compassion, making a difference

Jude 21-23 KJV

"Keep yourselves in the love of God, looking for the mercy of our Lord Jesus Christ unto eternal life. And of some have compassion, making a difference: And others save with fear, pulling them out of the fire; hating even the garment spotted by the flesh."

Allow God to give you *His* compassion

Elijah was willing to take on the whole nation out of his own spirit because he was able to hear from God. If you want more passion in your prayer life for your family, your city, and the generation, allow God to give you His compassion and you won't have any trouble thinking about what to say when you pray. Your heart will be broken for them and you will cry out to God with a new intensity for their salvation and the satisfaction of their needs.

Chapter 17

Pounding Prayer

START 3-9-21

Jesus said that men ought always to pray and not to faint.[185] There would be no fainting if we did not lose heart through prayerlessness. On the next page you will find a sample page for lists of "Pounding Prayers." These are areas where you may find resistance, like the man who went to his friend's house after midnight for bread.

Importunity principle of pounding prayer

Luke 11:5-9 KJV

"And [Jesus] said unto them, Which of you shall have a friend, and shall go unto him at midnight, and say unto him, Friend, lend me three loaves; For a friend of mine in his journey is come to me, and I have nothing to set before him? And he from within shall answer and say, Trouble me not: the door is now shut, and my children are with me in bed; I cannot rise and give thee. I say unto you, Though he will not rise and give him, because he is his friend, yet because of his importunity he will rise and give him as many as he needeth."

When we pray, we pray through to victory. Because God has given us the substance of faith, we are not playing praying. We are pressing through until something happens. We P.U.S.H., "Pray Until Something Happens." God already knows the end result. He is the Alpha and the Omega. He has commanded us to break up the fallow ground of our hearts. It is time for us to pray until righteousness is rained upon us.

[185]See Luke 18:1.

Pounding Prayer List

A list of requests to present to God on a consistent basis
until you see the results of your prayers
Jesus said, "I say unto you, Though he will not rise and give him,
because he is his friend, yet because of his importunity
he will rise and give him as many as he needeth" (Luke 11:8 KJV).

Prayer Requests	**Answers to Prayer**

Remember to be thankful. *"And Jesus answering said,*
Were there not ten cleansed? but where are the nine?
There are not found that returned to give glory to God,
save this stranger" (Luke 17:17-18 KJV).

Chapter 18

A Call to Personal All-Night Prayer

Here is an outline for something bold—schedule yourself to pray all night, just as Jesus did.

After all-night prayer, Jesus understood who should be His apostles

"One day soon afterward Jesus went up on a mountain to pray, and he prayed to God all night. At daybreak he called together all of his disciples and chose twelve of them to be apostles."[186]

More Scriptures Concerning All-Night Prayer

Genesis 32:24 KJV	*"And Jacob was left alone; and there wrestled a man with him until the breaking of the day."*
Psalm 22:2 KJV	*"O my God, I cry in the daytime, but thou hearest not; and in the night season, and am not silent."*
Mark 6:46 KJV	*"And when [Jesus] had sent them away, he departed into a mountain to pray."*

[186] Luke 6:12-13 NLT.

Personal All-Night Prayer Schedule

Jesus didn't use this format, but here is a suggestion for a profitable way to schedule your all-night time with God. The suggested time is 11:00 p.m. to 6:00 a.m.

First Hour 11 pm to 12 am **Confession and Repentance**	Everything you see about yourself that is sinful or not as intense as God wants it to be should bring you to repentance. *"If we confess our sins, he is faithful and just to forgive us our sins, and to cleanse us from all unrighteousness. If we say that we have not sinned, we make him a liar, and his word is not in us."*[187]
Second Hour 12 am to 1 am **Praise, Thanksgiving, and Worship**	Praise God. List what you have to give thanks for. Recite or read poetry. Worship in song. Listen to music, with a headset, if necessary. Sing along with music.[188] Use a song book. If you play an instrument, play and sing along. Create songs to your own tunes from the Psalms. *"O come, let us worship and bow down: let us kneel before the Lord our maker. For he is our God; and we are the people of his pasture, and the sheep of his hand."*[189]

[187] 1 John 1:9-10 KJV.
[188] As the Lord gives you a heart for songs in the night, you can download Christian songs from iTunes and Google Play and other sources. You will also find the lyrics to many songs and hymns at other places online such as the hymns of Charles Wesley and others in the Index.
[189] Psalm 95:6-7 KJV.

Third Hour 1 am to 2 am **Reading and Listening to the Bible**	Listen to the Bible recordings on any device and read along.[190] Record your favorite Scriptures in your own words for one hour. Use different versions of the Bible as you read. *"[Jesus] came to Nazareth, where He had been brought up. And as His custom was, He went into the synagogue on the Sabbath day, and stood up to read."*[191]
Fourth Hour 2 am to 3 am **Praying**	Use the priorities of personal prayer in *A Man's Journey with God*. Create personal prayer lists according to that model. Pray about your own visions and goals. *"But the end of all things is at hand; therefore be serious and watchful in your prayers."*[192]
Fifth Hour 3 am to 4 am **Writing Out Your Insights and Vision**	Spend time evaluating your vision and the things that God has told you to do in the past. Where are you in the process? *"And the Lord answered me, and said, Write the vision, and make it plain upon tables, that he may run that readeth it. For the vision is yet for an appointed time, but at the end it shall speak, and not lie: though it tarry, wait for it; because it will surely come, it will not tarry."*[193]

[190] Audio Bible read by Alexander Scourby is available. Bible on Amazon Kindle can be set to text-to-speech. The YouVerse app provides a read-aloud Bible on your phone. Many other options are now available.
[191] Luke 4:16 NKJV.
[192] 1 Peter 4:7 NKJV.
[193] Habakkuk 2:2-3 KJV.

Sixth Hour

4 am to 5 am

Planning Future Disciplines

Prayerfully decide what areas of our life need new habits of discipline—body, soul, and spirit. If you have determined to play a certain musical instrument, start an exercise program, read non-Christian books for research, etc., it will not happen by mistake. Make a decision to start doing something that you have been delaying. Commit to spend at least 15 minutes per day for the next 30 days to develop this new habit. Set your plan and keep your expectations high.

"Therefore if any man be in Christ, he is a new creature: old things are passed away; behold, all things are become new."[194]

Seventh Hour

5 am to 6 am

Praying Over the Lost

The lost are so important to God. Jesus died for them. Heaven rejoices over their salvation. Decree that they will be saved. It does not make sense not to pray for them in a consistent, disciplined way. Claim them for Christ.

"I say to you that likewise there will be more joy in heaven over one sinner who repents than over ninety-nine just persons who need no repentance."[195]

After all-night prayer, Jesus walked on water and so did Peter.

"Jesus insisted that his disciples get back into the boat and cross to the other side of the lake, while he sent the people home. After sending them home, he went up into the hills by himself to pray. Night fell while he was there alone.

"Meanwhile, the disciples were in trouble far away from land, for a strong wind had risen, and they were fighting

[194] 2 Corinthians 5:17 KJV.
[195] Luke 15:7 NKJV.

heavy waves. About three o'clock in the morning Jesus came toward them, walking on the water. When the disciples saw him walking on the water, they were terrified. In their fear, they cried out, 'It's a ghost!'

"But Jesus spoke to them at once. 'Don't be afraid,' he said.
'Take courage. I am here!'

"Then Peter called to him, 'Lord, if it's really you,
tell me to come to you, walking on the water.'

" 'Yes, come' Jesus said.

"So Peter went over the side of the boat and walked on the water toward Jesus. But when he saw the strong wind and the waves, he was terrified and began to sink. 'Save me, Lord!' he shouted.

"Jesus immediately reached out and grabbed him. 'You have so little faith,' Jesus said. 'Why did you doubt me?'

"When they climbed back into the boat, the wind stopped. Then the disciples worshiped him.
'You really are the Son of God!'
they exclaimed."[196]

Ask, and keep on asking
Matthew 7:7-8 KJV

"Ask [and keep on asking], and it shall be given you; seek [and keep on seeking], and ye shall find; knock [and keep on knocking], and it shall be opened unto you: For every one that asketh receiveth; and he that seeketh findeth; and to him that knocketh it shall be opened."

Prayer Is Essential to a Holy Life

Jonathan Edwards (1703-1758) understood the necessity for personal prayer not only for obtaining revelations as a pastor to preach to his congregation but also for living a holy life.

As a pastor, he was distressed about the spiritual state of his congregation and the nation and he placed the blame strongly on prayerlessness. He said, "A prayerless life is so far from being an holy life, that it is a profane life."

[196] Matthew 14:22-33 NLT.

Jonathan Edwards

(1703-1758)

Prayerlessness is inconsistent with a holy life

"But how is a life, in a great measure prayerless, consistent with an holy life? To lead an holy life is to lead a life devoted to God; a life of worshipping and serving God; a life consecrated to the service of God. But how doth he lead such a life who doth not so much as maintain the duty of prayer? How can such a man be said to walk by the Spirit and to be a servant of the Most High God? An holy life is a life of faith. The life that true Christians live in the world they live by the faith of the Son of God. ***But who can believe that man lives by faith who lives without prayer****, which is the natural expression of faith? Prayer is as natural an expression of faith as breathing is of life; and to say a man lives a life of faith, and yet lives a prayerless life, is every whit as inconsistent and incredible, as to say, that a man lives without breathing.* ***A prayerless life is so far from being an holy life, that it is a profane life.*** *He that lives so, lives like an heathen, who calleth not on God's name; he that lives a prayerless life, lives without God in the world."*[197]

"I Surrender All"[198]

Judson W. Van DeVenter (1855–1939), author of the lyrics to the hymn "I Surrender All," committed himself to ministry with these words:

"For some time, I had struggled between developing my talents in the field of art and going into full-time evangelistic work. At last the pivotal hour of my life came, and I surrendered all. A new day was ushered into my life. I became an evangelist and discovered down deep in my soul a talent hitherto unknown to me. God had hidden a song in my heart, and touching a tender chord, He caused me to sing."[199]

The composer who wrote the music to accompany those words, Winfield S. Weeden, composed many songs, but he chose "I Surrender All" to be placed on his tombstone. Here are these powerful lyrics:

[197] Jonathan Edwards, "Hypocrites Deficient in the Duty of Prayer." Located online at Thus Saith the Scripture http://www.whatsaiththescripture.com/Fellowship/Edwards.Hypocrites.in.Duty.html.
[198] Available at online sources.
[199] Judson W. Van DeVenter, "I Surrender All." Words available online. Music by Winfield S. Weeden (1847–1908).

I Surrender All

"All to Jesus, I surrender;
All to Him I freely give;
I will ever love and trust Him,
In His presence daily live."

Refrain
"I surrender all, I surrender all,
All to Thee, my blessèd Savior,
I surrender all."

"All to Jesus I surrender;
Humbly at His feet I bow,
Worldly pleasures all forsaken;
Take me, Jesus, take me now."

Refrain

"All to Jesus, I surrender;
Make me, Savior, wholly Thine;
Let me feel the Holy Spirit,
Truly know that Thou art mine."

Refrain

"All to Jesus, I surrender;
Lord, I give myself to Thee;
Fill me with Thy love and power;
Let Thy blessing fall on me."

Refrain

"All to Jesus I surrender;
Now I feel the sacred flame.
O the joy of full salvation!
Glory, glory, to His Name!"

Refrain

PERSONAL NOTES

Section 3

Daily Practices of Consecration

PERSONAL NOTES

Chapter 19

Beginning and Ending the Day with God

In *A Man's Journey with God,* you begin your day with God and at the end of your day you determine if you have completed all of His assignments before you ask, "May I go to sleep now, Father?" We are given only one day at a time. That is why we make every day count for God. You don't assume that you can sleep, as if it is your right. Sleep is earned. It assumes that you have done some work during the day.

Beginning the day with God

Sometimes people ask me if it makes any difference whether they pray and read the Bible in the morning or if they can wait until they go to bed. I believe it does make a difference. Jesus arose a great while before day. So did many of the saints of old. Don't try to enter the day without first spending time to give your day to God. Whatever you do in the evening is only a completion of that time in the morning.

Seek Me early and find Me *Proverbs 8:17 KJV*	*"I love them that love me; and those that seek me early shall find me."*
Jesus arose a great while before day *Mark 1:35 KJV*	*"And in the morning, rising up* ***a great while before day****, [Jesus] went out, and departed into* ***a solitary place****, and there prayed."*
God wakens me morning by morning *Isaiah 50:4 KJV*	*"[H]e wakeneth* ***morning by morning****,* he wakeneth mine ear to hear as the learned."

Ending the day with God—asking His permission to sleep

We live in a generation of Christians who no longer work through the day as if they were going to give an account to God at night. They just get by. They do the least possible work. If you have lived all day with an awareness of God, you are aware of Him at night. Just as you will have to answer to Him before the Judgment Seat of Christ, you are also willing to answer to Him each day. You want to finish well—one day or a lifetime.

When you stand before God in that Great Day, you will have a track record of day-by-day faithfulness.

When Lazarus died, Jesus said that he was asleep.[200] There is a spiritual analogy between sleep and death. You could also ask God, "May I go home now, Father?" at the end of your life. "Am I ready? Have I prepared myself on earth for the work that You have for me in heaven?" It takes time and practice to develop this heart for accountability and the willingness to ask God's permission to sleep.

Tomorrow is not promised to anyone, not even a child

The old folks lived with the awareness that each day belonged to God and that each night when they went to sleep might be their final night on earth. They prayed at night for introspection. They examined their day to see if there were any offenses against God that He might have against them so that their sleep would be sweet. They went to bed assuming that if they did not awaken they would be ready to meet God. We have to live each day as if it were our last. That is why fathers should teach their children to pray in such a way that they develop a consciousness that tomorrow isn't promised to us. They teach their children to pray for God's mercy on them as they sleep.

Holy calling of a dad to raise Christian children

The prayer on the next page comes from the New England Primer, a resource used by Christian parents in America's early history. Everyone agreed that being a father was a holy calling. Men took their responsibility seriously. It was part of their duty to the church and community.

---

[200] See John 11:11.

If I should die before I wake[201]

"Now I lay me down to take my sleep,
I pray the Lord my soul to keep;
If I should die before I wake,
I pray the Lord my soul to take."

Every man should ask, "May I go to sleep now, Father?"

At the end of the day when you ask the question "May I go to sleep now, Father?" that assumes that if God doesn't wake you in the morning you will be ready to stand before Him at the Judgment Seat. The old folks in church when I was growing up knew that. That is why they gave testimonies in the service making this simple prayer, "I thank you, Lord, for waking me up this morning and starting me on my way." My way where? My way to doing the will of God because God woke me up for that purpose.

God doesn't wake me up in the morning to make more money so that I can exist to fulfill my lusts. He wakes me up so that I can serve Him.

When you go to sleep in an attitude of prayer and accountability to God for your day, you are preparing yourself for another day where you are fulfilling the will of God. You are creating a spiritual legacy that can be built upon in the future.

Why you should take your child to church prayer meetings

When my mom first was saved and turned her life around, we used to go to prayer meetings at the end of the day. We were there almost every night at the church. We would sometimes pray for four or five hours, even if it was a school night. I would do my homework, but then they would expect me to be at the altar praying, even though I was a child. They knew I needed to be raised in an atmosphere of consecration. That would do more for me ultimately than being home in bed or at home watching TV. As a result, I was always advanced in my studies at school. A child can understand that tomorrow is not promised to you. When you live each day on earth as if you could face the Lord tomorrow, you go to sleep at night making sure that there are no outstanding issues between you and God.

---

[201] *New England Primer* 1784. Available at *Bartlett's Familiar Quotations* online at http://www.bartleby.com. This is the original text. A more familiar version is "Now I lay me down to sleep."

Writing to God at the end of the day

Building personal accountability to God is the purpose of *A Man's Journey with God*. You examine your life privately every day and determine if your heart has been pure and your life has been lived for Him.

Remember that a revolution begins with the spoken word, but it is carried by the written word. That also applies to your spiritual revolution. Your goal is a revolution inside of you that speaks to the world outside of you. You are someone who thinks like Christ, acts like Christ, and looks like Christ. You have a new dependency on God, willing for a new level of sacrifice. You are documenting your growth into a man—a man of God.

End-of-the-day accountability helps you to be more orderly and helps you to grow. Make notes all day in your 30-day journal, and at the end of the day, look over the notes and finish anything that is not completed in your daily quest for Christ-likeness. Some days write a summary paragraph with a personal evaluation of how you spent your day.

John Wesley prayed privately at the end of every day and he wrote down his prayers in his journal. He reviewed the affairs of the day, repented as necessary, and made new resolutions. Before he went to sleep, he recommitted himself to the care and protection of God. As a result, Wesley slept in peace and he also built the strength to reach the world with his faith in Jesus Christ.

Developing inner boundaries all day

We all need boundaries. *A Man's Journey with God* provides outward boundaries, but they point toward the development of inward boundaries of Christ-likeness. Inner boundaries come from the Creator. Those are the ones He is after ultimately.

Inward circumcision *Romans 2:29 KJV*	*"But he is a Jew, which is one inwardly; and circumcision is that of the heart, in the spirit, and not in the letter."*

Jesus was a person of regularity and order. He would go to the Temple, "as was His custom." We can be sure that His secret life was just as much in order as His public life, and more so. He is our model.

Reviewing your day

Here is a quick review of questions you can ask at the end of each day:

- Do I need to repent for anything?
- Do I need to pray for anyone?
- Do I have any reasons to bless God for my day?
- Are there any acts of kindness remaining to be done?
- Are my financial affairs in order for the following day?
- Have I neglected my reading, in the Bible or otherwise?
- Do I need to take a walk or otherwise complete my exercise?
- Did I control my time today, or did my time control me?
- Did my schedule reflect my commitment to do God's will?
- Did I make any appointments that offended God?
- Did I sleep too much? Eat too much?
- If I died tonight, would the Lord say to me, "Well done"?

Where you are unperfected in any area, be embarrassed about it, whether anyone else sees it or not. Cultivate such a pure relationship with the Holy Spirit that even the tendency to do something wrong is gone. God sees your heart. He can judge how genuine you are.

Praising God before you sleep

Before you go to sleep, give God praise! Thank Him for all that He has done in your life. Ask Him if there is anything more He wants to say to you, or anything else for you to do before your day is done.

Praise in the night watches
Psalm 63:5-6 KJV

". . . my mouth shall praise thee with joyful lips: When I remember thee upon my bed, and meditate on thee in the night watches."

When God is moving, you don't want to sleep. You don't want to miss God—not only by habits of physical sleep but also your tendency to fall asleep spiritually. Even if everyone else is asleep, He may want *you* awake. Jesus is your role model for prayer in the night season.

Jesus alone at evening, praying

Matthew 14:23 KJV

"And when [Jesus] had sent the multitudes away, he went up into a mountain ***apart*** *to pray: and when the* ***evening*** *was come, he was there* ***alone****."*

Invited to the mountain to pray, not sleep

Jesus invited Peter, James, and John up on the mountain to be with Him in prayer, but they became so heavy with sleep that they almost missed the visitation. They almost didn't see what happened to Jesus when God's glory came upon Him.

If you are still dealing with God at the level of survival instead of seeking the fellowship of intimacy in prayer, you are still asleep. You need to wake up and not only *see* the glory but also *receive* the glory. Jesus is calling you up into the Mount of Transfiguration to be changed from glory to glory. Wake up! It's not time to go to sleep yet!

Fully awake, they saw Jesus in His glory

Luke 9:28-32 NKJV

"Now it came to pass, about eight days after these sayings, that He took Peter, John, and James and went up on the mountain to pray. And as He prayed, the appearance of His face was altered, and His robe became white and glistening.

"And behold, two men talked with Him, who were Moses and Elijah, who appeared in glory and spoke of His decease which He was about to accomplish at Jerusalem. But Peter and those with him were heavy with sleep; and when they were fully awake, they saw His glory and the two men who stood with Him."

Chapter 20

Journaling Your Walk with God

As you write in your journal, be conscious of the lives of the Christians you are reading about in this book. Could your example of intimacy with God inspire others? In your secret time with God do you sense Him calling you to fulfill His will?

Private, intimate time with God is a privilege that comes about through yieldedness. It is rewarded by grace and power. The lifestyle in our generation is an enemy to quietness, but the Scripture says, "Be still and know that I am God."[202]

The word "know" is the same word used for sexual intimacy. You need intimacy with God more than you need more television, more entertainment, or even more time with friends. God, your greatest Friend, is calling you to be alone with Him.

Do you know the sweetness of prayer?
Do you love spending secret time with God alone?
What price are you willing to pay for the souls of sinners?

At the end of the day, complete your private checklist before you ask God for permission to sleep. Ask questions like these:

Was I devout today?
Was I prayerful?
Was I hungry for the Word?
Did I receive revelation today?
Was I strategic today? Was I a giver today?

[202] Psalm 46:10 KJV.

Journaling trains you for accountability. Consecration comes as a positive result of your commitment to judge yourself. The degree to which you judge yourself demonstrates how seriously you take your Christianity. By the Word and by the Spirit and by looking at what is documented at the end of the day, you can see yourself and evaluate your level of consecration.

> ***"I will stand upon my watch, and set me upon the tower, and will watch to see what he will say unto me, and what I shall answer when I am reproved. And the Lord answered me, and said, Write the vision, and make it plain upon tables."***[203]

Suggested Subjects for a Private Journal

Here are a few suggested areas that you might write about in your journal. You will discover others in this book. Some will be pointed out to you but others you will see by revelation.

1. Write about your growing understanding of Who God is.

Every journey with God begins with personal intimacy. You need to know God in order to be like Him in His holiness and to walk in His steps. When you get in a quiet place and consider before God the commitment level of the people you have read about in this book, you won't approach God in prayer as a Santa Claus, whose only purpose is to fulfill your personal desires. God does want to help you but He sees greater things for your life than meeting temporary needs. He wants you to grow up into Christ-likeness and become just like Him. As you seek Him through the daily disciplines of your journal, be conscious of how your view of Him is changing. When you are a young Christian you might spend all of your prayer time asking God to meet temporary needs like paying bills and buying new cars, but you know inside that there is something missing in your spiritual walk. You do need His help in practical ways and He wants

[203]Habakkuk 2:1-2 KJV.

to hear about what you are dealing with, but God wants you to get outside of your small world and let Him use you to do something great, just like the men of the Bible and other history.

Your discovery process of Who God really is will be a subject worth writing about for yourself and the generation. It will also be a test of your ability to define God by the standard of the Bible, not just your own thoughts, emotions or someone else's teaching.

David Brainerd liked to preach from his favorite chapter, Isaiah 53. Jesus as the Suffering Servant gave him the will to survive and fulfill his destiny and proved to be the message that helped him convert the Native Americans. Read Isaiah 53. What do *you* see there?

We hid our faces from him

Isaiah 53:4-5 KJV

"Surely he hath borne our griefs, and carried our sorrows: yet we did esteem him stricken, smitten of God, and afflicted. But he was wounded for our transgressions, he was bruised for our iniquities: the chastisement of our peace was upon him; and with his stripes we are healed."

2. Write about your journey into Christ-likeness

As you hide the Word of God inside of you, pray and come to know and serve God, you will grow into Christ-likeness. You will become an awesome Christian, and the world will be changed because you are in it. Wherever you go will be like heaven on earth.

3. Write about your increased patience in times of trial

To know God is to know what God knows *about you*. One of the ways that you discover what God knows about you, and therefore who you really are, is in crisis. Trials and testing expose the real you so that you can see yourself and discover the areas where you are really strong and the areas where you need to be changed.

4. Write about your passion to go after the lost

The salvation of the world is depending on you. Sinners are waiting for a word from you. The Bible says, "And we know that we are of God, and the whole world lieth in wickedness."[204]

> *"We know that we are children of God and that the world around us is under the control of the evil one.*
> *"And we know that the Son of God has come, and he has given us understanding so that we can know the true God."*[205]

The world's only hope is people like you. Do you believe that? Do you live as if that were true? Can you dedicate a portion of each day to growing in Christ-likeness for the sake of lost souls?

Writing Creatively in a Private Journal

Experiment. Be creative.
Try writing like Paul, David, Shakespeare, or a modern screen writer or novelist. Write poetry and prose. Add drawings and photos.

Turn your photos into a prayer journal.
Convert your photo album into a prayer journal or attach photos to your journal. Write near the pictures concerns that you want to remember when you pray for those people and also record God's answers.

Save interesting information.
You may read an interesting article or news story, song, or poem, or receive a special letter. You can attach it to your journal for further reflection.

In your Journal, you can create ways to reach the lost, share Christ with family and friends, and communicate through letters and other means. When the Holy Spirit guides your imagination, your creativity will be both spiritual and natural. You will need both.

---

[204] 1 John 5:19 KJV.
[205] 1 John 5:19-20 NLT.

Write about your works and what God will say

When you get to heaven, you will have to give an account of how you fulfilled the destiny that God created for you. If you want to hear on that Great Day "Well done!" you need to start preparing a worthy life now. One of the best ways to hold yourself accountable is to write down first what God expected of you and second what you did to please Him. This includes both your personal consecration and your lifestyle and outreach to others.

Go out and reach people in His name

Matthew 28:19-20 KJV.

"Go ye therefore, and teach all nations, baptizing them in the name of the Father, and of the Son, and of the Holy Ghost: Teaching them to observe all things whatsoever I have commanded you: and, lo, I am with you alway, even unto the end of the world. Amen."

When you get the revelation that everything you are doing is for God and to accomplish *His* purposes, you won't want to sit around. Being just a church attendee will not satisfy you. You will want to become a revolutionary.

The whole earth turning to the Lord

Psalm 22:27-28 KJV

"All the ends of the world shall remember and turn unto the Lord: and all the kindreds of the nations shall worship before thee. For the kingdom is the Lord's: and he is the governor among the nations."

Write the truth about yourself

Even if you keep your journal locked, you may still be tempted not to be truthful in what you write because someone else might read it.

That would be a mistake. Don't cover up the truth about yourself. Truth will serve you well in everything you do. Adam sinned, made excuses, and then covered up, but Jesus preached the value of openness, because *"the truth shall make you free."*[206]

Some philosophers claim that man invented God. Don't be guilty of doing that yourself. God was God before you came along, so find out Who He really is and honor Him as the great I Am. Honor Father, Son, and Holy Spirit as the only true and living God. The truth you uncover about God may not agree with your philosophy but always side with the Bible over philosophy.

Truthfulness and Transparency: John Wesley

When he saw the courage of Christians in a storm it changed this future founder of the Methodist Church[207]

John Wesley (1703-1791) was the young leader of a radical Bible study group while he was a college student at Oxford. However, during a perilous storm at sea in 1736 he realized that he did not truly know God.

When the storm arose, terror gripped the passengers and crew but the Moravian Christians onboard responded in the opposite way. They prayed and sang hymns and were totally unafraid.

As a result of this exposure to true, trusting faith, Wesley realized he was not truly born again. Later, on shore, he met one of the Moravian ministers, Rev. Spangenberg, who asked him, "Do you know Jesus Christ?"

Wesley recorded in his journal, "I paused and said, 'I know He is the Saviour of the world.' 'True,' replied he; 'but do you know He has saved you?' I answered, 'I hope He has died to save me.' He only added, 'Do you know yourself?' I said, 'I do.' But I fear they were vain words."

---

[206]John 8:32 KJV.
[207]See also *Dare to Hope* by Wellington Boone (Atlanta: APPTE Publishing, 2012).

John Wesley

(1703-1791)

Convicted!

The English were screaming as the storm buffeted the ship but the Moravian Christians were not afraid to die.

John Wesley saw when a crisis came that he truthfully did not know Jesus as he should. At the time that he confessed that, Wesley had been known for some time as a Christian leader.

Even though Wesley was convicted of his true spiritual state while on the ship, he had already started a significant work for Christ. His Holy Club for students at Oxford had high standards of Bible study, prayer, moral character, and service to the community. When Wesley recognized the truth about himself based on the truth of the Word of God, he was converted. Here is his testimony of how he gave his life to Christ as he recorded it in his journal:

Wesley's pathway to true conversion—a heart "strangely warmed"

Two years later, in May 1738, Wesley was back in England after completing his mission trip to Georgia and still searching his soul about his relationship with Jesus Christ. He described in his journal the moment when Christ became a reality to him.

"In the evening I went very unwillingly to a society in Aldersgate Street, where one was reading Luther's preface to the Epistle to the Romans. About a quarter before nine, while he was describing the change which God works in the heart through faith in Christ,

I felt my heart strangely warmed.

I felt I did trust in Christ, Christ alone, for salvation*;*
and an assurance was given me that He had taken away my sins, even mine, and saved me from the law of sin and death.

"I began to pray with all my might for those who had in a more especial manner despitefully used me and persecuted me. I then testified openly to all there what I now first felt in my heart. But it was not long before the enemy suggested, 'This cannot be faith; for where is thy joy?' Then was I taught that peace and victory over sin are essential to faith in the Captain of our salvation; but that, as to the transports of joy that usually attend the beginning of it, especially in those who have mourned deeply, God sometimes giveth, sometimes withholdeth, them according to the counsels of His own will.

"After my return home, I was much buffeted with temptations, but I cried out, and they fled away. They returned again and again. I as often lifted up my eyes, and He 'sent me help from his holy place.' And herein I found the difference between this and my former state chiefly consisted. I was striving, yea, fighting with all my might under the law, as well as under grace. But then I was sometimes, if not often, conquered; now, I was always conqueror.

"Thursday, 25.—The moment I awakened, 'Jesus, Master,' was in my heart and in my mouth; and I found all my strength lay in keeping my eye fixed upon Him and my soul waiting on Him continually. Being again at St. Paul's in the afternoon, I could taste the good word of God in the anthem which began, 'My song shall be always of the loving-kindness of the Lord: with my mouth will I ever be showing forth thy truth from one generation to another.' Yet the enemy injected a fear, 'If thou dost believe, why is there not a more sensible change?'

"I answered (yet not I), 'That I know not. But, this I know, I have now "peace with God." And I sin not today, and Jesus my Master has forbidden me to take thought for the morrow.'"[208]

[208]*The Journal of John Wesley*, available online at Christian Classics Ethereal Library, http://www.ccel.org/ccel/wesley/journal.i.html.

Understanding True Conversion

John Wesley had to come to a place of true conversion. Even though he could sense the presence of God when his heart was "strangely warmed" he knew he must also repent and admit that he was a sinner. He sought assurance from Jesus "that He had taken away my sins, even mine, and saved me from the law of sin and death." He had to resist the devil many times as Satan tried to cast doubt on his conversion.

When you come to Christ, repent for living a life away from God and accept the provision of Jesus' death on the cross to take away your sins. Resist the devil. Repent daily for every known sin. Turn your life over to Jesus to serve Him for the rest of your life in any nation of the world where He decides to send you.
That is true conversion.

Vulnerable and transparent like Jesus

In his journal entry John Wesley told the truth about his lack of real faith, his doubts, and the moment he found faith in Christ. Make a commitment to tell the truth about yourself in your journal so that you can see the areas where you are strong and the areas where you need to grow. Don't be like the first Adam, who covered up after the Fall and hid from God. Be like Jesus, Who is called the Last Adam. He was naked and vulnerable on the cross. He lived a transparent life before the Father.

Jesus said He is the Truth *John 14:6 NKJV*	*Jesus said to him, "I am the way, the truth, and the life. No one comes to the Father except through Me."*

Jesus is your role model. When you are vulnerable and transparent, you can become a role model for somebody else. Tell the truth. The truth is too important for you to be intimidated by what others might think. As Jesus said, the truth will set you free.[209]

[209] See John 8:32.

PERSONAL NOTES

Chapter 21

Scripture for the Day

"All Scripture is inspired by God and is useful to teach us what is true and to make us realize what is wrong in our lives. It corrects us when we are wrong and teaches us to do what is right. God uses it to prepare and equip his people to do every good work."[210]

Each daily devotional at the end of this book begins with Scripture. When I get an opportunity to preach the Scriptures, I am always excited. I hardly know where to begin and I don't always know how to stop. There is so much to give out. If I am that way with my small amount of insight, I can just imagine how God feels. He has all the wisdom of the universe and no one to listen to Him but Christians. Are you listening when He speaks?

Searched Scriptures
Acts 17:11-12 KJV

"These [Bereans] were more noble than those in Thessalonica, in that they received the word with all readiness of mind, and searched the scriptures daily, whether those things were so."

Bible—True, accurate, and the literal Word of God

One of the keys to receiving the greatest possible benefit from the Bible is acknowledging that it is true and accurate and the literal Word of God. At the time of the Protestant Reformation, one of the stands taken by Martin Luther (1483-1546), John Calvin (1509-1564), John Knox (1514-1572), and other Reformers was "*Sola Scriptura*"—Scripture Alone! Beginning with Luther's public stand for salvation by

[210] 2 Timothy 3:16-17 NLT.

grace alone—not by works dictated by the Church—the Reformers constantly reaffirmed the truth of the Scriptures beyond the interpretation of any man, even though it might mean persecution or even death.

Burden for the Bible: Jay Grimstead[211]

In 1976, Harold Lindsell published a bold book called *The Battle for the Bible* that exposed many arguments being presented by evangelical Christians, of all people, against the truth of the Bible. Jay Grimstead, founder of Coalition on Revival, said, "I had felt this prophetic, Jeremiah type burden over the church the previous five years as an actual pain and heaviness within my stomach almost constantly."[212] He had been suffering for some time over the disrespect of the Bible that he had seen among Christians, issues that were brought out in the open by this book.

As a scholar who had studied under Francis Schaeffer and a man with a heart to refute anything that would trouble the faith of America's youth, whom he had been discipling for 20 years through Young Life, he was motivated to take action. In February 1977 he held a conference on the authority of Scripture at Mount Hermon, California, with several major speakers on inerrancy.

Out of those meetings was launched an organization that came to be called the International Council on Biblical Inerrancy. In September 1977 a council of theologians and Christian leaders met in Chicago and drafted a group of white papers answering the major arguments that were being raised against the truth of the Bible. They scheduled a conference for October 1978 and Jay contacted Billy Graham, whose organization backed them financially.

In October, a group of 300 Christian leaders, theologians, and pastors met to launch the movement. Jay said, "During that conference, amidst much intense discussion and several all-night editorial sessions, we created together 19 articles on Biblical Inerrancy based upon a consensus agreement on the scholarly points made in the many white papers our team had written. These 19 articles were published as the historical Chicago Statement on Biblical Inerrancy. And it worked!"

211 The Coalition on Revival website is www.Reformation.net.

212 Dr. Jay Grimstead, "How the International Council on Biblical Inerrancy Began." Online at www.churchcouncil.org.

Many who had been afraid to take a stand came out publicly and signed it. Others loudly questionings the Bible became silent. Schools, churches, and organizations revised doctrinal statements to take a stronger stand. Scholars produced papers with proof. Jay said, "With the united front of the ICBI behind them, adherents of inerrancy came out of the 'closet' and more often than not saw that they were in the majority."

Jesus and These Great Men Said That the Bible Is True[213]

Jesus said that "the scripture cannot be broken" (John 10:35 KJV).

Jesus said that the Scriptures would continue to be fulfilled as long as heaven and earth remain (Matthew 5:18, 24:35; Luke 16:17).

Jesus said that His life fulfilled the Scriptures (Matthew 26:56, Luke 24:27, Luke 24:44-46).

Luke said that understanding of the Scriptures comes from Jesus (Luke 24: 45).

John said that Jesus' life fulfilled Scripture (John 19:28; 19:36-37).

Paul said to Timothy, "All scripture is given by inspiration of God, and is profitable for doctrine, for reproof, for correction, for instruction in righteousness: That the man of God may be perfect, throughly furnished unto all good works" (2 Timothy 3:16-17 KJV).

Peter said, "Knowing this first, that no prophecy of the scripture is of any private interpretation. For the prophecy came not in old time by the will of man: but holy men of God spake as they were moved by the Holy Ghost" (2 Peter 1:20-21 KJV).

Martin Luther said, "The great unthankfulness, contempt of God's Word, and willfulness of the world, make me fear that the divine light will soon cease to shine on man, for God's Word has ever had its certain course."[214]

---

[213]Many other references could be given. These are a few examples.
[214]Martin Luther, *The Table-Talk Of Martin Luther*, Translated By William Hazlitt, Esq. (Philadelphia: The Lutheran Publication Society), Part XV. Online source.

John Calvin said, "Scripture indeed is self-authenticating; hence, it is not right to subject it to proof and reasoning."[215]

Josephus wrote in his secular history written independently of the New Testament the same details of history we find in the Bible.

Dead Sea Scrolls are ancient fragments of parchment from the Old Testament Scriptures that were found in a cave in what was then Palestine and is now known as the West Bank. By dating fragments of Isaiah 53, for example, archeologists were able to confirm that prophecies of the Messiah that were fulfilled in Jesus' life were written before His birth.

Your Position on the Bible as Truth

As a Christian growing in spiritual maturity, always be ready to believe God's Word and receive from God through His Word. Take every natural step you can to make sure that you are in place, ready to receive what He is giving out to help you in your journey into Christ-likeness.

Each daily devotional in your journal begins with a reference from Scripture followed by a chart where you can record your four daily readings from eight areas from the Bible. Each day, if you take your Bible and find a secret place where you can read and listen to God alone, prayer and Scripture will become the anchors of your day. Like the Bereans of Acts 17, you will become known as "noble" as God fills you with understanding of the Scriptures that you read every day.

As your day progresses, if you are challenged by the storms of life, you will have an anchor in the Word of God and prayer. Storms will not move you. You will have heard His voice in the morning. You will have experienced His reality. All day long you will know that in the midst of the storm, He is keeping you. If you cry out to Him to save you, He will speak to the storm on your behalf, "Peace, be still."[216]

---

[215]John Calvin, *Institutes of the Christian Religion*, I, 7, 5.
[216]Mark 4:39 KJV.

All Scripture is inspired by God

2 Timothy 3:14-17 NKJV

"But you must continue in the things which you have learned and been assured of, knowing from whom you have learned them, and that from childhood you have known the Holy Scriptures, which are able to make you wise for salvation through faith which is in Christ Jesus. All Scripture is given by inspiration of God, and is profitable for doctrine, for reproof, for correction, for instruction in righteousness, that the man of God may be complete, thoroughly equipped for every good work."

How Billy Graham Answered the Question of Inerrancy

Those who know Billy Graham as an evangelist who has led millions of people to a saving knowledge of Jesus Christ might never suspect that he had to undergo a great trial to resolve whether or not he would take a public stand on the inerrancy of the Scriptures. Would he stake his reputation on stating that the Bible is true, regardless of how much pressure was on him to say that it had errors? Men around him argued that a stand for inerrancy was foolish.

While Billy was at the Forest Home Christian Conference Center in the mountains near Los Angeles, Chuck Templeton, a close friend who had worked with him in Young Life, said that Billy's position on inerrancy was "intellectual suicide" and pounded him with questions on passages that challenged his faith and belief in the truth of the Bible.

"Billy was deeply disturbed and hurt. After supper, instead of attending evening service, he retired to his log cabin and read again the Bible passages concerning its authority.

He recalled someone saying that the prophets used such phrases as 'the Word of the Lord came' or 'thus saith the Lord' more than two thousand times. He meditated on the attitude of Christ: 'He loved the Scriptures, quoted from them constantly, and never once intimated that they might be wrong.'

"Billy went out in the forest and wandered up the mountain, praying as he walked, 'Lord, what shall I do? What shall be the direction of my life?' He knew he had reached a crisis. He saw that intellect alone could not resolve the question of authority. He must go beyond intellect. He thought of the faith used constantly in daily life: Was it only in things of the Spirit that faith was wrong?

" 'So I went back and I got my Bible, and I went out in the moonlight. And I got to a stump and put the Bible on the stump, and I knelt down, and I said, "Oh, God; I cannot prove certain things, I cannot answer some of the questions Chuck is raising, but I accept this Book by faith as the Word of God." ' "[217]

Breakthrough followed by breakthrough

Six weeks after this crucial decision, Billy Graham broke through into national prominence when the success of his Los Angeles crusade provoked publisher William Randolph Hearst to tell his editors, "Puff Graham"—give him plenty of space in our newspapers. Wire services and then national publications picked up the stories on Graham's crusade and his life and ministry have never been the same.

Instead of causing him to be ridiculed, as his critics suggested, his position on the truth of the Bible caused him to achieve worldwide honor. He became one of the most respected men in the world, known as someone you could count on. He never wavered from his positions that you must be saved through Jesus Christ and that the Bible is true.

[217] John Pollock, *The Billy Graham Story* (Zondervan; Revised Updated Edition [May 3, 2011]).

The Chicago Statement on Biblical Inerrancy[218]

(Excerpt)

1. **God, who is Himself Truth** and speaks truth only, has inspired Holy Scripture in order thereby to reveal Himself to lost mankind through Jesus Christ as Creator and Lord, Redeemer and Judge. Holy Scripture is God's witness to Himself.

2. **Holy Scripture, being God's own Word**, written by men prepared and superintended by His Spirit, is of infallible divine authority in all matters upon which it touches: it is to be believed, as God's instruction, in all that it affirms, obeyed, as God's command, in all that it requires; embraced, as God's pledge, in all that it promises.

3. **The Holy Spirit, Scripture's divine Author**, both authenticates it to us by His inward witness and opens our minds to understand its meaning.

4. **Being wholly and verbally God-given, Scripture is without error** or fault in all its teaching, no less in what it states about God's acts in creation, about the events of world history, and about its own literary origins under God, than in its witness to God's saving grace in individual lives.

5. **The authority of Scripture is inescapably impaired if this total divine inerrancy is in any way limited or disregarded**, or made relative to a view of truth contrary to the Bible's own; and such lapses bring serious loss to both the individual and the Church.

[218]Created in 1978 at a gathering of Christian leaders. Available online at www.reformation.net. Emphasis added by author.

PERSONAL NOTES

Chapter 22

Reading through the Bible

Reading four chapters of the Bible every day

When I speak in the churches of many different denominations, one question always receives the same response. I ask, "How many of you read your Bible every day?" Fewer than 50 people ever raise their hands, even if the audience is in the thousands. When I ask those same people, "How many of you eat food every day?" All of them raise their hands. Which food will last you for eternity, physical food or spiritual food? Most people don't consider that what they are eating from the Word of God today is preparing them for tomorrow and also for eternity. They don't eat the Word of God as if their life depended upon it and as if the realm it represents is real.

God, give me Your word for today!

God desires to restore us back to His Word in an even greater measure than ever before, "that we might know the things that are freely given to us of God."[219] This knowing is intimate. It goes beyond mental knowing. It is a personal way of approaching God through the Bible.

In *A Man's Journey with God*, I am giving you a daily reading list of four chapters from eight different sections of the Bible. If you maintain this schedule, you can read through the entire Bible in 12 months. This is a consecration journey—an integral part of *A Man's Journey with God*.

When you open up your Bible, don't read it to fulfill religious duty but listen for the Lord's voice. Expect Him to speak. Cry out, "Give me your word for today!" You need to be just as committed to spiritual food as you are to natural food, and more so, because when you die the only food that will remain is what you ate from the substance of God during your lifetime. When you develop a taste for

[219] 1 Corinthians 2:12.

spiritual food, you find that you have a hunger that cannot be satisfied in any other way than eating from God's Word.

Jesus believed every Word from God *Matthew 4:3-4 KJV*	*"And when the tempter came to [Jesus], he said, If thou be the Son of God, command that these stones be made bread. But he answered and said, It is written, Man shall not live by bread alone, but by every word that proceedeth out of the mouth of God."*

Just as Israel in the wilderness ate manna from God every day,[220], we eat fresh manna from the Bible as our first meal of every day.

- "Bread from heaven"[221]
- "Angels' food"[222]
- "Spiritual meat"[223]

Four Chapters Daily From Eight Sections of the Bible

Pentateuch.[224] Genesis, Exodus, Leviticus, Numbers, Deuteronomy

History. Joshua, Judges, Ruth, 1 Samuel, 2 Samuel, 1 Kings, 2 Kings, 1 Chronicles, 2 Chronicles, Ezra, Nehemiah, Esther, Acts

Poetry. Job, Psalms, Ecclesiastes, Song of Solomon

Wisdom. Proverbs

Prophets. Isaiah, Jeremiah, Lamentations, Ezekiel, Hosea, Joel, Amos, Obadiah, Jonah, Micah, Nahum, Habakkuk, Zephaniah, Haggai, Zechariah, Malachi

Gospels. Matthew, Mark, Luke, John

[220]See Exodus 16:15, 31, 33; Numbers 11:6-9.
[221]Nehemiah 9:15 KJV.
[222]Psalm 78:25 KJV.
[223]1 Corinthians 10:3 KJV.
[224]Pentateuch *[pronounced PIN tuh tuke]. Greek term meaning "five-volumed," the first five books of the Old Testament. Also called Books of Moses, Book of the Law, the Law, the Torah.*

Epistles. Romans, 1 Corinthians, 2 Corinthians, Galatians, Ephesians, Philippians, Colossians, 1 Thessalonians, 2 Thessalonians, 1 Timothy, 2 Timothy, Titus, Philemon, Hebrews, James, 1 Peter, 2 Peter, 1 John, 2 John, 3 John, Jude

End Times. Daniel, Revelation

Jesus said, "To him that overcometh will I give to eat of the hidden manna."[225] A breakfast of hidden manna will make you into a champion for Christ with spiritual power. If you spend 30-60 minutes in meditation, Holy Spirit will come upon you in a supernatural way and line it up for you.

Here a little, there a little

Isaiah 28:13 KJV

"For precept must be upon precept, precept upon precept; line upon line, line upon line; here a little, and there a little."

You are building a holistic picture of the Bible, precept upon precept, as you read these sections. You will trust Holy Spirit as you have never trusted Him before. God will give you a picture of His Word that applies not only to your own life but also to your family, church, city, and nation. You will begin to see His purpose for the Church in history. He will open your eyes.

People who are not spiritual cannot receive the Bible as God's truth

1 Corinthians 2:12-16 NLT

"When we tell you these things, we do not use words that come from human wisdom. Instead, we speak words given to us by the Spirit, using the Spirit's words to explain spiritual truths. But people who aren't spiritual can't receive these truths from God's Spirit. It all sounds foolish to them and they can't understand it, for only those who are spiritual can understand what the Spirit means. Those who are spiritual can evaluate all things, but they themselves cannot be evaluated by others. For,

" 'Who can know the Lord's thoughts?
Who knows enough to teach him?'
"But we understand these things,
for we have the mind of Christ."

[225]Revelation 2:17 KJV.

When you read several parts of the whole Bible at one time with an open and yielded mind, you come to understand more of the greatness of God and the truth of His Word. You see how much of what He has said applies to you, personally, and to issues in today's news. You find themes and continuity and revelation in areas that you never knew were there. As you compare spiritual things with spiritual things, your spiritual understanding deepens beyond your natural understanding.

In supernatural ways the Spirit guides your reading

Your natural understanding puts limits on God and His Word, but God is supernatural. He is Spirit. He is far beyond your human understanding. If you could understand Him perfectly, He would no longer be God. It may seem foolish to you to read four chapters but spiritual things often seem foolish to our minds. You have to override the skepticism of your mind and allow God's Spirit to rule.

Let the Holy Spirit give you the symphony and the harmony of the Scriptures supernaturally. Most people have never learned to depend upon revelation in their Bible reading. They think they need only logical analysis. However, with your rational mind you cannot understand God fully. He has to make himself known to you supernaturally, beyond the ability of your puny mind.

Reading for a right revelation of Jesus

When Peter received a revelation of Jesus as "Christ, the Son of the living God,"[226] Jesus replied that "upon this rock [revelation] I will build my church; and the gates of hell shall not prevail against it."[227] Do you have a right revelation of Jesus? Do your reading priorities demonstrate that you see Jesus as Christ, the Son of the living God? They do if you feed daily on His Word. As you eat His Word, you become like Him. When you have read the Word each day, your life becomes a *living demonstration* that Jesus is Who He says He is.

[226]Matthew 16:16 KJV.
[227]Matthew 16:17-18 KJV.

Feeding on the Word to Become the Word

John 15:7-8 NKJV

"If you abide in Me, and My words abide in you, you will ask what you desire, and it shall be done for you. By this My Father is glorified, that you bear much fruit;
so you will be My disciples."

You yield your mind to His mind in order to have the mind of Christ.[228] You are a disciple who is not ruled by circumstances, people, and problems. You are ruled by the Spirit revealed through the Word.

Eat good food for your mind

Isaiah 55:2 NLT

"Why spend your money on food that does not give you strength? Why pay for food that does you no good? Listen to me, and you will eat what is good.
You will enjoy the finest food."

You are what you eat. When you read the Word, you become the Word on the inside. The Bible is more than new information. You are eating the substance of God's life and *applying* it to your life, building a spiritual momentum that carries you to places unknown. Man looks at the outside but God looks at the heart.[229] He works from the inside out. God created Adam's spirit before He built him a body. You are born again in the inside and then He forms your character that is seen on the outside. The more you eat internally, the more you grow in outward works.

Jesus reveals secrets to you that He does not reveal to others

Matthew 13:11-12 NLT

"[Jesus] replied, 'You are permitted to understand the secrets of the Kingdom of Heaven, but others are not. To those who listen to my teaching, more understanding will be given, and they will have an abundance of knowledge. But for those who are not listening, even what little understanding they have will be taken away from them.'"

[228] See 1 Corinthians 2:16.
[229] See 1 Samuel 16:7.

Don't Be Surprised by the Supernatural

I want you to move into a dimension where you're expecting God to move in your life and you don't know what He's going to do next. Open yourself up for God to surprise you. Make yourself available to Him so that the Spirit can speak into your spiritual ears.

You can't define the Spirit. Jesus said, "The wind blows where it wishes, and you hear the sound of it, but cannot tell where it comes from and where it goes. So is everyone who is born of the Spirit."[230]

Only the Spirit knows

1 Corinthians 2:11-12 NLT

"No one can know a person's thoughts except that person's own spirit, and no one can know God's thoughts except God's own Spirit. And we have received God's Spirit (not the world's spirit), so we can know the wonderful things God has freely given us."

You don't know when He will come upon you. He comes from places you do not know. He takes you places you have never been. He moves in ways you never expected. He is magnificent! When He says that "the Spirit searcheth all things, yea the deep things of God," He is talking about supernatural power—levels you cannot get to on your own.

The Lord will establish you and give you prosperity

Deuteronomy 28:11-13 NLT

"The Lord will give you prosperity in the land he swore to your ancestors to give you, blessing you with many children, numerous livestock, and abundant crops. The Lord will send rain at the proper time from his rich treasury in the heavens and will bless all the work you do. You will lend to many nations, but you will never need to borrow from them. If you listen to these commands of the Lord your God that I am giving you today, and if you carefully obey them, the Lord will make you the head and not the tail, and you will always be on top and never at the bottom."

[230]John 3:8 NKJV.

Chapter 23

Thought for the Day

When you become more consecrated, you hear God's voice more clearly. When you obey His voice, you have moved from external hearing to becoming like His nature. His Word has become seed for your spirit man that transforms you from the inside out. You are growing more and more to look like Jesus, think like Jesus, and act like Jesus—more holy, harmless, and undefiled. Hearing God and becoming more like Jesus are inevitable results of your consecration.

Each day in *A Man's Journey with God* you will receive a "Thought for the Day" like the one above that focuses on consecration and holiness, and what you can expect to receive as a result of your search for these character qualities of Christ.

Holiness is an internal state with no issues between you and God

"Beloved, if our heart does not condemn us,
we have confidence toward God."[231]

Holiness is your faith-life and self-sacrifice on the inside becoming progressively more visible on the outside.

"I have been crucified with Christ; it is no longer I who live, but Christ lives in me; and the life which I now live in the flesh I live by faith in the Son of God, who loved me and gave Himself for me."[232]

---

[231] 1 John 3:21 NKJV.
[232] Galatians 2:20 NKJV.

Outspoken Against Ungodliness: Billy Sunday

For seven years, Billy Sunday was a professional baseball player in the National League. He was converted to Christ through the street preaching of Harry Monroe of the Pacific Garden Mission in Chicago. For 20 years he preached hell-fire and brimstone all across America. During one crusade in Philadelphia, more than 2,300,000 people came. He preached against alcohol and helped pass the Eighteenth Amendment to the Constitution prohibiting its manufacture and sale, launching the era of Prohibition. In his final message, just before his death, 19 people were saved. He was still preaching against sin.

Billy Sunday
(William Ashley Sunday)
(1862-1935)

"I'm against sin.

"I'll kick it as long as I've got a foot, and I'll fight it as long as I've got a fist. I'll butt it as long as I've got a head. I'll bite it as long as I've got a tooth. And when I'm old and fistless and footless and toothless, I'll gum it till I go home to Glory and it goes home to perdition!"[233]

When you're holy, you're fearless. Only God's will can influence you.

"And do not fear those who kill the body but cannot kill the soul. But rather fear Him who is able to destroy both soul and body in hell. . . . Therefore whoever confesses Me before men, him I will also confess before My Father who is in heaven."[234]

God wants us to pray for character change in churches so that those who come will become more like God by becoming more like us.

[233]Quote from Billy Sunday is available online.
[234]Matthew 10:28, 32 NKJV.

"And be not conformed to this world:
but be ye transformed by the renewing of your mind,
that ye may prove what is that good, and acceptable,
and perfect, will of God."[235]

Stumbling Blocks into Stepping Stones: Richard Allen

Richard Allen
(1760-1831)
Founder of African Methodist Episcopal Church

In 1792, Richard Allen, a free Black preacher and a godly man, was praying in the balcony of St. George's Methodist Episcopal Church of Philadelphia, which he always attended and where he preached to the Blacks. He looked up to see his friend, the Rev. Absalom Jones, being forcibly pulled up off his knees by one of the White church trustees. "You must get up!" the White man exclaimed to the startled Black minister. "You must not kneel here!"

Apparently the seating arrangements had been changed and the Blacks had mistakenly entered a Whites-only section. Rev. Jones, a godly man, was asking if they might wait to change their seats until prayers were finished, but his question only provoked the man to threaten force. With that, Allen, Jones, and a group of other Black worshipers who had previously enjoyed respect at St. George's "all went out of the church in a body and they were no more plagued with us," Allen said later. "We were filled with fresh vigor to get a house to worship God in."

Bishop Francis Asbury ordains Richard Allen

Allen had been born a slave in 1760 but had bought his freedom from his master in 1777, the year he was converted. Allen said, "At length our master said he was convinced that religion made slaves better and not worse, and often boasted of his slaves for their honesty and

[235]Romans 12:2 KJV.

industry."[236] With the master's permission, the Methodist preacher came to the house, and before long the master was saved, turned against slavery, and allowed Allen to buy his freedom. Allen became a popular preacher to Blacks at St. George's Church and traveled to New Jersey and other locations in Pennsylvania. He was a favorite of Bishop Francis Asbury. As mentioned earlier, Asbury (1745-1816) was Bishop of the Methodist Episcopal Church in America. His ordination and endorsement of Richard Allen helped establish Allen's credibility as a Christian leader. Under the Methodist leadership of John Wesley and Bishop Asbury, there was no mistaking the standards required of every Christian, especially preachers. The Methodist Church provided ministers with clear documentation of Christian practices and beliefs in a book of *Doctrines and Discipline*.

From blacksmith shop to community activism

Allen and Jones saw the incident at St. George's Church not as a stumbling block but a stepping stone to the development of separate organizations to help Blacks. They formed the Free African Society in 1787 to serve practical needs of widows, fatherless children, and the sick. Allen's first church was a renovated blacksmith shop that he moved from another location to 6th and Lombard Streets in Philadelphia. Bishop Asbury led the dedication on July 29, 1794, for America's first Black Methodist society. In 1816, after years of challenges at St. George's, Allen established Bethel as an independent church and launched the first independent Black denomination in America—African Methodist Episcopal. Allen was consecrated as the first bishop.

Beginning in 1795 Bethel hid escaped slaves and integrated them into the community. They sent missionaries to Haiti to plant churches. Bishop Morris Brown, pastor of Emanuel AME Church in Charleston, SC, came under fire during an investigation of a slave uprising led by Denmark Vesey in 1821 that accused him of direct involvement. After a white mob burned down his church he escaped with his family to Philadelphia. He later succeeded Bishop Allen as the second bishop of the African Methodist Episcopal Church. Morris Brown College is named after Bishop Brown.

[236]Richard Allen, *The Life, Experience, and Gospel Labours of the Rt. Rev. Richard Allen*. Available online at Documenting the American South http://docsouth.unc.edu/ and http://Archive.org.

Chapter 24

My Insights (Revelations) For Today

"Write the things which you have seen,
and the things which are, and
the things which will take place after this."[237]

The revelations that come to you as you pray and seek God's face are worth writing down in a personal journal for yourself and for the generation. You may think that God already has enough other men teaching His Word, but that is not true. Somebody, somewhere, needs to know what you hear privately from God in the atmosphere of consecration and total surrender.

There are people in every generation who attend church yet never hear a fresh word from God, as it was with Israel in the days of Samuel, when the Bible says that "the word of the Lord was rare in those days; there was no widespread revelation."[238] People among your family, friends, and those you don't even know yet will die and go to hell unless you reveal the Word of God to them concerning their salvation. You need to seek God for fresh insight so that you can save them for an eternal destiny in heaven.

Rock of revelation on which you can help others to build

The foundational revelation of our faith is that Jesus is the Christ, the Son of the living God. Jesus told Peter that the revelation that He was Savior and God is the rock on which He would build His Church.

[237]Revelation 1:19 NKJV.
[238]1 Samuel 3:1 NKJV.

The rock on which we build—the revelation of the person of Jesus Christ

Matthew 16:13-19 KJV

"When Jesus came into the coasts of Caesarea Philippi, he asked his disciples, saying, Whom do men say that I the Son of man am? And they said, Some say that thou art John the Baptist: some, Elias; and others, Jeremias, or one of the prophets. He saith unto them, But whom say ye that I am? And Simon Peter answered and said, Thou art the Christ, the Son of the living God.

"And Jesus answered and said unto him, Blessed art thou, Simon Barjona: for flesh and blood hath not revealed it unto thee, but my Father which is in heaven. And I say also unto thee, That thou art Peter, and upon this rock I will build my church; and the gates of hell shall not prevail against it. And I will give unto thee the keys of the kingdom of heaven."

We need a revival of personal revelation.

Many Christians today do not believe that Jesus is truly God come in the flesh because they are not spending time with Him at the level that we have been talking about. If you know Him and believe that He came to save sinners, God will give you insight for yourself and for this generation. This insight will not draw them to you,(but to Christ, the source of your revelation, and theirs, if they know Him.)

Revelation comes as a fruit of your dedication and the time you spend praying and reading the Word of God. As you are faithful to seek Him, God will shape you and mold you into someone who is rock solid in your faith. The revelation of Who Christ is comes first by the Word (the Scriptures) and then by the Spirit. The Word without the Spirit is just the letter of the law, and the Bible says that "the letter kills, but the Spirit gives life."[239] Knowing the law and the principles of the Bible is not the same as revelation. Revelation comes when Christ reveals Himself to you in the midst of the law and principles.

When a principle comes alive to you, it has become a revelation. It is a source of life.

[239] 2 Corinthians 3:6 NKJV.

When Jesus said, "Man shall not live by bread alone, but by every word that proceedeth out of the mouth of God,"[240] He was speaking of the word revealed in your heart, not just the letter of memorizing what the Bible says.

Hearing from God by being quiet

God said that we should study to be quiet.[241] We need to ask Him to give us a heart to meditate on His Word and to listen to Him before we rush out into the day. Each day, He has new instructions for us that we need to hear.

Jesus said that His sheep hear His voice.[242] As you develop a listening ear, you will hear what He has to say, and your heart will be good ground where God can sow His insight. You will be the yielded vessel where He can deposit the substance of His mind and heart.

You perish spiritually when your ears are closed and your heart is not good ground to receive a prophetic revelation from God. Your ears are blessed when you hear from God.

"For the hearts of this people have grown dull. Their ears are hard of hearing, and their eyes they have closed, lest they should see with their eyes and hear with their ears, lest they should understand with their hearts and turn, so that I should heal them.' But blessed are your eyes for they see, and your ears for they hear."[243]

With every revelation from God, there is power in your life to bring to pass what He says.

"So shall My word be that goes forth from My mouth;
it shall not return to Me void, but it shall
accomplish what I please, and it shall
prosper in the thing for which I sent it."[244]

---

[240]Matthew 4:4 KJV.
[241] See 1 Thessalonians 4:1.
[242]See John 10:27.
[243] Matthew 13:15-16 NKJV.
[244]Isaiah 55:11 NKJV.

Confirming your revelations through the fivefold ministry

God will give you godly men in authority over you in the fivefold ministry to whom you can submit your revelations for confirmation, because as Jesus said "in the mouth of two or three witnesses every word may be established."[245]

Writing down the insights you personally hear from God

Each day, as you pray and read His Word and the "Thought for the Day," write down prophetic insights that God gives you. You can use the few lines in this journal and add other journals of your own. If you are free enough to write down what you see, then judge it honestly by the standard of the Word and other Christians. God will be able to develop in you a hearing ear and will begin to entrust you with His secrets.

Many years ago when I was alone in my bedroom I opened up a Bible that someone had given to me and saw the words of Isaiah 43:1, "I have called thee by thy name; thou art mine." God was speaking to me.

I cried out, "If there be a God, reveal Yourself to me!"

I was a fool but God had mercy on me. I had known God since I was a child but I had abandoned that relationship for the things of the world. The Bible says that only a fool would say there is no God. Even the demons know and tremble. But I was so far from God and at my wits end that I said, "If there be a God . . ."

God wasn't upset with my lack of eloquence. He knew in advance that when I reached the age of 25 a desperation would come upon me. I had a dysfunctional environment as a child, but the Lord found me. He delivered me and I am what I am by the grace of God.

Like Bishop Richard Allen, all my stumbling blocks became stepping stones when I found out that I could hear from God.

[245]Matthew 18:16 KJV.

Chapter 25

Servanthood for Today

"Let this mind be in you which was also in Christ Jesus, who, being in the form of God, did not consider it robbery to be equal with God, but made Himself of no reputation, taking the form of a bondservant, and coming in the likeness of men. And being found in appearance as a man, He humbled Himself and became obedient to the point of death, even the death of the cross. Therefore God also has highly exalted Him and given Him the name which is above every name."[246]

The Bible says that we are to follow Jesus' example in every way, which includes an awareness of how we can meet others' needs every day with humble acts of service.

At the Last Supper, Jesus demonstrated why God could exalt Him, because He humbled Himself. At the same time, Jesus called us to follow His example of humility and servitude.

Jesus washing their feet as a servant

John 13:13-15 KJV[247]

"Ye call me Master and Lord and ye say well; for so I am. If I then, your Lord and Master, have washed your feet; ye also ought to wash one another's feet. For I have given you an example, that ye should do as I have done to you."

Faithful Example of Serving the Poor: Salvation Army

William Booth's original plan was to send London's poor and outcasts he rescued to existing churches. However, they had no Sunday clothes and often no way to take a bath. They had been living

---

[246]Philippians 2:5-9 NKJV.
[247]The image of Jesus washing His disciples feet is the © logo of Wellington Boone Ministries.

below the standards of society and felt uncomfortable and unwanted. The Salvation Army plants churches and provides a biblical example of worldwide servitude to society for other churches to follow.

Salvation Army: [248] ***Servitude from Consecration***

Countries served: 124
Number of corps: 15,409
Number of officers: 26,359
Number of employees: 108,786

Soldiers: 1,150,666
Adherent members: 169,144
Junior soldiers: 368,749
Senior band musicians: 27,578
Songsters: 101,924
Sunday school members: 616,093

Community development programs: 10,859 (number of beneficiaries: 1,087,781)
Homeless hostels: 407 (capacity: 23,752)
Residential addiction dependency programs: 281 (capacity: 19,800)
Children's homes: 224 (capacity: 9,739)
Homes for elderly persons: 178 (capacity: 7,482)
Mother and baby homes: 45 (capacity: 1,308)
Refuges: 64 (capacity: 1,934)

Community day care centers: 611
Non-residential addiction rehabilitation centers: 91

Services to the armed forces: 86 projects
Disaster rehabilitation schemes: 180 (serving 1,035,396 people)
Prisoners visited: 230,113

General hospitals: 21
Maternity hospitals: 15 Specialist hospitals: 7

[248] Salvation Army international statistics (as of 1 January 2014). Source: 2014 Year Book. Online at http://www.salvationarmy.org/ihq/statistics.

Seeing that churches lacked a vision for servitude, the Salvation Army began meeting the needs of the poor in both social service ministries and their churches. Booth had become a Methodist pastor at age 23 but his passion was evangelism and service outside the church walls in the fields and on the streets so he eventually became independent. His message was a strong mix of eternal judgment and holiness but it was what the lost sinners needed. They saw it was salvation and accepted Jesus Christ as Savior and Lord.

Do you model out Jesus' example of evangelism and servitude in your home, church, or community? Could a social movement be based on your dedication?

I once heard someone ask a Salvation Army sergeant major in Atlanta how many people worked under him. Instead of giving the expected answer in numbers of people, he turned it around into a principle of servant leadership.

He said, "I serve 200 men now, and have served up to 2,000 men at a time in my course of duty." He understood the most important leadership principle of Jesus: if you want to be great, you should be a servant.

Servant Leadership in the Ghettoes: Dwight L. Moody

Someone else who understood the principle of servant leadership was Dwight L. Moody. He became a Christian as the result of a ManHunt by his Sunday School teacher.

Challenge to men—the ManHunt for Dwight L. Moody

Below is an excerpt about that event from his autobiography with a challenge to men: "*Young Christian men, go and lay your hand on your comrade's shoulder, and point him to Jesus tonight.*"

> *"When I was in Boston, . . . I used to attend a Sunday school class, and one day I recollect a Sabbath-school teacher came round behind the counter of the shop I used to work in, and put his hand on my shoulder, and talked to me about Christ and my soul. I had not felt I had a soul till then. I said: 'This is a very strange thing. Here is a man who never saw me until within a few days, and he is weeping over my sins, and I never shed a tear about them.'*

But I understand it now, and know what it is to have a passion for men's souls and weep over their sins. I don't remember what he said, but I can feel the power of that young man's hand on my shoulder tonight. Young Christian men, go and lay your hand on your comrade's shoulder, and point him to Jesus tonight. Well, he got me up to the school, and it was not long before I was brought into the kingdom of God."[249]

Dwight L. Moody became one of the most effective evangelists in the world in his day and became the founder of educational institutions and a church that still prosper today. However, like a true servant leader he started out serving—in his case, serving children of the ghettoes.

Sunday School of 1,500 in a freight car and a saloon

An anonymous writer told about Moody's servant lifestyle on behalf of the children of Chicago:

"At age 21, while working full time at a profitable secular job, Moody "started his own Sunday School in an abandoned freight car, then moved to an old vacant saloon on Michigan Street. A visiting preacher reported his favorable impressions seeing Moody trying to light the building with a half-dozen candles and then with a candle in one hand, a Bible in the other, and a child on his knee teaching him about Jesus. The school became so large that the former Mayor of Chicago gave him the hall over the city's North Market for his meetings, rent free. . . .

"The use of prizes, free pony rides and picnics along with genuine love for children soon produced the largest Sunday School in Chicago, reaching some 1,500 weekly. Moody supervised, recruited, and did the janitor work early Sunday morning, cleaning out the debris from a Saturday night dance, to get ready for the afternoon Sunday School."[250]

"It is a masterpiece of the devil to make us believe that children cannot understand religion. Would Christ have made a child the standard of faith if He had known that it was not capable of understanding His words?"

—D. L. Moody[251]

[249] M. Laird Simons, *Holding the Fort: comprising sermons and addresses at the Great Revival meetings conducted by Moody and Sankey, with the lives and labors of Dwight L. Moody, Ira D. Sankey, and P.P. Bliss* (Norwich, Connecticut: Henry Bill Publishing Co., 1877). Excerpts online at http://www.wholesomewords.org/biography/biomoody.html.

[250] Online at http://www.wilderness-cry.net/bible_study/bios/moody.html.

[251] Online at http://www.brainyquote.com/quotes/quotes/d/dwightlmo157631.html.

By the time that the Lord took him home, Moody, a man who began with such little education that he could barely read the Bible aloud to the children he served, had left in place a thriving ministry that is still changing lives worldwide today. His heart to win souls to Jesus at any cost of servitude produced an enduring legacy.

Decision to enter full-time ministry regardless of finances

Dwight L. Moody
(1837-1899)

"It was in June, 1860, that Moody decided to abandon secular employment and go into the Lord's work full time. He was now 23 and in only five years had built his income up to $5,000 annually and had saved $7,000.

Friends believed he could have become a millionaire had he concentrated his efforts in business. Income for the first year in his Christian ventures totaled no more than $300."[252]

Servitude in Home, Church, and Community

The Bible says that Christians are destined to be rulers—both in this world, and the next.[253] But before God can trust you with authority to rule, He will take you through a training program in humility. When you are humble, God can give you power because you won't use it for yourself. You will be a servant leader, not a self-serving leader nobody can touch.

[252]"Dwight Lyman (D.L.) Moody." Online at http://www.eaec.org/faithhallfame/dlmoody.htm
[253]See Revelation 22:5.

To be first, be a slave

Matthew 20:25-28 NKJV

"But Jesus called them to Himself and said, 'You know that the rulers of the Gentiles lord it over them, and those who are great exercise authority over them. Yet it shall not be so among you; but whoever desires to become great among you, let him be your servant. And whoever desires to be first among you, let him be your slave—just as the Son of Man did not come to be served, but to serve, and to give His life a ransom for many.'"

When you are a servant leader, you get behind people and push them past their level of mediocrity into excellence. You are more concerned with their level of achievement than your own. The kind of teachers and coaches that most of us remember happily from our schooldays are those who gave of themselves without a thought of recognition. They were there to serve us.

Consider full-time ministry

You have to become a front row seater in the Lord. You cannot be on the periphery anymore.

If we examine our hearts, almost all of us want to be used mightily We may have different jurisdictions. You may be in the academic community or the sports arena or family life, but you want to be used. You want to represent God in the most awesome way. You are not trying to look better than anybody else but to serve the Lord in the best way possible in heaven so that the angels are amazed. That is our potential in Christ. We are the body of Christ.

Many men who could be used mightily in full-time ministry hold back for one main reason—fear. If they are married and their wife is not a Kingmaker, they fear lack of money even more than any sense of danger. However, they have never seriously tried to raise money for ministry.

People give to people. If anybody in the world could be given anything, why couldn't those people be you? No one wants to give to an entity. They want to see who is on the board.

You give value to people's money because of your dedication to God. Some people's guilt will never be satisfied until they give to God and they can't give to God, so they give to people who serve God seriously.

You will have to become more holy before the Lord and the flood gates of finances will open and the money rushes in. You are not after money, but I guarantee that people will feel wonderful in giving to you when they know whom they are giving to is someone close to God.

Jesus is touched with a feeling of our infirmities.[254] He feels our pain and reaches out in mercy and compassion instead of judgment. That is what He wants us to do. Serving on earth is an important part of the training program for heaven. Serving others works humility in you.

When other people "use you," that's when you become most like Christ and least like the devil, whose pride eliminated him from consideration as a privileged being in heaven. When the devil became proud, God cast him out. That isn't what you want to happen to you, so you need to be humble and serve others.

Servitude in the home

When I teach about the need for husbands to out-serve their wives instead of expecting their wives to be their mommas,[255] I can tell from their startled looks and their wives' applause that most of them have never thought about how God looks at their arrogance in expecting their wives to serve them. I tell husbands that your wife may be serving you coffee on earth, but you will be serving her tea in heaven.

In most marriages, the wife out-serves the husband, but that is not Jesus' model. He doesn't let the Church out-serve Him. Jesus is the greatest Servant of all. If you want to be great, you should find ways every day to serve others, beginning in your home.

Servitude in the church

How well do you get along with other disciples of Jesus in your church? Would you wash their feet? Would you serve them? According to John 17:21, those in the world can judge if we are Christians by seeing whether or not we love one another in the Church. They can watch our relationships and decide whether they want to become Christians, which means they may decide to accept or reject Jesus as Savior based on what they see in your life. When unbelievers in the media report on quarrels within factions in the Church, that gives them an excuse to mock Christians. When atheists see that Christians can't hold their marriages

[254]See Hebrews 4:15.

[255] See *Your Wife Is Not Your Momma* by Wellington Boone (Atlanta: APPTE Publishing, 2011).

together and have more divorces than atheists, that becomes another excuse for them to reject a personal relationship with Jesus Christ.

Servitude in the community

When you are consecrated, you also look for opportunities to perform acts of benevolence outside the home, reaching out to the poor and those who are sick and in prison. As a Christian, you are called to give yourself away to your culture from a position of humility and servanthood.

Acts of servitude to those in need are acts of service to Jesus, the King

Matthew 25:34-40 NKJV

"Then the King will say to those on His right hand, 'Come, you blessed of My Father, inherit the kingdom prepared for you from the foundation of the world: for I was hungry and you gave Me food; I was thirsty and you gave Me drink; I was a stranger and you took Me in; I was naked and you clothed Me; I was sick and you visited Me; I was in prison and you came to Me.'

"Then the righteous will answer Him, saying, 'Lord, when did we see You hungry and feed You, or thirsty and give You drink? When did we see You a stranger and take You in, or naked and clothe You? Or when did we see You sick, or in prison, and come to You?'

"And the King will answer and say to them, 'Assuredly, I say to you, inasmuch as you did it to one of the least of these My brethren, you did it to Me.'"

You are called to give people answers—both spiritual and natural. Jesus said that when you serve the needs of the least of those in society, you are in reality serving Him.

Jesus washed the feet of Judas. Do you know any Judases?
Would you be willing to wash their feet?

Looking forward to the harvest of servitude

Your greatest witness for Christ is your lifestyle, not your words. Your life is lived out before individuals who might someday transform society because of what they have seen in you.

In the 18th century the Moravians didn't know that their selfless service on a ship on the way to Georgia would have an impact for eternity because of what one man, John Wesley, saw in their lives.

D. L. Moody didn't know that his service to the inner cities would result in a worldwide ministry of evangelism.

You will read of others who will have the testimony of servitude that produced a harvest when they get before God in that Great Day.

Are you grudgingly serving others,
or are you excited because
you can't wait to see the harvest of your love?

Unified to Serve Others in Love: Francis Schaeffer

Francis Schaeffer (1912-1984) and his wife Edith (1914-2013) influenced the conversion to Christ of leading intellectuals through their L'Abri community in Switzerland, books, and documentaries. Schaeffer was alarmed at society's trends away from biblical inerrancy and biblical standards. He challenged everyone to identify the presuppositions they used for making decisions and prove if there was any basis for the truth of their assumptions other than their own mind.

"Now comes the sobering part. Jesus goes on in this 21st verse [of John 17] to say something that always causes me to cringe. If as Christians we do not cringe, it seems to me we are not very sensitive or very honest, because Jesus here gives us the final apologetic. . . . 'that they all may be one, as You, Father, are in Me, and I in You; that they also may be one in Us, that the world may believe that You sent Me.' . . . .
In John 13:33-35 the point was that, ***if an individual Christian does not show love toward other true Christians, the world has a right to judge that he is not a Christian.*** *Here Jesus is stating something else which is much more cutting, much more profound:* ***We cannot expect the world to believe that the Father sent the Son, that Jesus' claims are true, and that Christianity is true, unless the world sees some reality of the oneness of true Christians.****"*[256]

Francis Schaeffer

(1912-1984)

As Christians, we should cringe at our lack of love for one another in the Church

Schaeffer went beyond intellectualism to application and confronted the Church with its ineffectiveness because of a lack of love. When people outside the Church look at the Church and see not love but sin, discord, jealousy, and back-biting, it brings shame on the Church and incurs God's wrath because our lack of love causes unbelievers to reject Christ. Schaeffer said that if we do not cringe at the lack of love among Christians, "it seems to me we are not very sensitive or very honest."

Love is more than an emotion.
It is essential for our lives as Christians.

[256]Francis Schaeffer, *Mark of a Christian*. Online at Christian Classics Ethereal Library, www.ccel.org.

Do Good to Show Others Peace with God—John Wesley

From the time he led the college Bible study called the Holy Club, John Wesley called Christians to serve others but always with a commitment to "do good to their souls" and "awaken those that sleep in death" and bring them to a knowledge of Christ's atoning blood.

"The Character of a Methodist"

Wesley wrote about this in "The Character of a Methodist":

"Lastly. As he has time, he 'does good unto all men;' unto neighbours and strangers, friends and enemies: And that in every possible kind; not only to their bodies, by 'feeding the hungry, clothing the naked, visiting those that are sick or in prison;' but much more does he labour to do good to their souls, as of the ability which God giveth; to awaken those that sleep in death; to bring those who are awakened to the atoning blood, that, 'being justified by faith, they may have peace with God;' and to provoke those who have peace with God to abound more in love and in good works. And he is willing to 'spend and be spent herein,' even 'to be offered up on the sacrifice and service of their faith,' so they may 'all come unto the measure of the stature of the fulness of Christ.'"[257]

Serving humbles you. You are forced to go down to the level of others and to go even lower as their servant in the likeness of Christ. This meekness causes the Church to grow in unity. When we become a people who are one in Christ through our love and serving, God will rejoice over His children who have come together to become a true family with His Son's spiritual DNA.

". . . he will rejoice over thee with joy; he will rest in his love, he will joy over thee with singing."[258]

[257] John Wesley, "The Character of a Methodist." Online at http://www.umcmission.org.
[258] Zephaniah 3:17 KJV.

The Low Road to Leadership

David took the low road to leadership. He was the youngest son. He had to take care of the sheep alone. When the prophet Samuel came to visit he was not even included in the dinner plans. When he went to take provisions to his brothers who were fighting the Philistines, they mocked him when he asked questions about the giant Goliath—until he killed him.

King Saul turned against him and eventually tried to kill him so he had to run for his life. He lived in caves with a ragtag band of men who followed him. While he was in the wilderness, he and his men helped protect the property of a man named Nabal, but all he received in return was ridicule and rejection.

Eventually Saul died and David became king, but because he had taken the low road to leadership he was a different kind of king from Saul. He had such a humble heart toward God that even when he turned away from God's ways and sinned with Bathsheba he broke down and repented. He was not a rebel like Saul, who sinned and made excuses. He was a child who knew that His Father's way was the right way.

David's kingdom lasted and flourished. He presided over a golden age for Israel full of wealth and peace with other nations. If you seek God's own heart and serve others, as David did, God will give you oversight over people, regardless of your humble circumstances. God can trust leaders who want to please Him.

Chapter 26

24-Hour Self-Accountability Journal

Jesus warned us to keep watch over every hour:

"Watch therefore, for you do not know what hour your Lord is coming. But know this, that if the master of the house had known what hour the thief would come, he would have watched and not allowed his house to be broken into. Therefore you also be ready, for the Son of Man is coming at an hour you do not expect."[259]

What plans do you have for today? Are they God's plans? Have you consecrated yourself first, before you decided how to schedule your day? That is the proper order for your schedule—first, consecration; then, plans for your day. As you follow the daily journal in *A Man's Journey with God,* order your day so that God is your earliest priority and your last thought at night.

This edition of *A Man's Journey with God* provides you with a daily 24-Hour Self-Accountability Journal where you will document every hour of your day so that you can look back and see how dedicated you are by how you spent your time. You can see yourself as God sees you.

Jesus told the people of His day that their priorities were out of order. He said they talked about the weather and watched for signs in the sky but they did not know the signs of the times—specifically related to Who He was as He lived among them.

Those who attend executive training seminars learn the importance of setting daily priorities. However, they won't teach you how to set God as a priority. Before you plan your work day, create your spiritual day. Then you will be ready to plan the appointments that God wants you to keep. Your daily schedule should represent the outworking of the will of God in your life.

[259]Matthew 24:42-44 NKJV.

Jesus calls us to the timetable of God

Matthew 16:2-3 KJV

"When it is evening you say, 'It will be fair weather, for the sky is red'; and in the morning, 'It will be foul weather today, for the sky is red and threatening.' Hypocrites! You know how to discern the face of the sky, but you cannot discern the signs of the times."

Giving God your schedule

Most of us are driven by the demands of our minds when we decide how to spend a day. However, your human mind is too limited to understand God's will. You can't put God on any kind of rational scale and try to figure him out logically. You have to know Him on the inside through yielding and spending intimate time with Him in the closet of total surrender before you can understand His timetable for you.

Time should be your tool instead of you becoming a tool of time.

Get alone with God before you decide on your appointment schedule. Unless you set up your schedule in the environment of prayer, your schedule will control you instead of you controlling your schedule.

Living daily in the realm of eternity

God is not limited by time. He lives in the realm of eternity. As you plan your schedule, consider what will count most when time is no more. Make practical lists of things to do in your day but when you decide what to do with these lists consider the significance of eternal reality. As you plan your schedule, remember that what God is able to do through you tomorrow is being formed in you today.

You won't find this standard for success in *Fortune* or *Ebony*, but the most truly successful people on earth are the ones who look like Jesus. God has ordained us to be like the Lord in thought, word, and deed. God is doing his part. Jesus is interceding for us and we must yield fully to Him.

Chapter 27

Daily Activity Checklist

"Search me, O God, and know my heart: try me, and know my thoughts: And see if there be any wicked way in me, and lead me in the way everlasting."[260]

David was willing to give God access to his heart. He pleaded with God to search his inner man to see if he had any wickedness. Will you evaluate your life daily by Jesus' standard of holiness, then grade yourself A, B, or C, or 1 to 10? Are you willing to give up anything in your lifestyle that is displeasing to God, regardless of the cost?

Pressing forward	*"But this one thing I do, forgetting those things which are behind, and reaching forth unto those things which are before, I press toward the mark for the prize of the high calling of God in Christ Jesus."*[261]

You may not know your specific calling, and you may not have any of the special knowledge you may need some day, but just by the level of your dedication—are you dedicated enough to press through until you accomplish God's will, whatever that may be? Do you have any areas where you need to repent for not following up on His will for you? That is the purpose of the end-of-the-day Personal Daily Checklist. If you have failed Him, humble yourself and call upon Him for His mercy. Then you can sleep, secure in the knowledge that tomorrow will be a new day, because His mercies are new every morning.[262]

Mercies of God

Charles Wesley, brother of John Wesley, founder of the Methodist Church, wrote this hymn about God's mercy.

---

[260] Psalm 139:23-24 KJV.
[261] Philippians 3:13-14 KJV.
[262] See Lamentations 3:23.

Depth of Mercy!

"Depth of mercy! Can there be
Mercy still reserved for me!
Can my God His wrath forbear,
Me, the chief of sinners, spare?

"I have long withstood His grace,
Long provoked Him to His face,
Would not hearken to His calls,
Grieved Him by a thousand falls. . . .

"There for me the Savior stands,
Shows His wounds and spreads His hands.
God is love! I know, I feel;
Jesus weeps and loves me still."[263]

Your Personal Self-Accountability Ratings

When you were a student in school, you had to perform at a certain level to keep from failing a class. If you were wise, you worked hard, not only to avoid failing but also to excel. You wanted to be an "A" student. The same should be true with how you perform for God.

In school, most of the time teachers would not let you grade your own paper because they knew your human tendency to make yourself look better than you really are. In grading yourself as a personal accountability exercise, no one will know your grade except you and God. Each day, evaluate yourself in each of these categories, and give yourself a grade of A, B, or C, or choose a number from 1 to 10.

Can you be honest? Do you know the consequences of lying to God? Most of us have never taken a careful account of ourselves in this much detail at the end of the day, but dedicated Christians of the past did it. They came up with their own accountability questions and their own standards for success, as they understood the will of God, and then they strove to meet them. In many cases, these types of questions helped them to disciple those under them to become accountable to God, as well.

[263]Charles Wesley, "Depth of Mercy." Words, music, and story available online.

Faithful to consider your ways

Charles Wesley was a student at Oxford University in England when his brother John returned. Their father was a pastor and they both attracted young Christian men around them. Although Charles was leading a group at the time, he welcomed the return of his brother to lead them.

As mentioned in the ministry of Richard Allen, once the denomination was established Wesley also devised systems for the growing Methodist movement that helped people to build holiness into their lives. This was a great asset to the freed slaves like Allen.

Another example is Jonathan Edwards. He not only kept himself accountable. He also taught his children, and they taught theirs, with the result that for many generations to follow the Edwards offspring were godly, successful members of society.

Faithful to represent Jesus in your integrity

The ultimate goal of accountability is shaping ourselves into Christ-likeness. You should be able to say with sincerity, "I represent Jesus." Your lifestyle should be such an example of righteousness that people would know a man of God was among them. You can be born again, saved from hell, but still live like the devil. What does that mean? You still have trouble with anger. You still have trouble with relationships with people. You still have deception and manipulation. You may call it circumlocution or being tactful, but it is manipulation and deceit. Eternally you are going to heaven, but unless you grow up and develop godly character formation, you will be largely irresponsible, not suited to rule and reign with him.

God is not primarily trying to get you to feed the poor, even though you can demonstrate Christ-likeness when you do. He is not first trying to get you rich. He is not trying to get you a husband or wife. He is not trying first to do any of that. His primary goal has never changed.

His goal is to qualify you for the next world.
That goal must become a reality for you.

You can never make your wife truly happy without Christ-likeness. The degree to which you are transformed is the degree to which you can have an impact. Everything you do in life centers around your yieldedness to Christ, because He is all and in all.

People of character, because we are like Christ

Colossians 3:9-11 KJV

"Lie not one to another, seeing that ye have put off the old man with his deeds; And have put on the new man, which is renewed in knowledge after the image of him that created him: Where there is neither Greek nor Jew, circumcision nor uncircumcision, Barbarian, Scythian, bond nor free: but Christ is all, and in all."

Faithful to fulfill responsibilities

In *Uncle Tom's Cabin,* Harriet Beecher Stowe gave an example of Christ-like character in the slave Uncle Tom. In the opening scene of the book, Tom's master, Mr. Shelby, is forced to sell Tom, his best slave, and secretly describes Tom's Christian virtues to a slave trader named Haley.

Mr. Shelby's commendation: *"Why, last fall, I let [Uncle Tom] go to Cincinnati alone, to do business for me, and bring home five hundred dollars. 'Tom,' says I to him, 'I trust you, because I think you're a Christian—I know you wouldn't cheat.' Tom comes back, sure enough; I knew he would. Some low fellows, they say, said to him—'Tom, why don't you make tracks for Canada?' 'Ah, master trusted me, and I couldn't,'— they told me about it. I am sorry to part with Tom, I must say. You ought to let him cover the whole balance of the debt; and you would, Haley, if you had any conscience."*[264]

Standards of Holiness—Your Personal Daily Checklist

The following pages will help you understand the personal daily checklist in A Man's Journey with God

[264]Harriett Beecher Stowe, *Uncle Tom's Cabin*, Chapter 1, p. 43. Available online at American Studies at the University of Virginia, http://etext.lib.virginia.edu/toc/modeng/public/StoCabi.html.

1. Time in Prayer

Praying without fainting

Luke 18:1 KJV

Jesus said that "men ought always to pray, and not to faint."

When a symphony orchestra assembles on stage, the musicians make quite a racket trying to tune their instruments. Before the conductor arrives, all of the professional musicians must prepare themselves to play by tuning their instruments to the same note. That is a requirement of the conductor before he will come on stage for the concert.

Do you know how to get in tune with God before you pray? Do you know how to stay in tune, not only during your assigned time of prayer but after you go about the business of the day?

The Bible gives instructions on how to develop your prayer life so that you are playing the tune that God desires. It speaks of cleansing your heart from sin, getting rid of your pride, becoming open and vulnerable, and humbling yourself so that He can speak to you. Prayer is something that is conducted by God.

God created you. God does not exist for your purposes. You exist for God's purposes. He is the One in charge. In prayer, you are always responding to God, never initiating. God initiates prayer, and you respond, to the degree that you know Him and are able to hear His voice.

Each day in *A Man's Journey with God* you will be evaluating how much time you gave to God in private prayer. How well did you prepare yourself? How well did you listen? How well did you walk out what He said to demonstrate that you heard Him? Your goal is not to be overbalanced by praying only for yourself. You can ask God for help but don't neglect others' needs. Your needs are practical and also spiritual. God has more wisdom than you do. He has more knowledge. He has an eternal perspective. When it is appropriate, He gives you what you ask for but when it is not appropriate, like any good parent, He says "No" or "Wait." Get alone with God, prepare your heart, and listen.

God's highest priority for prayer is that you would spend personal time with Him alone.

Go into your room and shut the door to pray.

Matthew 6:5-6 NKJV

"And when you pray, you shall not be like the hypocrites. For they love to pray standing in the synagogues and on the corners of the streets, that they may be seen by men. Assuredly, I say to you, they have their reward. But you, when you pray, go into your room, and when you have shut your door, pray to your Father who is in the secret place; and your Father who sees in secret will reward you openly."

It takes a commitment to quietness to hear God speak what He wants to say to you, that He is looking for a man like you, if you are holy. That is why you need to be alone with Him, so that the only voice you hear is God's voice.

Hindrances to Hearing from God about His ManHunt

"And I sought for a man among them, that should make up the hedge, and stand in the gap before me for the land, that I should not destroy it: but I found none"
(Ezekiel 22:30 KJV).

As you evaluate the level of your private prayer and grade yourself from A to C, or 1 to 10, consider which of these potential problems are hindering you from hearing that God is on a ManHunt for *you.*

Contention and strife. Isaiah 54:4-5. *"You fast, but at the same time you bicker and fight. You fast, but you swing a mean fist. The kind of fasting you do won't get your prayers off the ground" (Isaiah 58 The Message).*

Disobedience. Romans 5:12-19; Ephesians 5:6; Colossians 3:4-10

Disrespect of parents or elders. *"Honour thy father and thy mother: that thy days may be long upon the land which the LORD thy God giveth thee" (Exodus 20:12 KJV).* See also Peter 5:5-6.

Disrespect of wife by husband. *"Husbands, likewise, dwell with them with understanding, giving honor to the wife, as to the weaker vessel, and as being heirs together of the grace of life, that your prayers may not be hindered" (1 Peter 3:7 NKJV).*

Flesh-walking. Galatians 5:19-24

Heart turned away from God. Isaiah 29:13

Hiding your evil from God. Isaiah 29:15

Iniquity (wickedness). *"If I regard iniquity in my heart, the Lord will not hear me" (Psalms 66:18 KJV.)*

Lack of faith, unbelief. *"But let him ask in faith, nothing wavering. For he that wavereth is like a wave of the sea driven with the wind and tossed. For let not that man think that he shall receive any thing of the Lord" (James 1:6-7 KJV).* See also Hebrews 11:6.

Love for things in the world. I John 2:15

Lust of the flesh, lust of the eyes. 1 John 2:16

Manipulation—trying to trick God into doing things for you. Isaiah 48:1, Isaiah 58:3-4, Jeremiah 3:10, Matthew 15:7-9

Mistreatment of employees. James 5:1-6

Oppression of the poor. Proverbs 14:31, Luke 18:22-27

Pride. Psalm 12:3; Proverbs 6:16-19; James 4:10; 1 John 2:16 ". . . for every one that exalteth himself shall be abased; and he that humbleth himself shall be exalted" (Luke 18:14 KJV).

Proud of how you pray. Matthew 6:5-8; Luke 18:11-14

Rebellion. 1 Samuel 15:23; Proverbs 28:9

Resisting the Holy Spirit. Acts 7:51

Sin. Psalms 66:18; Isaiah 59:1-4 ; John 8:34-36

Strife. 1 Corinthians 3:3-9; Philippians 2:3-4; James 3:14-18
Unforgiveness. Matthew 6:14-15

Ungodliness. Psalm 1:1-6

Sin Separates Us from God

Some sins are premeditated and some are not. There are sins of omission and sins of commission in thoughts, words, and deeds.

(1) Thoughts: "Casting down imaginations, and every high thing that exalteth itself against the knowledge of God, and bringing into captivity every thought to the obedience of Christ."[265]

(2) Words: "But I say unto you, That every idle word that men shall speak, they shall give account thereof in the day of judgment. For by thy words thou shalt be justified, and by thy words thou shalt be condemned."[266]

(3) Deeds. "For if you live according to the flesh you will die; but if by the Spirit you put to death the deeds of the body, you will live."[267]

[265]2 Corinthians 10:5 KJV.
[266] Matthew 12:36-37 KJV.
[267]Romans 8:13 NKJV.

2. Time in Word of God

When you build on the rock of revelation, you become strong. You can prevail in the storms of life. You mature from a baby Christian, who is basically carnal, to a child, a young man, and a mature man of God.

Growing Up Spiritually by Feeding On God's Word

Babe, Baby Christian, Carnal, Milk-Drinking

"And I, brethren, could not speak unto you as unto spiritual, but as unto carnal, even as unto babes in Christ. I have fed you with milk, and not with meat: for hitherto ye were not able to bear it, neither yet now are ye able. For ye are yet carnal: for whereas there is among you envying, and strife, and divisions, are ye not carnal, and walk as men? For while one saith, I am of Paul; and another, I am of Apollos; are ye not carnal?" (1 Corinthians 3:1-4 KJV).

Little Child

"I write unto you, little children, because your sins are forgiven you for his name's sake" (1 John 2:12 KJV). "I write unto you, little children, because ye have known the Father" (1 John 2:13 KJV). "When I was a child, I spake as a child, I understood as a child, I thought as a child" (1 Corinthians 13:11 KJV).

Young Man

"I write unto you, young men, because ye have overcome the wicked one" (1 John 2:13 KJV).

Father, of Full Age, Man

"I write unto you, fathers, because ye have known him that is from the beginning" (1 John 2:13 KJV). "But strong meat belongeth to them that are of full age, even those who by reason of use have their senses exercised to discern both good and evil" (Hebrews 5:14 KJV).

"For when for the time ye ought to be teachers, ye have need that one teach you again which be the first principles of the oracles of God; and are become such as have need of milk, and not of strong meat. For every one that useth milk is unskillful in the word of righteousness: for he is a babe."[268]

3. Time for Personal Praise and Worship

Praise and worship are important expressions of respect and honor toward God, and they are also one of the means that God uses to accomplish His will, in earth as it is in heaven.

God inhabits your praises

Psalm 22:3 KJV

"But thou art holy, O thou that inhabitest the praises of Israel"

In praise and worship, you set up an atmosphere where God can come and do His will. You are responding to His presence in you. You are acknowledging the greatness of Who He is and your absolute dependency on Him for your salvation, and, in fact, your very life.

God's call to come up higher

In the book of Revelation, the Apostle John describes two godly prophets who are killed and their bodies left in public view to be mocked. However, God had the final word. He brought them back to life and then called them to come up higher to Him.

"But after three and a half days, God breathed life into them, and they stood up! Terror struck all who were staring at them. Then a loud voice from heaven called to the two prophets, "Come up here!" And they rose to heaven in a cloud as their enemies watched."[269]

God is calling all of us to come up higher right now so that we will be ready to ascend to him when we die. That's the call on the Church, to

[268] Hebrews 5:12-13 KJV.
[269] Revelation 11:11-12 NLT.

show people how to come up higher above the sins of earth. Come up to where God is so you can get a new anointing to deal with the darkness of your day. You are not ordained to be in the dark, nor are you ordained to be neutral. The Church cannot be sitting around while the world is falling apart. In prayer you must plead with God to let you be used.

During my momma's final illness, the doctor called me from the hospital and said, "We need to put more tubes in her. If we don't, she will die." He told me straight up, just like that. What do you think my answer was? Of course, unless God tells me something different. When I was in the ICU later with my assistant, Cynthia Ellenwood, who was also her caregiver, we sang to her a hymn by Fannie Crosby:

"Pass me not, O gentle Savior, hear my humble cry,
While all others thou art calling, Do not pass me by."

My momma couldn't speak because of a stroke and those tubes but she could still praise God! She was shaking her hand and joining with us. In spite of all those tubes that were coming out of my momma, she still had a passion for God on her deathbed. She could not sit up but she could arise inside in praise and worship to God, even without the ability to speak. She had a sense of God right there on that bed.

My momma was saved in a Pentecostal church when I was a child and from that moment on she was a changed woman. All of her Christian life she had identified with the language of dedication, the language of Jesus coming by. She did not want to die until His will was fulfilled in her life, but in that ICU she was also gripped by eternity.

Are you gripped by eternity? There's something fake in Christianity that causes a disconnect in praise and worship when you don't know my Friend, Holy Ghost. When you don't know and can't identify with what is right to do in the eyes of God, it's because you're not close enough to my Friend. The degree that you know Him is the degree to which His power is at work in your life.

This is not just a religious experience of talking in tongues, even though He brings a heavenly language with Him. It's the intimacy and reality of Jesus in your life every day through the Holy Ghost that leads you into a true relationship with God from now through eternity.

Your personal release through daily praise and worship

Praise and worship are something Christians can do every day at home, not just at camp meetings or on Sunday. You don't need a pastor or an evangelist or a group of musicians and singers at church to bring in

God's presence. His presence is already there if you are there, because you have Christ in you, the hope of glory.[270] In the morning and throughout each day, take time to speak and sing of God's greatness. Read the Psalms aloud to Him. Sing songs of praise and worship, even by yourself.

The word is already near you, in your mouth and in your heart.

Romans 10:6-10 NKJV

"Do not say in your heart, 'Who will ascend into heaven?' (that is, to bring Christ down from above) or, 'Who will descend into the abyss?' (that is, to bring Christ up from the dead). But what does it say? 'The word is near you, in your mouth and in your heart' (that is, the word of faith which we preach): that if you confess with your mouth the Lord Jesus and believe in your heart that God has raised Him from the dead, you will be saved. For with the heart one believes unto righteousness, and with the mouth confession is made unto salvation."

Taking your children to church—no exceptions

When I was growing up my momma would say emphatically, "You're going to church!" Too many fathers and mothers today let their children intimidate them. You don't even bring them to church on Wednesday night to children's programs. You don't come and they don't come. Or sometimes you come but slip in and slip out.

You can't let your children set their own standards when they are living with you and too young to decide! Don't abdicate your biblical role as a father to raise them up in the way they should go. Set standards for your kids and teach them to value fundamentals that are important to you.

I would whine to my momma, *"But I've got homework!"*

She would say straight to my face, "Look, you should have done your homework before this time. You're going to church right now and I want you to pay attention! You aren't going to sleep in there, either. You're going to church!" I have to admit she was right. Look at my life now!

God's Inner Presence: George Fox and William Penn

The state of Pennsylvania was founded by a devout Quaker named William Penn (1644-1718). While he was still in England he was

[270] See Colossians 1:27.

frequently imprisoned for speaking of his faith and taking a stand for other Quakers and against religious toleration. The 1701 Charter of Privileges of Pennsylvania bears the mark of his Christian faith.

Pennsylvania Charter of Privileges Acknowledges Jesus as "Saviour of the World" (1701)	*"AND that all Persons who also profess to believe in Jesus Christ, the Saviour of the World, shall be capable (notwithstanding their other Persuasions and Practices in Point of Conscience and Religion) to serve this Government in any Capacity, both legislatively and executively."*[271]

The average young person today has probably never heard of George Fox, founder of the Quakers, but he is an example for those willing to lay aside a right to do it "my way" and start doing things "God's way."

Commending George Fox **William Penn** (1644-1718) Quaker, Founder of Pennsylvania	*George Fox "was a man that God endowed with a clear and wonderful depth, a discerner of others' spirits, and very much a master of his own. And though the side of his understanding which lay next to the world, and especially the expression of it, might sound uncouth and unfashionable to nice ears, his matter was nevertheless very profound, and would not only bear to be often considered but the more it was so, the more weighty and instructing it appeared."*[272]

Like most Christians of his day, Fox believed in the historical evidence of Christ but that did not satisfy his longing for God and his seeming helplessness against sin. Theology left Jesus unreal and not present and he refused to be satisfied until he found the living God.

Fox took a strong stand against the Church of England's non-biblical requirements that all citizens must belong to the church and pay tithes. He was an example of radical Christianity in an age when appeasement in the mainstream church was driving revolutionary-minded Christians to take action.

[271] Thorpe, op. cit. Online at Constitution.org.

[272] "The Testimony of William Penn Concerning that Faithful Servant George Fox." Included in *George Fox, An Autobiography*. Available online.

George Fox

(1624-91)

Revolutionary and radical commitment challenged the coldness of the Church

"[Fox] emerges from the struggle with an absolute certainty in his own mind that he has discovered a way by which his soul has immediate dealings with the living God. The larger truth involved in his experience soon becomes plain to him, namely, that he has found a universal principle, that the Spirit of God reaches every man."[273]

Fox wrote, "I was taken up in the love of God, so that I could not but admire the greatness of His love."[274]

"The Church of that time was the result of compromise. It had inherited a large stock of medieval thought, and had absorbed a mass of medieval traditions.
The men of moral and religious earnestness were bent on some measure of fresh reform.
A spirit was abroad which could not be put down, and which would not be quiet."[275]

Quakers persecuted and risked their lives because they knew God

Contrary to hierarchy and formality he built a movement based on equality and universal love that became called "Society of Friends." In addition to refusing to attend Anglican services or pay tithes to the state church, Fox would stand outside the doors of the church dressed in leather and assail the people as they left, challenging them to follow the true Christ. In his journal he said that his group was called Quakers "because I bade them tremble at the word of the Lord." Thousands of Quakers were arrested, sold as slaves, beaten, imprisoned, and killed but the movement grew because of their genuine connection to God.

---

[273] George Fox, *Autobiography of George Fox* (Introductory material). Available online at Christian Classics Ethereal Library, www.ccel.org.
[274] Ibid. (Writings of George Fox).
[275] Fox, op. cit. (Introductory material).

One of the distinguishing marks of the Quakers was the belief that because each person can have a personal relationship with Jesus Christ—regardless of his station in life—he can hear the Spirit of God speaking to him.

They approach God with reverence. When the movement spread to America, many renounced any past association with slavery and risked their lives to rescue slaves escaping through the Underground Railroad.

Story of Quaker commitment appears in 19th century best-seller

Harriet Beecher Stowe based her anti-slavery novel *Uncle Tom's Cabin* on actual people and events. When she depicted the evils of slavery and the deep faith of the slaves she also gave space to Christians like the Quakers who demonstrated Christ-like character by assisting in the Underground Railroad.

In this fictional passage from *Uncle Tom's Cabin* George, an escaped slave, has just been reunited with his wife and child, who have escaped separately. George, the runaway, was bitter against God and his slave masters, but he broke through to faith in the humble home of Simeon and his family, the Quakers who helped his family to escape. Note the Quakers' traditional use of "thee" instead of "you."

"This, indeed, was a home, — home, — a word that George had never yet known a meaning for; and a belief in God, and trust in his providence, began to encircle his heart, as, with a golden cloud of protection and confidence, dark, misanthropic, pining atheistic doubts, and fierce despair, melted away before the light of a living Gospel, breathed in living faces, preached by a thousand unconscious acts of love and good will, which, like the cup of cold water given in the name of a disciple, shall never lose their reward.

"'Father, what if thee should get found out again?' said Simeon second, as he buttered his cake.

"'I should pay my fine,' said Simeon, quietly.

"'But what if they put thee in prison?'

"'Couldn't thee and mother manage the farm?' said Simeon, smiling.

"'Mother can do almost everything,' said the boy. 'But isn't it a shame to make such laws?'

"'Thee mustn't speak evil of thy rulers, Simeon,' said his father, gravely. 'The Lord only gives us our worldly goods that we may do justice and mercy; if our rulers require a price of us for it, we must deliver it up.'

"'Well, I hate those old slaveholders!' said the boy, who felt as unchristian as became any modern reformer.

"'I am surprised at thee, son,' said Simeon; 'thy mother never taught thee so. I would do even the same for the slaveholder as for the slave, if the Lord brought him to my door in affliction.'

"Simeon second blushed scarlet; but his mother only smiled, and said, 'Simeon is my good boy; he will grow older, by and by, and then he will be like his father.'

"'I hope, my good sir, that you are not exposed to any difficulty on our account,' said George, anxiously.

"'Fear nothing, George, for therefore are we sent into the world. If we would not meet trouble for a good cause, we were not worthy of our name.'"[276]

The real-life Quakers upon whom this home scene was based were tried for giving a ride to runaway slaves and unfairly convicted by a jury. When they were assessed a huge fine by the court, John Garret, the Quaker father, calmly rose and said that because of Christ he would willingly do the same thing again, and was even more committed to the cause of abolition. *Uncle Tom's Cabin* memorialized his dedication.

Underground Railroad: Helping Slaves Escape

White people went South to teach slaves escape routes to the North

Beginning three decades before the Civil War, at least 500 people were involved in the dangerous mission of training slaves how to follow the North Star and watch for hidden landmarks on the escape routes.

Estimated 60,000 to 100,000 escaped by end of Civil War

Slave masters sent dogs and bounty hunters after escaped slaves, punished them brutally, or killed them if they were caught. They tortured other slaves who might know where they were. Yet they still ran for freedom.

---

[276] Harriet Beecher Stowe, *Uncle Tom's Cabin*, op. cit., Chapter XIII, "The Quaker Settlement."

Departed in winter, when most people were indoors

They were taught to travel in the dark and cold when others would be less likely to see them. They had to cross the Ohio River to safety on the North side when the river was frozen, so they had to arrange to arrive there in winter.

Journey north took an average of one year

During the journey, they had to trust a network of people not only to hide them but also to feed them and provide for their basic needs.

Dangerous to slaves and also those who hid them

After the Fugitive Slave Law of 1850, Northerners had to break the law to hide slaves.

Guides, wagon drivers, ferry captains, and others became involved

Some slaves were old or became too ill to travel, but their guides or companions helped them to survive. Members of the Underground Railroad were so compassionate that they also helped the old and infirm.

Some had scruples against escaping

Uncle Tom's Cabin described Tom's unwillingness as a Christian to escape because of his integrity, and also because he knew that the others would be allowed to stay on the plantation if he sacrificed himself to be sold. However, Tom did endorse the escape of Eliza with her young son who was about to be sold. (Her husband George was the one converted in the Quaker home.)

What examples in your life compare to the sacrifice of these godly people? Do you know Jesus Christ as they did? Would you willingly suffer for a cause that was just?

Few people in history understood right away that slavery was wrong. The majority embraced it, especially if it was legal. This included slave owners in the American North and South. Even when slavery ended in the North owners heartlessly sold their slaves to the South.

You must give an account when you meet Christ in judgment

Just as the New Testament showed the wickedness of Saul for his murder of Christians before he was converted and called Paul, Christian authors need to continually tell the truth about sin in themselves and others and how they learned to rise above it by depending on God.

Praise in the midst of judgment and personal suffering

George Fox spoke often about God's judgment to the people of his day and he tried to call them to repentance. Often they responded not only with rejection but also with persecution. In this incident he was imprisoned. While he was in jail He saw God judge the people and mourned for their sins but he also praised God in the midst of suffering because their opinion of him did not affect him. He was able to stay true to the Lord.

> *"Great was the exercise and travail in spirit that I underwent during my imprisonment here, because of the wickedness that was in this town; for though some were convinced, yet the generality were a hardened people. I saw the visitation of God's love pass away from them. I mourned over them.*
>
> *"There was a great judgment upon the town, and the magistrates were uneasy about me; but they could not agree what to do with me. One while they would have sent me up to the Parliament; another while they would have banished me to Ireland. At first they called me a deceiver, a seducer and a blasphemer. Afterwards, when God had brought his plagues upon them, they styled me an honest, virtuous man. "But their good report and bad report were nothing to me; for the one did not lift me up, nor the other cast me down; praised be the Lord! At length they were made to turn me out of jail, about the beginning of winter, in the year 1651, after I had been a prisoner in Derby almost a year,—six months in the house of correction, and the rest of the time in the common jail."*[277]

[277] *Autobiography of George Fox* online at Christian Classics Ethereal Library, www.ccel.org.

4. Time for Thanksgiving

Do you take time to give thanks to God every day? When I was a child, I used to make fun of the old mothers who kept coming to church with the same old testimonies, over and over. Whenever it was time to stand up in the service and share something good that God had done, they would always say the same thing: *"Thank Him! He woke me up this mo'nin' 'n' He started me on mah way!"* When God finally got through to me years later, I realized that I was wrong and they were right. Their words of thanks were just the overflow of the attitude of thankfulness in their hearts. Their words were a pleasing aroma to God but my words of mockery stunk up the place. Now I am determined to express my thankfulness to God every day. Whether somebody else wants to make fun of me or not, I'm going to thank Him.

Giving thanks *Hebrews 13:15 KJV).*	*"By [Jesus] therefore let us offer the sacrifice of praise to God continually, that is, the fruit of our lips giving thanks to his name"*

Prayer of thanks for God's Word

Father, in Jesus name and in the anointing of the Holy Spirit, I thank you that we are blessed beyond measure as the people of the Lord. I declare blessings upon those who read, believe, and live the principles of Your Word. Because the Word of the Lord is true, thank You that Your Word follows us down throughout the years and people are changed. Thank You that as people read the Word and make it a reality in their lives, families are restored. Faith comes alive. Men repent and give their hearts to you and begin to live holy lives. They take steps into Your image, Lord Jesus, and allow You to correct them and perfect their ways. They take more steps and You use them to fulfill Your purposes for creating them.

Thank you, Lord, for what You are doing among the people of God in this hour. You have reserved for Yourself a remnant. Thank You that they will not be defeated because You are Almighty God!

We love you! In Jesus' name, I pray. Amen.

5. Time for Fasting[278] (with Isaiah 58 Fast)

You can find some way to fast for the sake of your consecration every day or at least every week. Prayer and fasting are a part of the walk of humility that brings you into Christ-likeness.

Fasting drives out unbelief

Matthew 17:14-21 NLT

(The quote to the right includes verse 21 which does not appear in all versions of this chapter.)

"At the foot of the mountain, a large crowd was waiting for them. A man came and knelt before Jesus and said, 'Lord, have mercy on my son. He has seizures and suffers terribly. He often falls into the fire or into the water. So I brought him to your disciples, but they couldn't heal him.

"Jesus said, 'You faithless and corrupt people! How long must I be with you? How long must I put up with you? Bring the boy here to me.' Then Jesus rebuked the demon in the boy, and it left him. From that moment the boy was well.

"Afterward the disciples asked Jesus privately, 'Why couldn't we cast out that demon?'

"'You don't have enough faith, Jesus told them. 'I tell you the truth, if you had faith even as small as a mustard seed, you could say to this mountain, "Move from here to there," and it would move. Nothing would be impossible.

"'But this kind of demon won't leave except by prayer and fasting.'"

Jesus said that certain victories on earth are only won with prayer and fasting.[279] He told His disciples that a fasted lifestyle builds your faith. It drives the unbelief out of you.

You cannot walk in the dominion of Christ without the walk of suffering, brokenness, and submission. If you do not walk His way, you will not have His dominion.

---

[278] See also Chapter 32, Fasting for Results. Check Index under "Fasting" for additional information.

[279] See Mark 9:29.

Blessed to endure suffering

James 5:10-11 NKJV

"My brethren, take the prophets, who spoke in the name of the Lord, as an example of suffering and patience. Indeed we count them blessed who endure."

God's kind of fasting—Isaiah 58

"No, this is the kind of fasting I want:
Free those who are wrongly imprisoned;
lighten the burden of those who work for you.
Let the oppressed go free,
and remove the chains that bind people.

"Share your food with the hungry,
and give shelter to the homeless.
Give clothes to those who need them,
and do not hide from relatives who need your help.

"Then your salvation will come like the dawn,
and your wounds will quickly heal.
Your godliness will lead you forward,
and the glory of the Lord will protect you from behind.

"Then when you call, the Lord will answer.
'Yes, I am here,' he will quickly reply.

"Remove the heavy yoke of oppression.
Stop pointing your finger and spreading vicious rumors!

Feed the hungry,
and help those in trouble.
Then your light will shine out from the darkness,
and the darkness around you will be as bright as noon."[280]

[280] Isiah 58:6-10 NLT.

In Isaiah 58:5, God condemns the type of fasting he has seen in Israel and then He spells out the right kind of fast, beginning in verse 6 when he says, "No, this is the kind of fasting I want" (NLT).

You may not have seen fasting this way before, but God lists eight categories of *benevolence* that He expects from those who fast. Most people who fast have in mind some benefit for themselves, but God is saying He is pleased when we fast for others. In other words, even though you are hungry, you make a decision to lay aside that desire for food and move from the need-based side to the resource side. That takes supernatural power. Fasting God's way is a supernatural experience.

You should meditate on this concept of fasting that results in benevolence. This understanding of fasting requires meditation until you see that what you can do for others is a greater result than what you can do for yourself.

Meditation is one of the habits you will develop through the course of completing your 30-day consecration journal. God told Joshua that meditation in His Word was a vital leadership practice when Joshua took over his new assignment of serving those multitudes after the death of Moses. God said:

> *"Study this Book of Instruction continually. Meditate on it day and night so you will be sure to obey everything written in it. Only then will you prosper and succeed in all you do" (Joshua 1:8 NLT).*

Eight practices of benevolence from Isaiah 58 fast:

1. Free those who are wrongly imprisoned. When someone is wrongly imprisoned, you are to be the vehicle to set them free.

2. Lighten the burden of those who work for you. You may be wealthy and yet you have people working for you who have a situation or circumstance in their lives where they need your help. God is saying that you should become their source. You should move outside of your assignments for them to show them your compassion.

3. Let the oppressed go free. In Black America you see a people group that has been oppressed for centuries. They need a release from people who fast and pray to set those oppressed people free.

4. Remove the chains that bind people. Become a resource person wherever you see people in chains—spiritual, physical, mental and emotional chains must be broken. Poverty keeps people in chains. So do alcoholism and drug addiction. How could you help break those chains?

5. Share your food with the hungry. During the Daniel fast that churches like ours participate in each year, we don't eat meat. However, you probably keep it in the freezer until the fast is over unless you are quitting meat and becoming a vegetarian. What about a different mentality to not only stop eating meat on a fast but also taking that meat to share with the hungry? It's probably a lot better than what their local food bank can supply.

6. Give shelter to the homeless. Jesus was homeless and so were His disciples. I don't know many people who reach out to the homeless with consistency. When you are fasting, consider people who have no home, no food, and no resources to get food. Do something to meet their needs. I don't think the church has taken enough responsibility at the level we should. We could do so much more. I know there are those who provide homeless houses or homeless shelters, but what about building a hotel? God could give you the facilities to provide that kind of shelter.

7. Give clothes to those who need them. Remember those pants and suits in your closet and the pairs of shoes that you can't count? How about giving some clothes to those who need them?

8. Do not hide from relatives who need your help. Probably at some point in your life you had somebody living with you. In some cases, it may have been your older children who lived with you much longer than they should. I know people who want to move out of town because their children are grown but they constantly have to be looking out for them. In Isaiah 58 God says don't hide from them. Maybe they still need to learn lessons of godliness from you. They may need to see you pray, fast, and show compassion to others.

God said "this is the fast I have chosen." God loves to see you do His Word.

You can become so aware of your own needs that you don't realize you are the person God wants to use to meet the needs of others.

During a fasting and consecration time you can fast for the right reasons and see a change in yourself as you become His vehicle to demonstrate His greatness.

Each of those eight categories of benevolence points to a new competence in you—the ability to help somebody else to get a release based on your sacrifice. The hunger from fasting along with a desire to please God can build compassion in you to think on the resource level.

All of these benefits are outside of you.

Almost all of it relates to what is going on with someone else's life. This is not about a 501(c)(3) ministry base. It's about your heart.

Once you heart gets right, you can look around and see all kinds of people who need you, even after the fast is over.

This is more than something to read about. You and I have to make a difference categorically in the world. The fast breaks us down so that we are not just thinking about what we are going through. Instead, whenever we are going through some crisis ourselves we are thinking about reaching out to make a difference for somebody else. We are being like Christ. As the Bible says, "Christ in you, the hope of glory" (Colossians 1:27 KJV).

Fulfill the reason God made you. We are not supposed to be comfortable all the way to heaven. We are ambassadors from heaven to those who need God.

6. Time with My Family

Everything starts in the family. Every one of us comes from a family and every family is a world. Even ghetto people understand that.

When you ask someone from the ghetto, "What's up?" they deflect that by saying, "It's your world." They mean that you are in control of your future. You have a certain DNA structure because you came from someone but in your family some things stuck and some things went right past you. Whatever stuck with you is what you are. You made choices.

When you establish a home with your wife and you have children, you are creating a world of your own. Your children carry your DNA and they also carry what you do for them and what you do with them as a family. Every child remembers what they did with their parents growing up. What will your children remember about you?

Healing for dysfunctional families

When you are seeking God and fasting and prayer are an important part of your Christian life, your encounter between you and God can fix anything that's negative in your past.

Jesus came to deal with past negatives so that your future could be way better. The latter is better than the former.

If your father was missing or even if he mistreated you, that doesn't stop you from being a good father. God knew about it. He knew your dad wouldn't be there so there is no use whining. God is greater than your daddy. You won't have a problem if you have consummated a vital relationship with God as your Creator. The Creator of daddies is better than your daddy.

I didn't meet my daddy until I was 35 and only because I went to see him at the suggestion of Bishop Garland Hunt. I was conceived out of wedlock and raised by my mom after she was not successful in trying to abort me. God preserved me and He is still keeping me.

Nobody in my church ever heard me whine about not having a father. My encounter with God was so real to me that I understood my dad was not a failure to me. He was a failure to God. I needed to be the example to him that he wasn't to me.

I went back to see him again when I was 52 years old. It was only the second time I had ever met him. I prayed for him and told him I never held anything else against him.

About a week later, my daddy died. I had already returned to Atlanta when I found out. He wasn't even sick. He was saved but somehow I believe that he needed that final blessing from me as his son.

The father's blessing

Every patriarch spoke over his children. A man of God should get insight from God in prayer so that he can speak destiny over his family. On a consistent basis he should lay hands on his wife and children and pray for them. He should teach them from the Scriptures. He should make sure that they attend services in the church.

A father should pronounce blessings over his wife and children. Give your son a "rite of passage" into manhood. Give your daughter the same rite into womanhood. They are both to commit themselves to chastity until marriage!

Words from God through a husband and father

Every man should be able to come to his family after prayer with a word from God. The direction of the household should come as a result of guidance that he receives in prayer.

In a family where the father is the head of the house, spiritual guidance begins through the leadership of the man. Unless your wife is in agreement with this from her own relationship with God, you better go back to the closet and make sure that you heard Him correctly before you make her submit to your guidance, "that in the mouth of two or three witnesses every word may be established."[281]

Your first priority of the day is time with God, and your next priority is time with your family. There should be no conflict with this. You can't use prayer as an excuse to escape your family.

If you don't enjoy spending time with your family, don't avoid them. Correct whatever is causing the division.

God created families and He created yours to be a blessing to you and those He placed around you. You can pray when they are sleeping and be ready for them when they awaken.

[281]Matthew 18:16 KJV.

Spiritual training by fathers[282]

Do you remember that children's story "The Three Little Pigs"? A couple of the pigs thought they could get by with quick construction.

They threw their houses together with straw and twigs. That was no problem for the big bad wolf. He just blew those houses down and ate the pigs. The third pig made his house of bricks. It took more time and money, but when he was finished it had the substance to protect him when the wolf came.

How much time do you spend building your spiritual house? If you're like most men, and I'm talking about most *Christian men*, you spend a whole lot of time building a career and very little time building your spiritual house. Everybody has to earn a living, but what is happening to your calling to minister to your family? Unless you get serious, your family won't have much more protection from the world, the flesh, and the devil[283] than those first two pigs had from the wolf.

God is calling you to take time out to build your house from the substance of a consecrated life. If you've built your house on anything but the rock-solid model of Jesus Christ, your house will be washed away. If you've built with wood, hay, and stubble, it's going to burn. Since Jesus is the head of your house, ask Him, "What are Your priorities?" and then do those things that He requires.

7. Time with My Friends

The Bible says, "Do not forsake your own friend or your father's friend."[284] George Müller was such a faithful friend that he prayed for the conversion of one man for 63 years. He said, "The great point is never to give up until the answer comes. . . . He is not converted yet, but he will be! How can it be otherwise? There is the unchanging promise of Jehovah, and on that I rest."[285]

The friend did not come to Christ in Müller's lifetime, but as soon as Müller died, the man was converted—even before the funeral! How many of your friends hear from you often about your Savior? How many know they can count on you in their day of adversity?

---

[282] See *Your Wife Is Not Your Momma* by Wellington Boone for an extensive discussion of the subject of spending time with your family (Atlanta: APPTE Publishing, 2011).

[283] *Book of Common Prayer,* ". . . and from all the deceits of the world, the flesh, and the devil, "Spare us, good Lord." Available online from many sources in various versions.

[284] Proverbs 27:10 NKJV.

[285] *The Kneeling Christian* (author unknown). From Chapter 8, "Does God Always Answer Prayer?" Online at Christian Classics Ethereal Library, www.ccel.org.

Brother born for adversity Proverbs 17:17 KJV	*"A friend loveth at all times, and a brother is born for adversity."*

Are you a fair-weather friend, or a deep-spirited friend? A true friend sees your weaknesses and says, "I know you are not there yet, but I don't love you because you are like me. I love you because you have purpose. God wants me to be an example of unconditional love to you."

Not a single person could meet the requirements of God's love in advance. Jesus died before any of us could ever do anything to earn his love. When our friendships demonstrate the unconditional love of God that is when we can give ourselves an "A" looking back over our day.

Our First Friend is Jesus. He said, "Henceforth I call you not servants; for the servant knoweth not what his lord doeth: but I have called you friends; for all things that I have heard of my Father I have made known unto you."[286]

Get friends by being a friend Proverbs 18:24 KJV	*"A man that hath friends must shew himself friendly: and there is a friend that sticketh closer than a brother."*

8. Time with the Lost (with Creeds and Scriptures)

The greatest need of society is a real encounter with the Person of Jesus Christ. Your lifestyle can win the lost to Jesus Christ as well as your words. Your consistent dedication will bring others into the kingdom. People are changed when they meet somebody like Jesus, but because we have been so unlike Him, nobody wants to be like Him, either. When people are not following you, something about you is not like Jesus.

[286] John 15:15 KJV.

That is the difference between soul-winning and winning by lifestyle. Why should Jesus want people to follow you when you don't show them dedication and love? You would only lead them into the flesh. That is why you need to let Him transform you into His image.

Paul made a habit of preaching the Gospel to the unreached. As you are committing yourself to the 30-day plan of consecration in *A Man's Journey with God*, you have two goals in mind:

(1) your own change through your growing relationship with God,
(2) reaching out to others for their change.

Because you are saved, you are a seed into the time when your family and the whole earth can be saved. Christians should be carriers of revival, not someone who is always looking for a revival to come. *You* need to be the revival that is coming. "And [John] said unto Him, Art Thou He that should come, or do we look for another?"[287] You are the one who comes in the name of Jesus. The world does not have to look for another.

In the home, a wife can reach her husband, who is saved by her love. "Wives, in the same way be submissive to your husbands so that, if any of them do not believe the word, they may be won over without words by the behavior of their wives, when they see the purity and reverence of your lives."[288]

You can reach the lowly by loving them and showing mercy on them. Jesus identified with the lowly. How many "low" people can you bring up another level in God? "Comfort the fainthearted, uphold the weak, be patient with all."[289] God has called us to pray without ceasing for those who are lost and to remember that He desires that all would be saved.[290] We should count prayerlessness as sin as it relates to the salvation of our loved ones and others who are lost.

Three major creeds of the Church that prepare you to win souls

As you pray for opportunities to speak about Jesus to unsaved people, review what you believe yourself, so that you will be prepared to speak clearly about your faith. Christian apologetics (your defense and proof of your Christianity) requires not only knowledge of the Scriptures but also familiarity with classic catechisms and creeds of the Church.

Here are three examples of Christian creeds.

[287] Matthew 11:3 KJV.
[288] 1 Peter 3:1-2 NIV.
[289] 1 Thessalonians 5:14 NKJV.
[290] See 1 Timothy 2:4.

Apostles' Creed (1st century A.D. and following years)[291]

"I believe in God the Father Almighty, Maker of heaven and earth. And in Jesus Christ his only Son our Lord; who was conceived by the Holy Ghost, born of the Virgin Mary, suffered under Pontius Pilate, was crucified, dead, and buried; he descended into hell; the third day he rose again from the dead; he ascended into heaven, and sitteth on the right hand of God the Father Almighty; from thence he shall come to judge the quick and the dead.

"I believe in the Holy Ghost; the holy catholic Church; the communion of saints; the forgiveness of sins; the resurrection of the body; and the life everlasting. Amen."

Nicene Creed (c. 325 A.D.)

"We believe in one God the Father Almighty, Maker of heaven and earth, and of all things visible and invisible.

"And in one Lord Jesus Christ, the only-begotten Son of God, begotten of the Father before all worlds, God of God, Light of Light, Very God of Very God, begotten, not made, being of one substance with the Father by whom all things were made; who for us men, and for our salvation, came down from heaven, and was incarnate by the Holy Spirit of the Virgin Mary, and was made man, and was crucified also for us under Pontius Pilate. He suffered and was buried, and the third day he rose again according to the Scriptures, and ascended into heaven, and sitteth on the right hand of the Father. And he shall come again with glory to judge both the quick and the dead, whose kingdom shall have no end.

"And we believe in the Holy Spirit, the Lord and Giver of Life, who proceedeth from the Father and the Son, who with the Father and the Son together is worshipped and glorified, who spoke by the prophets. And we believe one holy catholic and apostolic Church. We acknowledge one baptism for the remission of sins. And we look for the resurrection of the dead, and the life of the world to come. Amen."

The Nicene Creed is the most universal Christian creed and is used by the Roman Catholic, Eastern Orthodox, Anglican Communion, and many other Protestant denominations. The name is derived from the ecumenical Council of Nicea in A.D. 325. In the 6th century the words "and the Son" (Latin

[291] These creeds are available at multiple sources online. Note: The word "catholic" in the creeds is an ancient term that refers to the universal Christian church, not only the Roman Catholic Church.

Filioque) were added (third paragraph above) to read "the Holy Spirit . . . proceedeth from the Father *and the Son*" [italics added].

Athanasian Creed (c. 500 A.D.) (Excerpt)

". . . And in this Trinity, no one is before or after, greater or less than the other; but all three persons are in themselves, coeternal and coequal; and so we must worship the Trinity in unity and the one God in three persons.

"Whoever wants to be saved should think thus about the Trinity.
It is necessary for eternal salvation that one also
faithfully believe that our Lord Jesus Christ became flesh.
For this is the true faith that we believe and confess:
That our Lord Jesus Christ, God's Son, is both God and man.
He is God, begotten before all worlds from the being of the Father,
and he is man, born in the world from the being of his mother —
existing fully as God, and fully as man with a
rational soul and a human body;
equal to the Father in divinity, subordinate to the Father in humanity.
Although he is God and man, he is not divided, but is one Christ. . . .

"He suffered death for our salvation.
He descended into hell and rose again from the dead.
He ascended into heaven and is seated at the right hand of the Father.
He will come again to judge the living and the dead.
At his coming all people shall rise bodily to give an
account of their own deeds.
Those who have done good will enter eternal life,
those who have done evil will enter eternal fire.
This is the catholic faith.
One cannot be saved without believing this
firmly and faithfully."

The Athanasian Creed stresses the deity and equality of the Three Persons of the Trinity—Father, Son, and Holy Spirit—and includes warnings of eternal judgment for those who deny the truth. It is widely accepted by many Roman Catholic, Anglican, and Protestant churches but is used less often today than the Nicene Creed. You will find an excerpt from the Westminster Catechism at the end of the book.

We need a new passion for unsaved people

Whenever you are reading this, I can guarantee that in the past few weeks many people died and some went to hell, but hell was not made for them. They could have been saved. Somebody like you could have told them about Jesus. People are perishing from war, disease, and acts of terrorism. Some may be in your workplace, your neighborhood, or your family. That is why people all around you need to hear about Jesus.

Do you know what to say? Do you know how to pray? Do you understand that your lifestyle can attract people to Jesus?

While the President, Congress, the military, and every agency of the United States government is on alert, it cannot be business as usual in the Church. Jesus has called us to be martyrs, whether it is bloodless martyrdom—death to self (Acts 1:8, Galatians 2:20) that gives you the courage to talk about Jesus in unfriendly environments—or literal death.

This is war. Whether it is the bloodbaths in the Middle East or the killings in the streets of America's cities, you are called to be a revolutionary. You must reach the lost.

> *"Proclaim ye this among the Gentiles; Prepare war, wake up the mighty men, let all the men of war draw near; let them come up: Beat your plowshares into swords, and your pruning hooks into spears: let the weak say, I am strong. Assemble yourselves, and come, all ye heathen, and gather yourselves together. . . . Multitudes, multitudes in the valley of decision" (Joel 3:9-11,14 KJV).*

The good news of salvation is that God wants you to acknowledge your sin and repent for your wrongs, but His goal is restoration. His goal is never punishment and annihilation. I don't care what you've done and where you are right now. You're supposed to be restored and then become an example at the highest possible level that you will let God use you, with no ceilings. You're inwardly disciplined. You're personally devout. And you can be trusted. God wants to use you today!

Scriptures for Speaking the Name of Jesus to the Lost[292]

The world is bolder about their god than we are about Jesus. We have to reverse that trend. If you are ashamed of Jesus, Jesus will be ashamed of you.[293] Boldness it not just asking Jesus to be your Lord. It means being bold to speak about Jesus everywhere you go, forever.

When you mention Jesus to the world, Jesus mentions you to the Father. Jesus says if you want to be famous in heaven speak His name on earth and demonstrate in your manner of living that His life is in you. Then He will confess you before the Father.

"So they called the apostles back in and commanded them never again to speak or teach in the name of Jesus. But Peter and John replied, 'Do you think God wants us to obey you rather than him? We cannot stop telling about everything we have seen and heard.'"[294]

Creation and the role of God the Father, Son, and Holy Ghost. Genesis 1-2; John 1

Fall of man when sin entered the world. Genesis 3

Jesus is God. John 1, Hebrews 1

Jesus explains leaving Holy Spirit for us. John 3:6, 6:63, 14:16, 14:26

Ten Commandments. Exodus 20

God so loved the world that He gave His Son. John 3:16

"God so loved the world, that he gave his only begotten Son, that whosoever believeth in him should not perish, but have everlasting life" (KJV).

All have sinned. Romans 3:23

"For all have sinned, and come short of the glory of God" (KJV).

---

[292] See also Scripture charts throughout this book and read these verses in context for full revelation.
[293] See Matthew 10:32-33.
[294] Acts 4:18-20 NLT.

Jesus died for sinners. Romans 5:8

"While we were yet sinners, Christ died for us" (KJV).

Confession and forgiveness.1 John 1:9

"If we confess our sins, he is faithful and just to forgive us our sins, and to cleanse us from all unrighteousness" (KJV).

Sermon on the Mount. Matthew 5-7.

Beatitudes: "Blessed are . . ." Matthew 5

My Shepherd. Psalm 23

"The Lord is my shepherd; I shall not want" (KJV).

Repentance. Psalm 51

"Create in me a clean heart, O God; and renew a right spirit within me."

Humility. Psalm 22:6; Philippians 2

Hell. Rich man in hell, Luke 16:19-31; Revelation 22

Good Shepherd. Jesus' life given for the sheep, John 10

Prodigal Son. He was dead, and is alive, Luke 15

Good Samaritan. Who is my neighbor? Luke 10

Love. Greatest is love, 1 Corinthians 13

Birth of Jesus. Glory to God! Matthew 1-2, Luke 1-2

Cross and Resurrection. Matthew 26-28; Mark 14-16; Luke 22-24; John 18-21

Great Commission. Matthew 28:16-20; Mark 16:14-20

New Jerusalem; Bride of Christ. Revelation 21-22

How well known are you in heaven, based upon the witness that you give of Jesus in the earth? You may be better known in the earth than you are in heaven because you do not call out His name. You are ashamed of His name.

Jesus is God and everything was made by Him. The Word says in Philippians 2 that at His name every knee must bow. Jesus is that exalted name. His name carries authority, not only in this world, but also in the world to come.

Unsaved People Need to Know that Jesus Is God

God created the heavens and the earth. *"In the beginning God created the heavens and the earth."*[295]

Jesus made everything that exists. *"In the beginning was the Word, and the Word was with God, and the Word was God. The same was in the beginning with God. All things were made by him; and without him was not any thing made that was made."*[296]

Jesus—God, the Word—became a man for us. *"And the Word was made flesh, and dwelt among us."*[297]

9. Time to Eat Right

Jesus, Who made you, wants you to have the right perspective about every area of your life, including eating. The right foods are necessary for wholeness. There are basic building blocks for your body that are required for life and health. Food should not be your focus, however, especially the wrong food—things you know that you should not be eating. Demonstrate your sensitivity to the Holy Spirit by taking proper care of your body, which is His temple.[298] Maintain a biblical worldview perspective for your needs.

When Jesus' disciples found Him talking to the Samaritan woman, they offered Him some of the food that they had brought back, but He turned them down. They thought He must have already eaten.

[295] Genesis 1:1 NLT.
[296] John 1:1-3 KJV.
[297] John 1:14 KJV.
[298] See 1 Corinthians 3:16.

"But Jesus replied, 'I have a kind of food you know nothing about.'

"'Did someone bring him food while we were gone?' the disciples asked each other.

"Then Jesus explained: 'My nourishment comes from doing the will of God, who sent me, and from finishing his work.'"[299]

Jesus did not live to eat. He ate to live. His work was more important to Him than His physical food. Fasting was His lifestyle and it was also a permanent cure for overeating and overweight.

Inordinate craving for food

Never let food create an inordinate affection—lust—that dominates your thoughts. Physical food is for your physical body but your body is an instrument of your spirit. Whenever you let your appetites control what you think and do, you are in trouble. You are missing God. I am disturbed by how many people in the body of Christ who are overweight. Jesus said that overeating is as bad as drunkenness.

"And take heed to yourselves, lest at any time your hearts be overcharged with surfeiting [overeating], and drunkenness, and cares of this life, and so that day come upon you unawares."[300]

Right eating for health and focusing on the will of God

One of Jesus' foundational teachings from the Sermon on the Mount relates to how we look at food.

"Therefore I say unto you, Take no thought for your life, what ye shall eat, or what ye shall drink; nor yet for your body, what ye shall put on. Is not the life more than meat, and the body than raiment?"[301]

---

[299] John 4:32-34 NLT.
[300] Luke 21:34 KJV.
[301] Matthew 6:25 KJV.

Right eating is important to a healthy mind and a healthy spirit. Watch what you eat and drink, and notice how it affects you—sugar, excess caffeine, artificial sweeteners, soft drinks, fatty foods, etc.

Read the warnings of health professionals about additives and high cholesterol foods. Watch your salt intake. When you eat the wrong foods, you harm your body, hinder your thinking ability, and decrease your level of faith. You do not show the proper respect for your body, the temple of the Holy Spirit.[302]

At the end of each day, grade yourself on your eating.
Will what you ate provide the ideal substance for your health?
Are you overweight or underweight?
If Jesus sat at the table with you, would you eat the same foods?
Would Jesus think the thoughts about food on your mind today?

Jesus did not have to eat until the will of God was done. Having the right perspective on food means that we eat the proper foods for the health of our body, soul, and spirit. We don't lust after food. We don't live to eat. We eat to live.

10. Time to Exercise

When you are disciplined in your spirit, you are not lax in taking care of your body, the vessel that God is using to contain your spirit. It must be brought into the shape that God wants.

Decide on a routine of conditioning and stretching exercises that you can do at least three times a week. In the same way that you establish a routine of building and toning your spiritual strength on the inside, get in the habit of working out in a way that keeps your physical body in tip-top shape all the time.

God formed man. What form does God want you to be in physically? When you look in the mirror with no clothes on, do you see the shape that you want to build, or does it expose to you that you are being lax in some areas of godly discipline?

[302] See 1 Corinthians 3:16.

Disciplining my body so that I can win the race 1 Corinthians 9:24-27 NKJV	*"Do you not know that those who run in a race all run, but one receives the prize? Run in such a way that you may obtain it. . . . I discipline my body and bring it into subjection, lest, when I have preached to others, I myself should become disqualified"*

Godly exercise and body-shaping are profitable for your spirit. Don't give yourself any more excuses. Take care of your body, which is the temple of the Holy Spirit,[303] by eating, drinking, and exercising to the glory of God. "Whether therefore ye eat, or drink, or whatsoever ye do, do all to the glory of God."[304]

11. Time to Organize

When God created the heavens and the earth, He organized them by the laws of nature. The earth was formless but God put in place a certain structure to the earth. Structure and order also apply to you.

Without form until Spirit brought order *Genesis 1:2 KJV*	*"And the earth was without form, and void; and darkness was upon the face of the deep. And the Spirit of God moved upon the face of the waters."*

One of the goals of this prayer journal is to get you to think in an organized way about your daily life and your future. It is to help you to look at the end from the beginning, to set goals, and then work backward from your goals to see what you need to do to meet them.

"Take a lesson from the ants, you lazybones.
Learn from their ways and become wise!
Though they have no prince
or governor or ruler to make them work,
they labor hard all summer,
gathering food for the winter."[305]

303 See 1 Corinthians 6:19.
304 1 Corinthians 10:31 KJV.
305 Proverbs 6:6-8 NLT.

If you don't have an end in mind, you can't organize your present. You can't set priorities. When you allow yourself to stay disorganized, you lose the ability to dominate time. Instead, time dominates you. There is a better way!

There is a relationship between making your bed in the morning and good mental health. Daily diligence to details affects your clarity of thought and your ability to function at the level at which God has called you. This is both a natural and a spiritual principle.

God brought order to the earth by His Spirit

God is organized by the Spirit, but He applies it in the natural realm. The earth was "without form and void" but God's Spirit moved upon it and brought order. In the same way, you can move upon your life by your spirit and make changes that will help you to bring order to your environment.

Organization delivers you from the tyranny of the urgent—circumstances, trials, pressures that would try to force you to do things, whether or not you have decided that they are vital for reaching your goals. Make a commitment to bring order through your dedication to all of the five sovereign spheres that your life touches: self-government, family, church, civil government, free associations.

Godly government for your life

Before a contractor can build a house, he has to draw the plans so that everyone can see how it will look.

The Lord has a plan not only for time, but also for eternity and God has ordained that every model in the future would look like Jesus.

You are the model that God wants to change into the image of His Son. Because of what He saw in your life, He sowed his Son into your life to help you fulfill His plan. You have to sow into God's plan for you just as a contractor sows into the plans that he has for his house. In order to bring those plans into realization, He has to seed thinking into it. He has to sow time, money, and people into it. He could not realize what he saw without giving to it.

That is true for everything. If I am seeing reconciliation, revival and awakening, I have to seed into that in an orderly way. I have to find out what are the requirements for bringing it to pass. Whatever they are, I follow up on them and begin then to sow into that ground.

All governments are on His shoulders

The government shall be on His shoulders *Isaiah 9:6-7 KJV*	*"For unto us a child is born, unto us a son is given: and the government shall be upon his shoulder[s]: and his name shall be called Wonderful, Counsellor, The mighty God, The everlasting Father, The Prince of Peace. Of the increase of his government and peace there shall be no end, upon the throne of David, and upon his kingdom, to order it, and to establish it with judgment and with justice from henceforth even for ever. The zeal of the Lord of hosts will perform this."*

12. Time for Myself (Personal Intimacy with God)

Do you have a heart for getting alone with God? Don't let anything else get in the way. For most of the years of my ministry, I have taken time to walk away from the ministry to be alone with God and to fast and pray. I stay in isolation. I need that time alone with God to develop intimacy.

Holy Spirit is very sensitive. He knows when you are serious about cultivating your friendship with Him. He works first with every Christian alone and He's easily grieved when He is not given private attention.

Do you love spending intimate time with God?

Do you love spending time with God? Do you receive creative insight when you are together? David, the psalmist, knew God loved him, and he loved being with God. He wrote, "My meditation of him shall be sweet: I will be glad in the Lord."[306] God is jealous over anything that we choose instead of spending time with Him. In the KJV of James 4:5 it says He "lusts to envy."

[306] Psalm 104:34 KJV.

The Spirit is jealous of our time

James 4:4-8 NLT

"You adulterers! Don't you realize that friendship with the world makes you an enemy of God? I say it again: If you want to be a friend of the world, you make yourself an enemy of God. What do you think the Scriptures mean when they say that the spirit God has placed within us is filled with envy? But he gives us even more grace to stand against such evil desires. "As the Scriptures say,

" 'God opposes the proud
but favors the humble.'

"So humble yourselves before God. Resist the devil, and he will flee from you. Come close to God, and God will come close to you. Wash your hands, you sinners; purify your hearts, for your loyalty is divided between God and the world."

True intimacy with God develops primarily through these two character qualities:

(1) Transparency—willingness to open yourself up to God
(2) Vulnerability—tenderness of heart

(1) Becoming transparent and opening yourself up to God.

In Genesis 15 is a description of how Abram sacrificed animals to God and split them down the middle. What he did with the animals speaks of you opening yourself up. As someone has said, intimacy means "into me see."

"And it came to pass, that, when the sun went down, and it was dark, behold a smoking furnace, and a burning lamp that passed between those pieces. In the same day the Lord made a covenant with Abram."[307]

[307] Genesis 15:17-18 KJV.

(2) Becoming vulnerable, which means tenderness of heart.

The Bible says that you can't always trust your heart. Your destiny is heaven, which is where you come into His presence to be fully changed into His likeness. When your heart is tender, you can be taken into the true things of God. I remember hearing Joy Dawson of Youth With A Mission (YWAM) say, "Show me my heart, Lord, lest I die!"

"The heart is deceitful above all things, and desperately wicked: who can know it? I the Lord search the heart, I try the reins, even to give every man according to his ways, and according to the fruit of his doings."[308]

Jesus knocks at the door of your heart, which is closed:

"Behold, I stand at the door, and knock: if any man hear my voice, and open the door, I will come in to him, and will sup with him, and he with me."[309]

God asks you to humble yourself and look honestly at your heart. He wants you to look inside and see the pride in your own heart.[310] Jesus wants you to make your spiritual development the highest priority in your life—not whether you are loved or respected or appreciated. In that way every word spoken to you and every action for or against you becomes a tool in the Lord's hands to minister truth and growth in Christ-likeness. As Francis Schaeffer said, referring to the Bible, the mark of a Christian is love and a Christian carries, in Paul's words, "the sweet savor," or the essence, of Jesus Christ wherever we go.[311]

Instead of stinking up the place with our fleshly attitudes, we create the sweet-smelling environment of heaven on earth with our Christ-like lifestyle. When people hear us speak or watch our lives they should be able to witness the character of Christ in us because we have been accountable to nurture His nature within us by daily practices of consecration and self-accountability.

[308]Jeremiah 17:9-10 KJV.
[309]Revelation 3:20 KJV.
[310] See Mark 7:21-23.
[311] See 2 Corinthians 2:14-16.

Chapter 28

Expenses and Money Management

God wants you to be prosperous—not only spiritually but also economically. Piety does not have to mean poverty. God owns all the wealth in the world but most of those who control it are sinners. God wants Christians to steward His wealth, not sinners.

If you don't have much money to manage for God, maybe you haven't gone after it seriously enough. Maybe you have believed there was something sinful about having money even though you know you need money for supporting your family while you do the ministry.

If you are rich in prayer, rich in the Word of God, rich in consecration, why should there be anything wrong with also being rich in money? Somebody is handling the resources of the world. Why not you? You can be a bank instead of going to a bank. You can be a lender whom others come to, not a borrower begging for a loan. You can be empowering businesses and major ministries instead of looking for others to empower you. If your pastor wants a new building, you can be the first in line with a check. You just have to keep your heart right.

Seek knowledge and understanding as if they were money

Proverbs 2:3-6 NLT

"Cry out for insight,
and ask for understanding.
Search for them as you would for silver;
seek them like hidden treasures.
Then you will understand what it means to
fear the Lord,
and you will gain knowledge of God.
For the Lord grants wisdom!
From his mouth come knowledge and understanding."

When you are rich, doors open to you. You can become a person of influence. You can be a producer instead of a consumer. You can provide finances for other people of God so that they can be about the Father's business without becoming distracted by raising money. You can meet not only your own needs but also the needs of your family, church, and those in need. You can leave a godly inheritance—natural as well as spiritual. You can be like the patriarchs of the Bible.

If the love of money does not dominate your life, but the love of God's wisdom and the fear of the Lord, you can be trusted with handling money—both yours and someone else's. Even if you don't yet manage money well or if you haven't learned to see managing money as a demonstration of the orderliness of God, you can change!

Power to get wealth comes from God *Deuteronomy 8:18 KJV*	*". . . the Lord thy God: for it is he that giveth thee power to get wealth, that he may establish his covenant which he sware unto thy fathers, as it is this day."*

Faithfulness with money qualifies you to rule

Your daily accountability journal includes a place to record how you have spent and managed your money in a way that would cause the Master to say to you each day, "Well done," and give you cities to rule as His representative. Jesus said that your profitable handling of the money that He has entrusted to you will bring you future rewards. He will be able to watch what you do with the amounts that He has entrusted to you and see how well qualified you are to rule.

Jesus said you prove yourself qualified for leadership by how you handle money *Luke 19:17-19 NLT*	*"'Well done!' the king exclaimed. 'You are a good servant. You have been faithful with the little I entrusted to you, so you will be governor of ten cities as your reward.'* *"The next servant reported, 'Master, I invested your money and made five times the original amount.'* *"'Well done!' the king said. 'You will be governor over five cities.'"*

By contrast, if you misuse your wealth, or you are full of pride and arrogant toward the poor, judgment is coming upon you from God.

God will judge the rich for their arrogance

James 5

The Message

"And a final word to you arrogant rich: Take some lessons in lament. You'll need buckets for the tears when the crash comes upon you. Your money is corrupt and your fine clothes stink. Your greedy luxuries are a cancer in your gut, destroying your life from within. You thought you were piling up wealth. What you've piled up is judgment.

Many rich people have not considered the warnings in Scripture that our eternal judgment is affected by what we do with our resources. Money is for giving and receiving. Usually giving is weighted one way or the other. Someone may give much and receive little because he is creating resources to give. Someone else may receive much and give little, because he lacks a biblical vision for wealth.

Biblical vision for wealth

Before you can be accountable for your money, you have to get money. David started with nothing, but by the time he passed the kingdom to his son Solomon he had become rich.

It is totally biblical to have a vision for wealth. Most Christians have not seen that vision. Because of your relationship to God, the Owner of all wealth, you are able to create resources to give.

First in David's life came his personal devotion to God. He had already killed a lion and a bear with God's aid before the prophet Samuel anointed him to be king. He received the riches of a natural assignment.

He was anointed for the highest office in the land, a king appointed by God. Then he went through training and development. He was sent to Saul's house. God raised him up right in Saul's face. He was honored in war before Saul's men. He had respect and honor before the people of Israel. He was driven out of Saul's house into total dependency on God. People came who were in debt, distressed, and discouraged. He was a man without property or land but he was rich in God.

Those who came to David were in debt, discontented

1 Samuel 22:1-2 NLT

"So David left Gath and escaped to the cave of Adullam. Soon his brothers and all his other relatives joined him there. Then others began coming—men who were in trouble or in debt or who were just discontented—until David was the captain of about 400 men."

David also attracted those who were economically rich. Captains came to him, and other leaders of men.

Mighty men came to David

1 Chronicles 12:1,2,8,14 KJV

"Now these are they that came to David to Ziklag, while he yet kept himself close because of Saul the son of Kish: and they were among the mighty men, helpers of the war. They were armed with bows, and could use both the right hand and the left in hurling stones and shooting arrows out of a bow, even of Saul's brethren of Benjamin. . . . And of the Gadites there separated themselves unto David into the hold to the wilderness men of might, and men of war fit for the battle, that could handle shield and buckler, whose faces were like the faces of lions, and were as swift as the roes upon the mountains . . . These were of the sons of Gad, captains of the host: one of the least was over an hundred, and the greatest over a thousand."

Giving to the Unworthy

God says that you are called to personally meet the needs of the poor. You can't reach the poor with only prayers. You can't just say, "I'll pray for you so God will meet your needs." You have to look at how much is in your checking account.

Even if I have never been to your church, I can safely say that there are people in your church who have practical needs. They are living below the standard of God in the natural realm. They are not just poor. They are po'! If you are like most people I know, you have decided you would rather not give any money to these poor people in your church, or do anything else for them, because they will just "use" you. The same is true for someone who stops you on the streets of the city and asks you for "fifty cents" or says, "Have you got a dollar? I'm hungry."

When we become Christians we think we know something about "those people." They are not "like us." We rationalize that they became poor because they were bad stewards of their money, and besides, if we gave them any of our hard-earned money they would just waste it or use it to buy alcohol or a lottery ticket. With some that potentially is the case, but interestingly enough, the Bible says that you should give to them anyway—not because they need it, but *because you need to give.* You may not give *what* they ask, but you can give something.

When you give, you are obeying the Word, especially when you give to those who are undeserving. The Bible calls the Jubilee[312] the *Lord's* release. He does not need your rationalizing, your logic, and your reasoning to determine whether or not you are going to set these people free with your finances. He says, "Set them free!" and He sets *you* free.

When God presented Israel with the principle of the Jubilee, He told them, in effect, "Every seven years I want you to give people back their land. Give them back their property. Release them from all their debts. Set them free, because I am using you as My instrument. It is not *your* release to them. It is *My* release."

Releasing others' debts is a release of the Lord

Deuteronomy 15:1-2 NKJV

"At the end of every seven years you shall grant a release of debts. And this is the form of the release: Every creditor who has lent anything to his neighbor shall release it; he shall not require it of his neighbor or his brother, because it is called the Lord's release."

No shortages in God

When we give to the poor in obedience to God, we have responded to His challenge to obey Him. God says, in effect, "Can I use you to set poor people free? I don't have any shortages, and I am your Father, so you don't have any shortages, either. Can you be a father to them?"

[312] See Leviticus 25 and Deuteronomy 15.

Now that we are saved, God is telling us not to write off people and judge them as unworthy. He is telling us to take a hard look at *ourselves*. God says, "When I came to you, *you* were in shortage. I delivered *you* out of Egypt's bondage. You were not together when I saved you. Nothing about you was pleasing in my sight. Yet I still delivered you. You were a slave to sin. You deserved to be in bondage. You deserved to die because you were born under Adam, but I came to you because of My holy name's sake. Because of My unqualified love, I sent Jesus, a Man who was able to stand in My presence. I delivered you out with My mighty power, and I brought you unto myself.

He says, "My ultimate intent in releasing you is that I would bring you into My ways. I was not just bringing you to a land, I was bringing you to a lifestyle, with Me. This Jubilee was to be something I could do through you, to teach you my ways."

Stop looking at where a person is and begin to see them for where God is taking them. Be an instrument of blessing, even to those who, like yourself, are ill-deserving, because you need the release.

Jew Sets Standard for Christians: Julius Rosenwald

Julius Rosenwald (1862-1932), president of Sears and Roebuck in the early 20th century, gave in the spirit of the Jubilee when he donated $63 million, the equivalent of ten times that amount in today's dollars, to build rural schools for Blacks after slavery. Inspired by his association with Booker T. Washington of Tuskegee Institute, where he served on the board, he not only donated personal funds but also motivated others to give matching grants. In addition, he funded 25 chapters of the Young Men's Christian Association nationwide for Blacks, because in many cities the *Christians* were not allowing Blacks to join the same YMCA chapters as the Whites.

What dreams do you have for acquiring wealth beyond your own personal comfort? Can this generation depend on your personal giving to solve problems like illiteracy and discrimination? Take up those issues with God, and see what He tells you to do.

Chapter 29

May I Go to Sleep Now, Father?

"Hard and honest work earns a good night's sleep."[313]

Before the old folks went to bed at night, they examined their day to see if they had committed any offenses that God would have to hold against them, so that when they slept, their sleep would be sweet. They assumed that if they did not awaken again they would be ready to meet God. Before you go to bed at night, ask God, "May I go to sleep now, Father?" In addition to completing any unfinished areas of your personal accountability journal, ask the Holy Spirit to help you answer questions like these as truthfully as possible:

- Are there any places of disobedience in my life?
- Is there anything that I have left undone?
- Have I done everything that I should have done?
- Have I done anything that is not true to the nature and character of God?
- Do I need to repent for anything that I have done in thought, word, and deed?

When you have resolved questions like those, you can rest in the assurance that you are ready to meet God at any moment.

The Last Trumpet

1 Corinthians 15:52-53 KJV

"In a moment, in the twinkling of an eye,
at the last trump: for the trumpet shall sound, and the dead shall be
raised incorruptible, and
we shall be changed. For this corruptible
must put on incorruption, and this mortal
must put on immortality."

[313] Ecclesiastes 5:12, *The Message*.

If you expect a final judgment, your mind is set for the eternal dimension now. Your mind is made up. Your lifestyle proves it. If God doesn't come to get you, you will walk right out of this world into the heavenlies, there to abide forever. Enoch must not be the only one who has pleased God and did not see death, then made the Hall of Faith in Hebrews 11.[314] You are making yourself ready to please God, too. Your ways are more suitable for the heavenly realm than they are for the earthly. The words of this old song speak of holiness at day's end.

Now the Day Is Over

Sabine Bering-Gould ((1834-1924)

"Now the day is over,
Night is drawing nigh;
Shadows of the evening
Steal across the sky.

"Through the long night watches,
May Thine angels spread
Their white wings above me,
Watching round my bed.

"When the morning wakens,
Then may I arise
Pure, and fresh, and sinless
In Thy holy eyes."

Wholly given over to God

Henry Varley once spoke to D. L. Moody a challenge that reportedly originated with John Knox. He said, "It remains to be seen what God will do with a man who gives himself up wholly to Him." Moody replied, 'Well, I will be that man."

Will you be one who is totally given over to God?

[314] See Genesis 5:24 and Hebrews 11:5.

Section 4

Lifetime Exercises in Consecration

PERSONAL NOTES

Chapter 30

The Eightfold Anointing

Anointing Yourself Daily for Christ-likeness[315]

When the woman anointed Jesus' feet with oil from her alabaster box, He said she was anointing Him for His burial. He was being prepared symbolically for His death.

Jesus was anointed for burial

Matthew 26:7-12 KJV

"Meanwhile, Jesus was in Bethany at the home of Simon, a man who had previously had leprosy. While he was eating, a woman came in with a beautiful alabaster jar of expensive perfume and poured it over his head.

"The disciples were indignant when they saw this. 'What a waste!' they said. 'It could have been sold for a high price and the money given to the poor.'

"But Jesus, aware of this, replied, 'Why criticize this woman for doing such a good thing to me? You will always have the poor among you, but you will not always have me. She has poured this perfume on me to prepare my body for burial. I tell you the truth, wherever the Good News is preached throughout the world, this woman's deed will be remembered and discussed.'"

Just as she anointed Jesus for burial,[316] you can anoint yourself and recall that you are dead and your life is hid with Christ in God.

[315] Link to Words to Say with the Eightfold Anointing.
[316] See also Mark 14:8.

You are dead, hidden with Christ *Colossians 3:1-3 KJV*	*"If ye then be risen with Christ, seek those things which are above, where Christ sitteth on the right hand of God. Set your affection on things above, not on things on the earth. For ye are dead, and your life is hid with Christ in God."*

You are called to die, just like Jesus. You may not be called to die for your faith physically, in the flesh, but you are called to die to yourself, to the flesh, so that you can live once again in Christ-likeness.

Losing your life for Him *Luke 9:23-24 KJV*	*"And he said to them all, If any man will come after me, let him deny himself, and take up his cross daily, and follow me. For whosoever will save his life shall lose it: but whosoever will lose his life for my sake, the same shall save it."*

Jesus said in Acts 1:8 that His disciples would be His witnesses. The word "witnesses" is the same word as "martyrs." We may never have to be crucified, but we are still called to die. With us, it is bloodless martyrdom. We don't die *in* the flesh. We die *to* the flesh. If I am truly saved, I am a dead person, resurrected and walking in Christ-likeness.

Bloodless martyrdom of Christians *Acts 1:8 KJV*	*"But ye shall receive power, after that the Holy Ghost is come upon you: and ye shall be witnesses unto me both in Jerusalem, and in all Judea, and in Samaria, and unto the uttermost part of the earth."*

Sometimes I see Christians using the word "anointed" to describe themselves in press releases. I wonder if they realize that Jesus was anointed not only to be king and priest but also to die for the sins of the world. Death to self for the sake of others is Christ-like. When you are anointed, you become a bridge that others can walk on to get to God. You become a worm that does not strike back, but is easily crushed.

If you believe in Christ, you are saved from hell and going to heaven, but unless you die to yourself and become a disciple—a disciplined one—you may never develop Christ-like humility and apply the principles of the kingdom of God to your life.

Being a disciple requires sacrifice. It means laying yourself on the altar of total surrender and allowing God to have His way.

Sacrificial life *Psalm 50:5 KJV*	*"Gather my saints together unto me; those that have made a covenant with me by sacrifice."*

Anointed and set apart for God and the consecrated life

The Eightfold Anointing is a natural exercise that represents the spiritual reality of your being set apart for God and the consecrated life. It is a reminder that you belong to God. Your body is the temple of the Holy Spirit who is in you. You are not your own. You were bought with a price;[317] therefore you glorify God in your body and in your spirit, which are God's.[318] You have been set apart to be like Jesus today.[319]

Every morning, in acknowledgement of my death to self and my anointing to be like Jesus, set apart from the world, I anoint myself with fragrant olive oil. I recall that I have died to the flesh and come alive in the Spirit, and my life is hidden with Christ in God.[320] I am now dedicated to God. I am no longer my own. I was bought with the price of Christ's blood.[321]

Anointed for the Divine Business of Prayer

Jesus delivered the people of Israel out of their bondage to death, hell, and the grave. He destroyed the power of the devil. However, with all that He did, He still allowed Israel to stay in bondage to Rome. That was because He had given them something far more important than their physical deliverance from Rome. He had given them a spiritual deliverance. Instead of resolving their temporary condition, He dealt with divine business—their eternal condition.

---

[317] See 1 Corinthians 6:20.
[318] See 1 Corinthians 6:19-20.
[319] See Romans 8:29.
[320] See Colossians 3:3.
[321] See Acts 20:28.

Prayer is a ministry of the Holy Ghost where divine business is transacted in Jesus' name. His name is so powerful that someday every knee will bow and every tongue will confess that Jesus Christ is Lord.[322]

Several years ago I looked in the mirror and asked myself, "Do you understand that you must have the right attitude to approach Someone as great as God?" When I am making contact with God, is Jesus' blood sufficient or could God destroy me in a moment for approaching Him in the wrong way as He did in the Old Testament to those who displeased Him? Do I appreciate when I am praying that all of His resources are released to bring to pass again what Jesus began to accomplish on the earth?

I considered that since divine business is being transacted when God is moving, would God move for someone like me? God wants to work on my behalf but does God have to work against me because I am out of line? Is God serious while I am just religious?

In that mirror I had a little glimpse of reality. He didn't have to talk to me. He could choose not to. The fear of God came on me. I said I don't want to be perfunctory about this. I need to be more holy. From then on I implemented by the Holy Ghost certain practices including a daily anointing. Every day I anoint myself with oil and consecrate myself to serve the Lord. I want to share this revelation with you.

Anointed for a Sweet Aroma of Holiness from Your Life

A Christian brings "the sweet savour,"[323] or the essence, of Jesus Christ wherever we go.

When Mary anointed Jesus feet,[324] He said that she was anointing Him for His death. Ingredients in her aromatic anointing oil had been crushed to bring forth the odor of sweet perfume.

The ingredients of the holy anointing oil were also aromatic. The people could tell when Aaron and his sons had been anointed. If you let Holy Ghost crush you and break you down so that you get lost in Christ, a sweet aroma will come out of your life through that voluntary humiliation. You will create the aroma of heaven on earth.

---

[322] See Philippians 2:10-11.
[323] 2 Corinthians 2:15 KJV.
[324] See John 12.

"Our lives are a Christ-like fragrance rising up to God. But this fragrance is perceived differently by those who are being saved and by those who are perishing. To those who are perishing, we are a dreadful smell of death and doom. But to those who are being saved, we are a life-giving perfume."[325]

For my daily Eightfold Anointing I use a mixture of oil and my cologne as a reminder that the Bible says our lives have an aroma. To some who are not Christian, it smells like a deadly venom and they hate you, as they hated Jesus. To others on the pathway of Christ, your life is a sweet smelling aroma. Your life emits an odor that says something to people who either love being around you or would rather not be around you because you have become a reminder of what they are not living.

Anointed to Die to Your Self-Will

Dying to your flesh means that you don't want your own way. You have come to the place where you say as Jesus did in Gethsemane, "Not my will but Thy will be done, Father."[326] Your problem with fulfilling your anointing isn't primarily the devil. Your problem is your pride and self-will. Remember what Paul said:

"I am crucified with Christ: nevertheless I live; yet not I, but Christ liveth in me: and the life which I now live in the flesh I live by the faith of the Son of God, who loved me, and gave himself for me."[327]

Anointed as King

You are anointed as a king. When Saul proved himself unworthy to be king, God sent Samuel to find another king to replace him, and the sign that Samuel used to designate David as king was the anointing.

---

[325] 2 Corinthians 2:15-16 NLT.
[326] See Luke 22:42.
[327] Galatians 2:20 KJV.

Anointing a king for God

1 Samuel 16:1 NKJV

"Now the Lord said to Samuel, 'How long will you mourn for Saul, seeing I have rejected him from reigning over Israel? Fill your horn with oil, and go; I am sending you to Jesse the Bethlehemite. For I have provided Myself a king among his sons.'"

Anointed as Priest

The Bible says that we will be both kings and priests with Christ.[328] Aaron, as priest, had so much anointing oil poured over his head that it ran all the way down to his feet. God is extravagant about giving you the anointing. Aaron's anointing was only a type of what would come to us through Jesus Christ. Now all of us can serve as priests who are praying for ourselves, our families, and the world. The position of priest carried a tremendous responsibility for holiness. Any infraction of the laws, statutes, and ordinances would mean that God could kill you when you entered the Most Holy Place. Remind yourself of your need for holiness with the anointing before you go in to prayer.

Anointed for Unity in the Body of Christ

Priestly anointing for unity

Psalm 133:1-3 KJV

"Behold how good and pleasant it is for brethren to dwell together in unity! It is like the precious ointment upon the beard, even Aaron's beard: that went down to the skirts of his garments; As the dew of Hermon, and as the dew that descended upon the mountains of Zion: for there the Lord commanded the blessing,
even life forevermore."

The Bible relates Aaron's priestly anointing to the unity of God's people. When you anoint yourself, recommit yourself to the unity of the body of Christ, including those within your family and church.[329] When you anoint your body every day, you walk out a unified relationship with

[328] See Revelation 1:6.
[329] See Psalm 133:1-3. John 17:19-23.

other Christians. Every part of your body is as essential as every other part, and the same is true for the body of Christ. That takes death to self.

Throughout history, beginning with Pentecost, the Church has had moments when it really seemed possible that we could be unified. Azusa Street was one of them. So were the Cane Ridge camp meetings, the Welsh revival, and the Third Great Awakening. You have read about others in *A Man's Journey with God.* Why is it necessary 2,000 years after the resurrection for us to have reconciliation meetings? Why are we so divided? One of the problems is our unwillingness to die to our pride and our accustomed way of doing things and let God have His way.

Anointed for Supernatural Power

When Jesus said, *"The Spirit of the Lord* is *upon me because He hath anointed me,"*[330] the word "anointing" in Greek also means to smear. When you smear yourself daily with anointing oil it reminds you of the supernatural power of God within you. God is able to do exceeding abundantly above all that you can ask or think by the power that is at work within you.[331] The anointing represents what is happening to your spirit through Holy Ghost. This is a natural picture of a spiritual reality that is already true in heaven.

"Now unto him that is able to do exceeding abundantly above all that we ask or think, according to the power that worketh in us."[332]

Anoint yourself as a reminder that God said He would dwell in you. Your body is *"this dwelling where God lives by his Spirit."*[333] There is no telling what God might do through your life. You want every part anointed so that God can sanctify and use you. You anoint yourself daily because you are totally given over to your Friend, Holy Ghost.

[330] Luke 4:18 KJV.
[331] See Ephesians 3:20.
[332] Ephesians 3:20 KJV.
[333] Ephesians 2:22 NLT.

Anointed for Revival

In our generation, sometimes we focus so much on praying about our temporary needs that we forget the big picture of what God intended for us by giving us eternal life. We *look for* a revival, instead of *being* a revival. Revival means to bring back to life.

We need a reminder like the Eightfold Anointing to remember that God wants us to die to our earthly mentality and the domination of our flesh over our spirit, and bring us to life again in the eternal realm. We want to be restored to the place of fellowship where Adam was at the beginning of creation, before the Fall. He had a pure relationship with God that was restored through Christ.

Eight is the number for new beginnings and rebirth. On the next page are eight parts of your body to anoint daily:

Head. Mouth. Eyes. Ears. Nose. Hands. Feet. Body.

Words to Say with the Eightfold Anointing

Head. I anoint my head so that I will have the mind of Christ. 1 Corinthians 2:16. That I will mind spiritual things. Romans 8:5. That I will be transformed by the renewing of my mind. Romans 12:2; Ephesians 4:23. That my thoughts will be His thoughts and my ways will be His ways. Isaiah 55:8-9.

Mouth. I anoint my mouth for words of life because death and life are in the power of the tongue. Proverbs 18:21 KJV. With my mouth I shall decree a thing, and it shall be established. Job 22:28 KJV. I will speak no idle words, because Jesus said by my words I will be justified and by my words I will be condemned. Matthew 12:36-37 KJV. I anoint myself so that my words will be acceptable to God. Psalms 19:14. That they will bless, and not curse. That I will represent Jesus in what I say, but never *mis*represent Him. 2 Corinthians 5:20-21 That I will speak the Word and live the Word that I speak. James 2:14. That I will pray continually, 1 Thessalonians 5:17, so His presence will be always with me. John 15:7.

Eyes. I anoint my eyes so that I may have vision to see into the spirit world. That I may see the destiny of God. That I may see by revelation the will of God and the ways of God. That I will see what He sees from heaven. That I will see people not where they are, but where He has ordained them to be.

Ears. I anoint my ears so that they will be open to God. Psalm 40:6. That I will hear His voice. John 10:3. That my ears will be sensitive to spiritual things. [1] 1 Corinthians 2:13. That I will become pregnant in the womb of my ears with the seed of vision for myself, my family, and the generation. Isaiah 66:9.

Nose. I anoint my nose so that I will have discernment, wisdom, and judgment in my relationships with others and know what is right before the Lord. Christ is made unto me wisdom, and righteousness, and sanctification, and redemption. 1 Corinthians 1:30. If I lack wisdom, I will receive it from the Lord. James 1:5.

Hands. I anoint my hands that I might lay hands on others to bless and heal. Deuteronomy 10:8; 2 Samuel 6:20; Romans 12:14. That I might use my hands to anoint kings into office. 1 Samuel 16:13. That I might anoint the fivefold ministry into office. Ephesians 4:11-12.That I may work the works of Him that sent me, while it is day, because when the night comes, no man can work. John 9:4. That my work will bear fruit into eternity. Isaiah 37:31; John 15:4-5.

Feet. I anoint my feet that I might walk in the Spirit and not in the flesh. Galatians 5:16. That I may walk in His footsteps. 1 Peter 2:21. That I may walk with the weight of glory in my life. 2 Corinthians 4:17. That my footsteps might leave an imprint that the generation can follow and my walk would be pleasing to God, Colossians 1:10, in lowliness and meekness. Ephesians 4:1-2. That my life might be modeled after. 2 Thessalonians 3:9. That I would not walk in any place or destiny that is not ordained for me. That my walk and my lifestyle would take me into His perfect will forever. Colossians 1:9-10; Hebrews 13:21.

Body. I anoint my body, the temple of the Holy Spirit, for I am not my own. I was bought with a price. 1 Corinthians 6:19. Therefore I will glorify God in my body and in my spirit, which are God's. 1 Corinthians 6:20. I will fast and live a fasted lifestyle. Isaiah 58; Matthew 6:16-18; Mark 2:20.

I am anointed today to serve God and man, and to represent Jesus to the world! This is the day which the Lord has made. I will rejoice and be glad in it![334]

Anointed to Communicate Your Faith

"Next Moses took some of the anointing oil and some of the blood that was on the altar, and he sprinkled them on Aaron and his garments and on his sons and their garments. In this way, he made Aaron and his sons and their garments holy."[335]

Aaron and his sons were anointed for public ministry. His sons failed but they had the potential to please Him if they walked in holiness.

When you are anointed for holiness, creativity comes forth. Your emotions are turned into compassion. Your mind is anointed for new understanding. You are transformed by the renewing of your mind. You can think the thoughts of Jesus and communicate your faith openly.

"That the communication of thy faith may become effectual by the acknowledging of every good thing which is in you in Christ Jesus."[336]

My prayer for you. *Lord, I ask that those who take the time to practice this Eightfold Anointing daily will increase the holiness in their hearts. Let the anointing come upon them in a tangible way. Take them beyond just the letter of the law with its rules and practices and make their communion with you vital and real. In Jesus' name I pray. Amen.*

---

[334] See Psalm 118:24.
[335] Leviticus 8:30 NLT.
[336] Philemon 6 KJV.

Chapter 31

Personal Partaking of Communion

As a believer consecrating yourself, it is appropriate to partake of personal communion with the Lord. Communion is for believers, not the unsaved or unrepentant, lest they die.[337] Jesus said "as often as you do this." He will remind you of your union with Him and *koinonia* with Christians.

Greek Word for "Communion" also Means "Fellowship"	Koinonia *(Strong's number 2842) is the Greek word for "fellowship" in Acts 2:42 and "communion" in 1 Corinthians 10:16. It means partnership (including business relationships), mutual participation, social interaction, and mutual monetary benefit.*

Christ's Sufferings and Our Fellowship of Communion

"[T]he Lord's supper, like believers' baptism, is simplicity itself. It consists of bread broken, and wine poured out . . . a delightful picture of the sufferings of Christ for us, and of the fellowship which the saints have with one another and with Him. . . . As for the table, the very emblem of fellowship in all nations, for what expresses fellowship better than surrounding a table, and eating and drinking together?"[338]

Charles Spurgeon

(1834-1892)

[337] See 1 Corinthians 11.
[338] Charles Spurgeon, "Till He Come." Online source.

Biblical accounts of communion

Biblical accounts of the Last Supper and communion meals among Christians appear several times in the New Testament. The Passover meal that foreshadowed Jesus' death is referenced in the Old Testament. Jesus was the Passover Lamb of God, sacrificed for our sins, finishing the work that God gave Him to do in dying for us.

This is My Blood of the New Testament

Matthew 26:26-28 KJV

"And as they were eating, Jesus took bread, and blessed it, and brake it, and gave it to the disciples, and said, Take, eat; this is my body. And he took the cup, and gave thanks, and gave it to them, saying, Drink ye all of it; For this is my blood of the new testament, which is shed for many for the remission of sins."

Divine communion with God

As you read the following passage that comes from 1 Corinthians 11, meditate on the meaning of *divine communion*. The following is from the *Message* version of Paul's letter. Since the version is not as familiar as what is usually spoken over the elements in a church service, you may be able to give it fresh thought.

"Let me go over with you again exactly what goes on in the Lord's Supper and why it is so centrally important. I received my instructions from the Master himself and passed them on to you. The Master, Jesus, on the night of his betrayal, took bread. Having given thanks, he broke it and said,

"This is my body, broken for you.
Do this to remember me.

"After supper, he did the same thing with the cup:

"This cup is my blood, my new covenant with you.
Each time you drink this cup, remember me.

"What you must solemnly realize is that every time you eat this bread and every time you drink this cup, you reenact in your words and actions the death of the Master.

You will be drawn back to this meal again and again until the Master returns. You must never let familiarity breed contempt.

"Anyone who eats the bread or drinks the cup of the Master irreverently is like part of the crowd that jeered and spit on him at his death. Is that the kind of "remembrance" you want to be part of? Examine your motives, test your heart, come to this meal in holy awe.

"If you give no thought (or worse, don't care) about the broken body of the Master when you eat and drink, you're running the risk of serious consequences. That's why so many of you even now are listless and sick, and others have gone to an early grave. If we get this straight now, we won't have to be straightened out later on. Better to be confronted by the Master now than to face a fiery confrontation later."[339]

Eat His flesh and drink His blood

Jesus said that "he that eateth Me, even he shall live by Me."[340] There is a difference between *using* Jesus and *partaking* of Him just as there is a difference between *becoming* the substance of the Scriptures vs. *using* the Scriptures for your own agenda. When you eat the communion bread and drink the communion wine, you are partaking of the divine thinking and godly ways of the Lord. You are becoming like Him.

As you eat off His nature and become like Christ, people will live off what you believe. They will eat off your godly presuppositions and take into themselves your foundational thinking. They will partake of the way you live your life and become more like Christ, even as you are becoming more like Him.

When you are a consecrated Christian who eats the life of God and the principles of God and lives off of them, other people can see the

[339] 1 Corinthians 11:23-32, *The Message*. Bold emphasis added.
[340] John 6:57 KJV.

ways of the Lord through you. You do not have to pound them with your theology. You do not have to debate with them. They are caught up into your life and godliness. They receive life from you to live by.

Blessed, Broken, and Distributed

When Jesus blessed the bread, He said, "Take, eat; this is My body."[341] We also are His body. He blesses us. In Christ, the goal of God is to bless us, not to kill or condemn us. After Jesus blessed the bread, His body, then He broke it. He made it distributable. He gave Himself in brokenness to the whole world.

You are His body. He blesses you and then breaks you of your selfishness so that He can give you away. You are blessed for a reason greater than personal pleasure. You are blessed so that God can give you away to meet the needs of the world.

When you are blessed but unbroken, you keep the blessings for yourself instead of using yourself, your influence, ability, and your wealth for His purposes—those purposes that establish His covenant on the earth.[342] If God gives you a new house and you refuse to allow people to come inside who are not at your level, you are blessed but unbroken. If you don't give yourself in service to your church and your community, you are unbroken.

Gratitude—*Eucharist*. The Greek word *eucharisteo* (Strong's #2168) in the communion Scriptures of Luke 22 and 1 Corinthians 11 means giving thanks and expressing gratitude, as in grace at a meal.

"And he took the cup, and gave thanks."[343]

[341] Matthew 26:26 NKJV.
[342] See Deuteronomy 8:18.
[343] Luke 22:17 KJV.

Selected Communion Scriptures

Remembering Jesus and His death through communion. Luke 22:19; 1 Corinthians 11:24-26

Bread of life, Bread of heaven. John 6:35, 48-58

Breaking of bread by early church. Acts 2:42, 46; 20:7, 11

Cup of blessing, Communion of body and blood. 1 Corinthians 10:16

Death penalty for unworthy partaking of communion. 1 Corinthians 11:27-32

Eat Jesus' flesh and drink His blood. John 6:48-58

Examine yourself. 1 Corinthians 11:28-29. Literally, "prove" or "test" yourself, and partake of communion in a worthy manner.

Jesus' last supper before He was crucified. Matthew 26:17-30; Mark 14:12-26; Luke 22:1-23; John 13-17; 1 Corinthians 11:23-25

Communion of the blood of Christ and communion of the body of Christ. 1 Corinthians 10:16. *Greek word for communion, which also means fellowship, is* koinonia.

Lamb of God. John 1:29, 36. *John the Baptist's identification of Jesus as Lamb of God, God's sacrifice for the sin of the world.*

Lord's Supper. 1 Corinthians 11:20

Lord's Table. 1 Corinthians 10:21

New wine. Matthew 26:29 KJV. *"But I say unto you, I will not drink henceforth of this fruit of the vine, until that day when I drink it new with you in my Father's kingdom" (Matthew 26:29 KJV).*

Passover; Feast of Unleavened Bread. Exodus 12:1-13:16; Numbers 9:1-14; Leviticus 23:4-14; Deuteronomy 16:1-8. *Hebrew slaves in Egypt smeared lamb's blood on their doorposts so God would "pass over" their houses and spare them when He destroyed all the firstborn sons of Egypt. They ate unleavened bread because there was no time for the bread to rise before their escape.*

Christ, our Passover. 1 Corinthians 5:7; 11:26

Unleavened bread used at Passover. Matthew 16:6, 12; 1 Corinthians 5:6-8. *Leaven also symbolizes sin; no leaven, sinlessness.*

Humility—examining yourself. Before you take communion, you examine yourself to determine if you can approve yourself as worthy to partake of communion.

"So anyone who eats this bread or drinks this cup of the Lord unworthily is guilty of sinning against the body and blood of the Lord. That is why you should examine yourself before eating the bread and drinking the cup. For if you eat the bread or drink the cup without honoring the body of Christ, you are eating and drinking God's judgment upon yourself. That is why many of you are weak and sick and some have even died."[344]

Brokenness of Total Surrender

Brokenness deals with your total surrender to God's will. God insists that you become like His Son. That is how you become truly blessed and broken and others can eat off your life. Jesus gave Himself, was broken, and then He was given away. The substance of His life was so valuable that people are still eating off Him today.

We being many are one bread, and one body

1 Corinthians 10:14-17 KJV

"I speak as to wise men; judge ye what I say. The cup of blessing which we bless, is it not the communion of the blood of Christ? The bread which we break, is it not the communion of the body of Christ? For we being many are one bread, and one body: for we are all partakers of that one bread."

Many of the problems of Christians come not because they are not blessed but because they are not broken.

[344] 1 Corinthians 11:27-30 NLT.

Chapter 32

Fasting for Results

". . . but the days will come, when the bridegroom shall be taken from them, and then shall they fast." [345]

Dramatic results occur in earth as in heaven through the prayer and fasting of consecrated people. Consecrated people both pray and fast. Jesus fasted and He expected His disciples to fast.

Jesus said, ***". . . then shall they fast."*** *Matthew 9:15 KJV*	*"And Jesus said unto them, Can the children of the bridechamber mourn, as long as the bridegroom is with them? but the days will come, when the bridegroom shall be taken from them, and then shall they fast."*

Fasting brings results that are measurable. It increases the results of your prayers on behalf of your own needs and also your prayers on behalf of others.

In fastings often (Paul) *1 Corinthians 11:27 KJV*	*". . . in watchings often, in hunger and thirst, in fastings often."*

When you make a commitment not to eat, whether it is one meal, one day, or a week or more, and you make it through, you gain a satisfying sense of accomplishment in addition to any results you see from your prayers. Especially when you go on an extended fast, you become full of faith for what God can do for you supernaturally.

[345]Matthew 9:15 KJV.

Covenant of sacrifice

Psalm 50:5 KJV

"Gather my saints together unto me; those that have made a covenant with me by sacrifice."

In fasting you die to your self-will and stop accommodating the desires of the flesh. It takes God to help you not to eat, because your body is designed to demand food. When you deny that demand for a higher purpose, you receive a breakthrough in your spiritual life.

Fasting for Results

- Increase the quality and quantity of your prayer life.
- Dedicate yourself more fully to God.
- Seek higher levels of consecration.
- Study the Scriptures with a new intensity.
- Fulfill spiritual disciplines; seek God for new ones.
- Build spiritual strength privately, as God shows you.
- Overcome cravings that usually control your life.
- Focus on areas of personal spiritual change.
- Record specific, measurable goals for your fast on behalf of yourself and others.
- Record the results of your fast in the areas of your goals.
- Record unexpected but gratifying results of your fast.

Biblical Models of Fasting

On the next few pages are some examples of fasting from the Scriptures.

Jesus expected His disciples to fast[346]

Jesus said, "And <u>when</u> you fast *Matthew 6:16-18 NLT*	*"And when you fast, don't make it obvious, as the hypocrites do, for they try to look miserable and disheveled so people will admire them for their fasting. I tell you the truth, that is the only reward they will ever get. But when you fast, comb your hair and wash your face. Then no one will notice that you are fasting, except your Father, who knows what you do in private. And your Father, who sees everything, will reward you.*

Jesus fasted in the wilderness[347]

Before the onslaught of temptation from the devil, Jesus fasted.

Jesus ate nothing *Luke 4:1-2 NKJV*	*"Then Jesus, being filled with the Holy Spirit, returned from the Jordan and was led by the Spirit into the wilderness, being tempted for forty days by the devil. And in those days He ate nothing, and afterward, when they had ended, He was hungry."*

Jesus said that fasting drives out unbelief

Unbelief comes out through fasting *Matthew 17:19-21 KJV*	*"Then came the disciples to Jesus apart, and said, Why could not we cast him out? And Jesus said unto them, Because of your unbelief: for verily I say unto you, If ye have faith as a grain of mustard seed, ye shall say unto this mountain, Remove hence to yonder place; and it shall remove; and nothing shall be impossible unto you. Howbeit this kind goeth not out but by prayer and fasting."*

---

[346] See also parallel passages in Mark 2:19-20 and Luke 5:34-35.
[347] Matthew 4:2; Luke 4:2.

Daniel fasted from defiled food of the king

Daniel would not defile himself *Daniel 1:8 KJV*	*"But Daniel purposed in his heart that he would not defile himself with the portion of the king's meat, nor with the wine which he drank: therefore he requested of the prince of the eunuchs that he might not defile himself."*

Daniel fasted for revelation

Supplications with fasting *Daniel 9:3 KJV*	*"And I set my face unto the Lord God, to seek by prayer and supplications, with fasting, and sackcloth, and ashes."*

Daniel maintained his fast until the breakthrough

Spiritual powers hindered God's messenger until Daniel had prayed and fasted for 21 days.

21-day fast of Daniel *Daniel 10:12-14 KJV*	*"Then said he unto me, Fear not, Daniel: for from the first day that thou didst set thine heart to understand, and to chasten thyself before thy God, thy words were heard, and I am come for thy words. But the prince of the kingdom of Persia withstood me one and twenty days."*

Fasting for others was a normal part of early church life

Prayed with fasting, commending them to the Lord *Acts 14:23 KJV*	*"And when they had ordained them elders in every church, and had prayed with fasting, they commended them to the Lord on whom they believed."*

Fasting from sexual relations is a joint sacrifice by married couples

Consenting to abstinence during a time of fasting *1 Corinthians 7:5 KJV*	*"Do not deprive each other of sexual relations, unless you both agree to refrain from sexual intimacy for a limited time so you can give yourselves more completely to prayer. Afterward, you should come together again so that Satan won't be able to tempt you because of your lack of self-control."*

Restricting television and entertainment

It will be difficult for you to consecrate yourself if you feed yourself on television and movies during times of fasting. During your fast, try to look at all of the ways you spend your time and become more conscious of where you need to make adjustments.

Following your conscience and convictions

The precise details of your fast are between you and God. In Romans 14, the apostle Paul describes how we should relate in love to one another in the matter of what we eat or choose not to eat. He says, "Each person is free to follow the convictions of his own conscience."[348] If this is your first fast, you may not be able to endure as many restrictions as someone else who fasts frequently. In the future, live a "fasted lifestyle," increasingly accommodating God and not the flesh.

Make no provision for the flesh *Romans 13:14 NLT*	*"Instead, clothe yourself with the presence of the Lord Jesus Christ. And don't let yourself think about ways to indulge your evil desires."*

[348] Romans 14, *The Message*.

An End Result of Fasting—Changed by Humility

Fasting is a sacrifice that shows how dedicated you are to following the will of God. It is a voluntary step of humility, a very simple one that demonstrates you are not going to carry on business-as-usual. You want to be numbered among those whom God considers His saints who are in covenant with Him by sacrifice.

"But when Ahab heard this message, he tore his clothing, dressed in burlap, and fasted. He even slept in burlap and went about in deep mourning.
"Then another message from the Lord came to Elijah: 'Do you see how Ahab has humbled himself before me? Because he has done this, I will not do what I promised during his lifetime. It will happen to his sons; I will destroy his dynasty.'"

1 Kings 21:27-29 NLT

The prophet Huldah (a woman) sent a message to King Josiah that God was pleased with his humility and repentance:

King Josiah humbled himself before the Lord and He heard him
2 Kings 22:19 NLT

"You were sorry and humbled yourself before the Lord when you heard what I said against this city and its people—that this land would be cursed and become desolate. You tore your clothing in despair and wept before me in repentance. And I have indeed heard you, says the Lord."

Daniel Fast (21-Day Vegetable Fast)

Included in the Daniel Fast

- Vegetables, preferably fresh or frozen vegetables. Vegetables such as potatoes, beans, and soybeans will help provide substance.
- Nuts
- Pure fruit juices or fruit (no sweetened drinks or sweetened fruit): apple juice, orange juice, grapefruit juice, cranberry juice
- It is advisable to take vitamin, mineral, and possibly protein supplements.

Not included in the Daniel Fast

- Sugar and sugar products (desserts, soft drinks, heavily sweetened foods, etc.)
- Drinks containing caffeine (coffee, tea, etc.)
- Bread, grains, and rice
- Meats, fish, poultry, dairy products, eggs

Water

Drink 8 glasses of water daily throughout the fast. This is very important.

Side effects

You may experience moderate to severe headaches for the first day or two as your body rids itself of caffeine, salt, sugar, and various impurities. You may need to take an analgesic for pain such as aspirin, acetaminophen, or ibuprofen.

Important reasons you may need to modify your fast

Anyone with a medical condition related to eating or under the treatment of a physician must consult their doctor. Children, especially small children, will have special needs that must be considered. Under these conditions, find some sacrifice in the area of food that can be made without endangering health. Also, if you have extreme difficulty with the fast, such as impairment of your ability to work at your job, you will have to make adjustments. This is not a failure of will but is wisdom. Seek the Lord and discuss it with other Christians involved in the fast to find alternatives.

Chapter 33

Westminster Shorter Catechism

This excerpt is similar to the creeds that show how Christians have historically defined their faith in the form of sound doctrine. It was originally written in 17th-century England and Scotland but the questions and answers are still worth knowing today.

Question 1. What is the chief end of man?
Answer 1. Man's chief end is to glorify God and to enjoy Him for ever.

Question 2. What rule hath God given to direct us how we may glorify and enjoy Him?
Answer 2. The Word of God, which is contained in the Scriptures of the Old and New Testaments, is the only rule to direct us how we may glorify and enjoy Him.

Question 3. What do the Scriptures principally teach?
Answer 3. The Scriptures principally teach what man is to believe concerning God, and what duty God requires of man.

Question 4. What is God?
Answer 4. God is a Spirit, infinite, eternal, and unchangeable, in his being, wisdom, power, holiness, justice, goodness, and truth.

Question 5. Are there more Gods than one?
Answer 5. There is but one only, the living and true God.

Question 6. How many persons are there in the Godhead?
Answer 6. There are three persons in the Godhead; the Father, the Son, and the Holy Ghost, and these three are one God, the same in substance, equal in power and glory.

Question 7. What are the decrees of God?

Answer 7. The decrees of God are, his eternal purpose, according to the counsel of his will, whereby, for his own glory, he hath fore-ordained whatsoever comes to pass.

Question 8. How doth God execute his decrees?

Answer 8. God executeth his decrees in the works of creation and providence.

Question 9. What is the work of creation?

Answer 9. The work of creation is, God's making all things of nothing, by the word of his power, in the space of six days, and all very good.

Question 10. How did God create man?

Answer 10. God created man male and female, after his own image, in knowledge, righteousness, and holiness, with dominion over the creatures.

Question 11. What are God's works of providence?

Answer 11. God's works of providence are, his most holy, wise, and powerful preserving and governing all his creatures, and all their actions.

Question 12. What special act of providence did God exercise toward man in the estate wherein he was created?

Answer 12. When God had created man, he entered into a covenant of life with him, upon condition of perfect obedience; forbidding him to eat of the tree of the knowledge of good and evil, upon the pain of death.

Question 13. Did our first parents continue in the estate wherein they were created?

Answer 13. Our first parents, being left to the freedom of their own will, fell from the estate wherein they were created, by sinning against God.

Question 14. What is sin?

Answer 14. Sin is any want of conformity unto, or transgression of, the law of God.

Question 15. What was the sin whereby our first parents fell from the estate wherein they were created?

Answer 15. The sin whereby our first parents fell from the estate wherein they were created was their eating the forbidden fruit.

Question 16. Did all mankind fall in Adam's first transgression?
Answer 16. The covenant being made with Adam, not only for himself, but for his posterity; all mankind, descending from him by ordinary generation, sinned in him, and fell with him, in his first transgression.

Question 17. Into what estate did the fall bring mankind?
Answer 17. The fall brought mankind into an estate of sin and misery.

Question 18. Wherein consists the sinfulness of that estate whereinto man fell?
Answer 18. The sinfulness of that estate whereinto man fell, consists in the guilt of Adam's first sin, the want of original righteousness, and the corruption of his whole nature, which is commonly called Original Sin; together with all actual transgressions which proceed from it.

Question 19. What is the misery of that estate whereinto man fell?
Answer 19. All mankind by their fall lost communion with God, are under his wrath and curse, and so made liable to all miseries in this life, to death itself, and to the pains of hell for ever.

Question 20. Did God leave all mankind to perish in the estate of sin and misery?
Answer 20. God having, out of his mere good pleasure, from all eternity, elected some to everlasting life, did enter into a covenant of grace, to deliver them out of the estate of sin and misery, and to bring them into an estate of salvation by a Redeemer.

Question 21. Who is the Redeemer of God's elect?
Answer 21. The only Redeemer of God's elect is the Lord Jesus Christ.[349]

[349] Scripture sources plus additional questions and answers in the Westminster Catechism and Westminster Confession are online at several websites.

PERSONAL NOTES

Section 5

Resources and Index

Resources[350]

Books by Wellington Boone

A Man's Journey with God: Your personal accountability journal . . . between you and God takes men on a supernatural journey toward Christ-likeness. Using examples from great Christian men of the past, it increases your passion for knowing God and a newfound pleasure in pleasing Him, both now and in eternity. The coaching system in the 30-day journal provides practical daily exercises to grow in Christ. Inspiring stories; personal consecration; prayer and fasting guidelines; daily journaling; scheduling decisions; money management; and 24-hour accountability between you and God. Provides web links to resources, footnotes, evangelism instruction, annotated Index, Scriptures, and aggressive application of the Bible to marriage, family, church, civil government, and society. (Atlanta: APPTE Publishing, 2016). ISBN 13: 978-0984782178. Trade paper. $25.

Basic Black Journal—A Biblical Perspective on Black American History. This publication brings a biblical perspective to the historical triumphs and tragedies of Black Americans. Because of Jesus Christ and the historical role of the Church, it speaks of hope and the winds of change. Magazine format. Stitched. $7.00.

Breaking Through: Taking the Kingdom into the Culture by Out-Serving Others. The author writes, "For many Christians it would be an embarrassing moment if God called us to heaven for a spiritual evaluation." Contains profound insights into why most Americans say they believe in God yet are often unable to live godly lives among their friends and family. Historical vignettes. (Nashville: Broadman and Holman, 1996). ISBN 0-8054-5396-2. Hardback $20.00. Trade paper $10.00.

Dare to Hope: A 30-Day Journey to Hope. In Lamentations 3:21, Jeremiah was troubled but he said, "Yet I still dare to hope." Bishop Boone takes the reader on a 30-day journey to hope. Each day, you read inspiring vignettes, study the Bible, pray, and write in a journal. Pleasing God becomes your priority. You are preparing for that Great Day when you will be ready to hear God say "Well done" when you have sought His approval every day. (Atlanta: APPTE Publishing, 2012). ISBN: 978-0-9776892-8-6.

[350] **Website:** http://wellingtonboone.com; many resources are also available at www.Amazon.com.

Paperback $15.00. ***Hope Every Morning,*** based on this book, is a 30-day devotional with inspiring insights without the daily journal.

Holy Ghost Is My Friend: A Great Friend Who Must Never Be Ignored *Again,* a revolutionary new way to understand our relationship with God. Jesus left behind a Comforter, the Holy Spirit, or Holy Ghost, as He is called in the King James Version of the Bible, to take His place with the disciples. Bishop Boone wrote this book to help Christians develop their Friendship with the Holy Ghost, whom Bishop Boone calls the most ignored Person of the Trinity. Commentary on the Baptism with the Holy Ghost. 500 footnotes for personal study. Special Appendix with 272 Bible passages about the Holy Spirit. Christian Creeds defining and affirming the Deity of the Holy Spirit. (Atlanta: APPTE Publishing, 2011). ISBN-13: 9780984782109 Trade Paper. $15.00. Kindle $7.99.

Low Road to New Heights: What It Takes to Live Like Christ in the Here and Now is a proclaimed leadership guide that takes readers beyond success to significance. It teaches you how to think and act like Jesus by taking the low road of humility. It elevates those who are battered by discouragement, feel the sting of failure, and hunger for more of God. The daily practice of humility frees Christians to trust God enough to obey Him, to grow in spiritual maturity, to serve others, and to help lead others to Christ. (New York, NY: Doubleday, 2002). ISBN: 0-385-50087-4. Trade cloth. $20.00.

A Man's Journey with God— Men's training program for Christ-like authority. God said, "And I sought for a man among them, that should make up the hedge, and stand in the gap before me for the land, that I should not destroy it: but I found none" (Ezekiel 22:30 KJV). God is disappointed with men but he still says, "I sought for a man among them." You may be a long way from God but that doesn't mean He isn't seeking you. Scriptures, heroes of faith, timeline, footnotes, history of Church. Practical theology for living by faith and power. Includes a personal journal of 30 straight days of private consecration. (Atlanta: APPTE Publishing—ManHunt Ed., 2016). ISBN: 9780984782154. Trade paper. $25.00.

Women Are Kingmakers! Bishop Boone says boldly that women have been undervalued in our culture, but "God, the same One who gave man his purpose and value, also gave value and purpose to the woman." He chose the title Kingmakers because a woman has the ability to make others great. A Kingmaker is a lifter. She carries people higher from a position of humility—a position of lowliness. Bishop Boone says, "That's something Jesus does. I want to honor those who are like Jesus." Themes include faith, marriage, raising great children, family relationships, professional success, hospitality. (Revised ed. APPTE Publishing 2012). ISBN: 978-0-9847821-6-1. Trade paper. 235 pages. $15.00. www.Kingmakers.org.

Your Wife Is Not Your Momma: How You Can Have Heaven In Your Home. This book that wives love to buy for their husbands includes hilarious, thought-provoking biblical concepts for a brand new married life. It emphasizes the importance of husbands having Jesus as their First Love. It shows men how to go all out for their wives and develop a home-court advantage for their family. In-laws get vital insight about their roles. Singles find a checklist for choosing a mate. Divorced people see how to make it work the next time, Prayers, Bible-based teaching, challenging assignments and meditations, real-life examples and applications. Marriage is your most important preparation for the future! (Revised ed. Atlanta: APPTE Publishing, 2011). ISBN: 978-0-9776892-9-3. Trade paper. $15.00.

Your Journey with God. Originally published in 2002 at half the size, this book has been effective in transforming lives from lukewarm Christian attitudes to serious commitment to Christ and Christ-like consecration in the Christian life. It is built on multitudes of Scripture quotes and an inspirational history of the victories of the Christian church. Characterized by practical theology for living by faith and power. Includes a personal journal of 30 straight days of private consecration. If you miss a day, you start over again until you can complete 30 straight days. (Revised ed. Atlanta: APPTE Publishing, 2015). 464 pages. ISBN 13: 978-0984782178 Trade paper. $25.00.

What Others Are Saying about Wellington Boone

"This is an incredible man of God. Every time I'm in the presence of this guy, I sense two things. This is a man who is truly a man of tremendous faith and he's a man who is truly fearless. When I say a man who is fearless, this is a black man who is not afraid of any white man or what any white man thinks and even more than that, he's not afraid of any black man or what any black man thinks. He truly is a man called by God to speak today to issues that need to be addressed."

Bill McCartney—Co-founder, Promise Keepers
Former University of Colorado and Hall of Fame football coach

"First of all, the heart of your message that godly leadership rises out of Christian character is spot on. There is a great need for this teaching to be shared throughout Africa. . . . Second, I find a 'kingdom grace' in a Black American returning to the land of his forefathers with a powerful message of commitment to Christ and godly living."

Former Anglican Archbishop of Uganda Henry Orombi, a world leader in the Anglican Church

"This is not the prayer of superficial reconciliation, it is the kind of stuff which brings change to nations."

The Rt. Rev. Dr. Bill Atwood, GAFCON Ambassador

"If we truly understand these precepts and put them into practice, we will see revival. I join with Wellington Boone in his prayer that God would not let this generation pass without bringing his visitation to us."

Gordon Robertson, CEO of the Christian Broadcasting Network, Co-host of television's "The 700 Club"

"I appreciate the God-given vision of Wellington Boone. He is a man of conviction and passion for the Gospel of Jesus Christ."

Franklin Graham, President, Billy Graham Evangelistic Association and Samaritan's Purse

"Wellington epitomizes the phrase, 'Fall on the rock and be broken.' Only through brokenness can the fragrance fill the room."

Ricky Skaggs—Recording artist

Endorsing the book *Low Road to New Heights* by Wellington Boone

"The cry of Wellington Boone's heart is to help people follow the pathway to fruitfulness. That passion shines through from the first paragraph to the end of this exciting and thoughtful book,"

Tommy Barnett, Senior Pastor, Phoenix First Assembly reviewing Low Road to New Heights

"*The Low Road to New Heights* sets us on the path of humility, which is the heart of authentic Christianity."

Dr. John M. Perkins, President, John M. Perkins Foundation for Reconciliation & Development

"In *The Low Road to New Heights*, Wellington Boone reminds us of the importance of being liberated from self-absorption. May we all be challenged to become like Jesus, who came to serve, not to be served."

James Robison, Life Outreach International, TV co-host of "Life Today"

"Wellington Boone speaks to a generation with words that pierce to the heart of the matter. The power of his message comes from the depths of his commitment to Christ and to those he addresses."

Ben Kinchlow, Former co-host, "The 700 Club"

"America's need today is for revival that comes from fasting, prayer and seeking God's face. Wellington Boone is modeling and preaching this mandatory message."

Bill Bright, late founder of Campus Crusade for Christ

Endorsing the book *Your Wife Is Not Your Momma—How You Can Have Heaven In Your Home* by Wellington Boone (APPTE Publishing)

"It's got transforming power!"

James Robison, Host of "Life Today" television program

"Boone (*Breaking Through*), a nationally recognized pastor and speaker at Promise Keeper rallies, paints an engaging portrait of God's master plan for marriage relationships. The message is simple and, although directed at husbands, is for everyone, married couples, singles and divorcees. Foremost, we need to know who we are in God, and from that we can conclude who we are to be in our marriage."

Publisher's Weekly

Endorsing the book *Breaking Through—Taking the Kingdom into the Culture by Out-Serving Others* by Wellington Boone

"Wellington Boone has written a passionate, courageous and inspiring book."

Bill McCartney, Co-Founder of Promise Keepers

Former University of Colorado and Hall of Fame football coach

"*Breaking Through* is a must-read for anyone striving to be in right relationship with God and neighbor. No other recent book addresses with such clarity and conviction the importance and strength of being a yielded instrument before God and a wiling servant before our brothers in Christ." *New Man Magazine*

PERSONAL NOTES

Illustrations

Portraits (original art work by Avery Sean Bush) are noted above by shading.

Index

A. D. (from the Latin words *Anno Domini* that mean "In the year of our Lord"), 12, 39, 129, 264, 265. All of human history is divided into only two periods: B. C. (Before Christ) and A. D. Note that the pagan "CE" (Common Era) dating system denies the pivotal events of Christ's death, burial, and resurrection. CE dating recalls the Scripture that says, "When they heard Paul speak about the resurrection of the dead, some laughed in contempt, but others said, 'We want to hear more about this later.' That ended Paul's discussion with them, but some joined him and became believers" (Acts 17:32-34 KJV).

Abolition of slavery, 14, 89, 90, 124, 137, 138, 155, 250. See also Barnes, Gilbert H. *The Anti-Slavery Impulse 1830-1844* (New York: Harcourt, Brace & World Inc., 1933) for an historical perspective on how the Christian faith motivated those who dedicated themselves to the defeat of slavery in America.

Abortion, 14

Abraham (Abram), 72, 81, 160, 164, 275

Accountability and Accountability Journal, 16, 18, 19, 50, 136, 184, 185, 186, 190, 233, 236, 237, 276, 278, 283, 316-406, 434, 435. See also *Dare to Hope* by Wellington Boone (Atlanta: APPTE Publishing, 2012).

Adam, Adamic Nature, 57, 58, 59, 61, 62, 74, 75, 76, 141, 151, 194, 197, 211, 282, 294, 313,

Adams, John Quincy, 89

Aikman, David, 156. He is a Professor of History and Writer-in-Residence at Patrick Henry College, a Christian liberal arts college in Virginia. He is also a Christian journalist and former senior correspondent for *Time Magazine*. His book *Great Souls—Six Who Changed the Century* (Nashville: Word Publishing, 1998) includes biographies of Billy Graham, Mother Teresa, Aleksandr Solzhenitsyn, Pope John Paul II, Elie Wiesel, and Nelson Mandela.

Allen, Richard (1760-1831), 13, 111, 215, 216, 220, 237

Amazing Grace (song and film), 107, 119

American Missionary Association, 14, 89, 90, 91, 155

American Revolution (13) and American history from a biblical perspective are included throughout this book. See also Peter Marshall and David Manuel, *Light and the Glory* (Grand Rapids, Michigan: Fleming H. Revell, a division of Baker Books, 1977). See also Providence Foundation, Charlottesville, Virginia (founded by Mark Beliles and Stephen McDowell). "The Providence Foundation is a Christian educational organization whose purpose is to spread liberty, justice, and prosperity among the nations by instructing people in a Biblical philosophy of life."

American Sunday School Union, 13, 90

Amistad slave mutiny (1839), 13, 89, 91, . The Amistad Research Center on the Tulane University campus contains manuscripts for the study of ethnic history, culture, and race relations in the United States from that era to the present.

"And Can It Be that I Should Gain?" (hymn by Charles Wesley, 1738), 65

Anoint, Anointed, Anointing, 18, 24, 78, 279, 287-296, 316-404, 410, 417

Anointing, Eightfold, 18, 24, 287-296, 316-404, 410, 417

Apostle, 152, 158, 164, 173, 264, 267, 307, 418

Apostles' Creed (200-900 A.D.), 12, 264

Asbury, Francis (1745-1816), 13, 108-111, 116, 215, 216. See also George Preston Mains, *Francis Asbury* (1909). Available in Google Books. See also resources at Asbury University.

Assemblies Of God, 14, 102, 103

Athanasian Creed (c. 500 A.D.), 12, 265-266

Awakening 12, 13, 14, 29, 31, 33-42, 61, 66, 126, 133, 134, 293.

First Great Awakening (18th century). Led by pastors. Key figures were Theodore Frelinghuysen in New Jersey, Jonathan Edwards, George Whitefield, Francis Asbury. Prepared the nation spiritually for the American Revolution.

Second Great Awakening (early 19th century). Led by pastors. Key figures were Charles Finney, James McGready and Barton Stone and others in the camp meeting movement, Methodist circuit riders. Characterized by social action such as the abolition of slavery as well as evangelism and miraculous manifestations.

Third Great Awakening (mid-19th century). Led first by laymen such as Jeremiah Lanphier and businessmen at New York City prayer meetings. Pastors included Henry Ward Beecher. Prelude to American Civil War.

See also John Dawson, *Taking Our Cities for God* (Lake City, Florida: Charisma House, updated ed. 2002). Spiritual warfare and practical steps Christians can take to win their cities to Jesus Christ.

Azusa Street, 14, 100, 101, 102, 103, 194, 126, 293

Baptist, 12, 34, 41, 62, 89, 100, 117, 163, 165, 168, 218, 301, 417

Barnabas, 62

Bartleman, Frank (1871-1936), 101, 104. Unofficial historian of Azusa Street Revival. Several of his writings are available online at the Christian Classics Ethereal Library, www.ccel.org.

Beecher, Henry Ward (1813-1887), 13, 35. Congregational pastor, one of leaders of Second Great Awakening and activist for the abolition of slavery. He was famous for his leadership in abolition activity in "Bleeding Kansas." Abraham Lincoln sent him to Europe during the Civil War where he was effective in winning support for the Union over the Confederacy. Brother of Harriet Beecher Stowe (*Uncle Tom's Cabin*) and son of Lyman Beecher.

Beecher, Lyman (1775-1863), 13, 139, 140. He was a leading Calvinist Congregational and Presbyterian pastor and Christian reformer during the Second Great Awakening and the abolition of slavery. He also served as president of Lane Seminary. His children were also leading activists, including Henry Ward Beecher and Harriet Beecher Stowe, author of *Uncle Tom's Cabin*.

Benevolent Empire, 13, 89, 90, 138

Bible. The primary resource for all Christians for all time is the Holy Bible. The versions used in *A Man's Journey with God* are as follows: KJV *King James Version*, also known as the Authorized Version (1604-1611). NKJV *New King James Version*. NLT *New Living Translation*. *The Message*. (See reverse side of Title Page for copyright information.)

Bible Concordances. A standard reference book for finding where a word or verse is located in the King James Bible is *Strong's Concordance*, completed more than a century ago. Other concordances have been created for other versions of the Bible. Some citations in this book cite Strong's numbers in the Old Testament (Hebrew) and New Testament (Greek).

Bible resources. American Bible Society provides Bibles for sale individually or in cases at reduced prices. Bible Gateway: online at http://biblegateway.com/ offers multiple versions and languages in text and audio online. Biblos: online at http://biblehub.com also has many versions, translations, and study tools. Kindle and other e-versions of the Bible are available from www.Amazon.com and many other sources. Some Kindle versions and Adobe Acrobat have a text-to-speech feature that will read the Bible aloud to you as you read the text.

Biblical perspective or biblical worldview, see "Worldview"

Black America, 12-14, 26, 91, 99, 100, 101, 102, 103, 104, 111, 124, 138, 154, 155, 215, 216, 282, 434, 436. Some resources used in the preparation of this book include the following: *Breaking Through* by Wellington Boone (Nashville: Broadman and Holman, 1996). Association for the Study of African American Life and History, *International Library of Negro Life and History* (New York: Publishers Company, Inc., 1969). See also the exhibit "The African-American Mosaic" at the Library of Congress website, http://www.loc.gov. Thomas Sowell, *Ethnic America—A History* (New York: Basic Books, 1981). James Melvin Washington, *Conversations with God, Two Centuries of Prayers by African Americans* (New York: HarperCollins Publishers, Inc., 1994). John Dawson. *Healing America's Wounds* (Ventura, California: Regal Books, 1994). Raleigh Washington, Glen Kehrein, and Claude V. King, *Break Down the Walls: Experiencing Biblical Reconciliation and Unity in the Body of Christ* (Chicago: Moody Press, 1997), a study guide for groups to work through issues of reconciliation together.

Blackstone, William (1723-1780), 12, 136

Blood of Jesus, 53, 65, 73, 82, 83, 101, 102, 115, 116, 119, 120, 121, 122, 153, 230, 289, 290, 298, 299, 301, 302, 331

Booth, William (1829-1912), 13, 14, 67-69, 223. Founder of the Salvation Army. Wrote *In Darkest England and the Way Out* (Atlanta: Salvation Army, 1984). Originally published in 1890, this book gives his vision for redeeming people's lives—body, soul, and spirit. Online at Project Gutenberg.

Born Again, 52, 61, 75, 85, 86, 90, 93, 132, 144, 194, 211, 224, 237, 245, 266, 417

Boston, Massachusetts, 35, 91, 124, 139, 140, 253

Brainerd, David (1718-1747), 12, 36-42, 50, 129, 134, 191. Missionary to Native Americans. *The Life and Diary of the Rev. David Brainerd* by Jonathan Edwards (1703-1758) is available online at Christian Classics Ethereal Library, www.ccel.org. Edwards, a great American theologian, edited Brainerd's journal after Brainerd died in the Edwards home in 1747 at the age of 29.

Brokenness (spiritual state of repentance), 73, 125, 170, 255, 256, 300, 302

Bunyan, John (1628-1688), 7, 12, 407, 408. His book *The Pilgrim's Progress from This World to That Which is to Come*, a classic all-time best-seller written by a pastor imprisoned for his faith in 17th century England. He was both a Puritan and a Baptist which made him a nonconformist in an era of persecution.

Calvin, John (1509-1564), 12, 105, 106, 199, 201

Cane Ridge, Kentucky, Revival, 13, 116, 117, 293

Carey, William (1761-1834), 13, 38, 167, 168

Carnal (in the flesh, the opposite of godly), 243, 256

Catechism, Westminster, 12, 266, 311-312

Chambers, Oswald (1874-1917), 14, 52. See also Oswald Chambers, *My Utmost for His Highest* (Grand Rapids, Michigan: Discovery House Publishers). Some of his daily devotions are available online on a day-by-day basis.

Charismatic, 101, 104

Checklists and Priority Lists, 129-170, 233-276, 316-406, 410-412

Prayer Priority List, 129-170

1. Right Relationship with God, 135-140

Jesus spoke of God as His Father even though He was equal with God. As a man, His life was transparent before His Father. He always sought to please Him. He represented His Father perfectly before men.

Jesus is seated now on the right hand of the Father. He acknowledges us before the Father if we publicly acknowledge Him on earth. If we deny Jesus, He denies us before the Father in heaven.

Jesus said, *"Everyone who acknowledges me publicly here on earth, I will also acknowledge before my Father in heaven. But everyone who denies me here on earth, I will also deny before my Father in heaven" (Matthew 10:32,33 NLT).*

If we have to choose between obeying God and following the demands of our earthly father we must always choose God (see John 17:17-23) but we must be sure that we are hearing God and not just rebelling against the father he gave us on earth.

We represent our Father in our attitudes of love toward the lowly. We are fathers to the poor and we feed the hungry, take in the homeless, clothe the naked, and visit those in prison (see Matthew 25:34-40). When we do good deeds in humility, without looking for recognition, remembering our own lowliness before God, He gives us eternal rewards. (See also page 282.)

Each person has a natural father and carries his seed. Christians who make disciples are spiritual fathers. Their disciples carry their spiritual DNA. They should demonstrate a good example so that their children can become like them. Both natural and spiritual fathers want their children to grow up to be responsible.

Sometimes people reject their spiritual and natural fathers and also reject their Father in heaven.

A pioneer or apostle might be called the "father" of a movement. William Carey is called the "father of modern missions" (see page 167).

Fall, The (see Genesis 3), 151, 197, 294. Adam committed the first sin by eating from the Tree of the Knowedge of Good and Evil in the Garden of Eden in direct disobedience to God. The devil had tempted Adam's wife by contradicting what God had said. She was deceived and urged Adam to eat the fruit. The Bible says in 1 Timothy 2:14 that the woman was deceived but Adam was not deceived and willfully disobeyed God by eating the fruit.

Favor of God, 73, 275, 419

Fear of God, 15, 65, 66, 67, 106, 134, 170, 214, 249, 266, 277, 278, 290, 419

Fellowship of Finishers, 6

Finney, Charles (1792-1875), 13, 33, 35, 89, 91, 136-140, 142, 143. American revivalist, pastor, abolitionist, educator.

Fivefold Ministry (apostle, prophet, evangelist, pastor, teacher), 135, 151-158, 159, 220, 295, 316-406, 410-412

"Follow the Drinking Gourd," 44. Hidden message with information for slaves to escape.

Forgiveness, 17, 53, 96, 103, 115, 116, 120, 121, 122, 123, 124, 174, 242, 243, 264, 268, 419

Fox, George (1624-1691), 12, 247, 248, 253, 254. Founder of the Quakers (Society of Friends). *Autobiography of George Fox* is available online at the Christian Classics Ethereal Library, www.ccel.org.

Free, freedom, free will, 20, 21, 29, 37, 42, 43, 44, 45, 59, 65, 68, 73, 74, 89, 91, 94, 96, 106, 109, 116, 122, 123, 140, 153, 154, 155, 159, 179, 185, 194, 197, 207, 212, 215, 216, 220, 237, 238, 245, 246, 251, 256, 273, 281, 307, 312, 420, 435

Frelinghuysen, Theodore Jacob (1691-1747), 12, 29, 50

Fruit, fruit of the Spirit, fruitfulness, 28, 49, 59, 61, 66, 67, 116, 125, 126, 141, 145, 146, 157, 162, 211, 218, 254, 258, 276, 295, 301, 309, 313, 430, 436

The Bible says that you can't trust your own heart. Your heart can deceive you. Tenderness of heart toward God is the only way to know the truth. Tenderness takes humility. A proud heart blocks you from seeing God and discerning what is true.

"The heart is deceitful above all things, and desperately
wicked: who can know it? I the LORD search the heart, I
try the reins, even to give every man according to his
ways, and according to the fruit of his doings" (Jeremiah 17:9-10 KJV).

Jesus knocks at the door of your heart, which is closed:

"Behold, I stand at the door, and knock: if any man hear my voice, and open the door, I will come in to him, and will sup with him, and he with me" (Revelation 3:20 KJV).

Fasting and prayer

Focused on the will of God

Holiness, willing to be holy

Humility

Laid aside His rights

Praising and worshiping God

Reconciliation

Role model

Sanctify yourself

Time with the Lost

Total surrender

Victory over the devil

Church

Church is His Bride

He is head of the Church

He set in place the fivefold ministry of apostle, prophet, pastor, teacher, evangelist

The Church is His representative on the earth

The Church is to be preeminent, not the state

God owns the church and the state

Unity in the Church is Jesus' prayer

He will return for a glorious Church, without spot or wrinkle

Conqueror

Authority over the heavens and the earth

Outcome of wars

Reign over the devil, demons, world, flesh

Creator of man (Father, Son, and Holy Ghost)

Creates every person in God's image and likeness

Established Model of the Family

Imparts personal value and destiny

Prepared eternity for those who are saved

Deity of Jesus

God

The great I Am

Savior of the world

Worthy of all praise

Supernaturally conceived in Mary's womb by the Holy Ghost

Carrier of God's presence

Heaven

Alive forever in heaven

Gave believers a place in heaven through His blood

Seated on the right hand of the Father

Glorious on the throne

Rules and reigns

Will return to earth as King

History is His Story (Father, Son, and Holy Ghost)

America from colonial times to the present—from Christian covenants of our godly founders to rejection of Christ and His standards today; wars, conquests, nation-building, social programs usurping the church, suppression of minorities, legalized immorality such as abortion and homosexuality, suppressing the voice of the Church

Christian character focus in sports like basketball

Church, evangelists, biblical inerrancy, creeds, standards for a biblical worldview for all of life, reformation of society, mass movements like Promise Keepers, benevolence abdicated to government

Education—from Bible based to modern secularism

England—civil government, exploration, Christian global evangelism and missions

Global exploration and missions

Government, statesmen, kings, presidents, wars, Declaration of Independence, U.S. Constitution, three branches—executive, legislative, and judicial

Great spiritual revivals and awakenings

Israel and the Jews

People in the Bible

People in the history of the earth

Slavery, segregation, Black American heroes who followed Christ, Whites who ended slavery and empowered Blacks

Holy Ghost

With God from the beginning

Present at the creation of the earth (Genesis 1:2)

Jesus was filled with Holy Ghost

Holy Ghost drove Jesus into the wilderness to be tempted

Spiritual gifts and fruit come from Holy Ghost

Jesus sent Holy Ghost after His death to fill believers and be their Friend forever, filled with His power

Intercessory prayer ministry of Jesus

Spent much time in prayer alone with His Father

Prayed for people while on earth

Taught disciples to pray

Ever lives to make intercession for us in heaven

Judgment in Jesus' messages

Warned sinners of judgment

Taught on reasons for judgment

Will execute judgment

Provided a way of escape from judgment through His death

Lordship

Authority over nature

Authority over believers

Authority over the devil and demons

Commanding the elements to obey Him

Discipleship—brings you under authority

Healing, miracles, raising people from the dead

Obedience to the Father's will

Reading others' thoughts

Seeing events far off and interpreting them

Touch His garment and be healed

Marriage

Jesus worked His first miracle at the wedding in Cana

Jesus taught on lifetime marriage and gave the only grounds for divorce, contrary to Moses

Marriage represents the relationship between Christ and the Church.

The husband loves His wife as Christ loves the Church and gave His life for it

The wife reverences her husband similar to the way she respects Jesus

Jesus welcomed children to come to Him

Prayer

All night in prayer

Early in the morning seeking God

Obedient in His greatest trial before and during the crucifixion

Personal intimacy with God

Secret place of prayer

Seeking God on behalf of others

Seeking the Father's face

Thanksgiving, praise, worship, joy

Reconciliation

Reconciles us to God

Gives us the ministry of reconciliation

Road to forgiveness, humility, taking the low road, considering others first

Savior

Shows you way to repentance so you can be saved

Scapegoat who took away your sins

Martyr who died for your sins

Reconciled you with God

Saved you from the wrath of God by taking your punishment

Lamb of God who takes away the sin of the world

Communion sacrament recalls His sacrificial death for sinners

Scripture

History of Jesus as God with the Father and Holy Ghost from the beginning, alive in eternity before His birth as a man

Relationship of Jesus, Father, Holy Ghost

Jesus's words and deeds were written down and canonized

Jesus' life fulfilled prophetic Scriptures in the Old Testament

Jesus honored the Old Testament and quoted it as it applied to His life and ministry

We read through the Bible and read the Bible for revelation on how to live and how to reach and teach others and make disciples

See also Blood of Jesus, Cross, Crucify, Resurrection, Suffering Servant

Jews, 161, 162, 163, 164, 165, 186, 238, 282. See also Israel.

John the Baptist, 62, 165, 218, 301, 417

Joshua, 169, 170, 208, 358, 361, 415

Jubilee, 281, 282, 419

Judgment, 16, 105-109, 148, 149, 150, 153, 161, 184, 185, 223, 226, 242, 252, 253, 266, 274, 278, 279, 284, 295, 302, 352, 419, 420

Kingmaker, 91, 143, 260, 434

Knox, John (c.1514-1572), 12, 105-106, 199, 284. Scottish reformer and founder of the Presbyterian Church,. Links to books by John Knox are available online at Hanover College's Internet Archive of Texts and Documents.

Lake, John G. (1870-1935), 14, 78

Lanphier, Jeremiah (1809-?), 13, 33, 34

Lincoln, Abraham (1809-1865), 13, 160, 249

Lust, 135, 136, 185, 241, 270, 271, 274

Luther, Martin (1483-1546), 12, 96, 195, 199, 201

Man. See also Man of God, Inner man.

Whenever you read the word "man" it will not necessarily be referring to man as in gender but may mean "mankind" as in God's creation.

Sometimes "trust in man" (trust in people) is contrasted with "trust in God," the One Who created you. Genesis 2:7 (KJV) says, "And the Lord God formed man of the dust of the ground, and breathed into his nostrils the breath of life." From the text (page 73): "He knew when He created man that man would fail, but He made provision for our failure before He ever created us." In 1 Samuel 16:7 it says "for the Lord seeth not as man seeth; for man looketh on the outward appearance, but the Lord looketh on the heart."

Jesus was fully God and fully man, Son of God and Son of Man (see the creeds on pages 264-266 and Philippians 2:5-9, for example).

Sometimes "man" means husband, as in "man and wife" or "the man of the house" (page 142).

An ordinary man is contrasted with a man like Elijah with a passion for changing the destiny of his nation (see page 162).

Angels are always masculine in the Bible and sometimes an angel is called a "man," as in Genesis 32:24 (KJV), "And Jacob was left alone; and there wrestled a man with him until the breaking of the day."

Your "spirit man" inside does a work of transformation to make you more like Jesus (see page 213).

The "new man" is a person who has received Jesus Christ as Lord and Savior and is living for Him.

"Every man" (every person) who is born on earth is a descendant of the First Adam with Adam's seed of sin that separates all mankind from God. Therefore, every man must be redeemed from sin by the Last Adam—Christ—and Christ's death on the cross.

Fall of man (see Genesis 3). Adam committed the first sin by eating from the Tree of the Knowedge of Good and Evil in the Garden of Eden in direct disobedience to God. The devil had tempted Adam's wife by contradicting what God had said. She was deceived and urged Adam to eat the fruit. The Bible says in 1 Timothy 2:14 that the woman was deceived but Adam was not deceived and willfully disobeyed God by eating the fruit.

God judges every man. He can see his heart and sees how he handles the circumstances of life (see Jeremiah 17:9-10).

Man of God, men of God, godly man, 103, 117, 142, 160, 162, 168, 169, 201, 203, 215, 237, 243, 260, 436

Marriage, 42, 226, 260, 435, 436. See also Family, Husband, Wife.

Marriage Supper of the Lamb, 407, 408

Mason, Charles Harrison (C. H.) (1866-1961), 14, 99, 100, 101, 102, 103, 137, 246. Founder of Church of God in Christ, spiritual father of Assemblies of God and other Pentecostals worldwide. See also *Bishop C. H. Mason and the Roots of the Church of God in Christ* by Ithiel Clemmons (Lanham, MD: PneumaLife Publishing, 1997) that focuses on his vision, consecration, and ministry of reconciliation.

May I Go To Sleep Now, Father? 18, 21, 183, 185, 283-284, 316-406, 410-412

McCartney, Bill (1940-present), 14, 435, 437. See also Bill McCartney, *Sold Out: Becoming Man Enough to Make a Difference* (Nashville: Word Publishing, 1997) and other books. He is a former national championship head college football coach for the University of Colorado selected for induction into the College Football Hall of Fame in 2013. Many of his assistants on that team became head coaches at other colleges. In 1990 he became the co-founder of Promise Keepers, which is the most successful Christian men's movement in history, In his books for men Coach Mac tells what it means to be totally committed to following Christ with a crunch-time mentality for these times. He has also written about the responsibility of Christians to honor the Jewish people.

PERSONAL NOTES

A Man's Journey

with God

Seminar Edition

30-Day

Consecration

Journal

"If you miss a day, start over

A Man's Journey with God Day 1

Today's Date ____________________ ❑ Eightfold Anointing

DAY 1—God Looks for a Man to Stand in the Gap

"And I sought for a man among them, that should make up the hedge, and stand in the gap before me for the land, that I should not destroy it: but I found none" (Ezekiel 22:30 KJV)/

Today's Four Bible Chapters and Notes from Through the Bible Readings

____

____

____

____

Prayer Priority List

"And he spake a parable unto them to this end, that men ought always to pray, and not to faint" (Luke 18:1 KJV).

1. Right Relationship With God

____

____

____

____

2. Family Needs And Destiny

____

____

____

3. Fivefold Ministry

____

____

____

4. Leaders—Local, State, Nation, World

____

____

5. Other Needs

____

Thought for the Day

God used the prophet Ezekiel. Ezekiel was not the person God was talking to. *He was the man God was talking* through. *Could you be the Ezekiel of this day?*

24-Hour Self-Accountability

Jesus Christ left us an example, that we should follow in His steps (see 1 Peter 2:21).

Date		Planned Schedule	Actual Schedule and Notes
	12:00 A.M.		
	1:00 A.M.		
	2:00 A.M.		
	3:00 A.M.		
	4:00 A.M.		
	5:00 A.M.		
	6:00 A.M.		
	7:00 A.M.		
	8:00 A.M.		
	9:00 A.M.		
	10:00 A.M.		
	11:00 A.M.		
	12:00 NOON		
	1:00 P.M.		
	2:00 P.M.		
	3:00 P.M.		
	4:00 P.M.		
	5:00 P.M.		
	6:00 P.M.		
	7:00 P.M.		
	8:00 P.M.		
	9:00 P.M.		
	10:00 P.M.		
	11:00 P.M.		

Personal Daily Checklist

"For if we would judge ourselves, we should not be judged" (1 Corinthians 11:31 KJV).

Grade yourself, A, B, or C, for each one or rate yourself on a scale of 1 (lowest) to 10 (highest).

Checklist Item	Today's Score	Checklist Item	Today's Score
❑ Time in Prayer		❑ Time with My Friends	
❑ Time in Word of God		❑ Time with the Lost	
❑ Praise & Worship		❑ Time to Eat Right	
❑ Thanksgiving		❑ Time to Exercise	
❑ Fasting		❑ Time to Organize	
❑ Time with My Family		❑ Time Alone with God	

Today's Expenses and Money Management

"It is He who gives you power to get wealth, that He may establish His covenant (Deuteronomy 8:18 NKJV).

____

____

Servanthood for Today

Jesus said, "But he that is greatest among you shall be your servant" (Matthew 23:11 KJV).

____

____

My Insights for Today

Jesus said, "But he that is greatest among you shall be your servant" (Matthew 23:11 KJV).

____

____

May I Go To Sleep Now, Father?

"Hard and honest work earns a good night's sleep" (Ecclesiastes 5:12 The Message*).*

A Man's Journey with God Day 2

Today's Date ______________________ ❑ Eightfold Anointing

DAY 2—Will You Be the Man to Cleanse the Land?

"And the word of the Lord came unto me, saying, 'Son of man, say unto her, "Thou art the land that is not cleansed"'" (Ezekiel 22:23-24 KJV).

Today's Four Bible Chapters and Notes from Through the Bible Readings

Prayer Priority List

"And he spake a parable unto them to this end, that men ought always to pray, and not to faint" (Luke 18:1 KJV).

1. Right Relationship With God

2. Family Needs And Destiny

3. Fivefold Ministry

4. Leaders—Local, State, Nation, World

5. Other Needs

Thought for the Day

This is a message from God. "Thou art the land that is not cleansed, nor rained upon in the day of indignation. "What is the point of Man Hunt? Cleansing the land. But before you can cleanse the land you've got to get clean yourself. In Ezekiel God was talking—not through a perfect man but through a man who was willing to be cleansed.

24-Hour Self-Accountability

Jesus Christ left us an example, that we should follow in His steps (see 1 Peter 2:21).

Date		Planned Schedule	Actual Schedule and Notes
	12:00 A.M.		
	1:00 A.M.		
	2:00 A.M.		
	3:00 A.M.		
	4:00 A.M.		
	5:00 A.M.		
	6:00 A.M.		
	7:00 A.M.		
	8:00 A.M.		
	9:00 A.M.		
	10:00 A.M.		
	11:00 A.M.		
	12:00 NOON		
	1:00 P.M.		
	2:00 P.M.		
	3:00 P.M.		
	4:00 P.M.		
	5:00 P.M.		
	6:00 P.M.		
	7:00 P.M.		
	8:00 P.M.		
	9:00 P.M.		
	10:00 P.M.		
	11:00 P.M.		

Personal Daily Checklist

"For if we would judge ourselves, we should not be judged" (1 Corinthians 11:31 KJV).

Grade yourself, A, B, or C, for each one or rate yourself on a scale of 1 (lowest) to 10 (highest).

Checklist Item	Today's Score	Checklist Item	Today's Score
❑ Time in Prayer		❑ Time with My Friends	
❑ Time in Word of God		❑ Time with the Lost	
❑ Praise & Worship		❑ Time to Eat Right	
❑ Thanksgiving		❑ Time to Exercise	
❑ Fasting		❑ Time to Organize	
❑ Time with My Family		❑ Time Alone with God	

Today's Expenses and Money Management

"It is He who gives you power to get wealth, that He may establish His covenant (Deuteronomy 8:18 NKJV).

____

____

Servanthood for Today

Jesus said, "But he that is greatest among you shall be your servant" (Matthew 23:11 KJV).

____

____

My Insights for Today

Jesus said, "But he that is greatest among you shall be your servant" (Matthew 23:11 KJV).

____

____

May I Go To Sleep Now, Father?

"Hard and honest work earns a good night's sleep" (Ecclesiastes 5:12 The Message*).*

A Man's Journey with God Day 3

Today's Date ____________________ ❑ Eightfold Anointing

DAY 3—God's Power Will Make You Great, If You're Willing

"Thy people shall be willing in the day of thy power" (Psalms 110:3 KJV).

Today's Four Bible Chapters and Notes from Through the Bible Readings

Prayer Priority List

"And he spake a parable unto them to this end, that men ought always to pray, and not to faint" (Luke 18:1 KJV).

1. Right Relationship With God

2. Family Needs And Destiny

3. Fivefold Ministry

4. Leaders—Local, State, Nation, World

5. Other Needs

Thought for the Day

"God is looking for people who will give themselves willingly to Him so that He can make a difference in their lives and use them to do great things. This is the day that God wants to move and this is the day that you can build the greatness of God in you. There's not one negative thing that's going on that God would say to it, "I'm intimidated. There's no way I can fix this." Are you intimidated by life or do you demonstrate the greatness of God?

24-Hour Self-Accountability

Jesus Christ left us an example, that we should follow in His steps (1 Peter 2:21).

Date		Planned Schedule	Actual Schedule and Notes
	12:00 A.M.		
	1:00 A.M.		
	2:00 A.M.		
	3:00 A.M.		
	4:00 A.M.		
	5:00 A.M.		
	6:00 A.M.		
	7:00 A.M.		
	8:00 A.M.		
	9:00 A.M.		
	10:00 A.M.		
	11:00 A.M.		
	12:00 NOON		
	1:00 P.M.		
	2:00 P.M.		
	3:00 P.M.		
	4:00 P.M.		
	5:00 P.M.		
	6:00 P.M.		
	7:00 P.M.		
	8:00 P.M.		
	9:00 P.M.		
	10:00 P.M.		
	11:00 P.M.		

Personal Daily Checklist

"For if we would judge ourselves, we should not be judged" (1 Corinthians 11:31 KJV).

Grade yourself, A, B, or C, for each one or rate yourself on a scale of 1 (lowest) to 10 (highest).

Checklist Item	Today's Score	Checklist Item	Today's Score
❑ Time in Prayer		❑ Time with My Friends	
❑ Time in Word of God		❑ Time with the Lost	
❑ Praise & Worship		❑ Time to Eat Right	
❑ Thanksgiving		❑ Time to Exercise	
❑ Fasting		❑ Time to Organize	
❑ Time with My Family		❑ Time Alone with God	

Today's Expenses and Money Management

"It is He who gives you power to get wealth, that He may establish His covenant (Deuteronomy 8:18 NKJV).

Servanthood for Today

Jesus said, "But he that is greatest among you shall be your servant" (Matthew 23:11 KJV).

My Insights for Today

Jesus said, "But he that is greatest among you shall be your servant" (Matthew 23:11 KJV).

May I Go To Sleep Now, Father?

"Hard and honest work earns a good night's sleep" (Ecclesiastes 5:12 The Message*).*

A Man's Journey with God Day 4

Today's Date ____________________ ❑ Eightfold Anointing

DAY 4—God Is Judging Your Nation—What's Your Role?

"Therefore have I poured out mine indignation upon them; I have consumed them with the fire of my wrath: their own way have I recompensed upon their heads, saith the Lord God" (Ezekiel 22:31 KJV).

Today's Four Bible Chapters and Notes from Through the Bible Readings

____

____

____

____

Prayer Priority List

"And he spake a parable unto them to this end, that men ought always to pray, and not to faint" (Luke 18:1 KJV).

1. Right Relationship With God

____

____

____

____

2. Family Needs And Destiny

____

____

____

3. Fivefold Ministry

____

____

____

4. Leaders—Local, State, Nation, World

____

____

5. Other Needs

____

Thought for the Day

Most men in the church say today, "Lord, don't correct my behavior. Just bless me." But Christian men need to know that God is angry with what He sees in the nation. They won't find out unless a man tells them who knows God and His Word and hears God's voice in prayer. God judges nations in three ways: (1) Inclement weather. (2) An enemy stronger than you. (3) Destroying the nation from within. It's more serious than global warming. *This is the time of global warning. God is judging the nations.*

24-Hour Self-Accountability

Jesus Christ left us an example, that we should follow in His steps (1 Peter 2:21).

Date		Planned Schedule	Actual Schedule and Notes
	12:00 A.M.		
	1:00 A.M.		
	2:00 A.M.		
	3:00 A.M.		
	4:00 A.M.		
	5:00 A.M.		
	6:00 A.M.		
	7:00 A.M.		
	8:00 A.M.		
	9:00 A.M.		
	10:00 A.M.		
	11:00 A.M.		
	12:00 NOON		
	1:00 P.M.		
	2:00 P.M.		
	3:00 P.M.		
	4:00 P.M.		
	5:00 P.M.		
	6:00 P.M.		
	7:00 P.M.		
	8:00 P.M.		
	9:00 P.M.		
	10:00 P.M.		
	11:00 P.M.		

Personal Daily Checklist

"For if we would judge ourselves, we should not be judged" (1 Corinthians 11:31 KJV).

Grade yourself, A, B, or C, for each one or rate yourself on a scale of 1 (lowest) to 10 (highest).

Checklist Item	Today's Score	Checklist Item	Today's Score
❑ Time in Prayer		❑ Time with My Friends	
❑ Time in Word of God		❑ Time with the Lost	
❑ Praise & Worship		❑ Time to Eat Right	
❑ Thanksgiving		❑ Time to Exercise	
❑ Fasting		❑ Time to Organize	
❑ Time with My Family		❑ Time Alone with God	

Today's Expenses and Money Management

"It is He who gives you power to get wealth, that He may establish His covenant (Deuteronomy 8:18 NKJV).

____

____

Servanthood for Today

Jesus said, "But he that is greatest among you shall be your servant" (Matthew 23:11 KJV).

____

____

My Insights for Today

Jesus said, "But he that is greatest among you shall be your servant" (Matthew 23:11 KJV).

____

____

May I Go To Sleep Now, Father?

"Hard and honest work earns a good night's sleep" (Ecclesiastes 5:12 The Message*).*

A Man's Journey with God Day 5

Today's Date ____________________ ❑ Eightfold Anointing

DAY 5—You Can't Change God's Definition of a Family

"Thou shalt not lie with mankind, as with womankind: it is abomination"

(Leviticus 18:22 KJV).

Today's Four Bible Chapters and Notes from Through the Bible Readings

____

____

____

____

Prayer Priority List

"And he spake a parable unto them to this end, that men ought always to pray, and not to faint" (Luke 18:1 KJV).

1. Right Relationship With God

____

____

____

____

2. Family Needs And Destiny

____

____

____

3. Fivefold Ministry

____

____

____

4. Leaders—Local, State, Nation, World

____

____

5. Other Needs

____

Thought for the Day

God made me black. I cannot change the color of my skin, which to God is something good, but sodomites can change their sexual behavior, which God calls an abomination. When people try to force on us the acceptance of an unnatural restructuring of the family, we have this message for them—I cannot go against God.

24-Hour Self-Accountability

Jesus Christ left us an example, that we should follow in His steps (1 Peter 2:21).

Date		Planned Schedule	Actual Schedule and Notes
	12:00 A.M.		
	1:00 A.M.		
	2:00 A.M.		
	3:00 A.M.		
	4:00 A.M.		
	5:00 A.M.		
	6:00 A.M.		
	7:00 A.M.		
	8:00 A.M.		
	9:00 A.M.		
	10:00 A.M.		
	11:00 A.M.		
	12:00 NOON		
	1:00 P.M.		
	2:00 P.M.		
	3:00 P.M.		
	4:00 P.M.		
	5:00 P.M.		
	6:00 P.M.		
	7:00 P.M.		
	8:00 P.M.		
	9:00 P.M.		
	10:00 P.M.		
	11:00 P.M.		

Personal Daily Checklist

"For if we would judge ourselves, we should not be judged" (1 Corinthians 11:31 KJV).

Grade yourself, A, B, or C, for each one or rate yourself on a scale of 1 (lowest) to 10 (highest).

Checklist Item	Today's Score	Checklist Item	Today's Score
❑ Time in Prayer		❑ Time with My Friends	
❑ Time in Word of God		❑ Time with the Lost	
❑ Praise & Worship		❑ Time to Eat Right	
❑ Thanksgiving		❑ Time to Exercise	
❑ Fasting		❑ Time to Organize	
❑ Time with My Family		❑ Time Alone with God	

Today's Expenses and Money Management

"It is He who gives you power to get wealth, that He may establish His covenant (Deuteronomy 8:18 NKJV).

____

____

Servanthood for Today

Jesus said, "But he that is greatest among you shall be your servant" (Matthew 23:11 KJV).

____

____

My Insights for Today

Jesus said, "But he that is greatest among you shall be your servant" (Matthew 23:11 KJV).

____

____

May I Go To Sleep Now, Father?

"Hard and honest work earns a good night's sleep" (Ecclesiastes 5:12 The Message).

A Man's Journey with God Day 6

Today's Date ____________________ ❑ Eightfold Anointing

DAY 6—Jesus' Total Surrender

"Saying, Father, if thou be willing, remove this cup from me: nevertheless not my will, but thine, be done" (Luke 22:42 KJV).

Today's Four Bible Chapters and Notes from Through the Bible Readings

____

____

____

____

Prayer Priority List

"And he spake a parable unto them to this end, that men ought always to pray, and not to faint" (Luke 18:1 KJV).

1. Right Relationship With God

____

____

____

____

2. Family Needs And Destiny

____

____

____

3. Fivefold Ministry

____

____

____

4. Leaders—Local, State, Nation, World

____

____

5. Other Needs

____

Thought for the Day

Before Jesus went to the cross and shed His blood for us, He had already sacrificed Himself on the altar of total surrender to God's will. You don't know what is ahead of you. None of us do. We hope for the best. However, in uncertain times we must decide now that whatever is His will, even our death, we will do it. That is the message that you must receive from these daily disciplines of consecration. Lord, not my will but yours be done.

24-Hour Self-Accountability

Jesus Christ left us an example, that we should follow in His steps (1 Peter 2:21).

Date		Planned Schedule	Actual Schedule and Notes
	12:00 A.M.		
	1:00 A.M.		
	2:00 A.M.		
	3:00 A.M.		
	4:00 A.M.		
	5:00 A.M.		
	6:00 A.M.		
	7:00 A.M.		
	8:00 A.M.		
	9:00 A.M.		
	10:00 A.M.		
	11:00 A.M.		
	12:00 NOON		
	1:00 P.M.		
	2:00 P.M.		
	3:00 P.M.		
	4:00 P.M.		
	5:00 P.M.		
	6:00 P.M.		
	7:00 P.M.		
	8:00 P.M.		
	9:00 P.M.		
	10:00 P.M.		
	11:00 P.M.		

Personal Daily Checklist

"For if we would judge ourselves, we should not be judged" (1 Corinthians 11:31 KJV).

Grade yourself, A, B, or C, for each one or rate yourself on a scale of 1 (lowest) to 10 (highest).

Checklist Item	Today's Score	Checklist Item	Today's Score
❑ Time in Prayer		❑ Time with My Friends	
❑ Time in Word of God		❑ Time with the Lost	
❑ Praise & Worship		❑ Time to Eat Right	
❑ Thanksgiving		❑ Time to Exercise	
❑ Fasting		❑ Time to Organize	
❑ Time with My Family		❑ Time Alone with God	

Today's Expenses and Money Management

"It is He who gives you power to get wealth, that He may establish His covenant (Deuteronomy 8:18 NKJV).

____

____

Servanthood for Today

Jesus said, "But he that is greatest among you shall be your servant" (Matthew 23:11 KJV).

____

____

My Insights for Today

Jesus said, "But he that is greatest among you shall be your servant" (Matthew 23:11 KJV).

____

____

May I Go To Sleep Now, Father?

"Hard and honest work earns a good night's sleep" (Ecclesiastes 5:12 The Message)..

A Man's Journey with God Day 7

Today's Date ____________________ ❑ Eightfold Anointing

DAY 7—Christians Are Commanded to Change Nations by Preaching

Jesus told His disciples on the Mount of Olives, "And this gospel of the kingdom shall be preached in all the world for a witness unto all nations; and then shall the end come. (Matthew 24:14 NLT).

Today's Four Bible Chapters and Notes from Through the Bible Readings

____

____

____

____

Prayer Priority List

"And he spake a parable unto them to this end, that men ought always to pray, and not to faint" (Luke 18:1 KJV).

1. Right Relationship With God

____

____

____

____

2. Family Needs And Destiny

____

____

____

3. Fivefold Ministry

____

____

____

4. Leaders—Local, State, Nation, World

____

____

5. Other Needs

____

Thought for the Day

Jesus sent the disciples to disciple nations. Did He mean we should go there and change the whole nation, including the leader? Change them to what? They already have governments. They have historical authority structures. They have economic structures. But Jesus said clearly, Whatever I have taught you, you teach them and it's non optional. In other words, I will not go somewhere and negotiate with you. I will be your example and disciple you into Christ-likeness.

24-Hour Self-Accountability

Jesus Christ left us an example, that we should follow in His steps (1 Peter 2:21).

Date		Planned Schedule	Actual Schedule and Notes
	12:00 A.M.		
	1:00 A.M.		
	2:00 A.M.		
	3:00 A.M.		
	4:00 A.M.		
	5:00 A.M.		
	6:00 A.M.		
	7:00 A.M.		
	8:00 A.M.		
	9:00 A.M.		
	10:00 A.M.		
	11:00 A.M.		
	12:00 NOON		
	1:00 P.M.		
	2:00 P.M.		
	3:00 P.M.		
	4:00 P.M.		
	5:00 P.M.		
	6:00 P.M.		
	7:00 P.M.		
	8:00 P.M.		
	9:00 P.M.		
	10:00 P.M.		
	11:00 P.M.		

Personal Daily Checklist

"For if we would judge ourselves, we should not be judged" (1 Corinthians 11:31 KJV).

Grade yourself, A, B, or C, for each one or rate yourself on a scale of 1 (lowest) to 10 (highest).

Checklist Item	Today's Score	Checklist Item	Today's Score
❑ Time in Prayer		❑ Time with My Friends	
❑ Time in Word of God		❑ Time with the Lost	
❑ Praise & Worship		❑ Time to Eat Right	
❑ Thanksgiving		❑ Time to Exercise	
❑ Fasting		❑ Time to Organize	
❑ Time with My Family		❑ Time Alone with God	

Today's Expenses and Money Management

"It is He who gives you power to get wealth, that He may establish His covenant (Deuteronomy 8:18 NKJV).

____

____

Servanthood for Today

Jesus said, "But he that is greatest among you shall be your servant" (Matthew 23:11 KJV).

____

____

My Insights for Today

Jesus said, "But he that is greatest among you shall be your servant" (Matthew 23:11 KJV).

____

____

May I Go To Sleep Now, Father?

"Hard and honest work earns a good night's sleep" (Ecclesiastes 5:12 The Message).

A Man's Journey with God Day 8

Today's Date ____________________ ❑ Eightfold Anointing

DAY 8— Your Good Works—A Divine Assignment from Jesus

"Most assuredly, I say to you, he who believes in Me, the works that I do he will do also; and greater works than these he will do, because I go to My Father" (John 14:12 NKJV).

Today's Four Bible Chapters and Notes from Through the Bible Readings

____

____

____

____

Prayer Priority List

"And he spake a parable unto them to this end, that men ought always to pray, and not to faint" (Luke 18:1 KJV).

1. Right Relationship With God

____

____

____

____

2. Family Needs And Destiny

____

____

____

3. Fivefold Ministry

____

____

____

4. Leaders—Local, State, Nation, World

____

____

5. Other Needs

____

Thought for the Day

Jesus said that we would do greater works than He did (John 14:12). Why haven't men done good works at the level of Jesus? Because we have not been consecrated. The Lord has us here on a divine assignment. We are His ambassadors from heaven. That isn't just a nice Christian saying. We have actually been sent for a mission. Our hearts are becoming good ground for God to give us understanding and passion for our mission from heaven here on earth. That is why we live. You don't want to go another moment without the Lord clarifying that mission within your heart. Make that your prayer today.

24-Hour Self-Accountability

Jesus Christ left us an example, that we should follow in His steps (1 Peter 2:21).

Date		Planned Schedule	Actual Schedule and Notes
	12:00 A.M.		
	1:00 A.M.		
	2:00 A.M.		
	3:00 A.M.		
	4:00 A.M.		
	5:00 A.M.		
	6:00 A.M.		
	7:00 A.M.		
	8:00 A.M.		
	9:00 A.M.		
	10:00 A.M.		
	11:00 A.M.		
	12:00 NOON		
	1:00 P.M.		
	2:00 P.M.		
	3:00 P.M.		
	4:00 P.M.		
	5:00 P.M.		
	6:00 P.M.		
	7:00 P.M.		
	8:00 P.M.		
	9:00 P.M.		
	10:00 P.M.		
	11:00 P.M.		

Personal Daily Checklist

"For if we would judge ourselves, we should not be judged" (1 Corinthians 11:31 KJV).

Grade yourself, A, B, or C, for each one or rate yourself on a scale of 1 (lowest) to 10 (highest).

Checklist Item	Today's Score	Checklist Item	Today's Score
❑ Time in Prayer		❑ Time with My Friends	
❑ Time in Word of God		❑ Time with the Lost	
❑ Praise & Worship		❑ Time to Eat Right	
❑ Thanksgiving		❑ Time to Exercise	
❑ Fasting		❑ Time to Organize	
❑ Time with My Family		❑ Time Alone with God	

Today's Expenses and Money Management

"It is He who gives you power to get wealth, that He may establish His covenant (Deuteronomy 8:18 NKJV).

____

____

Servanthood for Today

Jesus said, "But he that is greatest among you shall be your servant" (Matthew 23:11 KJV).

____

____

My Insights for Today

Jesus said, "But he that is greatest among you shall be your servant" (Matthew 23:11 KJV).

____

____

May I Go To Sleep Now, Father?

"Hard and honest work earns a good night's sleep" (Ecclesiastes 5:12 The Message*).*

A Man's Journey with God Day 9

Today's Date ______________________ ❑ Eightfold Anointing

DAY 9—Jesus Christ Wants to Occupy Your Mind with His Work

"And he called his ten servants, and delivered them ten pounds, and said unto them, Occupy till I come" (Luke 19:13 KJV).

Today's Four Bible Chapters and Notes from Through the Bible Readings

____

____

____

____

Prayer Priority List

"And he spake a parable unto them to this end, that men ought always to pray, and not to faint" (Luke 18:1 KJV).

1. Right Relationship With God

____

____

____

____

2. Family Needs And Destiny

____

____

____

3. Fivefold Ministry

____

____

____

4. Leaders—Local, State, Nation, World

____

____

5. Other Needs

____

Thought for the Day

Jesus says in Luke 19:20, "Occupy until I come." Occupy is a military term. The spirit man inside of you has to occupy the inner motivations and reins of your heart in order to preserve your Christ-likeness. Consecration is the way the Lord knows those who are truly His people—not those who just go to church but those who consecrate themselves on the inside. When they pray, their hearts are pure because of their consecration.

24-Hour Self-Accountability

Jesus Christ left us an example, that we should follow in His steps (1 Peter 2:21).

Date		Planned Schedule	Actual Schedule and Notes
	12:00 A.M.		
	1:00 A.M.		
	2:00 A.M.		
	3:00 A.M.		
	4:00 A.M.		
	5:00 A.M.		
	6:00 A.M.		
	7:00 A.M.		
	8:00 A.M.		
	9:00 A.M.		
	10:00 A.M.		
	11:00 A.M.		
	12:00 NOON		
	1:00 P.M.		
	2:00 P.M.		
	3:00 P.M.		
	4:00 P.M.		
	5:00 P.M.		
	6:00 P.M.		
	7:00 P.M.		
	8:00 P.M.		
	9:00 P.M.		
	10:00 P.M.		
	11:00 P.M.		

Personal Daily Checklist

"For if we would judge ourselves, we should not be judged" (1 Corinthians 11:31 KJV).

Grade yourself, A, B, or C, for each one or rate yourself on a scale of 1 (lowest) to 10 (highest).

Checklist Item	Today's Score	Checklist Item	Today's Score
❑ Time in Prayer		❑ Time with My Friends	
❑ Time in Word of God		❑ Time with the Lost	
❑ Praise & Worship		❑ Time to Eat Right	
❑ Thanksgiving		❑ Time to Exercise	
❑ Fasting		❑ Time to Organize	
❑ Time with My Family		❑ Time Alone with God	

Today's Expenses and Money Management

"It is He who gives you power to get wealth, that He may establish His covenant (Deuteronomy 8:18 NKJV).

Servanthood for Today

Jesus said, "But he that is greatest among you shall be your servant" (Matthew 23:11 KJV).

My Insights for Today

Jesus said, "But he that is greatest among you shall be your servant" (Matthew 23:11 KJV).

May I Go To Sleep Now, Father?

"Hard and honest work earns a good night's sleep" (Ecclesiastes 5:12 The Message*).*

A Man's Journey with God Day 10

Today's Date ____________________ ❑ Eightfold Anointing

DAY 10—Spiritual Fitness Training for Good Works

"Therefore if anyone cleanses himself from the latter, he will be a vessel for honor, sanctified and useful for the Master, prepared for every good work"

(2 Timothy 2:20-21 NKJV).

Today's Four Bible Chapters and Notes from Through the Bible Readings

____

____

____

____

Prayer Priority List

"And he spake a parable unto them to this end, that men ought always to pray, and not to faint" (Luke 18:1 KJV).

1. Right Relationship With God

____

____

____

____

2. Family Needs And Destiny

____

____

____

3. Fivefold Ministry

____

____

____

4. Leaders—Local, State, Nation, World

____

____

5. Other Needs

____

Thought for the Day

Jesus says in Luke 19:20, "Occupy until I come." Occupy is a military term. The spirit man inside of you has to occupy the inner motivations and reins of your heart in order to develop your Christ-likeness. Consecration is the way the Lord knows which men are truly His people—not those who go to church but those who consecrate themselves on the inside. When they pray, their hearts are pure, because of their consecration.

24-Hour Self-Accountability

Jesus Christ left us an example, that we should follow in His steps (1 Peter 2:21).

Date		Planned Schedule	Actual Schedule and Notes
	12:00 A.M.		
	1:00 A.M.		
	2:00 A.M.		
	3:00 A.M.		
	4:00 A.M.		
	5:00 A.M.		
	6:00 A.M.		
	7:00 A.M.		
	8:00 A.M.		
	9:00 A.M.		
	10:00 A.M.		
	11:00 A.M.		
	12:00 NOON		
	1:00 P.M.		
	2:00 P.M.		
	3:00 P.M.		
	4:00 P.M.		
	5:00 P.M.		
	6:00 P.M.		
	7:00 P.M.		
	8:00 P.M.		
	9:00 P.M.		
	10:00 P.M.		
	11:00 P.M.		

Personal Daily Checklist

"For if we would judge ourselves, we should not be judged" (1 Corinthians 11:31 KJV).

Grade yourself, A, B, or C, for each one or rate yourself on a scale of 1 (lowest) to 10 (highest).

Checklist Item	Today's Score	Checklist Item	Today's Score
❑ Time in Prayer		❑ Time with My Friends	
❑ Time in Word of God		❑ Time with the Lost	
❑ Praise & Worship		❑ Time to Eat Right	
❑ Thanksgiving		❑ Time to Exercise	
❑ Fasting		❑ Time to Organize	
❑ Time with My Family		❑ Time Alone with God	

Today's Expenses and Money Management

"It is He who gives you power to get wealth, that He may establish His covenant (Deuteronomy 8:18 NKJV).

____

____

Servanthood for Today

Jesus said, "But he that is greatest among you shall be your servant" (Matthew 23:11 KJV).

____

____

My Insights for Today

Jesus said, "But he that is greatest among you shall be your servant" (Matthew 23:11 KJV).

____

____

May I Go To Sleep Now, Father?

"Hard and honest work earns a good night's sleep" (Ecclesiastes 5:12 The Message).

A Man's Journey with God Day 11

Today's Date ____________________ ❑ Eightfold Anointing

DAY 11—A True Disciple Seeks God Early and Earnestly

"I love them that love me; and those that seek me early shall find me"

(Proverbs 8:17 KJV).

Today's Four Bible Chapters and Notes from Through the Bible Readings

Prayer Priority List

"And he spake a parable unto them to this end, that men ought always to pray, and not to faint" (Luke 18:1 KJV).

1. Right Relationship With God

2. Family Needs And Destiny

3. Fivefold Ministry

4. Leaders—Local, State, Nation, World

5. Other Needs

Thought for the Day

When you consecrate yourself, you prepare yourself daily and diligently (Proverbs 8:17) to do everything God might call on you to do. As you seek God early and study His Word, ask Him to purify your heart, change your motivations, and help you to become more like Jesus. As the Holy Spirit sheds light on the unholy areas of your life, ask God to perfect you and get you in shape for the battles to come in the unknown future.

24-Hour Self-Accountability

Jesus Christ left us an example, that we should follow in His steps (1 Peter 2:21).

Date		Planned Schedule	Actual Schedule and Notes
12:00 A.M.			
1:00 A.M.			
2:00 A.M.			
3:00 A.M.			
4:00 A.M.			
5:00 A.M.			
6:00 A.M.			
7:00 A.M.			
8:00 A.M.			
9:00 A.M.			
10:00 A.M.			
11:00 A.M.			
12:00 NOON			
1:00 P.M.			
2:00 P.M.			
3:00 P.M.			
4:00 P.M.			
5:00 P.M.			
6:00 P.M.			
7:00 P.M.			
8:00 P.M.			
9:00 P.M.			
10:00 P.M.			
11:00 P.M.			

Personal Daily Checklist

"For if we would judge ourselves, we should not be judged" (1 Corinthians 11:31 KJV).

Grade yourself, A, B, or C, for each one or rate yourself on a scale of 1 (lowest) to 10 (highest).

Checklist Item	Today's Score	Checklist Item	Today's Score
❑ Time in Prayer		❑ Time with My Friends	
❑ Time in Word of God		❑ Time with the Lost	
❑ Praise & Worship		❑ Time to Eat Right	
❑ Thanksgiving		❑ Time to Exercise	
❑ Fasting		❑ Time to Organize	
❑ Time with My Family		❑ Time Alone with God	

Today's Expenses and Money Management

"It is He who gives you power to get wealth, that He may establish His covenant (Deuteronomy 8:18 NKJV).

____

____

Servanthood for Today

Jesus said, "But he that is greatest among you shall be your servant" (Matthew 23:11 KJV).

____

____

My Insights for Today

Jesus said, "But he that is greatest among you shall be your servant" (Matthew 23:11 KJV).

____

____

May I Go To Sleep Now, Father?

"Hard and honest work earns a good night's sleep" (Ecclesiastes 5:12 The Message).

A Man's Journey with God Day 12

Today's Date ____________________ ❑ Eightfold Anointing

DAY 12—Are You a Member of the Christian Special Ops?

"For many are called, but few are chosen" (Matthew 22:14 NLT).

Today's Four Bible Chapters and Notes from Through the Bible Readings

____

____

____

____

Prayer Priority List

"And he spake a parable unto them to this end, that men ought always to pray, and not to faint" (Luke 18:1 KJV).

1. Right Relationship With God

____

____

____

____

2. Family Needs And Destiny

____

____

____

3. Fivefold Ministry

____

____

____

4. Leaders—Local, State, Nation, World

____

____

5. Other Needs

____

Thought for the Day

Somebody's words allowed the earth to become what it is. Somebody's production strategy built the chair that you are sitting on right now. If God has said anything to you and has helped you, couldn't you say that to somebody else and help them, too? God never does anything significant with masses. He always does it with the remnant—the few, what they call the special ops in the military. The question is, who is the remnant? Is it you?

24-Hour Self-Accountability

Jesus Christ left us an example, that we should follow in His steps (1 Peter 2:21).

Date		Planned Schedule	Actual Schedule and Notes
	12:00 A.M.		
	1:00 A.M.		
	2:00 A.M.		
	3:00 A.M.		
	4:00 A.M.		
	5:00 A.M.		
	6:00 A.M.		
	7:00 A.M.		
	8:00 A.M.		
	9:00 A.M.		
	10:00 A.M.		
	11:00 A.M.		
	12:00 NOON		
	1:00 P.M.		
	2:00 P.M.		
	3:00 P.M.		
	4:00 P.M.		
	5:00 P.M.		
	6:00 P.M.		
	7:00 P.M.		
	8:00 P.M.		
	9:00 P.M.		
	10:00 P.M.		
	11:00 P.M.		

Personal Daily Checklist

"For if we would judge ourselves, we should not be judged" (1 Corinthians 11:31 KJV).

Grade yourself, A, B, or C, for each one or rate yourself on a scale of 1 (lowest) to 10 (highest).

Checklist Item	Today's Score	Checklist Item	Today's Score
❑ Time in Prayer		❑ Time with My Friends	
❑ Time in Word of God		❑ Time with the Lost	
❑ Praise & Worship		❑ Time to Eat Right	
❑ Thanksgiving		❑ Time to Exercise	
❑ Fasting		❑ Time to Organize	
❑ Time with My Family		❑ Time Alone with God	

Today's Expenses and Money Management

"It is He who gives you power to get wealth, that He may establish His covenant (Deuteronomy 8:18 NKJV).

____

____

Servanthood for Today

Jesus said, "But he that is greatest among you shall be your servant" (Matthew 23:11 KJV).

____

____

My Insights for Today

Jesus said, "But he that is greatest among you shall be your servant" (Matthew 23:11 KJV).

____

____

May I Go To Sleep Now, Father?

"Hard and honest work earns a good night's sleep" (Ecclesiastes 5:12 The Message).

A Man's Journey with God Day 13

Today's Date ____________________ ❑ Eightfold Anointing

DAY 13—No Matter How Weak You Feel, God Can Make You Mighty

"But God hath chosen the foolish things of the world to confound the wise; and God hath chosen the weak things of the world to confound the things which are mighty" (1 Corinthians 1:27 KJV).

Today's Four Bible Chapters and Notes from Through the Bible Readings

____

____

____

____

Prayer Priority List

"And he spake a parable unto them to this end, that men ought always to pray, and not to faint" (Luke 18:1 KJV).

1. Right Relationship With God

____

____

____

____

2. Family Needs And Destiny

____

____

____

3. Fivefold Ministry

____

____

____

4. Leaders—Local, State, Nation, World

____

____

5. Other Needs

____

Thought for the Day

Somebody is always exceptional in a day of mediocrity. When you are a real Christian and God is your Father, you still have potential in you that nobody has seen yet. I am talking about what God can do through vessels of clay like you. Those are the men God uses. He ordained it in the creative order to use humanity to show deity and usually the people He uses are the ones humble enough to say, "Even so, Lord, use me."

24-Hour Self-Accountability

Jesus Christ left us an example, that we should follow in His steps (1 Peter 2:21).

Date		Planned Schedule	Actual Schedule and Notes
	12:00 A.M.		
	1:00 A.M.		
	2:00 A.M.		
	3:00 A.M.		
	4:00 A.M.		
	5:00 A.M.		
	6:00 A.M.		
	7:00 A.M.		
	8:00 A.M.		
	9:00 A.M.		
	10:00 A.M.		
	11:00 A.M.		
	12:00 NOON		
	1:00 P.M.		
	2:00 P.M.		
	3:00 P.M.		
	4:00 P.M.		
	5:00 P.M.		
	6:00 P.M.		
	7:00 P.M.		
	8:00 P.M.		
	9:00 P.M.		
	10:00 P.M.		
	11:00 P.M.		

Personal Daily Checklist

"For if we would judge ourselves, we should not be judged" (1 Corinthians 11:31 KJV).

Grade yourself, A, B, or C, for each one or rate yourself on a scale of 1 (lowest) to 10 (highest).

Checklist Item	Today's Score	Checklist Item	Today's Score
❑ Time in Prayer		❑ Time with My Friends	
❑ Time in Word of God		❑ Time with the Lost	
❑ Praise & Worship		❑ Time to Eat Right	
❑ Thanksgiving		❑ Time to Exercise	
❑ Fasting		❑ Time to Organize	
❑ Time with My Family		❑ Time Alone with God	

Today's Expenses and Money Management

"It is He who gives you power to get wealth, that He may establish His covenant (Deuteronomy 8:18 NKJV).

Servanthood for Today

Jesus said, "But he that is greatest among you shall be your servant" (Matthew 23:11 KJV).

My Insights for Today

Jesus said, "But he that is greatest among you shall be your servant" (Matthew 23:11 KJV).

May I Go To Sleep Now, Father?

"Hard and honest work earns a good night's sleep" (Ecclesiastes 5:12 The Message).

A Man's Journey with God Day 14

Today's Date ____________________ ❑ Eightfold Anointing

DAY 14—Creation Awaits Our Consecration

"For the creation was subjected to futility, . . . the creation itself also will be delivered from the bondage of corruption into the glorious liberty of the children of God. For we know that the whole creation groans and labors with birth pangs together until now" (Romans 8:20-22 NKJV).

Today's Four Bible Chapters and Notes from Through the Bible Readings

____

____

____

____

Prayer Priority List

"And he spake a parable unto them to this end, that men ought always to pray, and not to faint" (Luke 18:1 KJV).

1. Right Relationship With God

____

____

____

____

2. Family Needs And Destiny

____

____

____

3. Fivefold Ministry

____

____

____

4. Leaders—Local, State, Nation, World

____

____

5. Other Needs

____

Thought for the Day

Your next level of Christian leadership will require increased consecration. The whole creation groans and travails in pain, waiting for the sons of God to be manifested (Romans 8:20-22). The world is waiting for you to become more consecrated so that you can lead them out of the mess that they are in. Because of the purity of your heart, you can be trusted to take them somewhere in God they couldn't get to on their own.

24-Hour Self-Accountability *Jesus Christ left us an example, that we should follow in His steps (1 Peter 2:21).*			
Date		**Planned Schedule**	**Actual Schedule and Notes**
	12:00 A.M.		
	1:00 A.M.		
	2:00 A.M.		
	3:00 A.M.		
	4:00 A.M.		
	5:00 A.M.		
	6:00 A.M.		
	7:00 A.M.		
	8:00 A.M.		
	9:00 A.M.		
	10:00 A.M.		
	11:00 A.M.		
	12:00 NOON		
	1:00 P.M.		
	2:00 P.M.		
	3:00 P.M.		
	4:00 P.M.		
	5:00 P.M.		
	6:00 P.M.		
	7:00 P.M.		
	8:00 P.M.		
	9:00 P.M.		
	10:00 P.M.		
	11:00 P.M.		

Personal Daily Checklist

"For if we would judge ourselves, we should not be judged" (1 Corinthians 11:31 KJV).

Grade yourself, A, B, or C, for each one or rate yourself on a scale of 1 (lowest) to 10 (highest).

Checklist Item	Today's Score	Checklist Item	Today's Score
❑ Time in Prayer		❑ Time with My Friends	
❑ Time in Word of God		❑ Time with the Lost	
❑ Praise & Worship		❑ Time to Eat Right	
❑ Thanksgiving		❑ Time to Exercise	
❑ Fasting		❑ Time to Organize	
❑ Time with My Family		❑ Time Alone with God	

Today's Expenses and Money Management

"It is He who gives you power to get wealth, that He may establish His covenant (Deuteronomy 8:18 NKJV).

____

____

Servanthood for Today

Jesus said, "But he that is greatest among you shall be your servant" (Matthew 23:11 KJV).

____

____

My Insights for Today

Jesus said, "But he that is greatest among you shall be your servant" (Matthew 23:11 KJV).

____

____

May I Go To Sleep Now, Father?

"Hard and honest work earns a good night's sleep" (Ecclesiastes 5:12 The Message).

A Man's Journey with God Day 15

Today's Date ____________________ ❑ Eightfold Anointing

DAY 15—Ignore the Mockers and Stay Focused

"Then Moses lifted his hand and struck the rock twice with his rod . . . Then the Lord spoke to Moses and Aaron, 'Because you did not believe Me, to hallow Me in the eyes of the children of Israel, therefore you shall not bring this assembly into the land which I have given them'" (Numbers 20:11-12 NKJV).

Today's Four Bible Chapters and Notes from Through the Bible Readings

____

____

____

____

Prayer Priority List

"And he spake a parable unto them to this end, that men ought always to pray, and not to faint" (Luke 18:1 KJV).

1. Right Relationship With God

____

____

____

____

2. Family Needs And Destiny

____

____

____

3. Fivefold Ministry

____

____

____

4. Leaders—Local, State, Nation, World

____

____

5. Other Needs

____

Thought for the Day

Moses was used mightily by God, but he had a gap in his consecration, and God called him to account. As they approached the Promised Land, God took Moses away because of his sin and turned over the leadership of those millions of people to Joshua, Moses' disciple. Never become so comfortable in your consecration that you take God for granted. Stay focused on His will—both for you and for those around you.

24-Hour Self-Accountability

Jesus Christ left us an example, that we should follow in His steps (1 Peter 2:21).

Date		Planned Schedule	Actual Schedule and Notes
	12:00 A.M.		
	1:00 A.M.		
	2:00 A.M.		
	3:00 A.M.		
	4:00 A.M.		
	5:00 A.M.		
	6:00 A.M.		
	7:00 A.M.		
	8:00 A.M.		
	9:00 A.M.		
	10:00 A.M.		
	11:00 A.M.		
	12:00 NOON		
	1:00 P.M.		
	2:00 P.M.		
	3:00 P.M.		
	4:00 P.M.		
	5:00 P.M.		
	6:00 P.M.		
	7:00 P.M.		
	8:00 P.M.		
	9:00 P.M.		
	10:00 P.M.		
	11:00 P.M.		

Personal Daily Checklist

"For if we would judge ourselves, we should not be judged" (1 Corinthians 11:31 KJV).

Grade yourself, A, B, or C, for each one or rate yourself on a scale of 1 (lowest) to 10 (highest).

Checklist Item	Today's Score	Checklist Item	Today's Score
❑ Time in Prayer		❑ Time with My Friends	
❑ Time in Word of God		❑ Time with the Lost	
❑ Praise & Worship		❑ Time to Eat Right	
❑ Thanksgiving		❑ Time to Exercise	
❑ Fasting		❑ Time to Organize	
❑ Time with My Family		❑ Time Alone with God	

Today's Expenses and Money Management

"It is He who gives you power to get wealth, that He may establish His covenant (Deuteronomy 8:18 NKJV).

____

____

Servanthood for Today

Jesus said, "But he that is greatest among you shall be your servant" (Matthew 23:11 KJV).

____

____

My Insights for Today

Jesus said, "But he that is greatest among you shall be your servant" (Matthew 23:11 KJV).

____

____

May I Go To Sleep Now, Father?

"Hard and honest work earns a good night's sleep" (Ecclesiastes 5:12 The Message).

A Man's Journey with God Day 16

Today's Date ____________________ ❑ Eightfold Anointing

DAY 16—Sanctify Yourself—Victory Is at Hand!

"Joshua said unto the people, Sanctify yourselves: for tomorrow the Lord will do wonders among you" (Joshua 3:5 KJV).

Today's Four Bible Chapters and Notes from Through the Bible Readings

Prayer Priority List

"And he spake a parable unto them to this end, that men ought always to pray, and not to faint" (Luke 18:1 KJV).

1. Right Relationship With God

2. Family Needs And Destiny

3. Fivefold Ministry

4. Leaders—Local, State, Nation, World

5. Other Needs

Thought for the Day

Joshua knew that sin could hinder them from crossing the Jordan, so he prepared himself, the priests, and the people by telling them, "Sanctify yourselves." They needed to be holy so they could hear from a holy God in the midst of battle. Sin hinders you from defeating your adversaries, so get rid of sin, then go on with God to win.

24-Hour Self-Accountability

Jesus Christ left us an example, that we should follow in His steps (1 Peter 2:21).

Date		Planned Schedule	Actual Schedule and Notes
	12:00 A.M.		
	1:00 A.M.		
	2:00 A.M.		
	3:00 A.M.		
	4:00 A.M.		
	5:00 A.M.		
	6:00 A.M.		
	7:00 A.M.		
	8:00 A.M.		
	9:00 A.M.		
	10:00 A.M.		
	11:00 A.M.		
	12:00 NOON		
	1:00 P.M.		
	2:00 P.M.		
	3:00 P.M.		
	4:00 P.M.		
	5:00 P.M.		
	6:00 P.M.		
	7:00 P.M.		
	8:00 P.M.		
	9:00 P.M.		
	10:00 P.M.		
	11:00 P.M.		

Personal Daily Checklist

"For if we would judge ourselves, we should not be judged" (1 Corinthians 11:31 KJV).

Grade yourself, A, B, or C, for each one or rate yourself on a scale of 1 (lowest) to 10 (highest).

Checklist Item	Today's Score	Checklist Item	Today's Score
❑ Time in Prayer		❑ Time with My Friends	
❑ Time in Word of God		❑ Time with the Lost	
❑ Praise & Worship		❑ Time to Eat Right	
❑ Thanksgiving		❑ Time to Exercise	
❑ Fasting		❑ Time to Organize	
❑ Time with My Family		❑ Time Alone with God	

Today's Expenses and Money Management

"It is He who gives you power to get wealth, that He may establish His covenant (Deuteronomy 8:18 NKJV).

____

____

Servanthood for Today

Jesus said, "But he that is greatest among you shall be your servant" (Matthew 23:11 KJV).

____

____

My Insights for Today

Jesus said, "But he that is greatest among you shall be your servant" (Matthew 23:11 KJV).

____

____

May I Go To Sleep Now, Father?

"Hard and honest work earns a good night's sleep" (Ecclesiastes 5:12 The Message).

A Man's Journey with God Day 17

Today's Date ____________________ ❑ Eightfold Anointing

DAY 17—The Greatest Love Is Laying Down Your Life for Others

"Greater love hath no man than this, that a man lay down his life for his friends" (John 15:13 KJV).

Today's Four Bible Chapters and Notes from Through the Bible Readings

____

____

____

____

Prayer Priority List

"And he spake a parable unto them to this end, that men ought always to pray, and not to faint" (Luke 18:1 KJV).

1. Right Relationship With God

____

____

____

____

2. Family Needs And Destiny

____

____

____

3. Fivefold Ministry

____

____

____

4. Leaders—Local, State, Nation, World

____

____

5. Other Needs

____

Thought for the Day

Christian songs and hymns of the past were about others—living your life to please God and ascending to receive your rewards. Today's songs are about you—your blessings, your feelings, and pleasing yourself—because musicians know that's what you want to hear. However, you're eliminated from becoming a resource person for the generation when you're need-based in your thinking. The true faith where you give up your life is Christianity, not Islam. All of the apostles except maybe John the Revelator died as martyrs.

24-Hour Self-Accountability

Jesus Christ left us an example, that we should follow in His steps (1 Peter 2:21).

Date		Planned Schedule	Actual Schedule and Notes
	12:00 A.M.		
	1:00 A.M.		
	2:00 A.M.		
	3:00 A.M.		
	4:00 A.M.		
	5:00 A.M.		
	6:00 A.M.		
	7:00 A.M.		
	8:00 A.M.		
	9:00 A.M.		
	10:00 A.M.		
	11:00 A.M.		
	12:00 NOON		
	1:00 P.M.		
	2:00 P.M.		
	3:00 P.M.		
	4:00 P.M.		
	5:00 P.M.		
	6:00 P.M.		
	7:00 P.M.		
	8:00 P.M.		
	9:00 P.M.		
	10:00 P.M.		
	11:00 P.M.		

Personal Daily Checklist

"For if we would judge ourselves, we should not be judged" (1 Corinthians 11:31 KJV).

Grade yourself, A, B, or C, for each one or rate yourself on a scale of 1 (lowest) to 10 (highest).

Checklist Item	Today's Score	Checklist Item	Today's Score
❑ Time in Prayer		❑ Time with My Friends	
❑ Time in Word of God		❑ Time with the Lost	
❑ Praise & Worship		❑ Time to Eat Right	
❑ Thanksgiving		❑ Time to Exercise	
❑ Fasting		❑ Time to Organize	
❑ Time with My Family		❑ Time Alone with God	

Today's Expenses and Money Management

"It is He who gives you power to get wealth, that He may establish His covenant (Deuteronomy 8:18 NKJV).

____

____

Servanthood for Today

Jesus said, "But he that is greatest among you shall be your servant" (Matthew 23:11 KJV).

____

____

My Insights for Today

Jesus said, "But he that is greatest among you shall be your servant" (Matthew 23:11 KJV).

____

____

May I Go To Sleep Now, Father?

"Hard and honest work earns a good night's sleep" (Ecclesiastes 5:12 The Message).

A Man's Journey with God Day 18

Today's Date ____________________ ❑ Eightfold Anointing

DAY 18—Pleasing God Is Your Goal, Not Pleasing People

"Obviously, I'm not trying to win the approval of people, but of God. If pleasing people were my goal, I would not be Christ's servant" (Galatians 1:10 NLT).

Today's Four Bible Chapters and Notes from Through the Bible Readings

____

____

____

____

Prayer Priority List

"And he spake a parable unto them to this end, that men ought always to pray, and not to faint" (Luke 18:1 KJV).

1. Right Relationship With God

____

____

____

____

2. Family Needs And Destiny

____

____

____

3. Fivefold Ministry

____

____

____

4. Leaders—Local, State, Nation, World

____

____

5. Other Needs

____

Thought for the Day

Let me just go on record. I don't want to stay the same. With no ceiling on the potential for growth, why would I want to just accomplish what I've accomplished so far when Almighty God is my Father? Why would I want to function as a mere human when I am born of God? Something has to break in me to be more and do more and no man can really define that level. You and I have got to satisfy the one who made us.

24-Hour Self-Accountability

Jesus Christ left us an example, that we should follow in His steps (1 Peter 2:21).

Date		Planned Schedule	Actual Schedule and Notes
	12:00 A.M.		
	1:00 A.M.		
	2:00 A.M.		
	3:00 A.M.		
	4:00 A.M.		
	5:00 A.M.		
	6:00 A.M.		
	7:00 A.M.		
	8:00 A.M.		
	9:00 A.M.		
	10:00 A.M.		
	11:00 A.M.		
	12:00 NOON		
	1:00 P.M.		
	2:00 P.M.		
	3:00 P.M.		
	4:00 P.M.		
	5:00 P.M.		
	6:00 P.M.		
	7:00 P.M.		
	8:00 P.M.		
	9:00 P.M.		
	10:00 P.M.		
	11:00 P.M.		

Personal Daily Checklist

"For if we would judge ourselves, we should not be judged" (1 Corinthians 11:31 KJV).

Grade yourself, A, B, or C, for each one or rate yourself on a scale of 1 (lowest) to 10 (highest).

Checklist Item	Today's Score	Checklist Item	Today's Score
❑ Time in Prayer		❑ Time with My Friends	
❑ Time in Word of God		❑ Time with the Lost	
❑ Praise & Worship		❑ Time to Eat Right	
❑ Thanksgiving		❑ Time to Exercise	
❑ Fasting		❑ Time to Organize	
❑ Time with My Family		❑ Time Alone with God	

Today's Expenses and Money Management

"It is He who gives you power to get wealth, that He may establish His covenant (Deuteronomy 8:18 NKJV).

____

____

Servanthood for Today

Jesus said, "But he that is greatest among you shall be your servant" (Matthew 23:11 KJV).

____

____

My Insights for Today

Jesus said, "But he that is greatest among you shall be your servant" (Matthew 23:11 KJV).

____

____

May I Go To Sleep Now, Father?

"Hard and honest work earns a good night's sleep" (Ecclesiastes 5:12 The Message).

A Man's Journey with God Day 19

Today's Date ____________________ ❑ Eightfold Anointing

DAY 19— Defeating Every Obstacle That Keeps Me from Hearing God

"The kings of the earth stood up, and the rulers were gathered together against the Lord, and against his Christ. . . . against thy holy child Jesus, whom thou hast anointed"

(Acts 4:26 KJV).

Today's Four Bible Chapters and Notes from Through the Bible Readings

____

____

____

____

Prayer Priority List

"And he spake a parable unto them to this end, that men ought always to pray, and not to faint" (Luke 18:1 KJV).

1. Right Relationship With God

____

____

____

____

2. Family Needs And Destiny

____

____

____

3. Fivefold Ministry

____

____

____

4. Leaders—Local, State, Nation, World

____

____

5. Other Needs

____

Thought for the Day

Christians fight a daily battle to take ground for God in their hearts. Our battles will never stop while we are on earth, because our enemies never stop trying to hinder us from hearing God and becoming more like His perfect, holy Child, Jesus.

24-Hour Self-Accountability

Jesus Christ left us an example, that we should follow in His steps (1 Peter 2:21).

Date		Planned Schedule	Actual Schedule and Notes
	12:00 A.M.		
	1:00 A.M.		
	2:00 A.M.		
	3:00 A.M.		
	4:00 A.M.		
	5:00 A.M.		
	6:00 A.M.		
	7:00 A.M.		
	8:00 A.M.		
	9:00 A.M.		
	10:00 A.M.		
	11:00 A.M.		
	12:00 NOON		
	1:00 P.M.		
	2:00 P.M.		
	3:00 P.M.		
	4:00 P.M.		
	5:00 P.M.		
	6:00 P.M.		
	7:00 P.M.		
	8:00 P.M.		
	9:00 P.M.		
	10:00 P.M.		
	11:00 P.M.		

Personal Daily Checklist

"For if we would judge ourselves, we should not be judged" (1 Corinthians 11:31 KJV).

Grade yourself, A, B, or C, for each one or rate yourself on a scale of 1 (lowest) to 10 (highest).

Checklist Item	Today's Score	Checklist Item	Today's Score
❑ Time in Prayer		❑ Time with My Friends	
❑ Time in Word of God		❑ Time with the Lost	
❑ Praise & Worship		❑ Time to Eat Right	
❑ Thanksgiving		❑ Time to Exercise	
❑ Fasting		❑ Time to Organize	
❑ Time with My Family		❑ Time Alone with God	

Today's Expenses and Money Management

"It is He who gives you power to get wealth, that He may establish His covenant (Deuteronomy 8:18 NKJV).

____

____

Servanthood for Today

Jesus said, "But he that is greatest among you shall be your servant" (Matthew 23:11 KJV).

____

____

My Insights for Today

Jesus said, "But he that is greatest among you shall be your servant" (Matthew 23:11 KJV).

____

____

May I Go To Sleep Now, Father?

"Hard and honest work earns a good night's sleep" (Ecclesiastes 5:12 The Message).

A Man's Journey with God Day 20

Today's Date ____________________ ❑ Eightfold Anointing

DAY 20—Be Fearless in the Face of God's Enemies

"Mine enemies would daily swallow me up: for they be many that fight against me . . . What time I am afraid, I will trust in thee. . . . I will not fear what flesh can do unto me" (Psalms 56:1-4 KJV).

Today's Four Bible Chapters and Notes from Through the Bible Readings

____

____

____

____

Prayer Priority List

"And he spake a parable unto them to this end, that men ought always to pray, and not to faint" (Luke 18:1 KJV).

1. Right Relationship With God

____

____

____

____

2. Family Needs And Destiny

____

____

____

3. Fivefold Ministry

____

____

____

4. Leaders—Local, State, Nation, World

____

____

5. Other Needs

____

Thought for the Day

Consecration is your pre-game preparation for the spiritual conflicts that you face each day in the game of life. Consecration is staying in shape to be a fearless champion who can defeat the enemies of God in your own life and then in the lives of others.

24-Hour Self-Accountability

Jesus Christ left us an example, that we should follow in His steps (1 Peter 2:21).

Date		Planned Schedule	Actual Schedule and Notes
	12:00 A.M.		
	1:00 A.M.		
	2:00 A.M.		
	3:00 A.M.		
	4:00 A.M.		
	5:00 A.M.		
	6:00 A.M.		
	7:00 A.M.		
	8:00 A.M.		
	9:00 A.M.		
	10:00 A.M.		
	11:00 A.M.		
	12:00 NOON		
	1:00 P.M.		
	2:00 P.M.		
	3:00 P.M.		
	4:00 P.M.		
	5:00 P.M.		
	6:00 P.M.		
	7:00 P.M.		
	8:00 P.M.		
	9:00 P.M.		
	10:00 P.M.		
	11:00 P.M.		

Personal Daily Checklist

"For if we would judge ourselves, we should not be judged" (1 Corinthians 11:31 KJV).

Grade yourself, A, B, or C, for each one or rate yourself on a scale of 1 (lowest) to 10 (highest).

Checklist Item	Today's Score	Checklist Item	Today's Score
❑ Time in Prayer		❑ Time with My Friends	
❑ Time in Word of God		❑ Time with the Lost	
❑ Praise & Worship		❑ Time to Eat Right	
❑ Thanksgiving		❑ Time to Exercise	
❑ Fasting		❑ Time to Organize	
❑ Time with My Family		❑ Time Alone with God	

Today's Expenses and Money Management

"It is He who gives you power to get wealth, that He may establish His covenant (Deuteronomy 8:18 NKJV).

____

____

Servanthood for Today

Jesus said, "But he that is greatest among you shall be your servant" (Matthew 23:11 KJV).

____

____

My Insights for Today

Jesus said, "But he that is greatest among you shall be your servant" (Matthew 23:11 KJV).

____

____

May I Go To Sleep Now, Father?

"Hard and honest work earns a good night's sleep" (Ecclesiastes 5:12 The Message).

A Man's Journey with God Day 21

Today's Date ____________________ ❑ Eightfold Anointing

DAY 21—Go and Make Disciples

"Therefore, go and make disciples of all the nations, baptizing them in the name of the Father and the Son and the Holy Spirit" (Matthew 28:19 NLT).

Today's Four Bible Chapters and Notes from Through the Bible Readings

____

____

____

____

Prayer Priority List

"And he spake a parable unto them to this end, that men ought always to pray, and not to faint" (Luke 18:1 KJV).

1. Right Relationship With God

____

____

____

____

2. Family Needs And Destiny

____

____

____

3. Fivefold Ministry

____

____

____

4. Leaders—Local, State, Nation, World

____

____

5. Other Needs

____

Thought for the Day

Jesus said, "Make disciples," but many who attend church today want religion more than a consecrated life. Those people like Sunday services. They like singing. They like good preaching. They like concerts with a Christian title. However, many of them aren't living anything. They need discipleship and you should prepare to give them that priceless gift.

24-Hour Self-Accountability

Jesus Christ left us an example, that we should follow in His steps (1 Peter 2:21).

Date		Planned Schedule	Actual Schedule and Notes
	12:00 A.M.		
	1:00 A.M.		
	2:00 A.M.		
	3:00 A.M.		
	4:00 A.M.		
	5:00 A.M.		
	6:00 A.M.		
	7:00 A.M.		
	8:00 A.M.		
	9:00 A.M.		
	10:00 A.M.		
	11:00 A.M.		
	12:00 NOON		
	1:00 P.M.		
	2:00 P.M.		
	3:00 P.M.		
	4:00 P.M.		
	5:00 P.M.		
	6:00 P.M.		
	7:00 P.M.		
	8:00 P.M.		
	9:00 P.M.		
	10:00 P.M.		
	11:00 P.M.		

Personal Daily Checklist

"For if we would judge ourselves, we should not be judged" (1 Corinthians 11:31 KJV).

Grade yourself, A, B, or C, for each one or rate yourself on a scale of 1 (lowest) to 10 (highest).

Checklist Item	Today's Score	Checklist Item	Today's Score
❑ Time in Prayer		❑ Time with My Friends	
❑ Time in Word of God		❑ Time with the Lost	
❑ Praise & Worship		❑ Time to Eat Right	
❑ Thanksgiving		❑ Time to Exercise	
❑ Fasting		❑ Time to Organize	
❑ Time with My Family		❑ Time Alone with God	

Today's Expenses and Money Management

"It is He who gives you power to get wealth, that He may establish His covenant (Deuteronomy 8:18 NKJV).

____

____

Servanthood for Today

Jesus said, "But he that is greatest among you shall be your servant" (Matthew 23:11 KJV).

____

____

My Insights for Today

Jesus said, "But he that is greatest among you shall be your servant" (Matthew 23:11 KJV).

____

____

May I Go To Sleep Now, Father?

"Hard and honest work earns a good night's sleep" (Ecclesiastes 5:12 The Message).

A Man's Journey with God Day 22

Today's Date ____________________ ❑ Eightfold Anointing

DAY 22—Your True Brothers Are Those Who Do God's Will

"Then Jesus' mother and brothers came to see him. . . . Jesus replied, 'Who is my mother? Who are my brothers? Then he looked at those around him and said, 'Look, these are my mother and brothers. Anyone who does God's will is my brother and sister and mother (Mark 3:31, 33-35 NLT).

Today's Four Bible Chapters and Notes from Through the Bible Readings

____

____

____

____

Prayer Priority List

"And he spake a parable unto them to this end, that men ought always to pray, and not to faint" (Luke 18:1 KJV).

1. Right Relationship With God

____

____

____

____

2. Family Needs And Destiny

____

____

____

3. Fivefold Ministry

____

____

____

4. Leaders—Local, State, Nation, World

____

____

5. Other Needs

____

Thought for the Day

When it was my time to transition out of pastoring, my natural son was not as qualified as my spiritual son to take over the church. He was in my bloodline, but that wasn't more important than having being a real disciple in my spiritual *bloodline. Jesus said, "Who is my mother and my brother? . . . Those who do the will of my Father."*

24-Hour Self-Accountability			
Jesus Christ left us an example, that we should follow in His steps (1 Peter 2:21).			
Date		**Planned Schedule**	**Actual Schedule and Notes**
	12:00 A.M.		
	1:00 A.M.		
	2:00 A.M.		
	3:00 A.M.		
	4:00 A.M.		
	5:00 A.M.		
	6:00 A.M.		
	7:00 A.M.		
	8:00 A.M.		
	9:00 A.M.		
	10:00 A.M.		
	11:00 A.M.		
	12:00 NOON		
	1:00 P.M.		
	2:00 P.M.		
	3:00 P.M.		
	4:00 P.M.		
	5:00 P.M.		
	6:00 P.M.		
	7:00 P.M.		
	8:00 P.M.		
	9:00 P.M.		
	10:00 P.M.		
	11:00 P.M.		

Personal Daily Checklist

"For if we would judge ourselves, we should not be judged" (1 Corinthians 11:31 KJV).

Grade yourself, A, B, or C, for each one or rate yourself on a scale of 1 (lowest) to 10 (highest).

Checklist Item	Today's Score	Checklist Item	Today's Score
❑ Time in Prayer		❑ Time with My Friends	
❑ Time in Word of God		❑ Time with the Lost	
❑ Praise & Worship		❑ Time to Eat Right	
❑ Thanksgiving		❑ Time to Exercise	
❑ Fasting		❑ Time to Organize	
❑ Time with My Family		❑ Time Alone with God	

Today's Expenses and Money Management

"It is He who gives you power to get wealth, that He may establish His covenant (Deuteronomy 8:18 NKJV).

____

____

Servanthood for Today

Jesus said, "But he that is greatest among you shall be your servant" (Matthew 23:11 KJV).

____

____

My Insights for Today

Jesus said, "But he that is greatest among you shall be your servant" (Matthew 23:11 KJV).

____

____

May I Go To Sleep Now, Father?

"Hard and honest work earns a good night's sleep" (Ecclesiastes 5:12 The Message).

A Man's Journey with God Day 23

Today's Date ______________________ ❑ Eightfold Anointing

DAY 23—Becoming a Spiritual Father

"For even if you had ten thousand others to teach you about Christ, you have only one spiritual father. For I became your father in Christ Jesus when I preached the Good News to you" (1 Corinthians 4:15 NLT).

Today's Four Bible Chapters and Notes from Through the Bible Readings

____

____

____

____

Prayer Priority List

"And he spake a parable unto them to this end, that men ought always to pray, and not to faint" (Luke 18:1 KJV).

1. Right Relationship With God

____

____

____

____

2. Family Needs And Destiny

____

____

____

3. Fivefold Ministry

____

____

____

4. Leaders—Local, State, Nation, World

____

____

5. Other Needs

____

Thought for the Day

Men are called to be both natural and spiritual fathers for this generation. One person can't do everything. Your son should be doing what you are clearly not ordained to do as effectively as he would do it. Even Jesus knew He would not be on earth forever. You should always be discipling spiritual sons to whom you can entrust the work you leave behind.

24-Hour Self-Accountability

Jesus Christ left us an example, that we should follow in His steps (1 Peter 2:21).

Date		Planned Schedule	Actual Schedule and Notes
	12:00 A.M.		
	1:00 A.M.		
	2:00 A.M.		
	3:00 A.M.		
	4:00 A.M.		
	5:00 A.M.		
	6:00 A.M.		
	7:00 A.M.		
	8:00 A.M.		
	9:00 A.M.		
	10:00 A.M.		
	11:00 A.M.		
	12:00 NOON		
	1:00 P.M.		
	2:00 P.M.		
	3:00 P.M.		
	4:00 P.M.		
	5:00 P.M.		
	6:00 P.M.		
	7:00 P.M.		
	8:00 P.M.		
	9:00 P.M.		
	10:00 P.M.		
	11:00 P.M.		

Personal Daily Checklist

"For if we would judge ourselves, we should not be judged" (1 Corinthians 11:31 KJV).

Grade yourself, A, B, or C, for each one or rate yourself on a scale of 1 (lowest) to 10 (highest).

Checklist Item	Today's Score	Checklist Item	Today's Score
❑ Time in Prayer		❑ Time with My Friends	
❑ Time in Word of God		❑ Time with the Lost	
❑ Praise & Worship		❑ Time to Eat Right	
❑ Thanksgiving		❑ Time to Exercise	
❑ Fasting		❑ Time to Organize	
❑ Time with My Family		❑ Time Alone with God	

Today's Expenses and Money Management

"It is He who gives you power to get wealth, that He may establish His covenant (Deuteronomy 8:18 NKJV).

Servanthood for Today

Jesus said, "But he that is greatest among you shall be your servant" (Matthew 23:11 KJV).

My Insights for Today

Jesus said, "But he that is greatest among you shall be your servant" (Matthew 23:11 KJV).

May I Go To Sleep Now, Father?

"Hard and honest work earns a good night's sleep" (Ecclesiastes 5:12 The Message).

A Man's Journey with God Day 24

Today's Date ______________________ ❑ Eightfold Anointing

DAY 24—Find Solitary Places to Be Alone with God

"At daybreak, Jesus went out to a solitary place. The people were looking for him and when they came to where he was, they tried to keep him from leaving them" (Luke 4:42 NIV).

Today's Four Bible Chapters and Notes from Through the Bible Readings

____

____

____

____

Prayer Priority List

"And he spake a parable unto them to this end, that men ought always to pray, and not to faint" (Luke 18:1 KJV).

1. Right Relationship With God

____

____

____

____

2. Family Needs And Destiny

____

____

____

3. Fivefold Ministry

____

____

____

4. Leaders—Local, State, Nation, World

____

____

5. Other Needs

____

Thought for the Day

When I pray, I go out in parking lot to be alone with God for hours. I'm not there to get a message to preach today. God comes on me. I'm out there getting filled with the reality of God. I'm feeding myself and growing. I'm not looking for sermons or acrostics. I need God. Find yourself a solitary place, as Jesus did, to prepare yourself for every responsibility He has ordained for you to accomplish and every life you need to be prepared to touch.

24-Hour Self-Accountability

Jesus Christ left us an example, that we should follow in His steps (1 Peter 2:21).

Date		Planned Schedule	Actual Schedule and Notes
	12:00 A.M.		
	1:00 A.M.		
	2:00 A.M.		
	3:00 A.M.		
	4:00 A.M.		
	5:00 A.M.		
	6:00 A.M.		
	7:00 A.M.		
	8:00 A.M.		
	9:00 A.M.		
	10:00 A.M.		
	11:00 A.M.		
	12:00 NOON		
	1:00 P.M.		
	2:00 P.M.		
	3:00 P.M.		
	4:00 P.M.		
	5:00 P.M.		
	6:00 P.M.		
	7:00 P.M.		
	8:00 P.M.		
	9:00 P.M.		
	10:00 P.M.		
	11:00 P.M.		

Personal Daily Checklist

"For if we would judge ourselves, we should not be judged" (1 Corinthians 11:31 KJV).

Grade yourself, A, B, or C, for each one or rate yourself on a scale of 1 (lowest) to 10 (highest).

Checklist Item	Today's Score	Checklist Item	Today's Score
❑ Time in Prayer		❑ Time with My Friends	
❑ Time in Word of God		❑ Time with the Lost	
❑ Praise & Worship		❑ Time to Eat Right	
❑ Thanksgiving		❑ Time to Exercise	
❑ Fasting		❑ Time to Organize	
❑ Time with My Family		❑ Time Alone with God	

Today's Expenses and Money Management

"It is He who gives you power to get wealth, that He may establish His covenant (Deuteronomy 8:18 NKJV).

____

____

Servanthood for Today

Jesus said, "But he that is greatest among you shall be your servant" (Matthew 23:11 KJV).

____

____

My Insights for Today

Jesus said, "But he that is greatest among you shall be your servant" (Matthew 23:11 KJV).

____

____

May I Go To Sleep Now, Father?

"Hard and honest work earns a good night's sleep" (Ecclesiastes 5:12 The Message).

A Man's Journey with God Day 25

Today's Date ____________________ ❑ Eightfold Anointing

DAY 25—You Don't Have Authority Until You Submit to Authority

"Obey them that have the rule over you, and submit yourselves: for they watch for your souls, as they that must give account, that they may do it with joy, and not with grief: for that is unprofitable for you" (Hebrews 13:17 KJV).

Today's Four Bible Chapters and Notes from Through the Bible Readings

____

____

____

____

Prayer Priority List

"And he spake a parable unto them to this end, that men ought always to pray, and not to faint" (Luke 18:1 KJV).

1. Right Relationship With God

____

____

____

____

2. Family Needs And Destiny

____

____

____

3. Fivefold Ministry

____

____

____

4. Leaders—Local, State, Nation, World

____

____

5. Other Needs

____

Thought for the Day

Do you hold a position of authority? Where did you receive that authority? When was the last time you were challenged? The Bible says, "Obey them that have the rule over you . . . for they watch for your souls." In the economy of God, you cannot have authority without being under authority. You can't fool God. You can't play games with submission in the economy of God and receive real authority. It's not going to happen.

24-Hour Self-Accountability

Jesus Christ left us an example, that we should follow in His steps (1 Peter 2:21).

Date		Planned Schedule	Actual Schedule and Notes
	12:00 A.M.		
	1:00 A.M.		
	2:00 A.M.		
	3:00 A.M.		
	4:00 A.M.		
	5:00 A.M.		
	6:00 A.M.		
	7:00 A.M.		
	8:00 A.M.		
	9:00 A.M.		
	10:00 A.M.		
	11:00 A.M.		
	12:00 NOON		
	1:00 P.M.		
	2:00 P.M.		
	3:00 P.M.		
	4:00 P.M.		
	5:00 P.M.		
	6:00 P.M.		
	7:00 P.M.		
	8:00 P.M.		
	9:00 P.M.		
	10:00 P.M.		
	11:00 P.M.		

Personal Daily Checklist

"For if we would judge ourselves, we should not be judged" (1 Corinthians 11:31 KJV).

Grade yourself, A, B, or C, for each one or rate yourself on a scale of 1 (lowest) to 10 (highest).

Checklist Item	Today's Score	Checklist Item	Today's Score
❑ Time in Prayer		❑ Time with My Friends	
❑ Time in Word of God		❑ Time with the Lost	
❑ Praise & Worship		❑ Time to Eat Right	
❑ Thanksgiving		❑ Time to Exercise	
❑ Fasting		❑ Time to Organize	
❑ Time with My Family		❑ Time Alone with God	

Today's Expenses and Money Management

"It is He who gives you power to get wealth, that He may establish His covenant (Deuteronomy 8:18 NKJV).

Servanthood for Today

Jesus said, "But he that is greatest among you shall be your servant" (Matthew 23:11 KJV).

My Insights for Today

Jesus said, "But he that is greatest among you shall be your servant" (Matthew 23:11 KJV).

May I Go To Sleep Now, Father?

"Hard and honest work earns a good night's sleep" (Ecclesiastes 5:12 The Message).

A Man's Journey with God Day 26

Today's Date ____________________ ❑ Eightfold Anointing

DAY 26—Stay Conscious of the Need to Please Jesus

"When the Son of Man returns, it will be like it was in Noah's day. . . . People didn't realize what was going to happen until the flood came and swept them all away. That is the way it will be when the Son of Man comes" (Matthew 24:37, 39 NLT).

Today's Four Bible Chapters and Notes from Through the Bible Readings

____

____

____

____

Prayer Priority List

"And he spake a parable unto them to this end, that men ought always to pray, and not to faint" (Luke 18:1 KJV).

1. Right Relationship With God

____

____

____

____

2. Family Needs And Destiny

____

____

____

3. Fivefold Ministry

____

____

____

4. Leaders—Local, State, Nation, World

____

____

5. Other Needs

____

Thought for the Day

Many of today's political candidates need to change from being a politician to being a statesman. One is ruled the tyranny of the masses. The other is character based. It's who you really are without the pretense. God is going to look at the cover-ups, the manipulation, and the pretenses you used to get where you are. That will count against you. I don't want God upset with me. I don't mind people being upset with me. But God, I can't beat God.

24-Hour Self-Accountability			
Jesus Christ left us an example, that we should follow in His steps (1 Peter 2:21).			
Date		**Planned Schedule**	**Actual Schedule and Notes**
	12:00 A.M.		
	1:00 A.M.		
	2:00 A.M.		
	3:00 A.M.		
	4:00 A.M.		
	5:00 A.M.		
	6:00 A.M.		
	7:00 A.M.		
	8:00 A.M.		
	9:00 A.M.		
	10:00 A.M.		
	11:00 A.M.		
	12:00 NOON		
	1:00 P.M.		
	2:00 P.M.		
	3:00 P.M.		
	4:00 P.M.		
	5:00 P.M.		
	6:00 P.M.		
	7:00 P.M.		
	8:00 P.M.		
	9:00 P.M.		
	10:00 P.M.		
	11:00 P.M.		

Personal Daily Checklist

"For if we would judge ourselves, we should not be judged" (1 Corinthians 11:31 KJV).

Grade yourself, A, B, or C, for each one or rate yourself on a scale of 1 (lowest) to 10 (highest).

Checklist Item	Today's Score	Checklist Item	Today's Score
❑ Time in Prayer		❑ Time with My Friends	
❑ Time in Word of God		❑ Time with the Lost	
❑ Praise & Worship		❑ Time to Eat Right	
❑ Thanksgiving		❑ Time to Exercise	
❑ Fasting		❑ Time to Organize	
❑ Time with My Family		❑ Time Alone with God	

Today's Expenses and Money Management

"It is He who gives you power to get wealth, that He may establish His covenant (Deuteronomy 8:18 NKJV).

____

____

Servanthood for Today

Jesus said, "But he that is greatest among you shall be your servant" (Matthew 23:11 KJV).

____

____

My Insights for Today

Jesus said, "But he that is greatest among you shall be your servant" (Matthew 23:11 KJV).

____

____

May I Go To Sleep Now, Father?

"Hard and honest work earns a good night's sleep" (Ecclesiastes 5:12 The Message).

A Man's Journey with God Day 27

Today's Date ____________________ ❑ Eightfold Anointing

DAY 27—Let God's Blessings Lead You to Repentance

"Don't you see how wonderfully kind, tolerant, and patient God is with you? Does this mean nothing to you? Can't you see that his kindness is intended to turn you from your sin?" (Romans 2:4 NLT).

Today's Four Bible Chapters and Notes from Through the Bible Readings

____

____

____

____

Prayer Priority List

"And he spake a parable unto them to this end, that men ought always to pray, and not to faint" (Luke 18:1 KJV).

1. Right Relationship With God	**3. Fivefold Ministry**
____________________	____________________
____________________	____________________
____________________	____________________
____________________	**4. Leaders—Local, State, Nation, World**
2. Family Needs And Destiny	____________________
____________________	____________________
____________________	**5. Other Needs**
____________________	____________________

Thought for the Day

Do the churches understand that God's judgment is coming? Because right now what you hear about is blessing. Lord, don't correct my behavior. Just bless me with me living in debauchery. No, the true blessings of God lead men to repentance. God can be so good it breaks you down because you know you ill deserve it. You say, "Oh God, I'm so sorry. I'm so blessed. You know I don't deserve it."

24-Hour Self-Accountability

Jesus Christ left us an example, that we should follow in His steps (1 Peter 2:21).

Date		Planned Schedule	Actual Schedule and Notes
	12:00 A.M.		
	1:00 A.M.		
	2:00 A.M.		
	3:00 A.M.		
	4:00 A.M.		
	5:00 A.M.		
	6:00 A.M.		
	7:00 A.M.		
	8:00 A.M.		
	9:00 A.M.		
	10:00 A.M.		
	11:00 A.M.		
	12:00 NOON		
	1:00 P.M.		
	2:00 P.M.		
	3:00 P.M.		
	4:00 P.M.		
	5:00 P.M.		
	6:00 P.M.		
	7:00 P.M.		
	8:00 P.M.		
	9:00 P.M.		
	10:00 P.M.		
	11:00 P.M.		

Personal Daily Checklist

"For if we would judge ourselves, we should not be judged" (1 Corinthians 11:31 KJV).

Grade yourself, A, B, or C, for each one or rate yourself on a scale of 1 (lowest) to 10 (highest).

Checklist Item	Today's Score	Checklist Item	Today's Score
❑ Time in Prayer		❑ Time with My Friends	
❑ Time in Word of God		❑ Time with the Lost	
❑ Praise & Worship		❑ Time to Eat Right	
❑ Thanksgiving		❑ Time to Exercise	
❑ Fasting		❑ Time to Organize	
❑ Time with My Family		❑ Time Alone with God	

Today's Expenses and Money Management

"It is He who gives you power to get wealth, that He may establish His covenant (Deuteronomy 8:18 NKJV).

____

____

Servanthood for Today

Jesus said, "But he that is greatest among you shall be your servant" (Matthew 23:11 KJV).

____

____

My Insights for Today

Jesus said, "But he that is greatest among you shall be your servant" (Matthew 23:11 KJV).

____

____

May I Go To Sleep Now, Father?

"Hard and honest work earns a good night's sleep" (Ecclesiastes 5:12 The Message).

A Man's Journey with God Day 28

Today's Date ____________________ ❑ Eightfold Anointing

DAY 28—My Goal of Oneness with God

"Now may the God of peace Himself sanctify you completely; and may your whole spirit, soul, and body be preserved blameless at the coming of our Lord Jesus Christ" (1 Thessalonians 5:22-23 NKJV).

Today's Four Bible Chapters and Notes from Through the Bible Readings

____

____

____

____

Prayer Priority List

"And he spake a parable unto them to this end, that men ought always to pray, and not to faint" (Luke 18:1 KJV).

1. Right Relationship With God

____

____

____

____

2. Family Needs And Destiny

____

____

____

3. Fivefold Ministry

____

____

____

4. Leaders—Local, State, Nation, World

____

____

5. Other Needs

____

Thought for the Day

Your calling is complete oneness with God—spirit, soul, and body. Sometimes that means that you will cannot be one with others. When He comes, your reward will be to hear Him say that you are blameless in the day of Jesus Christ.

24-Hour Self-Accountability

Jesus Christ left us an example, that we should follow in His steps (1 Peter 2:21).

Date		Planned Schedule	Actual Schedule and Notes
	12:00 A.M.		
	1:00 A.M.		
	2:00 A.M.		
	3:00 A.M.		
	4:00 A.M.		
	5:00 A.M.		
	6:00 A.M.		
	7:00 A.M.		
	8:00 A.M.		
	9:00 A.M.		
	10:00 A.M.		
	11:00 A.M.		
	12:00 NOON		
	1:00 P.M.		
	2:00 P.M.		
	3:00 P.M.		
	4:00 P.M.		
	5:00 P.M.		
	6:00 P.M.		
	7:00 P.M.		
	8:00 P.M.		
	9:00 P.M.		
	10:00 P.M.		
	11:00 P.M.		

Personal Daily Checklist

"For if we would judge ourselves, we should not be judged" (1 Corinthians 11:31 KJV).

Grade yourself, A, B, or C, for each one or rate yourself on a scale of 1 (lowest) to 10 (highest).

Checklist Item	Today's Score	Checklist Item	Today's Score
❑ Time in Prayer		❑ Time with My Friends	
❑ Time in Word of God		❑ Time with the Lost	
❑ Praise & Worship		❑ Time to Eat Right	
❑ Thanksgiving		❑ Time to Exercise	
❑ Fasting		❑ Time to Organize	
❑ Time with My Family		❑ Time Alone with God	

Today's Expenses and Money Management

"It is He who gives you power to get wealth, that He may establish His covenant (Deuteronomy 8:18 NKJV).

____

____

Servanthood for Today

Jesus said, "But he that is greatest among you shall be your servant" (Matthew 23:11 KJV).

____

____

My Insights for Today

Jesus said, "But he that is greatest among you shall be your servant" (Matthew 23:11 KJV).

____

____

May I Go To Sleep Now, Father?

"Hard and honest work earns a good night's sleep" (Ecclesiastes 5:12 The Message).

A Man's Journey with God Day 29

Today's Date ____________________ ❑ Eightfold Anointing

DAY 29—A Man's Battle to Stay Faith

"I have fought a good fight, I have finished my course, I have kept the faith: Henceforth there is laid up for me a crown of righteousness, which the Lord, the righteous judge, shall give me at that day" (2 Timothy 4:7-8 KJV).

Today's Four Bible Chapters and Notes from Through the Bible Readings

____

____

____

____

Prayer Priority List

"And he spake a parable unto them to this end, that men ought always to pray, and not to faint" (Luke 18:1 KJV).

1. Right Relationship With God

____

____

____

____

2. Family Needs And Destiny

____

____

____

3. Fivefold Ministry

____

____

____

4. Leaders—Local, State, Nation, World

____

____

5. Other Needs

____

Thought for the Day

As we grow up in God, we know how to sense when we are in the will of the Lord. We do not drift around wondering what He wants us to do. We see it, we obey, and we fight to the finish until His will is completed in our lives.

24-Hour Self-Accountability

Jesus Christ left us an example, that we should follow in His steps (1 Peter 2:21).

Date		Planned Schedule	Actual Schedule and Notes
	12:00 A.M.		
	1:00 A.M.		
	2:00 A.M.		
	3:00 A.M.		
	4:00 A.M.		
	5:00 A.M.		
	6:00 A.M.		
	7:00 A.M.		
	8:00 A.M.		
	9:00 A.M.		
	10:00 A.M.		
	11:00 A.M.		
	12:00 NOON		
	1:00 P.M.		
	2:00 P.M.		
	3:00 P.M.		
	4:00 P.M.		
	5:00 P.M.		
	6:00 P.M.		
	7:00 P.M.		
	8:00 P.M.		
	9:00 P.M.		
	10:00 P.M.		
	11:00 P.M.		

Personal Daily Checklist

"For if we would judge ourselves, we should not be judged" (1 Corinthians 11:31 KJV).

Grade yourself, A, B, or C, for each one or rate yourself on a scale of 1 (lowest) to 10 (highest).

Checklist Item	Today's Score	Checklist Item	Today's Score
❑ Time in Prayer		❑ Time with My Friends	
❑ Time in Word of God		❑ Time with the Lost	
❑ Praise & Worship		❑ Time to Eat Right	
❑ Thanksgiving		❑ Time to Exercise	
❑ Fasting		❑ Time to Organize	
❑ Time with My Family		❑ Time Alone with God	

Today's Expenses and Money Management

"It is He who gives you power to get wealth, that He may establish His covenant (Deuteronomy 8:18 NKJV).

____

____

Servanthood for Today

Jesus said, "But he that is greatest among you shall be your servant" (Matthew 23:11 KJV).

____

____

My Insights for Today

Jesus said, "But he that is greatest among you shall be your servant" (Matthew 23:11 KJV).

____

____

May I Go To Sleep Now, Father?

"Hard and honest work earns a good night's sleep" (Ecclesiastes 5:12 The Message).

A Man's Journey with God Day 30

Today's Date ____________________ ❑ Eightfold Anointing

DAY 30—Changed by the Touch of Jesus

"And, behold, there came a leper and worshipped him, saying, Lord, if thou wilt, thou canst make me clean. And Jesus put forth his hand, and touched him, saying, I will; be thou clean. And immediately his leprosy was cleansed" (Matthew 8:2-3 KJV).

Today's Four Bible Chapters and Notes from Through the Bible Readings

____

____

____

____

Prayer Priority List

"And he spake a parable unto them to this end, that men ought always to pray, and not to faint" (Luke 18:1 KJV).

1. Right Relationship With God

____

____

____

____

2. Family Needs And Destiny

____

____

____

3. Fivefold Ministry

____

____

____

4. Leaders—Local, State, Nation, World

____

____

5. Other Needs

____

Thought for the Day

Jesus is able to make you clean, if you recognize your need and ask Him for His help. He washes away all the after-effects of your sin. When you are cleansed from sin on the inside, you look different on the outside. Others will notice something different about your life.

24-Hour Self-Accountability

Jesus Christ left us an example, that we should follow in His steps (1 Peter 2:21).

Date		Planned Schedule	Actual Schedule and Notes
	12:00 A.M.		
	1:00 A.M.		
	2:00 A.M.		
	3:00 A.M.		
	4:00 A.M.		
	5:00 A.M.		
	6:00 A.M.		
	7:00 A.M.		
	8:00 A.M.		
	9:00 A.M.		
	10:00 A.M.		
	11:00 A.M.		
	12:00 NOON		
	1:00 P.M.		
	2:00 P.M.		
	3:00 P.M.		
	4:00 P.M.		
	5:00 P.M.		
	6:00 P.M.		
	7:00 P.M.		
	8:00 P.M.		
	9:00 P.M.		
	10:00 P.M.		
	11:00 P.M.		

Personal Daily Checklist

"For if we would judge ourselves, we should not be judged" (1 Corinthians 11:31 KJV).

Grade yourself, A, B, or C, for each one or rate yourself on a scale of 1 (lowest) to 10 (highest).

Checklist Item	Today's Score	Checklist Item	Today's Score
❑ Time in Prayer		❑ Time with My Friends	
❑ Time in Word of God		❑ Time with the Lost	
❑ Praise & Worship		❑ Time to Eat Right	
❑ Thanksgiving		❑ Time to Exercise	
❑ Fasting		❑ Time to Organize	
❑ Time with My Family		❑ Time Alone with God	

Today's Expenses and Money Management

"It is He who gives you power to get wealth, that He may establish His covenant (Deuteronomy 8:18 NKJV).

Servanthood for Today

My Insights for Today

May I Go To Sleep Now, Father?

"Hard and honest work earns a good night's sleep" (Ecclesiastes 5:12 The Message*).*

Conclusion

What's Next, Papa?

What to do now that your
30 days are completed

By this time you have completed 30 days of *A Man's Journey with God*. It is time to start on your next journey as you are becoming more like Christ and moving toward your ultimate destination of eternal life.

The allegory of Pilgrim's Progress

John Bunyan (1628-1688) wrote an allegory called *Pilgrim's Progress* that almost all Christian parents read to their children in the early history of America. Bunyan wrote about the journey of a character named Christian who set out on a journey for the Celestial City and met many dangers and distractions along the way. Children who grew up reading this book—as well as their parents—learned about the trials and temptations of life so that they would be prepared to meet them. They read about how Christian resisted evil, got rid of his burden of sin at the cross, and finally was welcomed joyfully into heaven (the Celestial City) for the marriage supper of the Lamb.

Below is a short excerpt from the joyful conclusion of his journey as Christian reaches heaven.

> *"Now while they were thus drawing towards the gate, behold a company of the heavenly host came out to meet them; to whom it was said, by the other two Shining Ones, These are the men that have loved our Lord when they were in the world, and that have left all for his holy name; and he hath sent us to fetch them, and we have brought them thus far on their desired journey, that they may go in and look their Redeemer in the face with joy.*

Then the heavenly host gave a great shout, saying, Blessed are they which are called unto the marriage supper of the Lamb. There came out also at this time to meet them, several of the King's trumpeters, clothed in white and shining raiment, who, with melodious noises, and loud, made even the heavens to echo with their sound. These trumpeters saluted Christian and his fellow with ten thousand welcomes from the world; and this they did with shouting, and sound of trumpet."

John Bunyan, *Pilgrim's Progress*

As you move forward on your journey, it is my prayer that you will bring the next revival. You will no longer think of Jesus as Someone outside of you. You will think of Him as Someone inside. You will recognize that it is your birthright to possess Jesus' spiritual DNA. Instead of trying to avoid danger, you will offer yourself to God for dangerous assignments until that day when you are welcomed with joy into your heavenly home.

Adventurous expectancy of the resurrection life

Romans 8

The Message

"This resurrection life you received from God is not a timid, grave-tending life. It's adventurously expectant, greeting God with a childlike, ***'What's next, Papa?'*** *God's Spirit touches our spirits and confirms who we really are. We know who he is, and we know who we are. Father and children. And we know we are going to get what's coming to us—an unbelievable inheritance!*
We go through exactly what Christ goes through. If we go through the hard times with him, then we're certainly going to go through the good times with him!"

The passage above from Romans 8 in *The Message* says our life is not for grave-tending. We are fully alive—expecting and greeting God, always ready for a new adventure. The Jesus in you and me is a real Jesus. His power is real. His life working through your life is dynamic and exciting. Every day holds new promise.

Maybe yesterday was a failure, but today is going to be awesome. You will take ground. God's mercy saw fit that you should awaken so there must be something that you and God are going to conquer today. He isn't trying to let you exist to barely make it. You are called, as the Bible says, to walk like Christ, because Christ is not only *in* your life. He *is* your life.

Newness of life *Romans 6:4-5* *KJV*	*"... that like as Christ was raised up from the dead by the glory of the Father, even so we also should walk in newness of life. For if we have been planted together in the likeness of his death, we shall be also in the likeness of his resurrection."*

Say this out loud—real loud!

From now on,
I will walk as if Jesus is real,
Because He is real.
And as if God were leading me,
Because He is leading me.
I have a new life, a resurrection life!
And I am not turning back to my old grave-tending life.

Now sing this!

I have decided to follow Jesus;
I have decided to follow Jesus;
I have decided to follow Jesus;
No turning back, no turning back.[351]

Now ask God this question!

What's next, Papa?

[351] These were the dying words of a 19th Century Christian martyr in India. They became a popular hymn attributed to S. Sundar Singh. The words express all-out commitment to Jesus regardless of the cost. Public domain.

Day 31—Starting a New Journey

Today's Date ____________________ ❑ Eightfold Anointing

DAY 31—Joy Gives You Strength for the Journey

"For this day is holy unto our Lord: neither be ye sorry; for the joy of the Lord is your strength. So the Levites stilled all the people, saying, Hold your peace,
for the day is holy" (Nehemiah 8:10-11 KJV).

Today's Four Bible Chapters and Notes from Through the Bible Readings

____

____

____

____

Prayer Priority List

"And he spake a parable unto them to this end, that men ought always to pray, and not to faint" (Luke 18:1 KJV).

1. Right Relationship With God

____

____

____

____

2. Family Needs And Destiny

____

____

____

3. Fivefold Ministry

____

____

____

4. Leaders—Local, State, Nation, World

____

____

5. Other Needs

____

Thought for the Day

You cannot carry the joy of the Lord and discouragement at the same time. When you make each day a holy day, you receive His joy and you are able to drive away discouragement. The joy of the Lord gives you strength for the journey every day.

24-Hour Self-Accountability

Jesus Christ left us an example, that we should follow in His steps (1 Peter 2:21).

Date		**Planned Schedule**	**Actual Schedule and Notes**
	12:00 A.M.		
	1:00 A.M.		
	2:00 A.M.		
	3:00 A.M.		
	4:00 A.M.		
	5:00 A.M.		
	6:00 A.M.		
	7:00 A.M.		
	8:00 A.M.		
	9:00 A.M.		
	10:00 A.M.		
	11:00 A.M.		
	12:00 NOON		
	1:00 P.M.		
	2:00 P.M.		
	3:00 P.M.		
	4:00 P.M.		
	5:00 P.M.		
	6:00 P.M.		
	7:00 P.M.		
	8:00 P.M.		
	9:00 P.M.		
	10:00 P.M.		
	11:00 P.M.		

Personal Daily Checklist

"For if we would judge ourselves, we should not be judged" (1 Corinthians 11:31 KJV).

Grade yourself, A, B, or C, for each one or rate yourself on a scale of 1 (lowest) to 10 (highest).

Checklist Item	Today's Score	Checklist Item	Today's Score
❑ Time in Prayer		❑ Time with My Friends	
❑ Time in Word of God		❑ Time with the Lost	
❑ Praise & Worship		❑ Time to Eat Right	
❑ Thanksgiving		❑ Time to Exercise	
❑ Fasting		❑ Time to Organize	
❑ Time with My Family		❑ Time Alone with God	

Today's Expenses and Money Management

"It is He who gives you power to get wealth, that He may establish His covenant (Deuteronomy 8:18 NKJV).

____

____

Servanthood for Today

Jesus said, "But he that is greatest among you shall be your servant" (Matthew 23:11 KJV).

____

____

My Insights for Today

Jesus said, "But he that is greatest among you shall be your servant" (Matthew 23:11 KJV).

____

____

May I Go To Sleep Now, Father?

"Hard and honest work earns a good night's sleep" (Ecclesiastes 5:12 The Message).

BibleGuide

Through-the-Bible-in-One-Year Reading Guide

Special Note: Although this is a dated reading guide, not everyone will be able to start this guide on January 1. Whenever you begin, simply find that date and start there. In that way, all of us will be reading the same chapters of the Bible together on the same days of the year. At the end of the year, keep reading until you have completed the entire Bible in one year.

In Chapter 22 of *A Man's Journey with God*, I introduced you to a plan of reading four chapters daily from eight different sections of the Bible. Four daily Bible readings are one of the disciplines incorporated into the 30-day Consecration Journal. If you maintain this schedule, you can read through the entire Bible in 12 months. Daily Bible reading is essential to your consecration journey.

You can start reading on any day. Although this is a dated reading guide, not everyone will be able to start on January 1. Whenever you begin, simply find that date and start there. In that way, we will read the same chapters together on the same days of the year. At the end of the year, keep reading until you have completed the entire Bible.

The Bible contains 1,189 chapters (Old Testament, 929 chapters; New Testament, 260 chapters). Reading four chapters per day, and repeating Proverbs and the End Times books of Daniel and Revelation, you can read every chapter in the entire Bible in 12 months.

Eight Divisions of the Bible Used in This Reading Guide

Pentateuch. Genesis, Exodus, Leviticus, Numbers, Deuteronomy

History. Joshua, Judges, Ruth, 1 Samuel, 2 Samuel, 1 Kings, 2 Kings, Ezra, Nehemiah, Esther *(1 and 2 Chronicles are read at the end of the Epistles. Acts is read after the Gospels.)*

Poetry. Job, Psalms, Song of Solomon *(Ecclesiastes is read at the end of the Prophets.)*

Wisdom. Proverbs *(repeated during the year)*

Prophets. Jeremiah, Lamentations, Ezekiel, Hosea, Joel, Amos, Obadiah, Jonah, Micah, Nahum, Habakkuk, Zephaniah, Haggai, Zechariah, Malachi *(Isaiah is read after the Gospels and Acts.)*

Gospels. Matthew, Mark, Luke, John *(followed by Acts and Isaiah)*

Epistles. Romans, 1 Corinthians, 2 Corinthians, Galatians, Ephesians, Philippians, Colossians, 1 Thessalonians, 2 Thessalonians, 1 Timothy, 2 Timothy, Titus, Philemon, Hebrews, James, 1 Peter, 2 Peter, 1 John, 2 John, 3 John, Jude *(followed by 1 and 2 Chronicles)*

End Times. Daniel, Revelation *(repeated during the year)*

Highlights of Your Monthly Bible Readings

In January you will read some of the great foundational books of the Bible about creation, man's Fall, and man's restoration to Friendship with God through the birth of Jesus, Who became our Savior.

God the Father. "In the beginning God created the heavens and the earth."[352]

God the Son. "Mary was found with child of the Holy Ghost."[353]

God the Holy Ghost. "And the Spirit of God moved upon the face of the waters."[354] *Man was made in the image of God*[355] but sinned and fell. Jesus reopened the door to Friendship with God by His death on the cross.

> *"For since our friendship with God was restored by the death of his Son. . . . now we can rejoice in our wonderful new relationship with God because our Lord Jesus Christ has made us friends of God."*[356]

In February, you will read about the gifts of the Holy Ghost that Paul described in 1 Corinthians Chapter 12: word of wisdom, word of knowledge, faith, healing, working of miracles, prophecy, discerning of spirits, speaking in unknown tongues, interpretation of tongues.[357]

All four Gospels speak of Jesus as the baptizer in the Holy Ghost. When you are baptized in the Holy Ghost, you are immersed in Him. You are lost in Him. Your deeds are His deeds. Your thoughts and

---

352 Genesis 1:1 KJV.
353 Matthew 1:18 KJV.
354 Genesis 1:2 KJV.
355 Genesis 1:26 KJV.
356 Romans 5:10-11 NLT.
357 See 1 Corinthians 12:7-10.

words come from Him. Your greatest goal is to obey Jesus, think like Him, and become like Him. The Baptism in the Holy Ghost is a gateway into your relationship with our Friend, Holy Ghost after you are born again and receive Jesus as your Savior and Lord. It is not the relationship, but it is the door you enter to Holy Ghost Friendship.

In March, you will read in the Gospel of Mark how John the Baptist prophesied that just as people were immersed in water in his baptism, they would be immersed in the Holy Ghost in Jesus' Baptism. The Greek word for baptize is *baptizo* [pronounced bap-tid'-zo] meaning to immerse, submerge, or make fully wet. It is a derivative of *bapto* [pronounced bap'-to'] that means "to overwhelm, i.e. cover wholly with a fluid . . . (by implication) to stain (as with dye); dip."[358]

"I baptize you with water, but he will baptize you with the Holy Spirit!"[359]

In April, you will read again about how Jesus was conceived when the Holy Ghost came upon Mary. You will see in Luke 3 how Jesus was full of the Holy Ghost Who led Him into the wilderness to be tempted by the devil. Jesus came out victorious in the power of the Spirit and then He was anointed by the Holy Ghost for public ministry in his own hometown synagogue. You will read in Ephesians about the emotions of the Holy Ghost—how He can be grieved by your bad character and lifestyle as well as your neglect of your Friendship with Him. You will read in Proverbs about the wisdom of God that calls out to us to be like Him. Holy Ghost is your Friend Who gave you life in your mother's womb, gave you new life when you were born again, and now empowers you to fulfill God's will.

If you have not received the Baptism in the Holy Ghost with visible manifestations, ask God to fill you with His power and anoint you for ministry.

In May, you will recall as you read earlier that God—Father, Son, and Holy Ghost—made man in His image to be His Friend, but man sinned[360] and fell away from God and lost the opportunity for that great Friendship offer. However, the Father's heart for the man He created was still so full of love that He laid out a plan of redemption. God was rejected but He was the one who reached out to restore Friendship through the sacrifice of His Son Jesus for our sins. Jesus spoke of that sacrificial love when he spoke to Nicodemus in John 3 as you will read this month.

---

[358] Strong's *Concordance*.
[359] Mark 1:8 NLT.
[360] See Genesis 3.

"For God so loved the world, that he gave his only begotten Son, that whosoever believeth in him should not perish, but have everlasting life."[361]

In June you will read how Jesus demonstrated the association between the word "to breathe" and the coming of the Holy Ghost when He breathed on His disciples and said, "Receive the Holy Ghost."[362] Holy Ghost is the breath of God Who blows wherever He wills. In Revelation, the Spirit is breathing on the churches and speaking to them the words of Jesus that they need to hear. We need the breath of the Holy Ghost and a word from Jesus just as they did.

In July you will read from the book "Acts of the Apostles" that could actually be called "Acts of the Holy Ghost." As you will read in July, the early Church was led by the Holy Ghost and filled with His power and they also conveyed this power to others through prayer and the laying on of hands. When David was convicted of his great sin with Bathsheba (Psalm 51), Holy Ghost spoke to him and caused him to cry out for a clean heart and a right spirit. Do you have any areas of your life where you lack power because of the condition of your heart and spirit? You can make things right with God today by yielding yourself to Him and allowing Jesus to baptize you in the Holy Ghost and fire.

In August you will read in John's letters how the Holy Ghost gives us faith to believe that Jesus is God even though He came as a man to die for our sins. You will read of forgiveness, cleansing, and fellowship with one another by the Holy Ghost working in us. In Leviticus 25 is the Year of Jubilee when all debts were canceled. Jesus read in the synagogue in Luke 4:19 and referred to the year of God's favor. America's founders placed words on the Liberty Bell to "proclaim liberty throughout all the land unto all the inhabitants thereof."[363] Hosea 10:12 says that "it is time to seek the Lord, till he come and rain righteousness upon you."

Have you experienced the liberty that comes when you are baptized in the Holy Ghost and released into the fulness of His power?

In September, as in the other months, you will read chapters in Revelation. You will read through the book of Revelation six times this year and you will see the working of the Holy Ghost in many supernatural ways. The same Holy Ghost is here today and He is available to you. Is your spirit filled with revelation like John? Do you hear a voice behind you as Isaiah did saying, "Whom shall I send, and who

[361] John 3:16 KJV.
[362] John 20:22 KJV.
[363] Leviticus 25:10 KJV.

will go for us?"[364] And if Holy Ghost asked you that question, would you respond, "Here am I; send me"?[365]

In October you will read about the outpouring of the Spirit in Isaiah 32 and the impact the Spirit's outpouring has on the environment. Has the Holy Ghost had an impact on the environment of your heart? What about the environment of your home and everywhere you go? When Belshazzar the king of Babylon was confronted with a fearful sign of God's judgment, the queen knew that Daniel would have the answer. He had a reputation as "a man in thy kingdom, in whom is the spirit of the holy gods."[366] In a time of national crisis, would anyone turn to you because you have so much of the Holy Ghost that everyone knows you are the man of the hour?

In November you will read words that Zechariah spoke that we should never forget: "Not by might, nor by power, but by my spirit, saith the LORD of hosts" (Zechariah 4:6 KJV). When you need power for change, God the Holy Spirit has the answer. As you read Deuteronomy consider that God has the power to move a whole nation of people from bondage to freedom, think not only of your own areas of bondage but also of people who are still in bondage. Some people in America are still in bondage, such as those in the inner city. They need not only human power and might but also the Spirit of God.

In December before you celebrate the birth of Jesus at Christmas you will read Isaiah 53 where the prophet gives us the picture of Jesus the Suffering Servant. He was born to die for our sins. He chose to be numbered with the transgressors—that means every one of us. Zechariah warns of God's judgment on sinners just like all of the Old Testament prophets. The last book of the Old Testament is Malachi. Without the New Testament, the Bible would have ended with the word "curse." Jesus came to redeem us from the curse of sin through the power of the Holy Ghost. Close out the year in triumph because you know Jesus Christ as Lord and Savior and the Holy Ghost has been your Friend all through the year. Go forward in great victory and Holy Ghost power and Friendship to make a difference in your generation.

Bible Readings Online in the Hyperlinked Digital Edition

In the separate Digital Edition of *A Man's Journey with God* you can choose to read your daily chapters of the Bible online. Each reading is linked to a web page at www.biblehub.com. You simply

---

[364] Isaiah 6:8 KJV.
[365] Isaiah 6:8 KJV.
[366] Daniel 5:11 KJV.

click the chapter and you will be taken to the chapter online. Bible Hub provides 25 versions of the Bible as well as many reference tools for further study. It is a free resource of the Christianbook Group, www.christianbook.com.

January

"And the Spirit of God moved upon the face of the waters" (Genesis 1:2 KJV).

Jan 1	❑Gen 1	❑Josh 1	❑Job 1	❑Prv 1
Jan 2	❑Gen 2	❑Josh 2	❑Job 2	❑Prv 2
Jan 3	❑Gen 3	❑Josh 3	❑Job 3	❑Prv 3
Jan 4	❑Gen 4	❑Josh 4	❑Job 4	❑Prv 4
Jan 5	❑Gen 5	❑Josh 5	❑Job 5	❑Prv 5
Jan 6	❑Gen 6	❑Josh 6	❑Job 6	❑Prv 6
Jan 7	❑Gen 7	❑Josh 7	❑Job 7	❑Prv 7
Jan 8	❑Jer 1	❑Matt 1	❑Rom 1	❑Dan 1
Jan 9	❑Jer 2	❑Matt 2	❑Rom 2	❑Dan 2
Jan 10	❑Jer 3	❑Matt 3	❑Rom 3	❑Dan 3
Jan 11	❑Jer 4	❑Matt 4	❑Rom 4	❑Dan 4
Jan 12	❑Jer 5	❑Matt 5	❑Rom 5	❑Dan 5
Jan 13	❑Jer 6	❑Matt 6	❑Rom 6	❑Dan 6
Jan 14	❑Jer 7	❑Matt 7	❑Rom 7	❑Dan 7
Jan 15	❑Gen 8	❑Josh 8	❑Job 8	❑Prv 8
Jan 16	❑Gen 9	❑Josh 9	❑Job 9	❑Prv 9
Jan 17	❑Gen 10	❑Josh 10	❑Job 10	❑Prv 10
Jan 18	❑Gen 11	❑Josh 11	❑Job 11	❑Prv 11
Jan 19	❑Gen 12	❑Josh 12	❑Job 12	❑Prv 12
Jan 20	❑Gen 13	❑Josh 13	❑Job 13	❑Prv 13
Jan 21	❑Gen 14	❑Josh 14	❑Job 14	❑Prv 14
Jan 22	❑Jer 8	❑Matt 8	❑Rom 8	❑Dan 8
Jan 23	❑Jer 9	❑Matt 9	❑Rom 9	❑Dan 9
Jan 24	❑Jer 10	❑Matt 10	❑Rom 10	❑Dan 10
Jan 25	❑Jer 11	❑Matt 11	❑Rom 11	❑Dan 11
Jan 26	❑Jer 12	❑Matt 12	❑Rom 12	❑Dan 12
Jan 27	❑Jer 13	❑Matt 13	❑Rom 13	❑Rev 1
Jan 28	❑Jer 14	❑Matt 14	❑Rom 14	❑Rev 2
Jan 29	❑Gen 15	❑Josh 15	❑Job 15	❑Prv 15
Jan 30	❑Gen 16	❑Josh 16	❑Job 16	❑Prv 16
Jan 31	❑Gen 17	❑Josh 17	❑Job 17	❑Prv 17

February

"The Spirit of God hath made me, and the breath of the Almighty hath given me life" (Job 33:4 KJV).

Feb 1	❑Gen 18	❑Josh 18	❑Job 18	❑Prv 18
Feb 2	❑Gen 19	❑Josh 19	❑Job 19	❑Prv 19
Feb 3	❑Gen 20	❑Josh 20	❑Job 20	❑Prv 20
Feb 4	❑Gen 21	❑Josh 21	❑Job 21	❑Prv 21
Feb 5	❑Jer 15	❑Matt 15	❑Rom 15	❑Rev 3
Feb 6	❑Jer 16	❑Matt 16	❑Rom 16	❑Rev 4
Feb 7	❑Jer 17	❑Matt 17	❑1 Cor 1	❑Rev 5
Feb 8	❑Jer 18	❑Matt 18	❑1 Cor 2	❑Rev 6
Feb 9	❑Jer 19	❑Matt 19	❑1 Cor 3	❑Rev 7
Feb 10	❑Jer 20	❑Matt 20	❑1 Cor 4	❑Rev 8
Feb 11	❑Jer 21	❑Matt 21	❑1 Cor 5	❑Rev 9
Feb 12	❑Gen 22	❑Josh 22	❑Job 22	❑Prv 22
Feb 13	❑Gen 23	❑Josh 23	❑Job 23	❑Prv 23
Feb 14	❑Gen 24	❑Josh 24	❑Job 24	❑Prv 24
Feb 15	❑Gen 25	❑Judg 1	❑Job 25	❑Prv 25
Feb 16	❑Gen 26	❑Judg 2	❑Job 26	❑Prv 26
Feb 17	❑Gen 27	❑Judg 3	❑Job 27	❑Prv 27
Feb 18	❑Gen 28	❑Judg 4	❑Job 28	❑Prv 28
Feb 19	❑Jer 22	❑Matt 22	❑1 Cor 6	❑Rev 10
Feb 20	❑Jer 23	❑Matt 23	❑1 Cor 7	❑Rev 11
Feb 21	❑Jer 24	❑Matt 24	❑1 Cor 8	❑Rev 12
Feb 22	❑Jer 25	❑Matt 25	❑1 Cor 9	❑Rev 13
Feb 23	❑Jer 26	❑Matt 26	❑1 Cor 10	❑Rev 14
Feb 24	❑Jer 27	❑Matt 27	❑1 Cor 11	❑Rev 15
Feb 25	❑Jer 28	❑Matt 28	❑1 Cor 12	❑Rev 16
Feb 26	❑Gen 29	❑Judg 5	❑Job 29	❑Prv 29
Feb 27	❑Gen 30	❑Judg 6	❑Job 30	❑Prv 30
Feb 28	❑Gen 31	❑Judg 7	❑Job 31	❑Prv 31

March

"I will pray with the spirit, and I will pray with the understanding also:
I will sing with the spirit, and I will sing with the understanding also"
(1 Corinthians 14:15 KJV).

Mar 1	❑Gen 32	❑Judg 8	❑Job 32	❑Prv 1
Mar 2	❑Gen 33	❑Judg 9	❑Job 33	❑Prv 2
Mar 3	❑Gen 34	❑Judg 10	❑Job 34	❑Prv 3
Mar 4	❑Gen 35	❑Judg 11	❑Job 35	❑Prv 4
Mar 5	❑Jer 29	❑Mark 1	❑1 Cor 13	❑Rev 17
Mar 6	❑Jer 30	❑Mark 2	❑1 Cor 14	❑Rev 18
Mar 7	❑Jer 31	❑Mark 3	❑1 Cor 15	❑Rev 19
Mar 8	❑Jer 32	❑Mark 4	❑1 Cor 16	❑Rev 20
Mar 9	❑Jer 33	❑Mark 5	❑2 Cor 1	❑Rev 21
Mar 10	❑Jer 34	❑Mark 6	❑2 Cor 2	❑Rev 22
Mar 11	❑Jer 35	❑Mark 7	❑2 Cor 3	❑Dan 1
Mar 12	❑Gen 36	❑Judg 12	❑Job 36	❑Prv 5
Mar 13	❑Gen 37	❑Judg 13	❑Job 37	❑Prv 6
Mar 14	❑Gen 38	❑Judg 14	❑Job 38	❑Prv 7
Mar 15	❑Gen 39	❑Judg 15	❑Job 39	❑Prv 8
Mar 16	❑Gen 40	❑Judg 16	❑Job 40	❑Prv 9
Mar 17	❑Gen 41	❑Judg 17	❑Job 41	❑Prv 10
Mar 18	❑Gen 42	❑Judg 18	❑Job 42	❑Prv 11
Mar 19	❑Jer 36	❑Mark 8	❑2 Cor 4	❑Dan 2
Mar 20	❑Jer 37	❑Mark 9	❑2 Cor 5	❑Dan 3
Mar 21	❑Jer 38	❑Mark 10	❑2 Cor 6	❑Dan 4
Mar 22	❑Jer 39	❑Mark 11	❑2 Cor 7	❑Dan 5
Mar 23	❑Jer 40	❑Mark 12	❑2 Cor 8	❑Dan 6
Mar 24	❑Jer 41	❑Mark 13	❑2 Cor 9	❑Dan 7
Mar 25	❑Jer 42	❑Mark 14	❑2 Cor 10	❑Dan 8
Mar 26	❑Gen 43	❑Judg 19	❑Ps 1	❑Prv 12
Mar 27	❑Gen 44	❑Judg 20	❑Ps 2	❑Prv 13
Mar 28	❑Gen 45	❑Judg 21	❑Ps 3	❑Prv 14
Mar 29	❑Gen 46	❑Ruth 1	❑Ps 4	❑Prv 15
Mar 30	❑Gen 47	❑Ruth 2	❑Ps 5	❑Prv 16
Mar 31	❑Gen 48	❑Ruth 3	❑Ps 6	❑Prv 17

April

"And grieve not the holy Spirit of God, whereby ye are sealed unto the day of redemption" (Ephesians 4:4, 30 KJV).

Apr 1	❑Gen 49	❑Ruth 4	❑Ps 7	❑Prv 18
Apr 2	❑Jer 43	❑Mark 15	❑2 Cor 11	❑Dan 9
Apr 3	❑Jer 44	❑Mark 16	❑2 Cor 12	❑Dan 10
Apr 4	❑Jer 45	❑Luke 1	❑2 Cor 13	❑Dan 11
Apr 5	❑Jer 46	❑Luke 2	❑Gal 1	❑Dan 12
Apr 6	❑Jer 47	❑Luke 3	❑Gal 2	❑Rev 1
Apr 7	❑Jer 48	❑Luke 4	❑Gal 3	❑Rev 2
Apr 8	❑Jer 49	❑Luke 5	❑Gal 4	❑Rev 3
Apr 9	❑Gen 50	❑1 Sam 1	❑Ps 8	❑Prv 19
Apr 10	❑Ex 1	❑1 Sam 2	❑Ps 9	❑Prv 20
Apr 11	❑Ex 2	❑1 Sam 3	❑Ps 10	❑Prv 21
Apr 12	❑Ex 3	❑1 Sam 4	❑Ps 11	❑Prv 22
Apr 13	❑Ex 4	❑1 Sam 5	❑Ps 12	❑Prv 23
Apr 14	❑Ex 5	❑1 Sam 6	❑Ps 13	❑Prv 24
Apr 15	❑Ex 6	❑1 Sam 7	❑Ps 14	❑Prv 25
Apr 16	❑Jer 50	❑Luke 6	❑Gal 5	❑Rev 4
Apr 17	❑Jer 51	❑Luke 7	❑Gal 6	❑Rev 5
Apr 18	❑Jer 52	❑Luke 8	❑Eph 1	❑Rev 6
Apr 19	❑Lam 1	❑Luke 9	❑Eph 2	❑Rev 7
Apr 20	❑Lam 2	❑Luke 10	❑Eph 3	❑Rev 8
Apr 21	❑Lam 3	❑Luke 11	❑Eph 4	❑Rev 9
Apr 22	❑Lam 4	❑Luke 12	❑Eph 5	❑Rev 10
Apr 23	❑Ex 7	❑1 Sam 8	❑Ps 15	❑Prv 26
Apr 24	❑Ex 8	❑1 Sam 9	❑Ps 16	❑Prv 27
Apr 25	❑Ex 9	❑1 Sam 10	❑Ps 17	❑Prv 28
Apr 26	❑Ex 10	❑1 Sam 11	❑Ps 18	❑Prv 29
Apr 27	❑Ex 11	❑1 Sam 12	❑Ps 19	❑Prv 30
Apr 28	❑Ex 12	❑1 Sam 13	❑Ps 20	❑Prv 31
Apr 29	❑Ex 13	❑1 Sam 14	❑Ps 21	❑Prv 1
Apr 30	❑Lam 5	❑Luke 13	❑Eph 6	❑Rev 11

May

"Quench not the Spirit" (1 Thessalonians 5:19 KJV).

May 1	❑Ezek 1	❑Luke 14	❑Php 1	❑Rev 12
May 2	❑Ezek 2	❑Luke 15	❑Php 2	❑Rev 13
May 3	❑Ezek 3	❑Luke 16	❑Php 3	❑Rev 14
May 4	❑Ezek 4	❑Luke 17	❑Php 4	❑Rev 15
May 5	❑Ezek 5	❑Luke 18	❑Col 1	❑Rev 16
May 6	❑Ezek 6	❑Luke 19	❑Col 2	❑Rev 17
May 7	❑Ex 14	❑1 Sam 15	❑Ps 22	❑Prv 2
May 8	❑Ex 15	❑1 Sam 16	❑Ps 23	❑Prv 3
May 9	❑Ex 16	❑1 Sam 17	❑Ps 24	❑Prv 4
May 10	❑Ex 17	❑1 Sam 18	❑Ps 25	❑Prv 5
May 11	❑Ex 18	❑1 Sam 19	❑Ps 26	❑Prv 6
May 12	❑Ex 19	❑1 Sam 20	❑Ps 27	❑Prv 7
May 13	❑Ex 20	❑1 Sam 21	❑Ps 28	❑Prv 8
May 14	❑Ezek 7	❑Luke 20	❑Col 3	❑Rev 18
May 15	❑Ezek 8	❑Luke 21	❑Col 4	❑Rev 19
May 16	❑Ezek 9	❑Luke 22	❑1 Ths 1	❑Rev 20
May 17	❑Ezek 10	❑Luke 23	❑1 Ths 2	❑Rev 21
May 18	❑Ezek 11	❑Luke 24	❑1 Ths 3	❑Rev 22
May 19	❑Ezek 12	❑John 1	❑1 Ths 4	❑Dan 1
May 20	❑Ezek 13	❑John 2	❑1 Ths 5	❑Dan 2
May 21	❑Ex 21	❑1 Sam 22	❑Ps 29	❑Prv 9
May 22	❑Ex 22	❑1 Sam 23	❑Ps 30	❑Prv 10
May 23	❑Ex 23	❑1 Sam 24	❑Ps 31	❑Prv 11
May 24	❑Ex 24	❑1 Sam 25	❑Ps 32	❑Prv 12
May 25	❑Ex 25	❑1 Sam 26	❑Ps 33	❑Prv 13
May 26	❑Ex 26	❑1 Sam 27	❑Ps 34	❑Prv 14
May 27	❑Ex 27	❑1 Sam 28	❑Ps 35	❑Prv 15
May 28	❑Ezek 14	❑John 3	❑2 Ths 1	❑Dan 3
May 29	❑Ezek 15	❑John 4	❑2 Ths 2	❑Dan 4
May 30	❑Ezek 16	❑John 5	❑2 Ths 3	❑Dan 5
May 31	❑Ezek 17	❑John 6	❑1 Tim 1	❑Dan 6

June

"But the Comforter, which is the Holy Ghost, whom the Father will send in my name, he shall teach you all things, and bring all things to your remembrance, whatsoever I have said unto you" (John 14:26 KJV).

Jun 1	❑Ezek 18	❑John 7	❑1 Tim 2	❑Dan 7
Jun 2	❑Ezek 19	❑John 8	❑1 Tim 3	❑Dan 8
Jun 3	❑Ezek 20	❑John 9	❑1 Tim 4	❑Dan 9
Jun 4	❑Ex 28	❑1 Sam 29	❑Ps 36	❑Prv 16
Jun 5	❑Ex 29	❑1 Sam 30	❑Ps 37	❑Prv 17
Jun 6	❑Ex 30	❑1 Sam 31	❑Ps 38	❑Prv 18
Jun 7	❑Ex 31	❑2 Sam 1	❑Ps 39	❑Prv 19
Jun 8	❑Ex 32	❑2 Sam 2	❑Ps 40	❑Prv 20
Jun 9	❑Ex 33	❑2 Sam 3	❑Ps 41	❑Prv 21
Jun 10	❑Ex 34	❑2 Sam 4	❑Ps 42	❑Prv 22
Jun 11	❑Ezek 21	❑John 10	❑1 Tim 5	❑Dan 10
Jun 12	❑Ezek 22	❑John 11	❑1 Tim 6	❑Dan 11
Jun 13	❑Ezek 23	❑John 12	❑2 Tim 1	❑Dan 12
Jun 14	❑Ezek 24	❑John 13	❑2 Tim 2	❑Rev 1
Jun 15	❑Ezek 25	❑John 14	❑2 Tim 3	❑Rev 2
Jun 16	❑Ezek 26	❑John 15	❑2 Tim 4	❑Rev 3
Jun 17	❑Ezek 27	❑John 16	❑Titus 1	❑Rev 4
Jun 18	❑Ex 35	❑2 Sam 5	❑Ps 43	❑Prv 23
Jun 19	❑Ex 36	❑2 Sam 6	❑Ps 44	❑Prv 24
Jun 20	❑Ex 37	❑2 Sam 7	❑Ps 45	❑Prv 25
Jun 21	❑Ex 38	❑2 Sam 8	❑Ps 46	❑Prv 26
Jun 22	❑Ex 39	❑2 Sam 9	❑Ps 47	❑Prv 27
Jun 23	❑Ex 40	❑2 Sam 10	❑Ps 48	❑Prv 28
Jun 24	❑Lev 1	❑2 Sam 11	❑Ps 49	❑Prv 29
Jun 25	❑Ezek 28	❑John 17	❑Titus 2	❑Rev 5
Jun 26	❑Ezek 29	❑John 18	❑Titus 3	❑Rev 6
Jun 27	❑Ezek 30	❑John 19	❑Phile 1	❑Rev 7
Jun 28	❑Ezek 31	❑John 20	❑Heb 1	❑Rev 8
Jun 29	❑Ezek 32	❑John 21	❑Heb 2	❑Rev 9
Jun 30	❑Ezek 33	❑Acts 1	❑Heb 3	❑Rev 10

July

"And they were all filled with the Holy Ghost, and began to speak with other tongues, as the Spirit gave them utterance" (Acts 2:4 KJV).

Jul 1	❑Ezek 34	❑Acts 2	❑Heb 4	❑Rev 11
Jul 2	❑Lev 2	❑2 Sam 12	❑Ps 50	❑Prv 30
Jul 3	❑Lev 3	❑2 Sam 13	❑Ps 51	❑Prv 31
Jul 4	❑Lev 4	❑2 Sam 14	❑Ps 52	❑Prv 1
Jul 5	❑Lev 5	❑2 Sam 15	❑Ps 53	❑Prv 2
Jul 6	❑Lev 6	❑2 Sam 16	❑Ps 54	❑Prv 3
Jul 7	❑Lev 7	❑2 Sam 17	❑Ps 55	❑Prv 4
Jul 8	❑Lev 8	❑2 Sam 18	❑Ps 56	❑Prv 5
Jul 9	❑Ezek 35	❑Acts 3	❑Heb 5	❑Rev 12
Jul 10	❑Ezek 36	❑Acts 4	❑Heb 6	❑Rev 13
Jul 11	❑Ezek 37	❑Acts 5	❑Heb 7	❑Rev 14
Jul 12	❑Ezek 38	❑Acts 6	❑Heb 8	❑Rev 15
Jul 13	❑Ezek 39	❑Acts 7	❑Heb 9	❑Rev 16
Jul 14	❑Ezek 40	❑Acts 8	❑Heb 10	❑Rev 17
Jul 15	❑Ezek 41	❑Acts 9	❑Heb 11	❑Rev 18
Jul 16	❑Lev 9	❑2 Sam 19	❑Ps 57	❑Prv 6
Jul 17	❑Lev 10	❑2 Sam 20	❑Ps 58	❑Prv 7
Jul 18	❑Lev 11	❑2 Sam 21	❑Ps 59	❑Prv 8
Jul 19	❑Lev 12	❑2 Sam 22	❑Ps 60	❑Prv 9
Jul 20	❑Lev 13	❑2 Sam 23	❑Ps 61	❑Prv 10
Jul 21	❑Lev 14	❑2 Sam 24	❑Ps 62	❑Prv 11
Jul 22	❑Lev 15	❑1 Kng 1	❑Ps 63	❑Prv 12
Jul 23	❑Ezek 42	❑Acts 10	❑Heb 12	❑Rev 19
Jul 24	❑Ezek 43	❑Acts 11	❑Heb 13	❑Rev 20
Jul 25	❑Ezek 44	❑Acts 12	❑James 1	❑Rev 21
Jul 26	❑Ezek 45	❑Acts 13	❑James 2	❑Rev 22
Jul 27	❑Ezek 46	❑Acts 14	❑James 3	❑Dan 1
Jul 28	❑Ezek 47	❑Acts 15	❑James 4	❑Dan 2
Jul 29	❑Ezek 48	❑Acts 16	❑James 5	❑Dan 3
Jul 30	❑Lev 16	❑1 Kng 2	❑Ps 64	❑Prv 13
Jul 31	❑Lev 17	❑1 Kng 3	❑Ps 65	❑Prv 14

August

"Hereby know ye the Spirit of God: Every spirit that confesseth that Jesus Christ is come in the flesh is of God: And every spirit that confesseth not that Jesus Christ is come in the flesh is not of God: and this is that spirit of antichrist" (1 John 4:2-3 KJV).

Aug 1	❑Lev 18	❑1 Kng 4	❑Ps 66	❑Prv 15
Aug 2	❑Lev 19	❑1 Kng 5	❑Ps 67	❑Prv 16
Aug 3	❑Lev 20	❑1 Kng 6	❑Ps 68	❑Prv 17
Aug 4	❑Lev 21	❑1 Kng 7	❑Ps 69	❑Prv 18
Aug 5	❑Lev 22	❑1 Kng 8	❑Ps 70	❑Prv 19
Aug 6	❑Hosea 1	❑Acts 17	❑1 Pet 1	❑Dan 4
Aug 7	❑Hosea 2	❑Acts 18	❑1 Pet 2	❑Dan 5
Aug 8	❑Hosea 3	❑Acts 19	❑1 Pet 3	❑Dan 6
Aug 9	❑Hosea 4	❑Acts 20	❑1 Pet 4	❑Dan 7
Aug 10	❑Hosea 5	❑Acts 21	❑1 Pet 5	❑Dan 8
Aug 11	❑Hosea 6	❑Acts 22	❑2 Pet 1	❑Dan 9
Aug 12	❑Hosea 7	❑Acts 23	❑2 Pet 2	❑Dan 10
Aug 13	❑Lev 23	❑1 Kng 9	❑Ps 71	❑Prv 20
Aug 14	❑Lev 24	❑1 Kng 10	❑Ps 72	❑Prv 21
Aug 15	❑Lev 25	❑1 Kng 11	❑Ps 73	❑Prv 22
Aug 16	❑Lev 26	❑1 Kng 12	❑Ps 74	❑Prv 23
Aug 17	❑Lev 27	❑1 Kng 13	❑Ps 75	❑Prv 24
Aug 18	❑Num 1	❑1 Kng 14	❑Ps 76	❑Prv 25
Aug 19	❑Num 2	❑1 Kng 15	❑Ps 77	❑Prv 26
Aug 20	❑Hosea 8	❑Acts 24	❑2 Pet 3	❑Dan 11
Aug 21	❑Hosea 9	❑Acts 25	❑1 John 1	❑Dan 12
Aug 22	❑Hosea 10	❑Acts 26	❑1 John 2	❑Rev 1
Aug 23	❑Hosea 11	❑Acts 27	❑1 John 3	❑Rev 2
Aug 24	❑Hosea 12	❑Acts 28	❑1 John 4	❑Rev 3
Aug 25	❑Hosea 13	❑Isa 1	❑1 John 5	❑Rev 4
Aug 26	❑Hosea 14	❑Isa 2	❑2 John 1	❑Rev 5
Aug 27	❑Num 3	❑1 Kng 16	❑Ps 78	❑Prv 27
Aug 28	❑Num 4	❑1 Kng 17	❑Ps 79	❑Prv 28
Aug 29	❑Num 5	❑1 Kng 18	❑Ps 80	❑Prv 29
Aug 30	❑Num 6	❑1 Kng 19	❑Ps 81	❑Prv 30
Aug 31	❑Num 7	❑1 Kng 20	❑Ps 82	❑Prv 31

September

"And I heard a voice from heaven saying unto me, Write, Blessed are the dead which die in the Lord from henceforth: Yea, saith the Spirit, that they may rest from their labours; and their works do follow them" (Revelation 14:13 KJV).

Sep 1	❑Num 8	❑1 Kng 21	❑Ps 83	❑Prv 1
Sep 2	❑Num 9	❑1 Kng 22	❑Ps 84	❑Prv 2
Sep 3	❑Joel 1	❑Isa 3	❑3 John 1	❑Rev 6
Sep 4	❑Joel 2	❑Isa 4	❑Jude	❑Rev 7
Sep 5	❑Joel 3	❑Isa 5	❑1 Chr 1	❑Rev 8
Sep 6	❑Amos 1	❑Isa 6	❑1 Chr 2	❑Rev 9
Sep 7	❑Amos 2	❑Isa 7	❑1 Chr 3	❑Rev 10
Sep 8	❑Amos 3	❑Isa 8	❑1 Chr 4	❑Rev 11
Sep 9	❑Amos 4	❑Isa 9	❑1 Chr 5	❑Rev 12
Sep 10	❑Num 10	❑2 Kng 1	❑Ps 85	❑Prv 3
Sep 11	❑Num 11	❑2 Kng 2	❑Ps 86	❑Prv 4
Sep 12	❑Num 12	❑2 Kng 3	❑Ps 87	❑Prv 5
Sep 13	❑Num 13	❑2 Kng 4	❑Ps 88	❑Prv 6
Sep 14	❑Num 14	❑2 Kng 5	❑Ps 89	❑Prv 7
Sep 15	❑Num 15	❑2 Kng 6	❑Ps 90	❑Prv 8
Sep 16	❑Num 16	❑2 Kng 7	❑Ps 91	❑Prv 9
Sep 17	❑Amos 5	❑Isa 10	❑1 Chr 6	❑Rev 13
Sep 18	❑Amos 6	❑Isa 11	❑1 Chr 7	❑Rev 14
Sep 19	❑Amos 7	❑Isa 12	❑1 Chr 8	❑Rev 15
Sep 20	❑Amos 8	❑Isa 13	❑1 Chr 9	❑Rev 16
Sep 21	❑Amos 9	❑Isa 14	❑1 Chr 10	❑Rev 17
Sep 22	❑Obad 1	❑Isa 15	❑1 Chr 11	❑Rev 18
Sep 23	❑Jon 1	❑Isa 16	❑1 Chr 12	❑Rev 19
Sep 24	❑Num 17	❑2 Kng 8	❑Ps 92-Ps 93	❑Prv 10
Sep 25	❑Num 18	❑2 Kng 9	❑Ps 94-Ps 95	❑Prv 11
Sep 26	❑Num 19	❑2 Kng 10	❑Ps 96-Ps 97	❑Prv 12
Sep 27	❑Num 20	❑2 Kng 11	❑Ps 98-Ps 99	❑Prv 13
Sep 28	❑Num 21	❑2 Kng 12	❑Ps 100-Ps 101	❑Prv 14
Sep 29	❑Num 22	❑2 Kng 13	❑Ps 102	❑Prv 15
Sep 30	❑Num 23	❑2 Kng 14	❑Ps 103	❑Prv 16

October

"Until the spirit be poured upon us from on high, and the wilderness be a fruitful field, and the fruitful field be counted for a forest" (Isaiah 32:15).

Oct 1	❑Jon 2	❑Isa 17	❑1 Chr 13	❑Rev 20
Oct 2	❑Jon 3	❑Isa 18	❑1 Chr 14	❑Rev 21
Oct 3	❑Jon 4	❑Isa 19	❑1 Chr 15	❑Rev 22
Oct 4	❑Micah 1	❑Isa 20	❑1 Chr 16	❑Dan 1
Oct 5	❑Micah 2	❑Isa 21	❑1 Chr 17	❑Dan 2
Oct 6	❑Micah 3	❑Isa 22	❑1 Chr 18	❑Dan 3
Oct 7	❑Micah 4	❑Isa 23	❑1 Chr 19	❑Dan 4
Oct 8	❑Num 24	❑2 Kng 15	❑Ps 104	❑Prv 17
Oct 9	❑Num 25	❑2 Kng 16	❑Ps 105	❑Prv 18
Oct 10	❑Num 26	❑2 Kng 17	❑Ps 106	❑Prv 19
Oct 11	❑Num 27	❑2 Kng 18	❑Ps 107	❑Prv 20
Oct 12	❑Num 28	❑2 Kng 19	❑Ps 108-Ps 109	❑Prv 21
Oct 13	❑Num 29	❑2 Kng 20	❑Ps 110-Ps 111	❑Prv 22
Oct 14	❑Num 30	❑2 Kng 21	❑Ps 112-Ps 113	❑Prv 23
Oct 15	❑Micah 5	❑Isa 24	❑1 Chr 20-1 Chr 21	❑Dan 5
Oct 16	❑Micah 6	❑Isa 25	❑1 Chr 22	❑Dan 6
Oct 17	❑Micah 7	❑Isa 26	❑1 Chr 23	❑Dan 7
Oct 18	❑Nah 1	❑Isa 27	❑1Chr 24-1 Chr 25	❑Dan 8
Oct 19	❑Nah 2	❑Isa 28	❑1 Chr 26	❑Dan 9
Oct 20	❑Nah 3	❑Isa 29	❑1 Chr 27	❑Dan 10
Oct 21	❑Hab 1	❑Isa 30	❑1 Chr 28	❑Dan 11
Oct 22	❑Num 31	❑2 Kng 22	❑Ps 114-Ps 115	❑Prv 24
Oct 23	❑Num 32	❑2 Kng 23	❑Ps 116-Ps 117	❑Prv 25
Oct 24	❑Num 33	❑2 Kng 24	❑Ps 118	❑Prv 26
Oct 25	❑Num 34	❑2 Kng 25	❑Ps 119	❑Prv 27
Oct 26	❑Num 35	❑Ezra 1	❑Ps 120-Ps 121	❑Prv 28
Oct 27	❑Num 36	❑Ezra 2	❑Ps 122-Ps 123	❑Prv 29
Oct 28	❑Deut 1	❑Ezra 3	❑Ps 124-Ps 125	❑Prv 30
Oct 29	❑Hab 2	❑Isa 31	❑1 Chr 29	❑Dan 12
Oct 30	❑Hab 3	❑Isa 32	❑2 Chr 1	❑Rev 1
Oct 31	❑Zeph 1	❑Isa 33	❑2 Chr 2	❑Rev 2

November

"Then he answered and spake unto me, saying, This is the word of the Lord unto Zerubbabel, saying, Not by might, nor by power, but by my spirit, saith the Lord of hosts" (Zechariah 4:6 KJV).

Nov 1	❑Zeph 2	❑Isa 34	❑2 Chr 3	❑Rev 3
Nov 2	❑Zeph 3	❑Isa 35	❑2 Chr 4	❑Rev 4
Nov 3	❑Hagg 1	❑Isa 36	❑2 Chr 5	❑Rev 5
Nov 4	❑Hagg 2	❑Isa 37	❑2 Chr 6	❑Rev 6
Nov 5	❑Deut 2	❑Ezra 4	❑Ps 126-Ps 127	❑Prv 31
Nov 6	❑Deut 3	❑Ezra 5	❑Ps 128-Ps 129	❑Prv 1
Nov 7	❑Deut 4	❑Ezra 6	❑Ps 130-Ps 131	❑Prv 2
Nov 8	❑Deut 5	❑Ezra 7	❑Ps 132-Ps 133	❑Prv 3
Nov 9	❑Deut 6	❑Ezra 8	❑Ps 134-Ps 135	❑Prv 4
Nov 10	❑Deut 7	❑Ezra 9	❑Ps 136	❑Prv 5
Nov 11	❑Deut 8	❑Ezra 10	❑Ps 137	❑Prv 6
Nov 12	❑Zech 1	❑Isa 38	❑2 Chr 7	❑Rev 7
Nov 13	❑Zech 2	❑Isa 39	❑2 Chr 8	❑Rev 8
Nov 14	❑Zech 3	❑Isa 40	❑2 Chr 9	❑Rev 9
Nov 15	❑Zech 4	❑Isa 41	❑2Chr 10-2 Chr 11	❑Rev 10
Nov 16	❑Zech 5	❑Isa 42	❑2Chr 12-2 Chr 13	❑Rev 11
Nov 17	❑Zech 6	❑Isa 43	❑2 Chr 14	❑Rev 12
Nov 18	❑Zech 7	❑Isa 44	❑2 Chr 15	❑Rev 13
Nov 19	❑Deut 9	❑Neh 1	❑Ps 138	❑Prv 7
Nov 20	❑Deut 10	❑Neh 2	❑Ps 139	❑Prv 8
Nov 21	❑Deut 11	❑Neh 3	❑Ps 140	❑Prv 9
Nov 22	❑Deut 12	❑Neh 4	❑Ps 141	❑Prv 10
Nov 23	❑Deut 13	❑Neh 5	❑Ps 142	❑Prv 11
Nov 24	❑Deut 14	❑Neh 6	❑Ps 143	❑Prv 12
Nov 25	❑Deut 15	❑Neh 7	❑Ps 144	❑Prv 13
Nov 26	❑Zech 8	❑Isa 45	❑2 Chr 16	❑Rev 14
Nov 27	❑Zech 9	❑Isa 46	❑2 Chr 17	❑Rev 15
Nov 28	❑Zech 10	❑Isa 47	❑2 Chr 18	❑Rev 16
Nov 29	❑Zech 11-Zech 12	❑Isa 48	❑2 Chr 19	❑Rev 17
Nov 30	❑Zech 13-Zech 14	❑Isa 49	❑2 Chr 20	❑Rev 18

December

"And the Spirit of God came upon Zechariah the son of Jehoiada the priest, which stood above the people, and said unto them, Thus saith God, Why transgress ye the commandments of the Lord, that ye cannot prosper? because ye have forsaken the Lord, he hath also forsaken you" (2 Chronicles 24:20 KJV).

Dec 1	❑Mal 1	❑Isa 50	❑2 Chr 21	❑Rev 19
Dec 2	❑Mal 2	❑Isa 51	❑2 Chr 22	❑Rev 20
Dec 3	❑Deut 16	❑Neh 8	❑Ps 145	❑Prv 14
Dec 4	❑Deut 17	❑Neh 9-Neh 10	❑Ps 146	❑Prv 15
Dec 5	❑Deut 18	❑Neh 11-Neh 12	❑Ps 147	❑Prv 16
Dec 6	❑Deut 19	❑Neh 13	❑Ps 148	❑Prv 17
Dec 7	❑Deut 20	❑Est 1	❑Ps 149	❑Prv 18
Dec 8	❑Deut 21	❑Est 2	❑Ps 150	❑Prv 19
Dec 9	❑Deut 22	❑Est 3	❑Song 1	❑Prv 20
Dec 10	❑Mal 3	❑Isa 52	❑2 Chr 23	❑Rev 21
Dec 11	❑Mal 4	❑Isa 53	❑2 Chr 24	❑Rev 22
Dec 12	❑Eccl 1	❑Isa 54	❑2 Chr 25	❑Dan 1
Dec 13	❑Eccl 2	❑Isa 55	❑2 Chr 26	❑Dan 2
Dec 14	❑Eccl 3	❑Isa 56-Isa 57	❑2 Chr 27	❑Dan 3
Dec 15	❑Eccl 4	❑Isa 58	❑2 Chr 28	❑Dan 4
Dec 16	❑Eccl 5	❑Isa 59	❑2 Chr 29	❑Dan 5
Dec 17	❑Deut 23-Deut 24	❑Est 4	❑Song 2	❑Prv 21
Dec 18	❑Deut 25-Deut 26	❑Est 5	❑Song 3	❑Prv 22
Dec 19	❑Deut 27	❑Est 6	❑Song 4	❑Prv 23
Dec 20	❑Deut 28	❑Est 7	❑Song 5	❑Prv 24
Dec 21	❑Deut 29-Deut 30	❑Est 8	❑Song 6	❑Prv 25
Dec 22	❑Deut 31-Deut 32	❑Est 9	❑Song 7	❑Prv 26
Dec 23	❑Deut 33-Deut 34	❑Est 10	❑Song 8	❑Prv 27
Dec 24	❑Eccl 6	❑Isa 60	❑2 Chr 30	❑Dan 6
Dec 25	❑Eccl 7	❑Isa 61	❑2 Chr 31	❑Dan 7
Dec 26	❑Eccl 8	❑Isa 62	❑2 Chr 32	❑Dan 8
Dec 27	❑Eccl 9	❑Isa 63	❑2 Chr 33	❑Dan 9
Dec 28	❑Eccl 10	❑Isa 64	❑2 Chr 34	❑Dan 10
Dec 29	❑Eccl 11	❑Isa 65	❑2 Chr 35	❑Dan 11
Dec 30	❑Eccl 12	❑Isa 66	❑2 Chr 36	❑Dan 12

PERSONAL NOTES

PERSONAL NOTES

PERSONAL NOTES

Made in the USA
Middletown, DE
04 April 2016